Putting Purpose Into Practice

Putting Purpose Into Practice

The Economics of Mutuality

Edited by
COLIN MAYER
and
BRUNO ROCHE

OXFORD
UNIVERSITY PRESS

OXFORD
UNIVERSITY PRESS

Great Clarendon Street, Oxford, OX2 6DP,
United Kingdom

Oxford University Press is a department of the University of Oxford.
It furthers the University's objective of excellence in research, scholarship,
and education by publishing worldwide. Oxford is a registered trade mark of
Oxford University Press in the UK and in certain other countries

First Edition published in 2021

Impression: 3

Published in the United States of America by Oxford University Press
198 Madison Avenue, New York, NY 10016, United States of America

British Library Cataloguing in Publication Data
Data available

Library of Congress Control Number: 2021930516

ISBN 978–0–19–887070–8

DOI: 10.1093/oso/9780198870708.001.0001

Printed and bound by
CPI Group (UK) Ltd, Croydon, CR0 4YY

Preface

This book is innovative not only in the message that it is seeking to convey about the purpose of business and the process of putting that purpose into practice. It is also unusual in terms of the way in which it has arrived at this message. It has done so through a partnership between a company, Mars Incorporated, and a university, Oxford University. This has been a multi-year partnership on which many of the conclusions of the book are based.

Over the years the partnership has broadened out from being between one company and one university to multiple companies and universities. It therefore draws on the experiences of many organizations and the knowledge of many academics and researchers around the world. The breadth and depth of the relationships between business and academia have provided an exceptionally rich source of information, data, and knowledge.

The content of the book is also unusual in seeking to convey a coherent, consistent message while at the same time drawing on the experience and understanding of the many companies and people that have participated in the programme. It is therefore edited by two people but written by multiple authors who are leading experts in their fields and acknowledged in the list of contents and contributors. Nevertheless, it is not a traditional edited volume of related but disparate articles but a radical call for reform of business spoken with one voice.

That could not have been achieved without the very constructive collaboration of all participants in the programme and the way in which they have responded to the process of editing to ensure the necessary degree of coherence and consistency. We would therefore like to begin by acknowledging the huge amount of work and support that all of the participants in the programme in Mars Inc., Oxford University and in the many other companies and universities have provided throughout.

It would also not have been achieved without the immense editorial support that Caroline Scotter Mainprize, Ben Jackson of Freud Communications, Kate Roll of Oxford University, and Jay Jakub and Francesco Cordaro of Mars Catalyst, the think-tank of Mars Inc., have provided. We are grateful to Mars Inc. for the funding of the six-year research programme on Mutuality in Business at the Saïd Business School which underpins the results of the research. We are extremely grateful to the researchers from Oxford University, Mars Inc., and many other universities and institutions around the world for authoring the chapters in Part II of the book. We are also very grateful to Alastair Colin-Jones, Justine Esta Ellis, Aida Hadzic, Francois Laurent, Sudhir Rama Murthy, Helen Campbell Pickford, Yassine El Ouarzazi, Judith Stroehle, and the fourteen companies involved in the case studies in Part III of the book for their immense assistance in their preparation. Finally, we would like to thank Adam Swallow at Oxford University Press, and two anonymous referees of our book proposal.

The book is in four parts. The first part comprises two chapters that introduce the subject and summarize the contents. The second part describes the different components of putting purpose into practice associated with the underlying business concept, known as the Economics of Mutuality. The third part is a set of case studies of companies from around the world in different sectors, at a variety of different stages of their development that have put purpose into practice. They reveal the extent to which companies are increasingly adopting the ideas of this book. The final part concludes and discusses other aspects of reform that will be required to put purpose into practice.

Colin Mayer and Bruno Roche

31 December 2019

Contents

List of Figures

List of Tables

List of Contributors

Bojan Angelov directs the culture practice and qualitative research at Catalyst—an internal think tank at Mars, Inc. Prior to this role, Bojan was the principal and founder of two lines and a dot, an innovation management and service design studio. He was also an adjunct professor at Parsons The New School for Design (New York) and a lecturer and research fellow at Polytechnic Institute of New York University. His research topics cover organizational culture, innovation and design management, and service design.Bojan holds a PhD in technology management from Polytechnic Institute of New York University, as well as an MS in management and an MS in electrical engineering from Polytechnic University (New York).

Richard Barker is professor of accounting at Saïd Business School, and tutor in management at Christ Church, Oxford University. An expert in financial reporting, Richard is a member of the Corporate Reporting Council, the UK advisory committee on accounting standards. He previously served as research fellow at the International Accounting Standards Board (IASB). Richard has degrees from Oxford and Cambridge and qualified as an accountant while working for AstraZeneca. He is currently researching issues of natural capital accounting, corporate sustainability, and institutional structures for regulating 'non-financial' corporate reporting. He serves on the Expert Panel of Accounting for Sustainability (A4S).

Helen Campbell Pickford researches learning in organizations, the development of best practice codes, relationships between investment funds, MNCs, and local communities in developing countries, and the impact of business-led social interventions. Her work is based on an ethnographic understanding of the ways people and organizations construct and distribute knowledge and meanings, particularly in policymaking.Helen comes from a background in development and education which has taken her to Sri Lanka, Kenya, Malaysia, the Democratic Republic of the Congo, and Oman. She has worked in engaging communities in schooling post-conflict, analysing the roles of businesses, NGOs, community stakeholders, and governments in education.

Alastair Colin-Jones joined Mars Catalyst in 2016 and is responsible for the day-to-day management of the joint research programmes between Mars Catalyst and various university partners around the world. He also supports the implementation of the Economics of Mutuality within large businesses on both the supply and demand side.Previously, he was the knowledge manager at the Skoll Centre for Social Entrepreneurship at Saïd Business School and prior to that helped to start a social enterprise in Oxford. Alastair has a first-class undergraduate degree and a graduate degree from the University of Oxford.

Francesco Cordaro has been part of the Economics of Mutuality programme since its beginning within Catalyst, the Mars internal think-tank. Over the last 12 years, he has been the architect of the metrics model behind the assessment of non-financial forms of capitals (Natural, Human and Social Capital) that are at the core of the Economics of Mutuality Foundation. Prior to that, Francesco led the data analytics lab in Mars Catalyst in Belgium and the US. Over his two decades-long tenure, he has led a portfolio of research projects in the business, such as analyzing weather forecasting applied to cocoa crop modeling in West Africa; developing key metrics to evaluate, predict and optimize the impact of TV advertising on sales and purchase behaviours; modelling of neurophysiological data from ads exposures responses and cognitive processes; applying real option approaches to assessing risk and opportunities in R&D projects.

Alain Desdoigts is a professor of economics at université Paris 1 Panthéon Sorbonne and a research associate at Développement & Sociétés (Institut de recherche pour le développement and Paris 1). Desdoigts received a MA in finance from université Paris Dauphine and a PhD in economics from the European University Institute (Florence, Italy). His main research interests are in economic growth and development, inequality, international economics, institutions, and family farming. His publications include articles in academic journals (*International Economic Review, Journal of African Economies, Journal of Economic Growth, Journal of International Economics, and others*), and chapters in edited volumes.

Catherine Dolan is on the faculty of anthropology at SOAS, University of London, and holds fellowships at the James Martin Institute and Green Templeton College, University of Oxford, and at the Royal Society for Arts, Manufacture and Commerce (RSA). Her research centres on the intersection of market and moral economies, particularly how corporations address ethical considerations through 'alternative' business models and market forms. Over the past fifteen years she has directed interdisciplinary programmes on ethical capitalism in relation to food, labour, poverty and gender in over ten African countries, with an emphasis on eastern Africa. Her recent books include the co-edited volumes, *The Anthropology of CSR* and *Digital Food Activism*.

Robert G. Eccles is a former tenured professor at Harvard Business School and is now a visiting professor of management practice at Saïd Business School, Oxford University. He is the founding chairman of the Sustainability Accounting Standards Board, an advisor to the Impact Management Project, and a member of the board of directors of the Mistra Center for Sustainable Markets at the Stockholm School of Economics. Eccles is a 'capital market activist' dedicated to ensuring that the capital markets support sustainable development through such mechanisms as integrated reporting. He is also a dedicated weight-lifter.

Yassine El Ouarzazi has a background in engineering. He has fourteen years of experience in various business-analytics-related positions in the consumer finance, automotive, and FMCG industries. For seven years, he spearheaded Mars' Evidence Based Marketing programme before turning to research in business model innovation. Since 2014, he has been developing and deploying Catalyst's signature Economics of Mutuality process to help businesses bring purpose to life—from ecosystem mapping, to intervention design, to metrics. Yassine is from Morocco. He graduated from a French engineering school (Ecole des Mines de Paris) in 2000. He has a passion for technology and education (and has contributed as a volunteer to the French translation of https://www.khanacademy.org.

Marcel Fafchamps is a senior fellow at the Freeman Spogli Institute for International Studies and a professor (by courtesy) for the Department of Economics at Stanford University. Prior to joining FSI, Fafchamps served as professor of development economics for the Department of Economics at Oxford University. He also served as deputy director and then co-director of the Center for the Study of African Economies. His research interests include economic development, market institutions, and social networks. His current research focuses on entrepreneurship, factor markets, and the efficiency of social networks in Africa and South Asia.

Justus von Geibler co-leads the research unit Innovation Labs in the Division of Sustainable Production and Consumption at the Wuppertal Institute, Germany. Based on more than twenty years of professional experience in sustainability assessment and innovation, his research focuses on sustainability standards, natural resource accounting, open innovation in companies and value chains, and living labs. He holds a PhD in economic geography from the Ruhr University Bochum, Germany, a master's degree in environmental management and policy from the University of Lund, Sweden, and a diploma in forest sciences from the University of Göttingen, Germany. He teaches natural resource management and sustainable supply chain management at several universities and is the author of several books and more than a hundred scientific publications.

Paul Gilbert is an anthropologist and lecturer in international development at the School of Global Studies, University of Sussex. His research interests fall into two primary areas: the role of private sector institutions, expertise and finance in international development; and environmental justice, violence, and environmental defenders around extractive industry projects. He has carried out ethnographic research in Bangladesh, the United Kingdom, and South Africa and has recently co-edited (with Jessica Sklair) a special issue of *Focaal* on 'Ethnographic Engagements with Global Elites: Mutuality, Complicity and Critique'.

Nicolas Glady is a doctor in econometrics, and professor and executive vice president at ESSEC Business School. His research work has been published in *Management Science*, the *International Journal of Research in Marketing* and the *Journal of Service Research* among others, and in managerial journals such as the *Financial Times*, *Harvard Business Review*, the *Huffington Post*, *Slate*, *Le Monde*, *Le Figaro*, *Les Echos*, etc. He advises companies in different sectors on these topics: banking and insurance, telecom, FMCG, distribution, pharmaceutics, and others. *Poets&Quants* identified him as one of the best forty under forty B-school professors in the world.

Andreas G. F. Hoepner is a financial data scientist working towards the vision of a conflict-free capitalism. While the vision is unlikely to be fully achievable, Andreas's view is that anyone can strive to make a regular contribution to reducing abusive conflicts of interests and thereby enhancing the fairness of our society and its financial system. Formally, Andreas is full professor of operational risk, banking, and finance at the Michael Smurfit Graduate Business School of University College Dublin (UCD). Since June 2018, Andreas has served on the European Union's Technical Expert Group on Sustainable Finance.

Jay Jakub is part of the Mars, Inc. think tank 'Catalyst'—created in the 1960s by Forrest Mars, Sr. to challenge conventional business thinking and to develop breakthrough capabilities for the firm. Born in Rahway, New Jersey—ironically the hometown of Milton Friedman, financial capitalism's founding father—Jay is the senior director for external research and co-manages the Economics of Mutuality initiative. Married to Eleni (Xanthakos) and father of two teenagers, Jay's doctorate is from St. John's College, Oxford University, and he is the co-author of *Completing Capitalism* (Berrett-Koehler, 2017 and CITIC Press in

Mandarin, 2018) and author of *Spies and Saboteurs* (Macmillan and St. Martin's Press, 1999).

Julie Kolokotsa worked for over twenty-five years in public policy in Washington DC, Brussels, and Athens, including as a campaign and NGO organizer, a journalist for a sustainable business magazine, and as a guest and adjunct lecturer on subjects including creating value with stakeholders on sustainability. She has co-developed research on how purposeful corporations can use business ecosystem orchestration to create social value alongside shareholder value. She has published articles in academic journals on policymaking and practitioner magazines on sustainability with stakeholders, has an undergraduate degree in politics/international relations, a master's in environmental management and sustainability, and is currently completing a PhD in politics and policymaking.

François Laurent is a senior Catalyst fellow based in Paris who holds a master's degree in business administration (EDHEC, France). He spent seven years in audit and consulting in Europe and Africa before becoming a finance director at Mars and Wrigley for eighteen years in a wide variety of geographic locations. As a former regional finance vice president in the Middle East, Central and Eastern Europe, Western Europe, and Asia-Pacific, Francois has acquired unique experience of managing and developing business in diverse market situations and cultural environments. He also has extensive experience in international accounting standards, financial reporting and audit.

Qian Li is a lecturer in sustainable business operations and public value engagement fellow at Cardiff Business School, Cardiff University. She previously worked as a postdoctoral researcher on the Mutuality in Business project at Saïd Business School, University of Oxford. Qian's current work focuses on the empirical links between ESG risks and shareholder value, the impact of NGO activism, and the drivers of human capital. Interdisciplinary in nature, her work spans corporate finance, strategic management, environmental economics and business ethics. Qian holds a PhD in business ethics and asset management from ICMA Centre, University of Reading.

Colin Mayer CBE FRA is the Peter Moores Professor of management studies at the Saïd Business School at the University of Oxford. He is a professorial fellow and sub-warden of Wadham College, Oxford and an honorary fellow of Oriel College, Oxford and St Anne's College, Oxford. He is a fellow of the British Academy and the European Corporate Governance Institute. He is a member of the UK Government Natural Capital Committee and the Board of Trustees of the Oxford Playhouse. He was appointed Commander of the Order of the British

Empire (CBE) in the 2017 New Year Honours for services to business education and the administration of justice in the economic sphere. He was chairman of Oxera Ltd. between 1986 and 2010 and assisted in building the company into what is now one of the largest independent economics consultancies in Europe. He is a director of the energy modelling company, Aurora Energy Research Ltd. He advises companies, governments, international agencies and regulators around the world, and he leads the British Academy enquiry into 'the Future of the Corporation'. He is the author of *Firm Commitment: Why the Corporation Is Failing Us and How to Restore Trust in It* and *Prosperity: Better Business Makes the Greater Good,* published by Oxford University Press in 2018.

Muhammad Meki is a post-doctoral research fellow at Pembroke College, University of Oxford. He completed his DPhil (PhD) in economics at St. John's College, University of Oxford. In his research he is interested in the effect of equity-like financial contracts, which involve profit and loss sharing and/or shared asset ownership, on the investment and growth of microenterprises in developing countries. Prior to academia, he worked for five years in the financial markets, for Bank of America in London and Deutsche Bank in Singapore, where he traded government bonds, fixed-income products, and foreign exchange derivatives.

Jonathan Michie is professor of innovation and knowledge exchange at the University of Oxford where he is director of the Department for Continuing Education and president of Kellogg College. He is a fellow of the Academy of Social Sciences. Prior to moving back to Oxford in 2008, he was dean of the Business School at the University of Birmingham; before that held the Sainsbury Chair of Management at Birkbeck, University of London, where he was head of the School of Management and Organisational Psychology; and before that was a lecturer in accounting and finance at the Judge Business School, Cambridge.

Jan Ondrus is an associate professor of information systems and currently serves as the associate dean of faculty, ESSEC Asia Pacific. Additionally, he is the director of research for the Center of Excellence in Digital Business. His interests cover digital business models and innovation, digital platforms and ecosystems strategy, mobile payment and FinTech, and strategy of IT. He currently serves as an associate editor of the journal *Electronic Commerce Research and Applications* (ECRA). In recent years, Jan has been visiting the University of Hawaii, Sungkyunkwan University, Mannheim University, University of Lausanne, Case Western Reserve University, Seoul National University, and Korea Development Institute (KDI). Professor Ondrus holds an MSc and a PhD in information systems from HEC Lausanne (University of Lausanne) in Switzerland.

Martyn Percy is a British Anglican priest and theologian. He has been Dean of Christ Church, Oxford since October 2014, and was previously Principal of Ripon College Cuddesdon, Oxford. Percy teaches in the Faculty of Theology and Religion. He is also Professor of Theological Education at King's College London and has served as Professorial Research Fellow at Heythrop College, University of London. He is an emeritus canon of Salisbury Cathedral, having previously served as an honorary canon. He has also been an honorary canon, serving later as Canon Theologian, at Sheffield Cathedral. He became a fellow of King's College London in 2018.

Simon Quinn is a researcher in development economics, with a particular interest in the role of firms. He is currently working as an associate professor at the University of Oxford Department of Economics, where he is also a deputy director of the Centre for the Study of African Economies. He is a member of St Antony's College.

Sudhir Rama Murthy is a research fellow at Saïd Business School, University of Oxford. He is also an early career research fellow at the Skoll Centre for Social Entrepreneurship, and a member of the Senior Common Room at St Antony's College, Oxford. His research interests are in sustainable manufacturing, circular economy, and stakeholder management. He was a recipient of the Dr Manmohan Singh Scholarship from St John's College, University of Cambridge, for his PhD in engineering. He holds a master's degree from the Indian Institute of Science. Sudhir's broad motivation is in sustainable industrialization of the developing world.

Sylvain Remyhas worked for twenty-five years as an economic and business analyst, researcher, teacher, and advisor in Europe and Asia. He was an information systems management consultant in Paris with leading service and financial multinationals. Later, he was posted in Seoul by the French Ministry of Finance, as an economic analyst and trade diplomat. With in-depth business and government experience, he turned to higher education in Singapore, where he has been involved in applied and academic research, course design and teaching, and programme development and direction around the topics of business networks and responsible business. He concurrently completed a PhD on the geography of entrepreneurship.

Bruno Roche is the founder and executive director of the Economics of Mutuality. He is the former Chief Economist of Mars, Incorporated and Managing Director of the Mars internal think tank 'Catalyst', a global thought leadership capability and internal corporate think tank to Mars which has been the laboratory for developing, testing, and incubating the Economics of Mutuality since 2006. In

2020, recognising its potential to reshape the landscape of business, finance and management education, Mars endorsed Bruno to re-deploy the Economics of Mutuality as a structurally independent public interest foundation with a management consultancy arm, able to grow beyond the boundaries of one company. Today, he leads the Economics of Mutuality globally from Geneva, Switzerland with the support of Mars as a key partner. He co-created the Economics of Mutuality Labs at the business schools of Oxford University (SBS) and CEIBS (Shanghai); he is a visiting lecturer in different universities and serves as an expert to the World Economic Forum. His education and academic research interests followed an applied maths path with a specialization in international economics & finance and management sciences. Bruno co-authored with jay Jakub *"Completing Capitalism: Heal Business to Heal the World"*, which has been published in both English and Chinese (Berrett-Koehler, 2017 and CITIC Press in Chinese, 2018).

Kate Roll is an Oxford political scientist concerned with power and vulnerability. With a background in international development, she is interested in the challenges and ethics of inclusive business, private sector approaches to poverty reduction, and the growing role of technology in these spaces. She has conducted field-based research on 'base of the pyramid' development programmes in Indonesia, the Philippines, and Kenya and on post-conflict transitions in Timor-Leste. At Saïd Business School, she contributes to the strategy and innovation curriculum and also serves as a lecturer in both politics and management.

Claudia Senik is professor of economics at the Sorbonne University and the Paris School of Economics. She is co-director of the Wellbeing Observatory at CEPREMAP, member of the IZA and of the Institut Universitaire de France. Educated at the Ecole normale supérieure, she received her PhD from EHESS. Her main research area is the economics of happiness, with a special interest in the relationship between income growth, income distribution, and subjective well-being, as well as well-being at work. She also conducts a research stream on gender gaps. She has published many articles in refereed journals, as well as several books, such as *L'économie du bonheur*, la République des idées, Seuil, 2014, and recently *Les Français, le bonheur et l'argent*, 2018, Presses de l'ENS, with Yann Algan and Elizabeth Beasley.

Judith C. Stroehle is a postdoctoral researcher at the Saïd Business School in Oxford, where her work primarily focuses on non-financial measurement and accounting, as well as sustainable investing and engagement strategies. Judith holds a PhD in economics and sociology from the University of Milan and has several years of industry work experience in the German online start-up scene and as a data strategy consultant for international channel marketing. Judith engages and works with several non-profits, companies, and asset managers on their non-financial strategies and reporting and measurement practices.

Case Study Contributors

Mike Barry, Marks & Spencer
Alexandra Berreby, Bel Explorer
Taryn Bird, Kate Spade
Helen Campbell Pickford, University of Oxford
Alastair Colin-Jones, Mars Catalyst
Yassine El Ouarzazi, Mars Catalyst
Justine Esta Ellis, University of Oxford
Aida Hadzic, (formerly) University of Oxford
Jamie Hartzell, Divine Chocolate
Ni Jing Hua, JD.com
Ben Jackson, Freud Communications
Genevieve Joy, University of Oxford
Lionel Khalil, Mars Catalyst
Jon Khoo, Interface Inc.
Louise Koch, Dell
Hugh Locke, Smallholder Farmers Alliance
Atlanta McIlwraith, Timberland
David Nash, Z Zurich Foundation
Lydia J. Price, CEIBS
Hannah Radvan, (formerly) Mars Catalyst
Sudhir Rama Murthy, University of Oxford
Stephen Roberts, Dell
Kate Roll, University of Oxford
Jean-Marie Solvay, Solvay Chemical
Caroline Sorlin, Bel Explorer
Judith C. Stroehle, University of Oxford
Miriam Turner, Zoological Society London
Vikram Vora, Sabka Dentist
Michel Washer, Solvay Chemical
Liu Xiaowen, JD.com
Ibon Zugasti, Mondragon

PART I

1
Introduction

Colin Mayer and Bruno Roche

'In Search of the Right Level of Profit'

This book is about purpose or rather the achievement of purpose, which is the realization of the highest form of aspiration of any organization or individual.

It is the argument of this book that the real battle our globalized world is facing today is not between liberalism and protectionism, or between China and the United States, or between globalization and nationalism, but rather between a sense of purpose and no purpose—between fulfilment and no fulfilment.

It is the argument of this book that the new rifts tearing apart the fabric of our society and planet—thriving cities versus rural areas, skilled elite versus the less educated, wealthy owners of financial assets versus the working class—are all rooted in an economic model (namely the Chicago School of Business) that was misconceived in its conception and has become more so over time. The nature of scarcity has changed radically from financial to other forms of capital while our economic models have not—making Chicago's profit maximization approach progressively less efficient and effective and more destructive of value creation.

It is the argument of this book that today's main actors of globalization are no longer nation states but a growing body of multinational corporations and large international non-governmental organizations (NGOs). These have gained power and influence over time and now have the means—if they so choose—to reshape the global agenda, but they lack

Colin Mayer and Bruno Roche, Introduction In *Putting Purpose Into Practice: The Economics of Mutuality.* Edited by: Colin Mayer and Bruno Roche, Oxford University Press (2021).
DOI: 10.1093/oso/9780198870708.003.0001

political legitimacy. However, their power and influence give multinational corporations (MNCs) a particular duty as well as opportunity to lead a transformation of business into a profitable force for good, that can partner with government to realign the regulatory environment for the new global context within which they operate.

It is the argument of this book that these new rifts have become so large—and the model and actors that together created them are so dysfunctional—that they cannot be addressed on the margin through conventional programmes of charity or corporate social responsibility (CSR) initiatives that incorporate philanthropy as a supplement to business. Instead, they demand a profound transformation of the very purpose of the firm, the extension of its effective boundaries beyond its legal ones, the redefinition of procedures for value creation beyond just the creation of financial capital for shareholders, and finally, the modes of profit construction. Only in this way will economists, academics, business practitioners, regulators, and policymakers have the tools and motivation to embrace their duty and opportunity to teach and practically implement needed changes within the context of the new macroeconomic and microeconomic paradigm.

But it is also the argument of this book that most successful organizations are those that choose to be driven by a sense of purpose that transcends self-interest—a sense of purpose that seeks to develop reciprocally beneficial obligations amongst a wide variety of relevant stakeholders—a sense of purpose that can transform business performance for the benefit of people, planet *and* profit (in that order)—in other words, *mutuality*.

Finally, it is the central argument of this book that the real issue today is not just having a purpose but fulfilling it. The achievement of purpose has become ever more necessary at a time when:

- Most MNCs articulate and communicate their corporate purposes beyond pure profit maximization but fail to realize them;
- There is a growing gap between purpose and practice—a dangerous and potentially explosive phenomenon that encourages cynical assessments of purpose as being 'sustainability Ponzi schemes', namely illusions of sustainable practices without the capability to deliver them;

- The level of trust society in business and the leaders of business is eroding rapidly.

This is not an abstract issue, but rather is a real living, breathing conflict that every responsible leader in business, finance, and business academics must now face. This is the very essence of modern economics and management: a battle for purpose in a world of rapidly increasing complexity and confusion—not just having a purpose but making that purpose real at every level of the organization, especially when the odds are so often resolutely stacked against it.

This is the objective of what we call the *Economics of Mutuality*, which is about:

1. Putting purpose into practice through a new definition of the boundaries of the business ecosystem of the firm, a more complete definition of performance, a more comprehensive process of value creation, and profit construction that go beyond financial profit alone;
2. Inspiring corporations with a tested means to access untapped resources to improve business performance in a holistic manner for people, planet, and profit;
3. Identifying how business and finance can restore their roles in society and the planet.

There are periodic revolutions in business: the emergence of the joint stock company, limited liability, the market for corporate control, lean manufacturing, and just-in-time management are some examples. They fundamentally affect not just business and the corporate sector but customers, employees, investors, economies, societies, and the environment at large. They have profound effects on our lives, well-being, prosperity, and our environment.

We are going through such a period now. There are two forces at work. The first is technology: the so-called fourth industrial revolution is fundamentally altering ways of working, consuming, living, and flourishing. It is providing new means of communicating, socializing, thinking, producing, and distributing. And it is connecting us with each other, with information and knowledge in ways that were unimaginable only a few years ago.

The second force at work is the central subject of this book, and that is the nature of business itself. In the face of profound and rapid changes, the nature of business has to evolve rapidly if it is to remain relevant to society at large. The last sixty years have seen the rise and dominance of a particular view of business that has shaped the nature of the way in which it conducts its activities. This view has been widely accepted as the sole paradigm for how good business should be done and what makes for success—a genuine success that has indeed enabled the emergence of a global middle class lifting hundreds of millions out of poverty in the midst of a doubling of the world population, famines, plagues, wars, the collapse of the Berlin Wall and most of the ideologies that have disfigured the twentieth century, the advent of the fourth industrial revolution, and the rise of MNCs.

Yet this success has been accompanied by an unbalanced distribution of value creation to the benefit of financial capital owners and highly educated workers at the expense of the less educated; an unprecedented and continuously rising consumption of natural resources—humanity is currently depleting the environment 1.7 times faster than our planet's ecosystems can regenerate; and a rising and alarming level of societal mistrust in business and government.

In this context, the 2008 crisis was a wake-up call that has started to shake the pillars of society and the economy. It has been a milestone that has begun to highlight the excesses of the relentless pursuit of profit maximization and its consequences—the widening of inequalities, public distrust, and environmental degradation. The gains of financial capitalism and unbridled globalization are increasingly being extinguished by exclusion, populism, nationalism, and protectionism, which themselves are fuelled by fear of others, the evolution of work imposed by the fourth industrial revolution, the decline of the middle class, and threats to the planet.

Despite a plethora of papers, books, gatherings, forums, summits, initiatives like the United Nations Sustainable Development Goals, the World Economic Forum, movements like inclusive capitalism, creating shared value, conscious capitalism, and purpose beyond profit, the status quo prevails. Such has been the plethora of ideas for promoting responsible business that if 'the road to hell is paved with good intentions' then responsible business risks becoming the source of our damnation. However, the last few years have seen a growing recognition that business needs to change. The question is no longer whether business should reform or why, but how and now. How should business change to meet the requirements of the twenty-first century?

That is precisely the question this book seeks to answer. It attempts to move beyond general exhortations for change, fine words, and good intentions to describe how change should occur and how business can bring this about itself. It is about how some of the most enlightened, successful corporations are striving to achieve change and what their experiences of it have been. It is not about intentions but vision and actions. How business can and should adapt in the twenty-first century to make good its power to do good, not necessarily for a worthy higher cause but because it is simply good business. It is about what works and what doesn't work and why.

The book therefore has elements of a 'how to' volume. But it is much more than that. It is based on an extensive programme of research that Mars Catalyst, the internal think tank of Mars Incorporated, the food and beverage company, has been undertaking since 2007 in conjunction with several universities, including the Saïd Business School at Oxford University as part of a programme of research funded by Mars Inc.

That research programme has provided profound insights into the nature of the corporation, its purposes, its process of value creation, and above all its potential to promote economic, environmental, and social well-being in ways that are reciprocal. This book sets out both the intellectual contribution of the research programme as well as the practical insights it provides into the means by which companies can adopt practices that are mutually beneficial for themselves, the societies they serve, and the environment in which they operate.

In these two introductory chapters we set the scene by describing the background to this volume based on the erosion of trust in business, the reasons for this, including the failings of the conventional business paradigm, the nature of the new paradigm based on the economics of mutuality, and its different components. We describe the contents of the book and the way in which it attempts to combine conceptual ideas with practical evidence from a large number of case studies.

Trust and Trustworthiness of Business

The current state of business is paradoxical. It is by most measures booming. Up to the period of writing this book, growth in many parts of the world has been high, unemployment low, and inflation modest. By conventional economic criteria these are in many respects halcyon days. Furthermore, technological advances are offering extraordinary opportunities for business to transform our lives for the better in numerous areas—communications, computing, energy, food, medicine, and transport, to name a few.

And yet despite the successes and the opportunities, the standing of business in societies around the world has never been lower. The latest figures of the Edelman Trust Barometer (a nineteen-year-old instrument designed by the public relations Firm Edelman to detect and document large opinion shifts globally), for example, confirms an alarming yet consistent pattern: 'Only one in five feels that the system is working for them, with nearly half of the population believing that the system is failing them' and a growing divide of trust in business, government, NGOs, and media between the informed public (a proxy for highly educated people) and the rest of the population. Yet, despite the bleak context, the 2019 barometer also highlights that people are looking to business leaders to promote the change that is needed.

Every year for the past thirty-five years IPOS-Mori, the market research company, has undertaken a survey of 1,000 people in Britain on which professions they trust to tell the truth. The 2018 survey recorded that business leaders came near the bottom—just above estate agents, professional footballers, the media, and politicians. They came below trade union officials and 'the man or woman in the street'.

This is not just a bankers' phenomenon, because bankers are recorded separately and come slightly above business leaders. Nor is it just a post-financial-crisis result because it has been true from the start of the survey. Mistrust in business is profound, pervasive, and persistent. Why?

The answer can be found in two books recently published by the editors of this book.

What Has Gone Wrong?

In *Prosperity: Better Business Makes the Great Good,* Colin Mayer (2018) describes how business fundamentally shifted its focus over the last sixty years. For nearly all of its two-thousand-year history since the corporation was created under Roman law to perform public works, such as collecting taxes and minting coins, it has combined a public with a commercial function. It is only over the last sixty years since Milton Friedman first expounded his doctrine that 'there is one and only one social purpose of business . . . to increase profits so long as it stays within the rules of the game' that profits have emerged as the sole purpose of business.

This was a consequence of mounting concern during the first half of the twentieth century about a lack of accountability of management arising from a separation of ownership and control created by the growing dispersion of shareholdings of companies listed on stock markets. The response was markets for corporate control, first in the form of hostile takeovers, and more recently hedge-fund activism, that have resulted in an increasing preoccupation in boardrooms with profits.

The Economics of Mutuality

In *Completing Capitalism—Heal Business to Heal the World,* Bruno Roche and Jay Jakub (2017) describe how the context in which business operates has fundamentally shifted over the last sixty years—and highlight the need for the economic/business model to adjust. On the basis that economics is about managing scarcity and that the nature of scarcity has changed since financial capitalism emerged fifty years ago and became the dominant model for business operations, the authors argue that this model is today redundant in the current context of there being an overabundance of what was once scarce (money) and a growing deficit of what was once abundant (natural resources and talent matching the jobs being created). The world has changed, but the dominant model continues to deliver a form of value that is in surplus while largely ignoring what is in deficit.

In business, as the old adage goes, only what is measured is managed. With financial capitalism, business has only the tools to measure and manage a single form of capital—money—among multiple forms of capital—social, human, and natural. These other 'capitals' have considerable value but their value is not expressed in conventional monetary terms, and businesses that fail to account for such forms of value underemploy them. Roche and Jakub (2017) demonstrate how business can mobilize more of the value at its disposal to create greater value for society and nature, and by so doing so, also generate more profit than it can by maximizing profit alone.

In their book on *Completing Capitalism,* Roche and Jakub (2017) set out the vision, context, objectives, roots, principles, and ideas behind the Economics of Mutuality. They position it as a management innovation designed to empower business to outperform while restoring its positive impact on society and the planet and highlight the duty, the opportunity, and most importantly the responsibility of business leaders and business schools to take the lead in recasting the role of business. They describe the central aspects of the Economics of Mutuality methodology in terms of ecosystem building and mapping (to identify the effective and relevant boundaries of the firm with regards to its purpose), pain-point identification (to identify opportunities for impact), innovative management practices (to deliver against these aforementioned opportunities), innovative metrics and measurement of performance, and finally new modes of profit construction—namely the concept of a mutual profit and loss statement (to help assess what the right level of profit should be, to then align purpose and practice). The book also highlights real business experiments where Economics of Mutuality has been implemented.

This book elaborates on this simple yet powerful idea—that many of the world's most pressing societal and environmental challenges can be solved through business by using integrated business model approaches to drive positive social and environmental impact, while simultaneously delivering strong financial performance—and describes how in practice

Economics of Mutuality can and has been adopted and the experiences and lessons that have been learnt from doing so.

It further describes the core elements of the Economics of Mutuality methodology in the next chapter and fifteen cases where firms have implemented Economics of Mutuality in one form or another. It illustrates the very diverse set of businesses and sectors to which Economics of Mutuality has been relevant. It discusses its performance in extending the boundaries of the firm and embracing capitals beyond material and financial capital to include human, social, and natural capital.

First, the Purpose of Business Is Not Profit

There is nothing wrong with profits. On the contrary, profits are the lifeblood of business. They are needed to sustain business and to provide it with resources to fund growth, investment, and research. Without them business is dependent on philanthropy, and, as Grameen Bank founder Muhammed Yunus once said, a charity dollar only has one life while a business dollar (profits reinvested in business) can have multiple and potentially indefinite lives.

As *Prosperity* (Mayer 2018) argues, it is not profits per se that are the problem; it is the maximization of profit for the benefit of the shareholders at the expense of other stakeholders that is a mistake, as well as the presumption that profits are the 'be all and end all' of business and its sole purpose. Profits are not the sole purpose of business. The purpose of business is 'to produce profitable solutions to the problems of people and planet, and not to profit from producing problems for people and planet'. In the process, business produces profits. But profits are not per se the purpose of business and business should not profit from producing problems for people and planet.

Everyone who runs successful businesses knows this to be the case. What they do is to recognize the importance of trust and trustworthiness in upholding the commitment of the company to its corporate purposes. They commit to the corporate purpose and to those who contribute to creating the common purpose. Those people in turn commit to the common purpose.

It is this that gives rise to reciprocal relations of trust between the firm and the different parties to the firm—its 'stakeholders'. This in turn creates mutual benefits for the firm as well as its stakeholders. It gives rise to more loyal customers, more engaged employees, more reliable suppliers, and more supportive shareholders and societies. This results in higher revenues, lower costs, and therefore more profits.

This is the essence of mutual benefits—to the firm in the form of higher profits as well as to society in the form of the well-being of customers, employees, suppliers, creditors, shareholders, and communities.[1] It is the basis of what is termed the Economics of Mutuality.

Second, the Effective Boundaries of the Firm Are Not the Legal Ones

In an increasingly global, complex, and interconnected world, business leaders are recognizing that they can no longer solely rely only on their own resources and ideas and still remain competitive. In particular, they are seeing that innovation can come from anywhere, often from outside the firm's linear value chain.

In that context, what modern business is about is building relationships of trust not just within a firm but within society and in synergy with the environment. By trust we mean connection, recognition, and support of a mutual purpose for which we all work, and from which we all benefit, thereby providing an economic justification of social cohesion. In that context, the emphasis of the corporate purpose must shift—from the company being a mere vehicle for the capital market (to be traded, bought, and sold as a commodity) towards a vision of the company as a community of partnership in which each relevant stakeholder, including the planet, has a stake. The corporate ecosystem must be enlarged to go beyond the legal boundaries of the firm and be aligned with the effective boundaries of the firm (as determined by its purpose)—to encompass all relevant stakeholders; in a word: mutuality.

Notions of reciprocal relations are not new in business and are not in themselves a particular innovation. However, what marks out the Economics of Mutuality from other similar ideas in relation to responsible business is its notion of what constitutes the firm, and also (most importantly, perhaps) its pragmatic approach to defining the effective boundaries of the firm, to measuring non-financial performance with a set of simple, stable, and actionable metrics, and to leveraging the power of management and accounting to position mutuality at the core of the firm.

The conventional view of the firm is that it comprises a set of assets, such as buildings, plant and machinery, and land, over which it has property rights of control. It then contracts with a variety of parties, such as customers, suppliers, distributors, employees, and investors through contractual arrangements that bind them together with the firms' assets. Together property rights and contracts define the boundary of the firm.

What is not owned or contracted by the firm is external to the firm and gives rise to 'externalities'. These impose benefits or costs on the firm for which it is not charged or rewarded and, because they are externalities, they create a misallocation of resources resulting from the failure of markets to reward or penalize companies for them.

However, this conventional 'nexus of contracts' view of the firm is misleading. First, as is generally recognized, contracts are very incomplete. At best they are only a partial reflection of the factors that are relevant to the relation of firms with those with whom they interact. Second, contracts are in many cases infeasible. It is, for example, infeasible for firms to write contracts with future generations that may not yet be born but can be affected significantly by the activities of the firm, not least through their environmental consequences.

Most seriously of all, the nexus of contracts fails to recognize that most relations are not based on contracts at all but on trust, by which one party believes that another party will respect their interests without there being any contractual obligation on them to do so. That belief derives from an assessment of the trustworthiness of the other party.

What business is about is building relationships of trust and trustworthiness well beyond the boundaries of the firm to areas where ideas of property rights and contracts are an illusion. It allows companies to internalize activities that would conventionally be regarded as externalities and therefore the source of market failures.

The Economics of Mutuality is about how to create such reciprocal relations of trust and trustworthiness in areas that conventional business would not allow firms to trespass. It produces creative forms of doing business that do not do good for the sake of it or just for the benefit of others but for the reason that it is simply better business. It is a way of tapping into untapped resources, of mobilizing hitherto hidden capabilities, and of creating markets and profitable activities that other firms fail to recognize.

Once one thinks in these terms of extending the boundaries of the firm by creating reciprocal relations of trust then opportunities open up that previously were inconceivable. The purpose of the firm becomes the profitable solving of the problems of people and planet because people and planet provide profitable opportunities from which firms as well as people and planet benefit.

It is this notion of internalizing some of the most relevant externalities that underpins this book and the Economics of Mutuality and it is this that the subsequent chapters will explore. It will describe in principle and in practice how firms can and do create these profitable opportunities.

Putting purpose at the centre rather than the financial profit of a single firm means that an ecosystem can be designed to contribute to the overall welfare of communities while also leveraging multiple forms of capital, from financial to human, social, and natural, multiplying benefits for all. To do this, firms need to move beyond classical positioning strategies to embrace new approaches that bring into view wider perspectives that, in turn, focus on system-shaping strategies.

A starting point for implementing the Economics of Mutuality, therefore, is combining the principle of mutuality with the fact that companies are parts of larger business ecosystems and as such, have responsibilities to individuals, communities, and resources that contribute to business performance.

Third, We Need New Management Metrics to Measure Non-Financial Performance

In business, you manage what you measure and can expect good performance with good management. The issue we face today is that business tends to measure only financial capital—and only its own performance (ignoring the performance of others in the ecosystem in which it operates). Broadly speaking, business has managed its financial performance very well, but is left wanting in other areas. Although business has generally lacked interest in measuring—and therefore managing—non-financial capitals, it has been active in their creation and destruction.

The problem, however, is not business' preoccupation with measurement. Rather, it is business' obsession with the measurement of financial capital in the short term at the expense of non-financial forms of value without which the firm cannot operate effectively. The aim of the Economic of Mutuality's non-financial metrics, therefore, is not to offer new metrics for measurement's sake. Nor is it about using measurement of non-financial capitals to address sustainability issues and impact, although these are legitimate applications of the approach.

First and foremost, Economics of Mutuality metrics are designed to be simple, pragmatic, stable, and actionable tools for business to manage. They are analogous to financial metrics and are intended to drive management practices and decisions that positively impact people, planet, *and* profit. In other words, for business to be purposeful about becoming a force for good in society, it needs the metrics, management practices, and incentives that will drive corporate behaviour towards this goal. Without business enlarging the core of what it measures, mobilizes, and manages, it will never truly change its behaviour.

Fourth, We Need Management Accounting of Mutuality

The final core element of Economics of Mutuality is the mutual profit and loss (P&L), which integrates non-financial metrics and new practices through the use of existing accounting tools to efficiently manage performance across people, planet, and profit at the very core of the business.

The mutual P&L is a proposed change in the management account P&L, designed for internal use, that will modify the presentation of the financial P&L to take into account a business unit's impact on selected human, social, and environmental capital issues. The challenges of accounting for non-financial capitals are many and in a large part due to the fact that natural, human, and social capitals are priceless in the sense that they cannot be assigned a dollar value in a non-arbitrary and/or reductive way. A further challenge is that such capitals are external to the business, they are shared resources and do not belong to the company in the same way that buildings or machinery do. Therefore, there is little prospect of including them in the P&L by converting these non-financial capitals into a tangible asset with a financial value. However, it is possible through the Economics of Mutuality approach to:

- Avoid the pitfall of remunerating non-financial capital with financial capital (e.g. give a monetary value to human, social, human capital), hence positioning in an arbitrary fashion one capital above the others;
- Empower business to remunerate each capital with its own kind (e.g. remunerate financial capital with financial capital, natural capital with natural capital etc.);
- Account for the cost of maintaining and growing non-financial capitals, connecting the associated cost of doing so in the P&L; and
- Hence, calculate a single bottom line that incorporates financial and non-financial forms of value that are created and destroyed (and can be leveraged) by businesses across the most relevant stakeholders in the ecosystems in which they operate.

Doing this requires classifying two types of activity:

For External Capital Depletion: one should extend the operating P&L to reflect costs of replacing depleted capital. The 'mutual' profit will be lower than the traditional operating profit because of this adjustment. Any measurable improvement (i.e. reduction of external capital depletion) will be monitored using metrics (described above) and will entail an improvement year-on-year of the mutual P&L, encouraging doing 'right' for the durability of the business model.

For External Capital Creation: change the presentation of the operating P&L to treat related costs of interventions (budgets, people costs, etc.) as investments not as operating expenses. These costs will be removed from the mutual P&L with an effect similar to existing accounting practices, such as capitalization on internal R&D or IT costs or reclassification 'below-the-line' of one-time costs for restructuring. Mutual profit will be higher than traditional operating profit due to this adjustment. This modified presentation of the P&L can help relieve budgetary tensions at the unit level that are obstacles to strategic initiatives with short-term costs and long-term impact.

The P&L modifications described above can be shown as a simple reclassification in the management accounts P&L in a way similar to the treatment of non-operating costs. This is a simple, pragmatic step to incorporate non-financial metrics in management accounts. It will promote decision-making and performance management across multiple forms of capital; present an alternative mode of profit construction away from a pure financial profit maximization; remove the tension between the idea that there must be a trade-off between 'delivering the P&L' and doing what is responsible long term for human, social, and natural capital issues; and make it possible to adjust the incentive system and dividends accordingly so that doing the right thing aligns with the firm's objective and how it rewards employees and shareholders, shifting variable pay incentives from financial to mutual profit.

The next chapter will summarize the main learning that has come out of these experiences to date and the insights that Parts II and III of the book provide on the conceptual and practical adoption of the Economics of Mutuality. It is worth noting at this point that the significance of the Economics of Mutuality extends well beyond business theory and practice at the micro level to macroeconomic considerations of the role of business in addressing performance of economies as well as firms.

The significance of extending the boundaries of the firm beyond their conventional confines is that it empowers parties to engage in economic activity from which they were previously excluded. The exclusion does not just come from the traditional concerns of macroeconomics in relation to aggregate demand and money supply but from the ability of individuals and organizations to realize their productive supply capabilities.

The pain points that are identified in ecosystem mapping are not only those of consumers in terms of meeting their consumption needs but also employees, suppliers, communities, and the environment in delivering the goods and services of which they are capable. These parties are constrained by their access to knowledge, training, skills, as well as finance and material inputs. These resources are not available to them from existing arrangements, but they are precisely the contribution that other companies are capable of providing, once they realize the potential profitable opportunities from doing so.

In other words, analogous to the demand constraints that afflict consumers in making their notional demands effective are limitations on individuals and organizations to make their notional supplies effective. They are supply constrained in a way that mirrors the demand constraints of Keynesian economics. These constraints are not a function of the capabilities of individual agents but a reflection of the systemic coordination and cooperation between multiple parties. No one agent acting individually is capable of realizing their potential supplies without the contribution of others. There is a need to orchestrate the contribution of different parties in such a way as they can meet their collective purposes.

Interventions by companies in building ecosystems that embrace constrained organizations therefore not only enhance human, social, and natural welfare and the performance of participating firms but also stimulate levels of supply and the growth and development of economies as a whole. The success of previously constrained organizations in turn allows them to engage with and assist other parties, which thereby alleviates the constraints that they in turn face. There is therefore a multiplier effect from one organization promoting Economics of Mutuality that permits others to follow suit.

The Limitations to Economics of Mutuality

While the book attempts to describe the case for Economics of Mutuality as clearly as possible, it strives to do so in an objective and balanced way. The partnership between a company—Mars Incorporated—and an academic institution, such as Oxford University, has been important in that regard. It has given access to information on the underlying activities and performance of firms which otherwise would not have been available, while ensuring that objective independent assessments of them are made.

It has also given access to knowledge and capabilities that would not have been available to create new knowledge, to implement it in business, teach it in business schools, and disseminate it through books, academic publications, and forums.

Such partnerships inevitably pose risks and problems, for example, of academic capture by commercial interests. However, one of the insights to come from the Oxford–Mars programme has been how to manage such academic–business partnerships in a way that provides insights while maintaining independence. The book does not claim to provide definitive answers on the merits or deficiencies of this particular model of doing business but it does suggest that it is worthy of serious consideration and in-depth analysis and scrutiny by others.

First, as conventionally understood in some circles, mutuality is a source not a solution to the problem.[2] To the extent that it is associated with free exchange then mutually beneficial transactions to which parties voluntarily contribute cannot be divorced from the power imbalances and concentrations of control that frequently underpin them. To create a mutually beneficial outcome that confers nearly all the gains on the rich and powerful while only improving the lot of the impoverished by a miniscule amount is certainly not inspiring and may be positively detrimental in exacerbating inequality and disparities of wealth.

It is therefore important to understand that the conception of mutuality here goes beyond this conventional notion of exchange to embrace the idea of promoting positive and significant benefits for others as well as the self. Putting purpose as the driver, with purpose being directed towards solving problems appropriately identifies problem solving as the source of economic performance and social well-being.

A second limitation is that, in its current form, Economics of Mutuality is a management innovation that is limited to business. It does not address the macroeconomic and policy-making questions that will be necessary to frame the upcoming Economics of Mutuality grassroots movement and ensure that there will be no confusion between the role of business (which has no democratic legitimacy), civil society, and government. In that context, the topic of the politics of mutuality is separate from its economics but of utmost importance and will requires politics, similarly to business, to shift the paradigm and tilt it in two directions: first, to strengthen the core of purpose (drawing inwards to a core meaning); and second to embrace the power of participation (pushing outwards to engage) and develop leadership capabilities to unite inner purpose and outer engagement.

A third limitation is that, in its current form, because Economics of Mutuality is a business model innovation that works for business, it is not (yet) designed to be used in finance as an investment model, though conversion of Economics of Mutuality from a business model tested in the fast-moving consumer goods space into a financial investment model is the next step in our plans for the Economics of Mutuality. Given the overwhelming power of finance (over the real economy), one could argue that until Economics of Mutuality addresses the world of finance, it will never be a transformational movement.

A fourth limitation is that Economics of Mutuality should not be regarded as a panacea for the failings of companies in relation to society or the environment or a means by which companies are assured of improved performance. As with any business innovation, it has its pitfalls as well as advantages in terms of the impact that it can have on companies as well as the societies and environments in which they operate, and this book seeks to set out a balanced account of these drawbacks as well as advantages.

In particular, in so doing the research programme has brought out the importance of recognizing the two elements associated with purposeful business, namely not only 'to produce profitable solutions to the problems of people and planet' but also 'not to profit from producing problems for people and planet'. The latter is important in avoiding the adverse consequences that doing well by doing good can create. That is to say, extending the boundaries of the firm beyond its property and contractual rights can be an intensified source of doing well by doing bad as well as good.

Two examples will illustrate this. The 'gig economy' and the sharing instead of ownership of assets for the provision of taxi, delivery, property rental, and other services around the world provide forms of 'employment' with a greater degree of flexibility than previously existed. However, they also lack the security, protection, and insurance of traditional employment and risk exploiting vulnerable members of society with few or no alternatives available to them. Whether the gig economy is enabling or exploitative remains highly controversial.

Second, companies may enhance human and social capital by bringing employment to parts of the world where it is in short supply but involve the production, distribution, and supply of goods and services with adverse consequences associated with them, for example addictive products such as alcohol, drugs, fast foods, and tobacco.

In both cases, companies may appear to be benefiting—earning profits—by doing good—creating employment—where they are producing bad—insecurity and addiction. The profits are therefore illusory and do not satisfy the condition of avoiding producing one set of problems at the same time as they are solving others.

The approach of arguing for companies taking enlightened and innovative approaches to the way in which they conduct their business also raises questions about whether companies can and should be making ethical and welfare judgements. The traditional view of business, as expounded by Milton Friedman, is that there should be a clear separation between the roles of business in seeking to profit, and governments in setting the regulatory rules of the game by which companies are expected to abide. Mixing and confusing the two risks placing welfare judgements in the hands of those without elected mandates to exercise them. It therefore subverts the democratic process by conferring disproportionate authority on owners and executives of corporations in relation to the rest of society.

There therefore remains a primary role for governments and regulators in setting and enforcing the standards by which companies are required to behave, for example in relation to the terms and conditions on which people are employed. However, many of the obligations on companies will reflect not only formal systems of regulations but also socially acceptable norms, as, for example, set out in the United Nations Sustainable Development Goals.

In particular, regulation has an important role to play in not only setting the rules by which companies should abide but also aligning corporate purposes with public purposes in organizations that perform public functions and provide public goods and services. This applies in particular to utilities—energy, telecoms, transportation, water companies—

infrastructure providers, companies engaged in public–private partnerships and private finance initiatives, and companies with significant market power. In all these cases, companies perform public alongside private, commercial functions and need to align their corporate with their public purposes.

Conclusion

In our world of increasing complexity and confusion, the achievement of purpose in business becomes steadily more difficult but is also more necessary; and our world needs mutuality more than ever, even if the forces that oppose the achievement of mutuality are becoming more powerful.

In its current form, Economics of Mutuality is a first step in that direction that can be applied in business and helps shape a grassroots movement of business and business leaders to adopt a responsible form of capitalism, fairer and more efficient than the purely financial one dominating business practice today. Through the Economics of Mutuality, one can achieve a more equal, social and environmentally oriented economy that is actually more profitable than a purely financial one. To rediscover its vocation, business does not need to focus exclusively on short-term financial capital remuneration to survive and thrive.

This book avoids responsible business paving the way to hell with good intentions by converting those intentions into actionable realities and compelling visions. It describes how it can, should, and has been done. It sets out the evidence on the way in which companies can do well by doing good and avoid doing well by doing bad.

In particular, the book sets out the reasons why this works. It is centred round corporate purposes that go beyond the pursuit of profits to solutions to people and planet problems. It emphasizes the importance of trust and trustworthiness beyond property ownership and contracts. It describes the process of ecosystem building, pain-point identification, and human, social, and natural capital promotion, measurement, and rewarding.

However, above all it points to the importance of extending the boundaries of the firm beyond property and contractual control rights to areas that traditionally would have been viewed as external to the firm. By internalizing such externalities, it encourages companies to address market failures themselves that previously have been the remit of governments.

The significance of this is not just for firms and the societies with which they interact but economies as a whole. What the Economics of Mutuality does is to establish the macroeconomic as well microeconomic significance of mutuality. It does this by allowing not only those who are demand constrained to be able to make their notional demands effective, but also those who are supply constrained to make their notional supplies productive. It does this by providing them with the skills, relations, and financial resources that they require to do it.

This book is therefore of significance not just in addressing the defects of corporations, solving problems of people and planet, and avoiding problems that are currently imposed on people and planet, but also in promoting the functioning of national and international economies. Putting purpose into practice potentially provides a process for promoting aggregate as well as individual well-being. At the heart of this is a new paradigm for business and finance driven by new modes of profit construction and a new relationship between business, society, the environment and work.

Notes

1. For evidence of superior financial performance of purpose driven firms, see Gartenberg, Prat, and Serafeim (2016). For evidence that firms which treat their workers well perform better see, for example, De Neve, Krekel, and Ward (2019).
2. Rangan (2015, 2018).

2

Overview

Colin Mayer and Bruno Roche

Mutuality and Mars

Part II of the book begins in Chapter 3 with some thoughts on the ideas of mutuality and economics from a philosophical and theological perspective. It explores the changing relationships between business, finance, social flourishing, and morality, suggesting that: 'We are increasingly coming to see that the myopia of the market economy rests on a set of values and assumptions that prioritize the individual over the social, and wealth over wider concepts of flourishing.' It describes the values that promote human flourishing and how they have come to be condensed in a single value of profit that has progressively dominated our lives and societies.

Chapter 4 describes the history of how Economics of Mutuality emerged as a concept in Mars. It describes its roots back in the 1940s when Forrest Mars, son of Frank, the founder of Mars, set out the mutuality of benefits in a letter on 'the Objective of the Company'. Those objectives were framed in terms of a mutuality of services and benefits among consumers, distributors, competitors, suppliers, government, employees, and shareholders.

What was striking about this was the emphasis that the company placed on the interests of parties other than the shareholders—the 'stakeholders' rather than the shareholders. That was the basis of the study that Mars Catalyst, the think tank of Mars Inc., then undertook in the first two decades of the twenty-first century.

Colin Mayer and Bruno Roche, Overview In *Putting Purpose Into Practice: The Economics of Mutuality.* Edited by: Colin Mayer and Bruno Roche, Oxford University Press (2021).
DOI: 10.1093/oso/9780198870708.003.0002

The book discusses the meaning of mutuality in Chapter 5. In particular, it looks at how people in Mars regard the concept of mutuality as it is applied within the organization. What emerges is a considerable diversity of views about what it means and its significance. Even amongst the most senior levels of management and within the Mars family there is a significant divergence of attitudes towards it.

While this ambiguity might be thought to be a source of confusion, it has also allowed different approaches to its adoption to be pursued resulting in a greater degree of experimentation and innovation than might have prevailed in a more monoculture. To some, it is perceived as being predominantly about inclusive growth for the benefit of all parties; to others, it is the fact that it is neither charity nor amoral pursuit of profit that defines it; and to a third group, it is the long-term orientation predicated on enduring relationships that is of most significance.

This observation on diversity and ambiguity raises an important question about the leadership and implementation of responsible business programmes. Some people might argue that it is the role of the board and senior management to ensure that there is a consistent set of purposes and values in an organization that reflect its fundamental objectives. However, what Mars illustrates is more of a 'letting many flowers bloom' approach that devolves decision-taking to individual units to determine the extent to which they believe it appropriate to adopt mutuality principles. In turn, over time, as experiments succeed and fail then a more consistent set of views as to what is appropriate for the company as a whole might emerge.

Economics of Mutuality and Responsible Business Theories

Chapter 6 places Economics of Mutuality (EoM) in the context of a wider set of responsible business concepts, such as stakeholder theory and creating shared value (CSV).[1] It considers whether these ideas represent fundamental 'paradigm' shifts in business or whether they are essentially just old wine in new bottles. It concludes that stakeholder theory was a significant shift away from shareholder centric views of the firm, whereas CSValue retains a firm-centric, financially driven concept of business.

In line with stakeholder theory, EoM places corporate purposes other than shareholder value at the heart of the firm and derives business practices on the basis of that. But it differs from stakeholder theories in emphasizing the importance of relations with stakeholders in delivering corporate purposes not the interests of stakeholders themselves. It also differs from existing models in looking at the boundaries of the firm beyond traditional ownership rights and contractual arrangements. It is therefore a problem-solving view of the firm as against a financially or stakeholder driven concept that embraces shareholders and stakeholders but does not put corporate purpose at the heart of either of them.

EoM is fundamentally different from corporate social responsibility (CSR), which regards responsible business as an add-on to the existing activities of the firm—philanthropic, societal, benevolent, and worthy—but not the core of what the business does. Real responsible business is the business. It is embedded in the corporate purpose and it drives the structure, conduct, and performance of the business.

Corporate Purpose and Ecosystem Orchestration

Chapter 7 begins by setting out the nature and importance of corporate purpose. The power and effect of corporate purpose depend on its authenticity and way in which it is specified. Striking a balance between breadth and vision, and specificity and precision determines its relevance and impact. Authenticity involves living the corporate purpose and translating it effectively into corporate actions. It should not be preserved in aspic but instead evolve steadily over time to promote its relevance.

Chapter 7 then argues that it is not only the internal organization of a company that should be aligned with its purpose but so too should its external ecosystem. Ecosystems include other businesses, non-profit organizations, local communities, and governments. Pharmaceutical companies, for example, are closely linked to patient organizations, hospitals, and government health agencies.

The co-creation of products and ideas depends on an alignment of the corporate purposes of participating organizations. They commit to devoting their resources to a common purpose and the term ecosystem orchestration refers to the coordination of multiple stakeholders in pursuit of a common purpose. It thereby extends the purpose beyond the individual corporation to a range of external as well as internal parties who help to internalize externalities. As Chapter 7 states, ecosystem orchestration 'redefines a stakeholder's "stake" in the corporate purpose as a forward-looking opportunity to co-create value, instead of a backward-looking opportunity to capture value created by the corporation on its own'.

The case in Part III of Sabka Dentist, which is the largest chain of dental clinics in India, is an illustration of the importance of clarity of purpose. The company's mission is to provide affordable dental care to all people in India, with an emphasis on the poorest members of the urban population. At the heart of its business model is a high degree of standardization that involves fitting out clinics with pre-specified units that allow the company to set up a new clinic within three weeks. It invests heavily in training programmes and provides interest-free funding to patients. It measures its performance in terms of the number of patients it treats, its in-house audit scores, patient satisfaction, and average revenue per patient.

Chapter 8 describes the process of ecosystem orchestration in more detail. It sets out an eight-step process around: (a) establishing a purpose, (b) designing metrics that measure the purpose, (c) identifying the relevant stakeholders, (d) mapping their objectives, capabilities, relationships, and pain points (i.e. problems), (e) selecting the pain points in the ecosystem that the organization should address, (f) measuring the baseline performance metrics before the intervention, (g) identifying, testing, and implementing the interventions to address the pain points, and (h) measuring the impact of the interventions on purpose and performance.

The chapter emphasizes that the process of ecosystem orchestration involves the company placing the interests of the ecosystem and the ecosystem's purpose as against the company's own self-interest at the centre of its own purpose. In so doing, the company should embrace the creation of mutuality of benefits not for enlightened self-interest but on a commitment to delivering the ecosystem purpose. This involves the company acting as an orchestrator not a dictator of the ecosystem and performing this function by developing the right tools and partnerships. In the process, the company will create a strategic advantage for itself as well as the other members of the ecosystem.

The case of Mahindra Firstchoice in Part III provides a clear description of the process of ecosystem orchestration in the context of the second-hand car market in India. It describes how Mahindra Firstchoice mapped the ecosystem in relation to six key parties—consumers who were buyers, consumers who were sellers, car manufacturers, independent used-car dealers, independent car service workshops, and banks. It then identified the bottlenecks and 'pain points' that afflicted the six parties.

The used-car market did not function properly because of lack of trust, information, and transparency and Mahindra Firstchoice worked with the parties to identify solutions to the market failures. These involved, amongst other things, the creation of third-party car inspection services, the establishment of a multi-brand car dealer franchise, a warranty system, a bluebook of second-hand prices and transactions, and a car diagnosis and repair system.

Through building a clear understanding of the nature of the problems in the ecosystem, Mahindra Firstchoice was able to provide precise responses that allowed for cost-effective responses to the problem. It thereby avoided the higher costs associated with buying out the players in the ecosystem.

One of the most serious pain points that people and communities face is flooding. As Part III of the book describes, Zurich is one of the world's leading insurance groups with a mission to help customers to 'understand and protect themselves from risks'. It is seeking to reduce flood risk through preventive action and in 2013 it launched a global flood resilience programme. This involved building partnerships with several organizations including the Red Cross and Red Crescent, and Wharton Business School. It runs interventions with communities in Mexico, Indonesia, Nepal, Peru, and Bangladesh. Zurich believes that for every dollar spent on flood-risk reduction, five dollars are saved through avoided and reduced losses.

Chapter 9 examines the creation of cross-sector partnerships in more detail. These partnerships involve building unconventional relations between organizations that have traditionally not worked closely together, in particular between businesses and non-profit organizations. To achieve this, the different objectives and participating organizations need to be acknowledged and reflected in appropriate key performance indicators (KPIs). For example, a company may be concerned with the number of bars of soap sold and the non-profit organization with the number of people responding to a hygiene awareness campaign. The partnership's purpose is captured in the number of people addressing hygiene problems through thorough washing with soap.

Cross-sector partnerships go through several stages of development that move from philanthropy to transactions in the form of reciprocal exchanges between the partners, integration of the values and objectives of the partners, and transformation of these into values at the societal or community rather than the individual partner level. The most complex stage of development is the transition from transaction to integration and in many cases partnerships get stuck there. Completing the process of a full transformation of the partnership takes time and requires a sufficiently long horizon on the part of the partner organizations.

The case of the Bel Group in Part III of the book documents the way in which the company has worked together with a variety of different parties in marketing and selling its Laughing Cow brand in many countries around the world. The process began with investigating the structures and patterns of existing street vendors and then identifying those with whom it wished to partner. It involved running focus groups to determine pain points in the ecosystem and then providing training, health insurance, financing, and access to the formal sector of taxation, social security, and migrant registration. The programme became profitable within two years of its launch, graduated more than four hundred micro-entrepreneurs from training courses and provided health insurance to a thousand people. It is currently targeting eighty thousand street vendors around the world by 2025.

The case in Part III of Timberland, which designs, manufactures, and sells footwear, clothes, and accessories for the outdoor is a good example of a business–non-profit partnership. It has partnered with a Haitian non-profit organization, the Smallholder Farmers Alliance, with a view to creating a new supply chain to reintroduce organic Haitian-grown cotton and incentivize farmers to plant trees. From the start of the programme in 2010 it has grown to more than six thousand members in three thousand farms.

Metrics and Measurement

Chapter 10 turns to the measurement of performance in delivering corporate and ecosystem purposes. The metrics are designed to capture the pain points in the ecosystem that need to be addressed and the success of the intervention in addressing them. This requires measures of non-financial as well as financial performance.

Chapter 10 provides an overview of measurements of non-financial forms of capital: natural, human, and social. In examining natural capital, it contrasts input measures that record the amount of natural resources that are used in the production process and output measures that examine the impact of the inputs on products, emissions, waste, etc. It notes that measuring inputs is in general more straightforward than outputs and it therefore argues that natural capital metrics should be constructed around inputs rather than outputs.

An example is the resources used in producing a cup of coffee. This involves raw materials, air emissions, biodiversity and land used in agriculture processes, and raw materials, energy, water and waste production in packaging, distribution, and drinking. In essence, this approach measures the resources used at different stages of production from farm to consumption and seeks to diminish the environmental and natural capital input of the entire value chain.

The circular economy, in which manufacturers of products take responsibility for their disposal by recycling them back into the production process for their reuse in new products, is an example of mutually beneficial diminution of environmental and natural capital inputs across the value chain. As described in Part III, the computer manufacturer Dell runs the world's largest electronics take-back programme. It has recovered more than 800,000 tonnes of electronics since 2008. In the case of individual consumers it partners with freight companies in retrieving equipment from consumers' homes and partners with Goodwill, a not-for-profit organization that seeks to make people independent through education and training, in running two thousand locations across the United States where consumers can drop off any brand of used electronics.

Interface, a billion-dollar corporation and one of the world's largest manufacturers of carpet tiles, is another example of a circular economy company. It uses discarded fishing nets to make carpets. Through a social enterprise, Net-Works, it collects and sells discarded fishing nets from local communities in the Philippines and Cameroon, generating income for the local communities, reducing the environmental impact of the discarded nets and providing an input for the manufacturer of new carpets.

Chapter 11 looks in detail at social capital, which it defines as 'the quality of the social context in which exchange and teamwork take place: does the social context promote efficiency and coordination, or is it an impediment to trade and a source of distrust?' Key to this is trust and the trustworthiness of parties to a relationship and exchange. This involves creating a group identity that promotes collective as against individual interests. Leadership and social norms are critical to the creation of group identities.

Chapter 11 notes that social capital can be detrimental as well as beneficial to firm performance if it encourages allegiances outside the firm, for example, in the form of corruption and nepotism. Avoiding this requires creating a sense of common purpose and values that embrace partners rather than either exploiting them or pandering to particular interest groups. As Chapter 11 concludes, 'fostering mutual investment in reciprocal relationships has been practised by human societies since time immemorial to build social capital and achieve mutually beneficial exchange. The difference is that the approach here is applied to the market realm, which is known to be such a powerful mobilizer of human dynamism and ingenuity. It is this combination of old and new that makes mutuality such a promising avenue to joint prosperity.'

Three indicators of social capital appear to be particularly important: (a) inclusion and cohesion; (b) trust, solidarity, and reciprocity, and

(c) collective action and cooperation. They account for a high proportion of social capital in vulnerable farming communities around the world and they are associated with the productivity of these communities. There is also evidence of a relationship between these measures of social capital, exchange of information and learning, and adoption of new agricultural practices.

JD.com is one of China's largest e-commerce companies, capturing more than a quarter of the country's $600 billion B2C market in 2017. Part III describes how it is seeking to become one of the world's most trusted companies and is working with local farmers' cooperatives, the Chinese, and a local internet business owner to create a programme called Running Chicken to source free-range chickens at scale from low-income farmers in Wuyi County in northern Hebei Province. JD buys chickens at three times the average market price provided that strict standards are adhered to and monitored. The result has been increased farmer incomes that have raised hundreds of families out of poverty and removed Wuyi County from the national poverty list. Pilots are underway to replicate the programme in other poverty-stricken counties of China.

As Part III discusses, Novo Nordisk, the Danish multinational pharmaceutical company, has taken an innovative approach to addressing diabetes around the world in a programme known as 'Cities Changing Diabetes'. This involves partnering with patients, policy-makers, health care professionals, and non-government organizations to find policies based on life-style changes that help people living in urban environments to avoid, manage, and treat the onset of Type 2 Diabetes. Community engagement with health, health promoting policies, and health system strengthening were the types of initiatives that were trialled, and impact measurements were undertaken to evaluate the performance of the programme.

Chapter 12 turns to human capital. Human capital is typically associated with the stock of skills and experience that an employee accumulates through education and training. However, the chapter refers to it in a broader context of well-being at work. This is affected not just by wages and working hours but also by the degree of hierarchy in an organization, management style, wage differences, prospects for upward mobility, and corporate identity. Alongside hierarchy, status, career progression, and inclusiveness, corporate culture (defined as shared beliefs, understanding, values, goals, and practices) plays a key role in determining well-being at work. The chapter records that it is possible to construct actionable metrics of well-being at work based on these factors that can be used to identify pain points within firms and the actions that are needed to address them.

The case of Kate Spade in Part III is a good illustration of a company that has sought to create human capital in the form of women's economic empowerment in an employee-owned social enterprise in Rwanda. The purpose of the company is to produce high-quality, high-end products for the global fashion industry by investment in training and skills that empowers women to promote positive change in their communities. The lowest artisan salary in the business is higher than the median salary in the private sector in Rwanda and the company generated a positive net income in 2017.

The case of Marks and Spencer in Part III illustrates how the company has used a sustainability scorecard that awards provisional, bronze, silver, and gold ratings to participating suppliers to promote its sustainability programme. The scores are based on environment, human resources, and ethical trade, and lean manufacturing. Suppliers undertake self-assessments of the scorecard at least once a year, which are subject to audit and assurance. The programme has delivered substantial savings through waste reduction and environmental efficiency amounting to over £600 million since 2007. Marks and Spencer aims to source all of its products from silver- and gold-level suppliers by 2020.

Accounting

Chapter 13 sets out the principles that lie behind designing a system of accounting for responsible business. It considers this in the context of accounting for natural capital. It describes how accounting in a mutual context has to be intrinsic in the sense of promoting the enhancement of natural capital for its own ends, not extrinsic to shareholder interests in being motivated by a desire to enhance profit and shareholder value.

That might be a consequence of the enhancement of natural capital but it should not be the motive. Secondly, the accounting system should reflect the full impact of a company on natural capital, not just reporting the improvements that are being achieved but also recording the detriments. It needs to recognize that the starting level of a firm's natural capital may not be sustainable because it has fallen below a level at which it is capable of regenerating itself. Investment in natural capital may therefore be required to restore it to a minimum critical threshold.

Third, accounting needs to recognize the strong non-linearities in natural capital—for example, threshold levels below which it is prone to collapse—the complex nature of biological ecosystems, and their time dependency on external conditions—for example, growth might result in a deterioration in a company's natural capital at the same time as it makes substantial improvements to its utilization and maintenance of natural capital.

Finally, and linked to the first point, accounting for natural capital should reflect a corporate purpose that places the intrinsic benefits of natural capital at its heart. While one might not be able to manage what one does not measure, one does not necessarily appropriately manage what one measures. There is therefore a limit to what accounting can achieve without the determination of corporations to achieve it.

Chapter 14 records how Mars is seeking to implement a mutual profit and loss (P&L) statement in its management accounts. It is being used to align the management systems of Mars with its purpose and signal to the business that performance in terms of human, social, and natural capital is as important as financial performance.

The mutual P&L reflects the observation made above that the boundary of the firm should not be restricted to its legal and contractual rights and obligations but should also embrace the ecosystem that is relevant to the delivery of its purposes. It includes expenditures in the ecosystem as part of its activities and crucially recognizes these as investments not just current operating expenditures where they contribute to human, social, and natural capital as well as material and financial capitals. In line with traditional accounting methods, it values these investments at cost not at market values.

As Chapter 14 states: 'the mutual P&L is an extension of the financial P&L that takes into account selected human, social, and environmental issues that are relevant for the organization and its ecosystem toward a stated purpose.' It describes four phases in the construction of a mutual P&L. The first is selection of relevant material issues; the second is the measurement of the creation and depletion of human, social, and natural capitals; the third is the valuation of impacts at cost as capital investments or depletion; the final stage is the integration and presentation of the mutual P&L in the company's management accounting system.

Chapter 14 then describes how Mars and Oxford University are monitoring the impact that adoption of mutual P&L management accounting is having on the management of different parts of the Mars business. Incorporating expenditures as investments in human, social, and natural capital is expected to encourage management to engage in activities that have effects on, amongst other things, sourcing supplies, packaging, and storage. It encourages the leadership to promote activities that at present are discouraged by concerns about the firm's bottom line but in future will be recognized for what they are, namely investments in assets that contribute to the delivery of the corporate purpose. The chapter acknowledges that this process will be constrained not only by the adoption of appropriate accounting systems but also by the degree to which the firm's financial, investment, ownership, and engagement arrangements are conducive to the adoption of innovative practices and investments.

The mutual P&L is one example of many attempts that are being made to incorporate non-financial considerations in company accounts. Integrated reporting is another and Solvay, a global chemical company headquartered in Belgium with revenues in 2017 of €10 billion discussed in Part III, is an example of a company that is seeking to adopt integrated reporting. It has developed a sustainable portfolio management tool to assist the company with reducing the environmental and social risks of its products and producing an integrated financial report. The tool maps the environmental footprint and costs and risks to society of all products, investments, research and innovation projects, and potential mergers and acquisitions.

Finance, Investment, Ownership, and Engagement

One way in which sharing traditionally occurs is through financial instruments. Equity is the form in which different parties to a firm share its risks and rewards. Over the past two decades, there has been an explosion in funding in the form of debt that has been available to micro-entrepreneurs and borrowers through microfinance around the world. This has allowed individuals and communities to promote the development of new businesses and entrepreneurial activities that were previously unfunded. However, it has also driven people into debt for consumption as well as investment purposes and placed substantial repayment obligations on those with little means to meet them.

Equity in principle offers the potential for more mutual funding arrangements. Chapter 16 describes an experiment that is in progress in Kenya to encourage entrepreneurial activity through financing investment by micro-equity rather than micro-debt. The experiment involves individuals distributing Wrigley chewing gum products alongside other goods in Kenya, in particular in areas of the country which were previously impenetrable by existing distribution mechanisms. To assist with their activities, funding arrangements were put in place to allow the distributors to purchase bicycles.

The study investigates what happens when the distributors were offered alternative forms of finance ranging from traditional debt instruments to more equity forms of risk (revenue) sharing. At the time of writing, a pilot study has been undertaken which reveals that equity financing performs better than debt in terms of repayments. If confirmed in a larger study this will have important implications for designing financing instruments for promoting activities beyond traditional boundaries of the firm (in this case the self-employed distributors of Wrigley products) and for evaluating the benefits that may be conferred from developing more mutual sharing funding arrangements.

Important though finance is, mutuality encompasses much more than just risk-sharing funding. Indeed, it has been traditionally associated with particular types of organizations (mutual organizations) that were established to prioritize the interests of their customers and employees. Mutual ownership was viewed as key to aligning the interests of businesses with their members in contrast to stock corporations where shareholder interests diverged from those of their stakeholders.

But as Chapter 17 describes, the concept of mutuality described in this book extends well beyond that of mutually owned businesses. Mars itself is entirely owned by the Mars family. Many of the companies described in Part III of the book are stock corporations with external shareholders. One of the ways in which family firms can retain a focus on the common purpose of the business after the family has withdrawn or sold out to other shareholders is through 'industrial foundations' that confer a substantial fraction of the ownership of firms on foundations. These are particularly commonplace in Denmark and Germany, and some of the most successful companies in the world, such as the shipping company Maersk and the media firm Bertelsmann have these ownership forms.

The principle of the Economics of Mutuality is about aligning the interests of diverse parties to a common purpose. This can be adopted in companies with any type of ownership but where it takes the form of, for example, mutuals or foundations, then it creates a commitment to the common purpose that may not be observed to the same degree elsewhere.

Divine Chocolate, a UK-based Fairtrade confectionary company described in Part III, has an innovative ownership model in which a Ghanaian farmer-owned co-operative supplies its cocoa and owns 44 per cent of the Divine Chocolate business. The co-operative shares in the profits of the business and has a say in the running of the company, including being represented on the board of Divine Chocolate. It thereby seeks to address the numerous challenges facing the chocolate industry of farmers' income, low productivity, price instability, child labour, and deforestation, driving many people to leave cocoa farming.

Mondragon in Part III is a federation of industrial co-operative associations with over 260 company subsidiaries in thirty-five countries, founded in 1959 in Spain's Basque Region. Today it employs seventy-five thousand workers producing revenues of approximately $14 billion. Membership of the co-operative gives employees equal rights to vote and ownership; management boards consist of employees from all levels of the organization; the highest managers earn no more than six times the salary of the lowest paid workers; no more than 20 per cent of workers can be temporary contractors; and the general assembly of worker-owners decides how to distribute 70 per cent of profits after tax. An illustration of the effect of the structure came with the collapse of the white goods manufacturer and one of Mondragon's largest co-operatives, Fagor. With 1,800 jobs at risk, Mondragon invested in cross-training employees to take on different roles at other co-operatives, transferred capital from stable to vulnerable co-operatives and placed 1,500 people in other co-operatives in the group.

At the other end of the spectrum from microfinance institutions are the institutional investors, such as the mutual funds, pension funds, and life insurance companies. Their importance stems not only from the financing that they provide but also from the governance that they exercise over companies by virtue of their ownership of corporate equity. The concern that this has raised is the failure of institutional investors to recognize their responsibilities as owners as well as their rights as shareholders. Those responsibilities relate to the stewardship function of their corporate investments, promoting corporate purposes, and ensuring that companies have the resources and support they need to fulfil them, and correcting their management when they fail to do so.

In particular, the dispersed ownership systems of the United Kingdom and the United States are associated with a plethora of institutional investors each holding a small proportion (e.g. less than 5 or 10 per cent) of the shares of large listed companies. As a result, they have little incentive to engage in active governance of the companies in which they invest. Instead, they 'free ride' on markets in corporate control from hostile takeovers and hedge-fund activism to intervene on their behalf at lower cost.

However, there is increasing interest amongst some institutional investors in more engagement with their corporate investments. A number of Canadian pension funds and several countries' sovereign funds are leading the way in this regard. Chapter 18 describes the approach that these funds are taking. It involves them acquiring significant blocks of shares in companies that are held for extended periods of time and managed directly by asset owners themselves instead of by intermediary asset managers.

Critical to this is the way in which the performance of their investments are monitored and measured. Alongside measuring financial performance over longer periods of time than is conventionally the case, performance needs to be assessed in relation to other indicators of performance related to human, social, and natural capital. Increasing weight is being placed on environmental, social and governance (ESG) measures of performance in this regard and there is mounting evidence of a positive association of ESG with financial performance over the longer term. There are, however, limitations of the reliability of ESG metrics and the application of mutual P&L statements may provide a more useful management tool for institutional investors as well as corporations.

It is not only institutional investors that should exert influence over companies to promote the adoption of corporate purposes that extend beyond profit. Consumer groups, employee forums, and non-governmental organizations (NGOs) are also increasingly being recognized as powerful influences over corporate activities. Chapter 18 describes the work of NGOs in aligning corporate with social and environmental purposes.

Historically, the relationship between corporations and NGOs has been antagonistic. However, as Chapter 9 describes increasingly corporations and NGOs are working in partnership to achieve common goals. The role of NGOs in influencing corporate activities is not restricted to such partnerships. They have been adopting activist campaigns to achieve desired outcomes in a form that is not dissimilar to those of institutional investors. Indeed, in some cases, they have acquired shares to strengthen their influence over companies.

These campaigns have often been seen by companies to be shareholder-value destroying. Chapter 19 records that this is by no means always the case and NGO campaigns can be mutually beneficial for firms as well as society. It sets out how NGOs can bring knowledge of a local community or a technical and legal expertise nature that firms may lack. They execute projects in common with companies, set agendas for various constituencies, exchange complementary knowledge in diverse areas, and provide access to networks.

Conclusion

The book documents how EoM offers a powerful approach to putting purpose into practice. At the heart of it lies a clear articulation of corporate purposes and an alignment of different constituencies associated with the firm in the delivery of those purposes. What distinguishes EoM from other responsible business concepts is its recognition of the need in the process to extend the boundaries of the firm beyond their legal and contractual limits to achieve the full potential for delivering corporate purposes.

Ecosystem creation and mapping, and pain-point identification are critical to the internalizing of these external engagements of companies. They are the reason why it is feasible for companies to internalize what are traditionally regarded as externalities and to address the market failures that have previously been regarded as the remit of governments to solve. In the process, they often involve companies working with local and national public bodies, not just in the form of the public organization setting the rules of the game and the private one implementing them, but as true mutually beneficial partnerships.

Alongside ecosystem creation and mapping, measurement and metrics are crucial to the fulfilment of corporate purposes. These measures extend beyond financial and material assets to include human, social, and natural capital. The measurement of these involve the accumulation of very different data from financial and material capital but are capable of being evaluated in a form that permits their practical adoption by companies in their management processes.

These measures should furthermore be incorporated in companies accounting systems to develop mutual profit and loss statements. These appropriately recognize expenditures on human, social, and natural capital as investments that should be capitalized and depreciated in an analogous manner to material assets. They also create liabilities that reflect the obligations on companies to preserve and promote non-financial forms of capital.

The Economics of Mutuality involves not just innovative types of partnering, measurement, and accounting but also financial instruments, forms of ownership, institutional engagement, and ways of working with civil society. In particular, outside bodies such as institutional investors and NGOs need to adopt some of the practices and forms of measurement and management that are required of corporations. They too should recognize the importance of investments in human, social, and natural capital and the potential financial as well as societal benefits that can thereby be derived.

Note

1. See Porter and Kramer (2011).

PART II

3

Bread and Honey

Social Flourishing, Mutuality, and Economics

Martyn Percy

Introduction

Mutuality, charity, and a concern for economic justice marked out the very first Christian communities. Stephen, the first Christian martyr, was a deacon with special responsibility for the daily distribution of alms to widows and orphans (Acts 6: 1–3), reflecting the commitment of the church to charity and service advocated in the gospels. In character, the first churches, although diverse in practice and belief, appear nevertheless to have exhibited a radical openness to mutuality, parity, and inclusion. Indeed, the term for 'church' is the simple Greek word *ekklesia*, meaning the 'assembly of the people' who belong to but are called out of their community. All over the Mediterranean world, assemblies determined the politics, polity, and civic ordering of communities and cities. But they were usually only open to citizens, and the power to speak and vote was normally confined to men.

The assemblies of the New Testament church—the deliberate adoption of the more internationalist term which must have caused confusion to some potential converts, as well as making a point—were, in contrast, inclusive bodies and models of mutuality. In these *ekklesia*, women were admitted, as were slaves (c.f. Paul's Letter to Philemon), children, foreigners, and other visitors. In other words, the character of the New Testament *ekklesia* represented and embodied a different kind of spiritual and social

Martyn Percy, Bread and Honey: Social Flourishing, Mutuality, and Economics In *Putting Purpose Into Practice: The Economics of Mutuality.* Edited by: Colin Mayer and Bruno Roche, Oxford University Press (2021).
 DOI: 10.1093/oso/9780198870708.003.0003

ordering that eschewed discrimination on grounds of race, gender, and other criteria.

The very term 'economics' is rooted in the Greek word *oikos*—the concept of a well-managed, stewarded household. *Oikos* was one of the early terms for 'church'—literally, the 'household of faith'. In terms of etymology, the management of the household was linked to the budget. It is no accident that Jesus told so many parables about stewardship and money, linked to the church. The *oikos* known in the first-century world of Jesus was different from our modern focus on the nuclear family: it was a household comprising servants, slaves, distant relatives, perhaps a tutor for the children, and other workers. The *oikos* was, in other words, a small social unit that transcended biological-family relations. The *oikos* had a care for the poor, and for the destitute; it cared for its members. As did the church later.

The Power of Latency

Linked to this, therefore, we often find that churches foster and focus distinctive values that are derived from the process of training (often through hidden curricula rooted in shaping virtues and character) that then go on to provide leaven in complex contexts. Here, faith communities often find themselves promoting forms of goodness that secular and utilitarian organizations might miss. In this respect, Bruce Reed explains how mutuality and ministry partly functions by drawing on an analogy from nature:

> If bees could talk, and we came across them busy in a flower garden and enquired what they were doing, their reply might be: 'Gathering nectar to make honey.' But if we asked the gardener, he would most certainly answer: 'They are cross pollinating my flowers.' In carrying out their manifest function to make food, the bees were performing a latent function of fertilizing flowers. The mutual dependence of bees and flowers is an analogue of churches and society.[1]

Here, Reed offers us a vivid picture of mission and ministry that we might recognize. Through a simple ministry of 'deep hanging out' with the people we serve, attentiveness, hospitality, care and celebration, celebration, ministers often do more good for the parishes, communities, and institutions they serve than they can ever know. This may simply be through the offering of regular lunches, simple visiting, or open house for tea and coffee at any time. These are manifest intentions. But the potency of the gesture and practice lies more in their latency, and is significant for ministry. Much as Jesus set an example in this respect, simply by walking from place to place, and developing his ministry through seemingly casual encounters, rather than through overt planning.

The practice of being engaged in an occupation of this kind says something about the possibilities for different kinds of spaces in communities—social, pastoral, intellectual, spiritual, to name but a few. They open up a different side of the humanity of a community or institution to those individuals within it. In being there with programmes and events, as well as in being purposefully hospitable, churches actually begin to enable that work of becoming the social transcendent communities they are called to be.

Economic intentionality can be highly focused and immensely productive. But sometimes, values and 'soft' forms of valuable social capital come out of time and space that might at first sight seem 'unproductive'. This is a subtle concept to grasp. According to John Kay, the concept of obliquity describes a simple process: that of achieving complex objectives indirectly.[2] One thinks of Polonius's speech in Hamlet, suggesting we reach our wisdom and goals through indirect means:

> And thus do we of wisdom and of reach,
> With windlasses and with assays of bias
> By indirections find directions out.

Kay discusses the verdict of Charles Jencks, the architectural commentator, who opined that modernism ended at 3.32 pm on 15 July 1972. That is the date when contractors detonated fuses that blew up a housing development in St Louis. Only two decades earlier, such housing—high rise tower blocks, most notably—had been feted by Le Corbusier, who famously claimed such buildings were the supreme expression of modernism, and that a house was (merely) 'a machine for living in'.

But as Kay points out, the modernists knew less than they thought. A house is not simply a machine to live in. Indeed, there is a difference between a house and a home. The utility of property and its actual functionality is only one element in design. The spaces that we inhabit are formational. They say things about individuals and groups. They arrange social living. Buildings have aesthetics that can promote subtle qualities and values. Some prompt alienation and individualism. Others, in contrast, can foster civic sociability, generosity, and mutual flourishing.

Kay's concept of obliquity is more fertile than it may at first appear, to take intentional church growth as an example: is this best achieved by clear aims and objectives, and with clarity on programmes and activities? Or, is growth better achieved through oblique means? To some extent, the answer will depend on what is meant by 'growth'. If measurable numerical growth is the primary goal, and is rooted in a concept of member-based organization, then yes, straight, direct and forthright programmes will be cherished and valued. The missional activity will have manifest intent, and a clarity to its aims, objectives, and outcomes that is often 'measurable'. And then there is that question: what do the bees think they are doing? And what are they actually doing?

So much for the honey mentioned earlier, but what about the bread? It is worth looking at Abby Day's prescient study of 'Generation A' women who, born in the 1920s and 1930s, have provided the backbone to organizations such as the Mother's Union.[3] Day's analysis picks up on the function of these laywomen in churches who are often found providing support through 'soft' forms of pastoral care and, in particular, through their catering. Specifically, she writes about them baking together.

Day shows how through activities such as communal baking—which are technically uneconomic—nonetheless provide an environment that promotes mutual care, flourishing, prayer, and pastoral well-being. It is obviously cheaper to buy the cakes and buns at any supermarket. But the communal baking fosters something else. The obliquity lies in the gap between the manifest and latent function of the activities Day so richly describes. The manifest intention of the communal baking is to provide a supportive catering service to the church and community. The latent intent that emerges is the thick pastoral care that the gatherings engender, which also produce deeper and richer spiritual lives. It makes no economic sense, please note, to bake buns like this. The value lies in the actual and apparent *inefficiency*—which leads to deeper, unintended rewards; and goals no-one aimed at.

The Early Church and Mutuality

The early church had form on this count. It is a little-known fact that part of the Edict of Milan (313), which was an agreement between the emperors Licinius and Constantine to recognize the legal personality of churches, treat all religions equally, and to restore lands and property confiscated under persecution, also made provision for donkeys. According to the agreement, Christians, calling on all others of good will, were to see that beasts of burden were not abused in transporting heavy loads uphill. Such concerns may seem trivial to modern readers, but the Edict provided an early piece of evidence to support the view that the Christian faith had extensive interests in contributing to mutuality and social order—even in the minutiae of everyday life. Generations of Christians would follow suit on other issues where prevailing standards and social constructions of reality had to be undermined and cast aside if justice was to be done. The emancipation of slaves (Samuel Wilberforce), equality for those sweltering under the yoke of oppression in America's deep south (Martin Luther King), or the alleviation of poverty in Victorian London (William Booth) are but a few examples.

The Edict of Milan is widely regarded as the point at which the foundation for established Christianity was first laid, although the Edict did not establish Christianity in the formal sense. The emerging Constantinian settlement did, however, provide a paradigm that was to influence much of Europe as it embraced Christianity. This was to link civic governance, religion, and the economy in the interests of providing sustainable patterns of social ordering that were of benefit to communities (e.g. such as the prohibition on usury). In England, for example, the relationship between a parish and its church was intrinsic to the identity of a place. Communities that were economically and socially viable were able to sustain a church and the ministry that issued from it, which in turn guaranteed a certain level of moral welfare, social improvement, and pastoral provision (including the availability of the sacraments). Or, put another way, the very existence of a parish church within a community confirmed the identity of the place, conferring it with recognizable significance that invited a form of social ordering in which (amongst other things) the needs of the poor and other matters of moral concern could be addressed on behalf of the community.[4] Churches were early agents of mutuality.

Similarly, the genesis of many hospitals, schools, hospices, and other agencies for welfare (e.g. adoption, fostering, etc.) began their life as an extension of the pastoral provision of the churches, intended for the common good. Throughout Christian history, there have been many movements and individuals whose faith has spawned something particular that has directly contributed to the re-ordering of society. Christianity has been especially prominent in healthcare, welfare, and education, but has taken no less interest in the moral well-being of society.

Challenging the Assumptions of Late Capitalism

The global financial crisis, coupled with the collapse of major banks and the effective insolvency of countries—Greece and Iceland come to mind—have prompted a new wave of ethical, economic introspection that is focused on the limits of capitalism in relation to the human condition and social flourishing. David Hare's play, *The Power of Yes*, which deconstructs the inner dynamics of the financial crises of the twenty-first century—economic growth transformed into an apotheosis—neatly encapsulates the issues:

> Once Bradford and Bingley became a bank, I remember taking an immediate dislike to a new non-exec who said, 'I want one thing from this company.' He said, 'What I want is regular, incremental growth.' In other words, he was saying '*This company must grow every year*.' Now that we all know that nothing in the world shows regular incremental growth. You know that. I know that.[5]

In his prescient work[6] David Sainsbury reflects on the private equity bid for Sainsbury's, the family business that he had once run. In his view, the bid for the business was nothing more than an attempt to acquire the company, sell off the firm's property portfolio, and take on additional debt in the process of acquisition (in much the way that new wealthy owners of Premier League football club might do). Sainsbury maintains that the bidders for his family business had no pretence of seeking to improve the performance of the company. The bid was, in other words, not about the flourishing of individuals, the company or the communities they serve. It was, rather, purely about profit for those driving the bid. In the face of this kind of dynamic, Sainsbury has become a staunch advocate of progressive capitalism. By this he does not mean to imply the state intervention of government, nor of shrinking government and deregulation. Rather, he means to infer better and more intelligent government that can be simultaneously nimble and strong, and, crucially, knows when to intervene and when to stand aside.

Sainsbury's reflections belong to a burgeoning genre of critical texts that have begun to cast some doubt on the implicit assumptions relating to the nature of humanity and society embedded in late capitalism. Sue Gerhardt, for example, writes as a psychotherapist and social commentator, and in her *The Selfish Society* she muses on the consequences of a society focused on individual acquisition, independent of the concerns and needs of our neighbours and wider society: 'selfishness is often a symptom of a failure of human connection.'[7] It is a failure of mutuality and our common life.

At issue here, perhaps, is the relationship between business, finance, social flourishing, and morality. In Stephen Green's *Good Value*, he considers how capitalism, though obviously flawed, might take a wider account of spiritual and social needs.[8] For Green, who writes as both a banker (former chair of HSBC) and an Anglican priest, the financial services industry has responsibilities to the people it serves. Echoing Sainsbury, he suggests that that businesses have a duty to society that go beyond the creation of profit. Whilst he acknowledges that 'open market capitalism' may be the best hope for creating wealth, this in itself does not prescribe how individuals are to work together for the common good. This is especially so in an increasingly urban, connected, and demanding world, where the intense and pluralistic pressures on morality and spirituality—which foster value and character in individuals and society—are threatened by the drive to individualistic self-improvement. Green, in other words, is another 'soft advocate' of balancing the 'private' (i.e. business) with the wider 'public' sphere. And he recognizes, in a similar vein to David Hare's play, *The Power of Yes*, that the future of social flourishing lies in seeing the distinctive contributions each sphere can make.

Here in the play, Hare has an imaginary conversation between a pro-privatization banker and someone in public service, who works in an institution. The character speaking puts it like this:

> I come from the private sector myself but I do get tired of a certain private-sector (organizational) arrogance. When people say, 'Oh get some private-sector people into the schools, that'll sort them out.' Actually I doubt if there are many jobs in finance as hard as teaching a class of fourteen-year-old boys in a tough school. Because business is in some way quite simple, it has clearly defined aims. The aim is to make money. So you have a measure against which to judge all the subsidiary actions which add up to the overall result. Managing a hospital is rather more complex. Because it's very hard to know what your objective is. There's no money-metric to help make the choice between better cancer care or having a better A & E. It's a judgement call. And running a hospital is an endless series of judgement calls where the criteria and objectives are very far from clear. So don't tell me that's easier than making money.[9]

What is appealing about Hare's play is the way in which he sets about questioning the assumptions and values we place on money and economics, appearing not to notice that economics—indeed economic systems—cannot be value-neutral. Carried within any philosophy of economics is a set of values that have implications for individuals, communities, and wider social flourishing. We should be cautious about assuming any immutability in the current economic systems that we have come to take for granted.[10]

The nub of the problem with the current unchallenged dominance of capitalism within most developed-world socio-economic systems is that capitalism has become a kind of 'fundamental' of human existence. Theologians such as Kathryn Tanner have even gone so far as to suggest that capitalism, as an outlook and philosophy, is something of a belief system.[11] It is almost as though God said 'let there be markets', and 'lo, they were created, grew, and multiplied'. Yet one should not simply read economics as a faux-religious creed. It can also be clothed in the rhetoric of 'hard science'—and indeed we note how the term 'political economy', a phrase which Marx and Engels would have understood—has been morphed into the simpler, apparently more humble 'economics'.

The consequences of this are serious, as 'economics', as a 'science', can then simply reduce everything to the realm of commodification: labour, services, relationships . . . and even religion. Drawing on the work of Michael Sandel, Rowan Williams singles out education as a sphere that is particularly under threat from commodification: 'that education could have some value other than improving profits seems to be unthinkable.'[12] Sandel himself thinks the balance may have tipped:

> we believe that civic duties should not be regarded as private property but should be viewed instead as public responsibilities. To outsource them is to demean them, to value them in the wrong way . . . without quite realizing it, without ever deciding to do so, we have drifted from *having* a market economy to *being* a market economy.[13]

Sandel is keen to proscribe the limits of the free market economy. We cannot 'buy' friends, for example,[14] as friendship is constituted by certain norms, virtues, and attitudes that are beyond pricing: sympathy, generosity, thoughtfulness, and attentiveness cannot be replaced by market values. To attempt to purchase such characteristics as commodities would be to simultaneously destroy them in the very act of procurement.

Conclusion

Money can't buy love; and it can't buy true friendship either. Yet the marketplace has an uncanny knack of developing and producing simulacrums that replace the slow, patient business of building relationships and developing reticulation with something that is quick and instantly gratifying. Richard Sennett's essay, 'Together'[15] cites the example of Phillipa, a teenager who has 639 friends on Facebook, and claims to know the vast majority of them. Sennett points out that if all 639 friends sent one message or image each and received a reply, that would be 816,642 messages to digest—simply impossible.[16] Sennett is alive to the limits of capitalism and market economies. In a world where relationships are increasingly stretched by the demands of economic life, friendship, education, family life, and love emerge as forms social bonding and human flourishing that put the market economy back where it belongs: something that society has, rather than something that 'has' society.

There are signs of hope in the midst of this current phase of our human existence. Churches, theologians, and campaigning groups have recently begun to focus on issues such as transparency (in business and government), fair trade, and taxation. Money and markets are not neutral in terms of their values. We are increasingly coming to see that the myopia of the market economy rests on a set of values and assumptions that prioritize the individual over the social, and wealth over wider concepts of flourishing. In calling government, business, and financial services to account, the twenty-first century may yet see theologians playing a key and prophetic role in enabling society to see that what it might initially desire may not be what people actually need, and that tempting though wealth and individual autonomy may be, we are all connected. Our mutuality and social flourishing is all about the bread and honey, and the obliquity of economics. No one is an island.

Notes

1. Reed (1978: 139).
2. Kay (2010).
3. Day (2017).
4. Pounds (2001).
5. Hare (2009: 37).

6. Sainsbury (2013).
7. Gerhardt (2010: 115).
8. Green (2009).
9. Hare (2009).
10. For an example of this argument see, Berry (2003: 207–8).
11. Tanner (2010).
12. Williams (2012: 75).
13. Sandel (2012: 10).
14. Sandel (2012: 137–41).
15. Sennett (2012).
16. Sennett (2012: 145).

4

The Roots of the Economics of Mutuality

Jay Jakub

Introduction

> It is clear ... that Mars, Incorporated is exploring the path to becoming a long-run investor in a holistic business future as opposed to a short-sighted, profit-only driven entity.
>
> Mars External Peer Review Panel, July 2013

The roots of the Economics of Mutuality (EoM) management innovation can be found deeply embedded in the DNA of Mars, Incorporated—a global food and beverage company whose origins date to 1911, when founder Frank Mars, Snr. began selling butter creams from his kitchen in Tacoma, Washington. The Mars-O-Bar company was launched in Minneapolis, Minnesota in 1922, and relocated to Chicago in 1929, shortly before the start of the Great Depression. In 1932, Frank's son Forrest left his father's company under the condition that any business he set up would be outside the United States. With $50,000 and the family's candy formulas, he moved to England to start his own Mars chocolate business in the industrial town of Slough, with a dream to build a business based on the objective of promoting 'a mutuality of service and benefits' for all stakeholders.

Forrest's 'mutuality of benefits' approach to business was later codified in a Mars personnel manual that he drafted,[1] and in his 1947 letter titled, 'The Company's Objective' (Figure 4.1).[2] This approach was more formally expressed in 1982 by his heirs as the 'Mutuality Principle'—one of

DOI: 10.1093/oso/9780198870708.003.0004

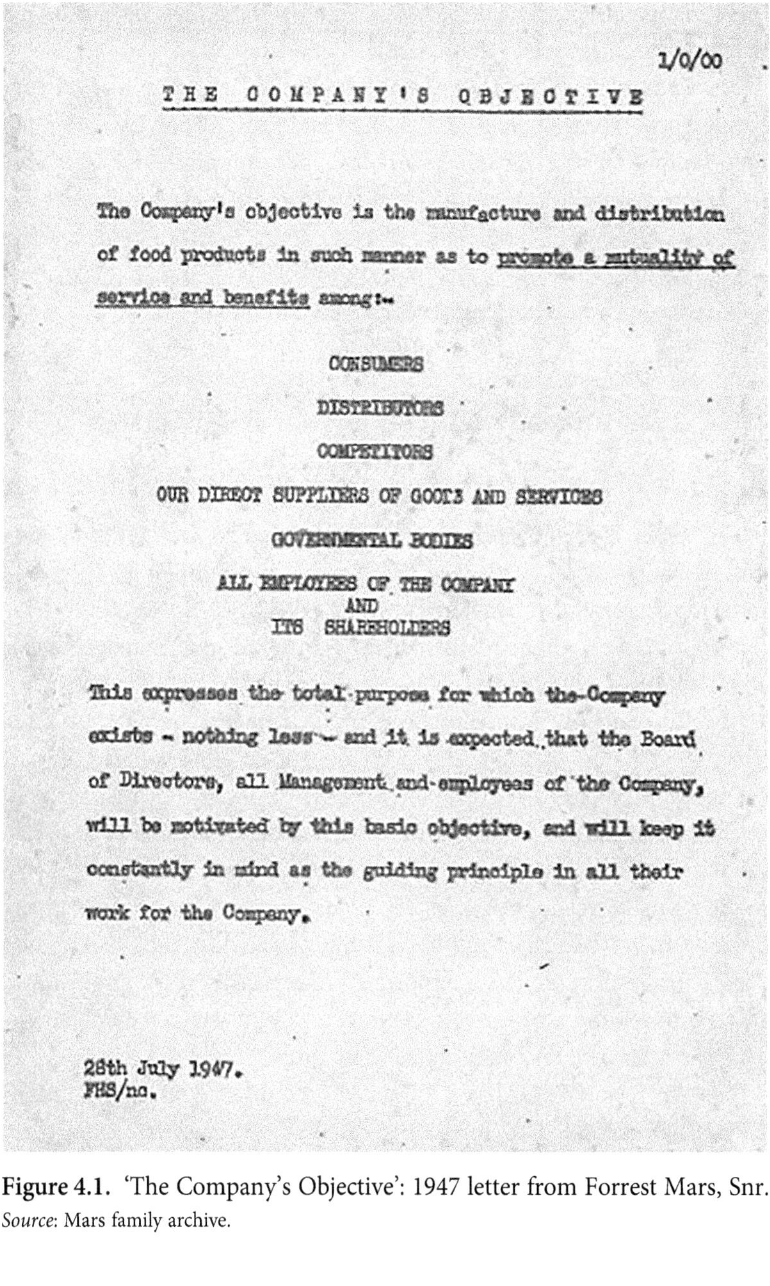

1/0/00

THE COMPANY'S OBJECTIVE

The Company's objective is the manufacture and distribution of food products in such manner as to promote a mutuality of service and benefits among:-

CONSUMERS

DISTRIBUTORS

COMPETITORS

OUR DIRECT SUPPLIERS OF GOODS AND SERVICES

GOVERNMENTAL BODIES

ALL EMPLOYEES OF THE COMPANY
AND
ITS SHAREHOLDERS

This expresses the total purpose for which the Company exists - nothing less - and it is expected that the Board of Directors, all Management and employees of the Company, will be motivated by this basic objective, and will keep it constantly in mind as the guiding principle in all their work for the Company.

28th July 1947.
FHS/nc.

Figure 4.1. 'The Company's Objective': 1947 letter from Forrest Mars, Snr.
Source: Mars family archive.

five core operating principles of Mars along with quality, responsibility, efficiency, and freedom—that remain in effect today.[3]

Mars has now grown into one of the world's largest and most successful corporations, operating in more than eighty countries across 420 sites. It employs over 100,000 'associates',[4] has over one hundred factories, and generates in excess of $35 billion in annual revenues across five business segments. These cover petcare, confectionery, food, and an entrepreneurial unit established in 2018 called Mars Edge that is exploring new opportunities at the nexus of data and nutrition.

The Future Mars Laboratory for EoM: Catalyst Think Tank

In the 1960s, Forrest Mars personally established an internal think tank for his company to challenge orthodox business thinking. This unit, Catalyst, currently led by the Mars chief economist, continues to have a purpose closely aligned with Forrest's intuition that 'management is about applying mathematics to economic problems.'[5]

The Economics of Mutuality programme, launched by Catalyst at the start of 2007 after preliminary research begun in late 2006, is the most expansive example of Forrest, Snr.'s vision of the role of management science in business. A much earlier illustration dates to the 1970s when Catalyst addressed what was then a major challenge for Mars of commodity procurement involving the cocoa supply. Catalyst helped the business by introducing weather and climate data into the existing crop yield's forecasting models to improve the accuracy of the predictions, thereby providing a better risk assessment against market fluctuations. This was very new for the business at the time.

This early work on cocoa led Catalyst into other quantitative disciplines, such as statistics, times series analysis, econometrics, and data mining that, in turn, gave birth to robust metrics for what had previously been thought to be unmeasurable—the impact of marketing on sales. The advertising evaluative approach Catalyst pioneered yielded a doubling of the efficiency of Mars advertising, bringing huge savings and giving the company advanced capabilities that competitors of Mars continue to try to replicate.

The EoM Journey Starts with an Unusual Shareholder Question

> What should be the right level of profit for Mars?
>
> John Mars, shareholder—question posed to Mars CEO & CFO in late 2006

The EoM journey at Mars can be traced back to a conversation in late 2006 between John Mars (son of Forrest), then Mars CEO Paul Michaels, and then CFO Olivier Goudet, during which John asked what the right level of profit should be for the company. This was a remarkable question coming from a shareholder, as most would define the 'right' level of profit as the maximum that can be extracted from a value chain to ensure continued growth, and for distribution as shareholder dividends.

But far from implying that the Mars family shareholders demanded higher profits, John Mars in 2006 was troubled that the company's profits might be too high. He was concerned that if the firm extracted more than its right from its value chain partners, this could create a squeezing effect whereby one stakeholder would be driven to squeeze another for more margin, and so on, ultimately creating a disequilibrium that would disadvantage Mars. As he explained to the co-chairman of the Mars Science Advisory Council (who later led two external peer reviews of the EoM programme), 'If you take care of the left [downstream] part of the value chain [growers, processors, etc.], it will take care of the right [upstream] part of the value chain [manufacturers, distributors, consumers].'[6]

This profit question was delegated by the Mars leadership team to the Catalyst think tank, thereby opening the door for the EoM programme, which started with the broadly accepted premise that *businesses only manage what they measure*. Therefore, Catalyst hypothesized that the question of the 'right level of profit' must address management incentives because incentives largely govern the behaviour of managers.[7] And to do this properly, an examination of what is of value to business and can be used by business to create more value—beyond just monetary profits (financial capital)—would be necessary. This, in turn, led to the development of non-traditional (for business) metrics to account—in ways that were simple enough for business managers to use, stable across markets, and robust scientifically—for the value of non-monetized forms of capital for people (human and social capital) and the planet (natural capital).[8]

Back to the Future: Sowing the Seeds for EoM in the Mars DNA

> The impact of founders' beliefs, values, and assumptions is the most important source of an organization's culture, which does not form spontaneously or accidentally.[9]
>
> Professor Edgar Schein, MIT

While the story of EoM at Mars began with the question about the right level of profit, the mutuality approach to business that provided such fertile ground for these principles to emerge was fostered by John's father, Forrest.

The culture that Forrest, Snr. modelled, and that was carried forward by his offspring and now by their own children, was characterized not only by mutuality, but also by a long-term perspective; continuous shareholder reinvestment back into the company; patience; risk tolerance; and a willingness to fund a unit (Catalyst) for half a century and counting to continue to challenge the status quo inside the firm.

In his 1947 letter, 'The Company's Objective', it is notable that Forrest reversed the typical order of precedence that in most corporations puts the interests of the shareholders foremost, sometimes mentioning the consumers, but often leaving out many other key stakeholders without whom the company would be unable to operate. By contrast, Forrest put shareholders (himself alone in 1947) last, with even competitors placed above himself in order of precedence. Specifically, his letter stated:

> The company's objective is the manufacture and distribution of food products in such a manner as to promote a mutuality of services and benefits among: *consumers, distributors, competitors, our direct suppliers of goods and services, governmental bodies, all employees of the company and its shareholders.*[10]

The substance of this letter reflected Forrest's personal business values. These values were very likely to have been influenced by his experiences learning the chocolate business in the United Kingdom of the Great Depression era. He would have had the opportunity to observe the practices of a particular sub-set of family-owned confectionery firms, of which seven of the ten largest were owned by practising Quakers.[11]

Of these, the best known are Cadbury's and Rowntree's, whose businesses were influenced at every level by their beliefs. Cocoa and drinking chocolate were produced as alternatives to alcohol, which was viewed as among the causes of poverty and deprivation. Both George Cadbury and Joseph Rowntree were known for their honesty and paternalistic way of caring for their workforce, and the ethical way in which they conducted their businesses. As the Rowntree Trust explains, 'Quakers didn't wring every penny out of a business.'

Mars was and remains a strictly secular company, yet some of the more socially oriented approaches to business of his early chocolate competitors to which Forrest was exposed in the 1930s almost certainly resonated with him as 'good business sense'. This would have been further reinforced by the unarguable financial success of such competitor UK firms, even during this time of severe economic downturn, making it logical for Forrest to infuse his own company's culture with his personal morals and ethics, which in his case included mutuality.

Forrest's ideas may also seem to have something in common with the 'cooperative' and 'mutual' businesses that emerged in the United Kingdom in the nineteenth century. There is a similar emphasis on long-term relationships and on sharing benefits and services amongst a range of stakeholders in such firms. However, it is important to understand that in these companies mutuality refers to ownership and governance. Cooperatives developed as groups of workers, or small shopkeepers decided to work together and pool resources. Effectively, each member contributes equity capital and shares in the control of the firm. A so-called mutual is more usually a financial organization (building society or life assurance firm) owned by its clients or policyholders—in other words, customers. In a widely cited 1991 paper on mutuals, the economist John Kay describes different types of firms in terms of the way they prioritize stakeholders when distributing the added value earned from their activities: 'An employee-controlled organization will... seek to create added value, but will then distribute it primarily among workers. In the agricultural sector we often observe supplier cooperatives, which return the added value which they create to that group of stakeholders. A mutual organization stresses the claims of its customers in the distribution of added value.' So, while the absence of external shareholders may make it easier for what are traditionally known as mutuals to practise mutuality as it is understood by Mars, the two concepts are not the same.

The family-owned nature of Mars in the United Kingdom and the United States during the challenging economic times of the 1930s—with Forrest's notably frugal way of living, investing much of his ownership dividend back into the business year after year—gave greater flexibility to manage for the long term than publicly traded companies. The latter, for example, faced intense shareholder pressure to deliver returns on a short-term quarterly basis. Forrest's long-term orientation at Mars, in turn, relied for its financial success in large part on a loyal, motivated, high-performing workforce. 'It's not only the right thing to do morally, [looking after one's workforce and operating in mutually beneficial ways], it's also a good thing to do for business. You have incredible intelligence from people at all different levels of an organization and if you can really build their loyalty and motivation for the benefit of the company, then you will have a market advantage.'[12]

From a Research Project to a Game-Changing Innovation with Broad Application

> In electing to undertake the [EoM program], Mars is positioning itself for leadership in the new scientific revolution focused on

> business and economics. The groundbreaking work started by the Catalyst organization has the potential for creating an enduring legacy of corporate shared value nested within an environment of competitive advantage.[13]
>
> Mars External Peer Review Panel, July 2013

Catalyst launched EoM at the start of 2007 initially as an 'evenings and weekends'[14] type of research project. In subsequent years, the promising progress of the initiative would transform it from a casual project into the Catalyst raison d'être—purpose of existence.

The challenge of determining the 'right level of profit', Catalyst initially assessed, was one with both moral and social dimensions beyond the purely financial. Catalyst was also asked as part of the profit issue to consider two corollary questions posed by the Mars CEO and CFO regarding whether there is a relationship between profit and growth, and if there exists an optimum profit level to ensure resilience and durability over generations.

In investigating these questions, Catalyst found—based on an analysis of the performance over a forty-year period of some 3,500+ companies—no evidence at all of a relationship between past growth and future profitability, or between past profitability and future growth. The only evidence found was a relationship between past and future profitability.[15] Accordingly, the corporate think tank proposed that the very definition of the prosperity Mars and other companies generate should not be confined to the narrow financial performance metrics most widely used by businesses, including Mars, but should address the holistic value created and/or destroyed and then leveraged by business across the three pillars (3Ps) of performance, people, and planet within the business ecosystems in which firms operate.

While Catalyst quietly went much deeper from a research perspective into the topic in 2007–08, the global economic crisis that began in October 2008 generated intense discussion across the world[16] about whether the Friedman 'Chicago School' model of financial capitalism favouring shareholder returns at the expense of all other stakeholders had run its course and had become systemically dysfunctional. Such debate gave Catalyst's nascent new business model research programme important forward momentum in parts of Mars[17] that, in turn, led to formalizing the approach as a series of experimental business pilots across different Mars segments that are continuing and multiplying in number today.

Piloting EoM in Mars

The 24-month long Mars Drinks (coffee) EoM pilot concluded at the end of 2011. It was divided into a number of work streams covering performance (shared financial capital), people (human and social capital), and planet (natural capital) across the entire coffee value chain, from farmer to consumer. This project is discussed in more detail in Chapter 10.[18]

The Catalyst team, with its Mars Drinks and external academic partners, found that human, social, natural, and shared financial capital could in fact be measured with enough simplicity for business to make use of them; with sufficient robustness and uniformity across different cultures, markets; and on both the demand and supply sides of the company. The findings of the pilot proved to be foundational for the EoM pilots that followed, and in 2011, the external co-chair of the Mars Science Advisory Council was asked to lead what became an extensive nine-month external peer review of whole initiative.

The first external peer review panel included seasoned leaders from business, academia, and non-governmental organizations. It completed its work in 2012 and issued a report to Catalyst and the Mars leadership in July 2013 strongly endorsing both the science underpinning EoM and the potential for application to business.[19] A further internal Mars review of the initiative was conducted soon after, noting inter alia that the Catalyst team's human capital work 'provided a substantial amount of insight which will be used [at Mars] in developing this overall strategic lever, [and the team] unearthed a very significant new insight that shows a strong correlation between social capital [and] the productivity and ability of communities to develop'.[20] Armed with the encouraging findings of the distinguished external peer review panel and with sufficient support from those senior executives involved in the internal Mars senior leaders review that followed, Catalyst was able to launch its next pilots, expanding the programme to different parts of the Mars ecosystem.

The Ivorian EoM Cocoa Pilots (2012–13/2014–15)

In 2012–13, then again in 2014–15, Catalyst conducted two field pilots to identify and measure social capital in a number of cocoa farming communities in Ivory Coast, where the largest proportion of the world's cocoa is grown. The outcome of these pilots confirmed the pattern in cocoa discovered across the related pilots in coffee of the same three variables—simplified here as trust, social cohesion, and capacity for collective action—together accounting for over 80 per cent of what constitutes social capital in a given community, and in yet another geography that had a distinctively different cultural context than the previous piloting work. Moreover, the research team achieved another breakthrough through its Ivorian pilots. From the data of the two cocoa pilots, Catalyst identified a significant correlation between the amount of social capital in a given farming community with that community's agricultural productivity and with the farmers' propensity for modifying their agronomic practices to improve crop yields. Catalyst, therefore, concluded that social capital (and later human capital) is a potentially critical element in any intervention aimed at increasing output along with sustaining quality-of-life enhancements.[21]

The Wrigley Kenya Pilot (2012–13)

Building on what was learned in prior EoM pilots in Mars Drinks, and as the first Ivorian cocoa exploratory pilot was underway, the Mars Wrigley Kenya pilot was launched in 2012 following a Catalyst–Wrigley workshop in Zurich, Switzerland.[22] It was the first attempt to introduce some of EoM's non-monetized metrics (human and social capital) as key performance indicators (KPIs) and new management practices to create a new type of route-to-market business for a Mars segment—in this instance, Mars Wrigley in East Africa where Wrigley's only African chewing gum factory was located. The Mars leadership identified a key motive and objective for this pilot as: 'Aspiring to make a difference to People and Planet through our Performance. As we build and grow the business the [Mars Wrigley] segment will also take steps to firstly aid decisions and measure impact using the learning from the PIA [Principles-in-Action] metrics [aka EoM] pilots.'[23]

The Kenya pilot initially comprised five independent but interrelated workstreams covering the Kenyan market. The most important of the workstreams, which soon subsumed the others, became what is called 'Maua'.[24] Today Maua is a profitable, fast-growing, socially oriented micro-distribution business for Wrigley chewing gum operating in the slums outside Nairobi and in some rural areas in Kenya that traditional distribution methods are unable to reach.[25] Maua challenged traditional route-to-market (RTM) approaches, which typically use a master distributor rather than micro-distributors and seek to maximize profit for shareholders rather than to address stakeholder needs as the means to the end of a healthy business. In many ways, Maua was a true business breakthrough for EoM and for the sponsoring Mars business segment, demonstrating how by using non-traditional (non-financial) KPIs that put the interest of stakeholders ahead of maximizing profit for shareholders, highly performing businesses that are both scalable and deliver measurable social value are possible.[26]

Catalyst learned through Maua that by unlocking a successful and sustainable RTM, the construction of a business ecosystem that addresses the needs of individuals, their communities, and the need for partnering with new, non-traditional (for business) institutions is required. It also necessitated a rethink of the traditional metrics, incentives, and accountability systems used to support, measure, and reward long-term success.

In June 2018, the Mars Wrigley segment took the decision to globally scale up Maua, taking full ownership and investing further in growth of existing Maua programmes in Kenya and the Philippines that started as Catalyst pilots in 2013 and 2014, respectively, as well as initiating a plan to expand Maua into Tanzania, Egypt, Nigeria, India, and China.[27]

Partnership with Oxford University

In June 2014, Mars Catalyst entered a five-year joint research partnership with Oxford University's Saïd Business School called the Mutuality in Business (MiB) programme.[28] The aim of the hybrid arrangement, which began its fifth year on 1 October 2018, has been to further advance EoM research and to begin to build a global movement around this approach to making business more responsible in ways that are measurable, profitable, and scalable, unlike the typical corporate social responsibility programme, the vast majority of which do none of these things, however beneficial they may be at a local level.

Conclusion

> The story of EoM in many ways is in fact currently at the 'end of the beginning', but with a still very long way ahead...

As this book is being assembled, the two largest Mars business segments—Mars Petcare and Mars Wrigley—have sponsored multiple new EoM pilots to test the approach in different market and segment situations:

- The Maua micro-distribution route-to-market approach, powered by EoM, is, as was noted earlier, being globally expanded by Mars to countries in Africa, South and East Asia.
- The Maua approach is being further tested by Catalyst in India as a way to bring a new Mars affordable nutrition product to market to provide, in addition to good job opportunities, a health and wellness benefit.
- In China, an EoM pilot on human capital across multiple Mars segments identified the true drivers of well-being among the entire Mars workforce there and several other new EoM China pilots have just been commissioned and will soon be scoped.
- In Ivory Coast, where a great deal of the world's cocoa is grown, yet farmers continue to suffer severe impoverishment, the newly

created Mars Cocoa Enterprise is now partnering with Catalyst to explore how EoM approaches can be applied to help mitigate farmer poverty, while helping to secure the cocoa supply chain.

- The fast-growing premium petfood business, Royal Canin, has sponsored a pilot in the very mature market of Europe as has the Mars Pet Nutrition Poland business.
- The Mars Veterinary Healthcare business is now sponsoring new EoM pilots, including the first EoM foray into North America.
- A new EoM 'mutual profit P&L' single bottom line accounting approach is now ready for practical business testing, including for how such an expanded P&L alters manager behaviour.[29]
- At the time of this writing, Catalyst is in the midst of its first EoM pilot for a non-Mars company—a global retail conglomerate based in Europe—to explore new business ecosystems and to share EoM learnings that can be seeded in this way into another sector of the economy, yielding new learnings to advance the approach.

Putting Purpose into Practice at Mars

Grant Reid, president and chief executive officer, Mars, Incorporated

Over the last few years at Mars we've invested a good bit of time and energy considering what it is that distinguishes us as a private, family business. In today's world, it is more important than ever to be able to articulate what you stand for. It's important to our associates (we don't use the word employees), consumers, customers, and the public. The outcome of this self-reflection, as well as conversations with our stakeholders about what's unique about Mars, is our purpose statement: '*The world we want tomorrow starts with how we do business today.*' This simple, powerful articulation connects our history as a family-owned company guided by five principles (quality, responsibility, mutuality, efficiency, freedom) to the future we want for ourselves and the world. It's more than a tagline. It is supported by a commitment to measure our performance against our purpose on multiple dimensions. The Mars family is holding the Mars board of directors and leadership accountable for delivering across multiple dimensions including financial performance metrics, our positive societal impact and the trust we earn with our stakeholders.

For us, profit without purpose isn't meaningful. Equally, purpose without profit isn't possible. Our belief is that business can and should make the world a better place while delivering superior business performance. We're not alone, research indicates that purpose-oriented companies outperform the average. For Mars, business has never been a zero-sum game where one can only win if someone else is losing. On the contrary, we have sought to create enduring, shared value for Mars and our stakeholders—this is the very definition of our 'mutuality' principle first described by Forrest Mars, Snr. in 1947. The challenges the world faces today are different than those in the post-world-war 1940s, but they are just as daunting. Poverty, water stress, climate change, human rights abuses, and other societal and environmental issues are holding back the potential of people, communities, and business. Business absolutely has a role and a responsibility in addressing these challenges—because it is the right thing to do—and because business can't hope to prosper in an environment where society and the planet, upon which we all depend, are not.

The Economics of Mutuality is a powerful concept that reflects the value for society and the environment can be created (or compromised) based on how a business operates, and that business needs non-financial forms of capital (human, social, natural) as much as it needs financial capital to operate. There are a number of case studies outlined in greater detail in this chapter that help bring this to life. For example, EoM-inspired business models like the 'Maua' micro-distribution route-to-market business discussed later in this book, is helping Mars deliver quality growth in emerging geographies and hard-to-reach communities, while creating enduring opportunity within those communities.

Business management requires making choices about how to leverage finite resources for maximum impact. By providing meaningful measures of non-financial forms of value to supplement traditional financial capital measures, business can help equip managers with a fuller set of data points. This, in turn, can change the conversation on return on investment and make clearer the interdependencies between these forms of capital and the impact that they have on resilient business performance.

In today's world, the workforce and the general public are looking to business to lead, not just as drivers of economic growth, but as institutions that are helping the world address its challenges. Reinventing management practices to take a holistic view of profit and purpose will help us live up to these expectations while creating enduring business benefits. I'm excited about the future this can create for Mars and business at large.

The future for EoM looks bright, and Mars has to date viewed learning from the programme not as intellectual property, but rather as intellectual capital to be shared openly with similarly purposed organizations. In many ways Catalyst sees EoM is a non-rival good, in that Mars (and others who adopt the approach) will gain more by sharing it than by keeping it to themselves. The next step of the journey, therefore, will be partnering in an open collaborative space starting in January 2019, and this will be discussed elsewhere in this book.

Notes

1. Extracted from the Mars Personnel Manual, Mars Slough UK Site, 1947, Mars Museum, McLean, Virginia.
2. 'The Objective of the Company', letter by Forrest Mars, Snr., 1947, Mars family archives.
3. Five Principles of Mars, see https://www.youtube.com/watch?v=7PniaEqe478.
4. Mars, Incorporated refers to its employees as 'associates' to emphasize the personal stake each employee has in the success of the enterprise.
5. 'The Sweet Secret World of Forrest Mars', *Fortune Magazine*, 1967.
6. John Mars comments in conversation about his 2006 'right level of profit' question with Frank Akers, chairman, Mars Science Advisory Council, 2012.

7. The Catalyst emphasis on the need to address management incentives began at the very start of the EoM programme with the exploration of new non-financial forms of capital, but was codified more recently in 2017–18 through work partnering with Oxford University on introducing non-financial metrics into the P&L of piloting business units to turn what was heretofore a purely financial P&L into a 'mutual P&L'. This work is ongoing and is covered in depth elsewhere in this book.
8. 'The Economics of Mutuality Explained', internal Mars Catalyst briefing paper drafted by Jay Jakub, Alastair Colin-Jones, Francois Laurent, and Bruno Roche et al. for senior Mars managers, Spring 2018.
9. Schein (2010).
10. 'The Purpose of the Company', letter by Forrest Mars, Snr., 1947, Mars family archives.
11. 'Quakers are members of the Religious Society of Friends, a faith that emerged as a new Christian denomination in England during [the] mid-1600's and is practiced today in a variety of forms around the world... [Quakers practice] testimonies of pacifism, social equality, integrity, and simplicity... Today, many [Quakers] include stewardship of [the] planet as one of [these] testimonies.' Extracted from the Quaker Information Center, http://www.quakerinfo.org/index.
12. Ibid, p. 21, quoting Peter Holbrook, chief executive of Social Enterprise UK, in an interview with Tom Woodin.
13. Mars Economics of Mutuality/Principles-in-Action Metrics External Peer Review Summary report, internal Mars document delivered by Frank Akers, July 2013.
14. Frequent observation of Mars chief economist and Catalyst managing director Bruno Roche, as conveyed to the author.
15. Internal Mars Catalyst analysis using Baysian classifier algorithmic and other techniques of data from 3,500+ public and private companies with revenues of > $1bn spanning four decades, S&P, 2007.
16. While there were hundreds of news stories worldwide questioning the viability of the financial capitalism model in the months immediately following the October 2008 economic meltdown, it is notable that this intense debate extended into what were widely recognized as the media bastions of the Friedman model, such as the *Financial Times*, which later launched a series called 'The Future of Capitalism.'
17. The loud public discourse in late 2008, early 2009 about the future viability of the financial capitalism approach in its present form prompted some of the harshest critics at Mars of the multi-capital approach being explored by Catalyst to withdraw or otherwise quiet their objections, allowing for EoM to be formally brought to the attention of the Mars Leadership Team and members of the Mars family in an internal Mars symposium in April 2009 at the firm's global headquarters in McLean, Virginia. This symposium prompted the Mars

Drinks and Mars Food presidents to volunteer to host the first EoM pilot, with Mars Drinks being selected, mostly on the basis of its very small size, the limited ability of Catalyst's small team to run multiple pilots simultaneously while continuing the work of its Marketing and Culture Laboratories, and the shared passion of the Drinks Leadership Team for the topic. It is noteworthy that members of that Drinks Leadership Team from 2009 today include the executive vice president of Mars who services also as the Mars Wrigley Confectionery president (Martin Radvan); the president of Mars Global Services (Angela Mangipane); and the CFO of Mars Petcare—the company's largest segment (Jacek Szarzynski). And the current global vice president for corporate affairs at Mars, Andy Pharoah, was the overall Wrigley coordinator of the first experimental EoM RTM pilot in Africa while serving as head of corporate affairs for the Wrigley segment.

18. Further details can also be found in Roche and Jakub (2017).
19. Mars Economics of Mutuality/Principles-in-Action Metrics External Peer Review Summary report, internal Mars document delivered by Frank Akers, July 2013.
20. 'PiA [Principles in Action, aka Economics of Mutuality] metrics conclusions and recommended next steps', internal Mars document drafted by Mars Science Advisory Council co-chairman Frank Akers, summarizing key findings of a high-level internal Mars review of the EoM programme on 22 October 2013. Note that this document is undated, but almost certainly was written and delivered in the week following the 22 October 2013 review in plenary if not on the day of or after that review.
21. Mars Economics of Mutuality/Principles-in-Action Metrics External Peer Review Summary report, internal Mars document delivered by Frank Akers, July 2013.
22. The author has personal knowledge of this workshop by virtue of having attended it and having helped organize it.
23. 'PiA [Principles in Action, aka Economics of Mutuality] metrics conclusions and recommended next steps', internal Mars document drafted by Mars Science Advisory Council co-chairman Frank Akers, summarizing key findings of a high-level internal Mars review of the EoM programme on 22 October 2013. Note that this document is undated, but almost certainly was written and delivered in the week following the 22 October 2013 review in plenary if not on the day of or after that review.
24. Maua is a Swahili word meaning 'blossoming flower'. It was suggested by one of the micro-distributors in the programme because the sales territories were flower shaped. As Maua has been replicated elsewhere and is now the subject of a Mars Wrigley Confectionery global scale-up effort, this Swahili 'branding' of this EoM RTM model is now the standard.

25. See chapter x for further details. See also the Maua case study, 'Uncovering Hidden Riches: Project Maua Kenya—A Demand Side Business Model', economicsofmutuality.com website. And see Roche and Jakub (2017).
26. See the 'Project Maua, Kenya: A Demand Side Business Model' case study, posted both on the website of Oxford University's Saïd Business School (https://www.sbs.ox.ac.uk) and on the website https://eom.org. Note: Maua is also discussed in detail in Roche and Jakub (2017).
27. 'Economics of Mutuality, Route to Market Rollout: A Global Opportunity', internal Mars PowerPoint deck prepared by the Mars Wrigley Global Confectionery Maua Scale Up Team with support from Mars Catalyst, June 2018.
28. See 'Agreement for the Sponsorship of a Research Project', master agreement between Mars, Incorporated and Oxford University's Saïd School of Business, June 2014. See also 'Heads of Terms Agreement', specifying the joint intent of Mars and Saïd Business School to undertake a five-year partnership to advance EoM, June 2014 (executed by Stephen Badger from the Mars board of directors for Mars, Incorporated and by Peter Tufano, dean of Saïd Business School, for Oxford University).
29. Harvard's Robert Eccles, widely known as the inventor of integrated accounting, is Catalyst's main partner in this work on mutual profit, along with Oxford's Saïd Business School through the MiB programme noted earlier.

5
The Meaning of Mutuality

Catherine Dolan, Bojan Angelov, and Paul Gilbert

Introduction

Approaches to ethical capitalism have flourished in recent decades, circulating new regimes of accountability and sustainability in business. The corporation, in particular, has been at the forefront of efforts to 'remoralize' capitalism, seeking to mitigate potentially harmful effects of business through new initiatives, from corporate social responsibility (CSR) to cause-related marketing, that orient firms around more than the pursuit of profits. Recently, the ethical mandate of business has constellated around efforts to 'humanize' supply chains, witnessed in the recent emphasis on empowerment, partnership, and shared value. Within this context we find Mars, Inc.'s distinctive model of ethical capitalism founded on the principle of mutuality.

Mars, Inc.'s commitment to mutuality preceded the wave of CSR standards that fanned out through global supply chains in the 1990s. In 1947 Forrest Mars, Snr. wrote that the company's 'objective' and 'total purpose' was to manufacture and distribute food products in 'such a manner as to *promote a mutuality of service and benefits*' among consumers, distributors, competitors, suppliers, government, and the company's employees and shareholders (emphasis in original) (see Chapter 3). Mutuality has since become a key structuring principle of the business and moved to the forefront of corporate ambitions in 2014 when Mars announced its intention 'to be the most mutual company in the world'. Yet despite the elevation of the principle, and its prime

Catherine Dolan, Bojan Angelov, and Paul Gilbert, The Meaning of Mutuality In *Putting Purpose Into Practice: The Economics of Mutuality.* Edited by: Colin Mayer and Bruno Roche, Oxford University Press (2021).
 DOI: 10.1093/oso/9780198870708.003.0005

importance to the company, what such a declaration means in practice has been less easy to parse, spawning a multi-year research programme between Mars Catalyst and the Saïd Business School, Oxford, on 'conceptualizing and enacting mutuality', upon which this chapter is based. The research, it was hoped, would generate a broader understanding of mutuality as an economic model and management theory which could offer an alternative to the orientation towards 'maximizing shareholder value' of existing corporate capitalism (Lazonick and O'Sullivan 2000).

The question the research posed was simple: how do individuals within Mars conceptualize mutuality? This question, however, was linked to a broader set of questions, including what does it mean to say that the business aligns its decisions with the principle of mutuality? How do we recognize mutuality's presence, and indeed its absence in business interactions? Does mutuality represent a value that is understood similarly across Mars' supply chains or one that is adapted to suit different contexts but nonetheless retains enough shared meaning to be recognizable across the company's sites?

This chapter, based on interviews with employees ('associates') and contractors at Mars,[1] tracks our efforts to define and locate mutuality. Rather than assuming that different actors within Mars and its value chain were talking about the same thing when they referred to mutuality, we sought to draw out the differences, as well as the similarities, in the way actors used mutuality. We found that despite an over-arching sense of the principle as the Law of Moral Reciprocity, that is, 'Do unto others as you would have them do unto you' (Gewirth 1978), in practice mutuality incorporated multiple meanings that were at times competing and contradictory, as individuals, both within and beyond the corporation, invested mutuality with different capacities. While the business school partners treated mutuality as a new principle central to an emergent ethical capitalism, Mars' management claimed mutuality as a long-established value unique to their company. While associates tethered mutuality to norms of obligation and reciprocity, among the 'micro-entrepreneurs' that are part of a pilot programme (Maua) launched in Kenya,[2] the principle came closer to notions of patronage and dependence. Yet rather than creating confusion and discordance, we suggest that the ambiguousness of mutuality serves as a strategic resource for constellating unevenly shared interests, ambitions, and purposes. It is, we suggest, the mutability of mutuality that is key to its stability over time and that makes it useful when enacted both in internal and external relationships. In the remainder of the chapter, we discuss how the ambiguity of mutuality surfaces in the Mars ecosystem of relationships and identify *six underlying attributes*[3] *of mutuality in business* that enable its coherence as a corporate and organizing principle.

The 'Mutual' Corporation

Economic philosophers have long acknowledged that the contingent deployment of ethics can improve capitalism by removing inefficiencies that result from unethical behaviour (Kustin et al. 2018). This reasoning also underpinned Forrest Mars' rationale for placing the mutuality of benefits at the heart of the business: the company, he believed, could only be successful if all stakeholders were successful, if there was a 'mutual flourishing of the company and all those associated with it' (Mayer 2015: 3). Hence, the mutuality principle was conceived as neither an alternative to, nor additional to capitalism, but rather as a re-visioning of the corporation and its relationship with wider society; a belief that the incorporation of social and environmental values into business practice and decision-making would stem the damaging consequences of 'non-mutual', corporate excess (Brady 2014), and catalyse transformational change in business–society relations (Roche and Jakub 2017).

Understood in this way, Mars' project to remake capitalism through the 'Mutuality in Business' (MIB) approach bears a striking resemblance to corporate value regimes such as corporate social responsibility (CSR). Yet, as we will discuss, both Mars management and associates sought to differentiate the MIB approach from other ethical business models, whether they be CSR, corporate philanthropy, shared value, or the long tradition of 'mutual businesses' for which membership is dependent on commitment, and benefit is dependent on membership (see Chapter 16). Most notably, they also distinguished the MIB approach from the ideology of shareholder value, defining corporate success 'in much broader terms than profits for shareholders', in part because the company retains independence as a private, family business (Badger 2014: 2), which allows it to reinvest profits in the business, rather than simply liquidating them into dividends (Kustin et al. 2018). Nonetheless, as Mayer notes, 'the mutual sharing of profits is central to the generation of profits that in turn are critical to mutual arrangements,' and '[p]rofit is required to promote commitment and reciprocal participation that is of mutual benefit to all parties' (Mayer 2015: 9–11; also Mayer 2014). Hence, while the mutuality principle accords weight to profit and competitive advantage, its explicit moral imperative diverges from the normative neoclassical model of individual self-interest, privileging instead the benefit that 'endures'.

Meanings of Mutuality at Mars

Mutuality often refers to the kind of distinctive ethical and economic relationships found among members of the same kinship group, and which are based on reciprocity and responsibility (Pina-Cabral 2013; Gudeman 2009). Mutuality thus entails a shared register of meaning, a normative expectation of how members of a community should behave towards one another. This conception of mutuality—as a mechanism of inclusion that guides interactions in the present as well as the future—is also implicit in Mars' approach to ethical business. At an organizational level, mutuality was portrayed as a fundamental aspect of corporate identity, linked by associates[4] to the Mars family and to the distinctive family ownership, which enabled the company to deliver value (social, human, natural, and financial) across its supply chains. This was explained by one associate who said that '[in contrast to] other companies maybe where they write a manifesto or set of principles or values of a mission statement [that] sits on the wall or it sits in the drawer and no one really lives it . . . mutuality . . . holds us together as a business and the way we treat each other and the way we treat associates, the way we treat other stakeholders. So it's a very powerful narrative.' Indeed, a common theme among our interviews with Mars senior leaders, as well as with associates at Mars Wrigley in Kenya, was the distinctive position that mutuality occupied as one of Mars' Five Principles: quality, responsibility, mutuality, efficiency, and freedom. One senior leader—a regional president for one of Mars' four segments—noted that:

> you'll find a lot of the other companies, you know, that are, you know, what I call in the premier league, talk about efficiency, talk about quality, talk about responsibility, but I think the mutuality principle and the freedom principle are sort of kind of unique to the way we are owned and structured and heavily influence the way we operate.

For this senior leader quality, efficiency, and responsibility are unremarkable, everyday 'standards of services for business' rather than organizational values that guide 'ethical manager behaviour or employee action' (Williams 2011: 316). In contrast to these commonplace 'values', mutuality was viewed as a touchstone for organizational practice and a mobilizing element of corporate culture that cohered diverse actors, functions, and interests.

Nevertheless, while mutuality is a powerful signifier that circulates among associates located in different segments, regions, and sub-cultures of Mars, when asked to define the concept, associates offered varied interpretations. As one associate noted, '[m]utuality means so many different things to different people. We can read what's on every wall about what mutuality means, but mutuality might mean a certain thing [in abstract], but it also means something different to individuals.' Mutuality emerged as a decidedly amorphous concept, able to carry diverse meanings, which in turn—as we argue—afforded it stability over time and performed an important job; it made mutuality useful by allowing for situational enactment. This aspect of mutuality *as a principle that carries diverse meanings and is generative of organizational identity* is the first of six attributes that we found gave coherence to mutuality in business and helped to internalize the principle among diverse actors in the company.

In the following, we examine these varied interpretations, focusing on how different attributes of mutuality were emphasized by senior leaders and associates in Mars, and by associates and micro-entrepreneurs involved in Mars/Wrigley's project Maua in Kenya to: (1) strengthen organizational identity; (2) make sense of the relationship between mutuality and growth; (3) mark Mars' approach to mutuality as distinct from philanthropy/charity and amoral market transactions on the one hand, and corporate social responsibility and 'shared value' approaches on the other; (4) to accommodate contradictions; (5) embed fairness within the business model; and (6) consider the possibilities and limitations of mutuality expressed over time. As becomes evident, there are tensions between the ways different actors talk about mutuality as either the property of a relationship or as an approach—in other words, whether mutuality is understood as something that can be enacted only by both parties to a relationship simultaneously, or unilaterally by Mars as a 'way' of doing business.

Mutuality and Growth

'Mutuality talk' infuses all manner of staff communications at Mars. It is built into 'The Essence of Mars' induction course and performance evaluations, is referenced continuously in Mars documents and everyday encounters, and is hyper-visible on the walls of hundreds of Mars offices and manufacturing sites. Yet despite its ubiquity, some senior leaders found it difficult to speak about mutuality as a stand-alone principle and instead tied mutuality to growth. In the words of one regional president, 'I could work with growth we're proud of, that would be sufficient to me, and leave the five principles where they are.' For others, mutuality could only be instituted if the company performed well (above the industry average) and grew in a competitive market. 'I think mutuality only exists when we're talking about growing the pie,' a senior leader with a global role said, 'you know, about having the ability to make what we do bigger than what it is today. And if you go in there with that mindset, then you realize I can afford to be mutual. If you go in with a mindset of saying OK, I need to carve up what we have today differently, then that could never be mutual.' For another senior vice president, mutuality was tied to growth because of the shared benefits derived from enduring and mutually reinforcing business relationships, where both Mars and their partners require each other's success in order to grow themselves: 'And so I think, so mutuality I think has always been there and this idea that we want to have mutual benefits and, you know, our growth of our business needs to be the growth of others, and honestly we wouldn't have the positions we have in stores if it wasn't mutually advantageous for our customers.' In this sense, mutuality is manifested through the growth of all actors in the relationship(s). Indeed, it is precisely the tension between the pursuit of economic activity 'for its own sake' (i.e. competition and growth) as opposed to 'for the sake of something else' (i.e. mutuality broadly defined), that underpins the diverse conceptions of mutuality across the supply chain. We argue that *focusing on growth for all actors in the ecosystem of mutual relationships* is the second underlying attribute of mutuality in business that gives it coherence as an organizing principle.

Mutuality Is Not Charity

Mars associates carefully distinguished mutuality from forms of charity on the one hand and single-minded profit-maximizing 'business as usual' on the other, as logically opposed forms of economic action. Staking the 'business case' one senior leader commented, '[o]ne thing that has really kept us in the game is that it's not a charity.' Yet, several senior leaders expressed concern that the distinction between mutuality and charity or philanthropy was becoming blurred, or as one senior leader put it: 'misinterpreted mutuality could lead to the business being too philanthropic.' Others differentiated mutuality from philanthropy or charity by emphasizing the difference between value transfer and mutual value creation. Thus, for one regional president, the immediate concern was 'how could we do more together with other corporations, something that is truly mutual but not charitable.' Value creation was the key to avoiding activities that were charitable rather than mutual:

> When you just transfer value, you don't activate, and I truly believe in the concept of value being created by activities, actions, and how companies or how Mars can create activities that create value and in such a way that obviously this value is shared amongst those that participate in activities. So, and how can this value be shared in a fair

> way so that, you know, all participants feel like their level of contribution is rewarded with value they create and it's fair.

Project Maua was often mentioned by senior leaders as an exemplar of mutuality. This sought to enact mutuality by providing 650 informal micro-entrepreneurs the opportunity to distribute and sell confectionery products (including those of Mars' competitors) to small shops and kiosks in hard-to-reach slums and rural communities of Kenya. Micro-entrepreneurs (deemed 'uplifters'), who hail from these communities, were rewarded with a small commission on each product sold, supplemented with an end-of-the-month commission-based bonus. Mars framed the initiative as a pioneering test case for the economics of mutuality, with the potential for replication across emerging markets (Roll and Dolan nd).

Yet while Project Maua was considered among senior leaders to be a pioneering approach of mutuality in the context of global business—and a distinctively Mars one at that—it was enabled by Mars/Wrigley staff in Kenya, for whom the boundaries between mutuality as philanthropy and mutuality as business were less clear-cut. One Mars/Wrigley associate working closely on Maua described her on-going efforts to remind staff that the project was about 'social benefits', not just sales:

> There's always tension for finance and sales [department] and us at Maua, because at Maua, we try the social agenda more. The sales team wants to see in-market sales numbers growing higher and higher every day, and they don't understand why we have share-outs [with entrepreneurs].

A senior manager added:

> Everybody wants to jump in and say, 'Okay, let's turn it into a selling tool,' and I say, 'No, no, no, it's not a selling tool, we are looking at the social and economic benefit to the people. We have so many other tools to sell; we have our field sales rep, the other wholesalers, but this is about improving people's lives.' I constantly have to keep everybody in check.

Here too, we see the contradictions of mutuality, as associates wrestled with the relationship between economic and moral imperatives, revealing the third attribute of mutuality in business: *mutual relationships are expected to be distinct from both charity and amoral market transactions, as well as from CSR and shared value* (discussed below). However, it is in offering the space to address these very contradictions where mutuality becomes visible, revealing the fourth attribute of mutuality in business: *mutuality has the capacity to accommodate contradictions* and evolve given the specific sociocultural contexts in which relationships in Mars' ecosystem are enacted.

Mutuality Is Not CSR or Shared Value

A common theme running through the interviews with Mars leaders was the portrayal of mutuality as a distinctive (and superior) approach to ethical business that offered a new form of 'moral' capitalism. Models of CSR, for example, were considered a step backwards from the economics of mutuality. In a graph illustrating the evolution of the corporation's social and environmental impact, CSR was plotted as an earlier and by implication less-evolved iteration of the moral corporation, associated in the captions with 'writing cheques', 'risk management', and driving only 'some positive change' (Roll and Dolan nd). Senior leaders also distanced the Mars mutuality approach from the shared value model, espoused by Michael Porter and Mark Kramer (2011) and adopted by Nestlé, a competitor of the company. Mutuality, suggested one senior leader, constituted a 'higher bar' than shared value, because mutuality is 'seeking fairness':

> The farmer is living in poverty, I can go and create some shared value by giving him some training, that will create some shared value, he'll be better off and he'll produce a bit more product. That's created shared value, but is that fair? No, I don't think so, he's still living in poverty... it'll be mutual when he's doing well and he is getting an appropriate return from the work he puts in. Now what does that mean? It almost certainly means more poverty, but it means at least a living wage, it

> means he's getting, you know, he's significantly more successful than he was before. It's difficult to decide but it's not just sharing a bit of value, it's seeking fairness.

Here, mutuality or 'fairness' is neither separate from, nor additional to the business model, but *is firmly embedded within it.* We recognize this as the fifth attribute of mutuality in business.

Mutuality and Time

Running through the various interpretations of mutuality is a sense that Mars' status as a family-owned company, and the long-term orientation this affords, enables business (whether the focus is on ethics or strategy) to be done differently. 'Above all,' the company explains, 'our private ownership gives us the freedom to take a long-term perspective on making investments, building businesses and providing for the well-being of our associates' (Mars 2017), unconstrained by the short-term mandates of the financial quarter (Kustin et al. 2018). This points to the *long-term time orientation and enduring relationships* as the sixth underlying attribute of mutuality in business that we recognized in the Mars ecosystem. As a sales manager explained:

> So every decision that I make when dealing with a new customer, I'm trying to think about mutuality, so what is right for them, what will make them the most profit and not leave them in a difficult situation of having to clear stock... in other companies it would have been 'sell, sell, sell', and I think partly because you are targeted in sales in other companies on a quarterly basis on your results, and I think Mars, obviously we have those targets but I think there's a longer-term view and I think that can come from being family owned rather than owned by shareholders, who are after immediate results. Whereas with us, we can play the long game and build better, longer-lasting relationships.

Yet, though Mars' longer-term orientation can facilitate enduring expressions of mutuality, time may also foreclose the ethical possibilities of mutuality. Like most multinationals, Mars draws significantly on (skilled and unskilled) contract labour across its global supply chains, whose relationship with the company is typically short term. Because relationships between contractors and Mars are delimited in time, the nature and scope of mutuality can differ. As a human resources associate noted, contractors pose challenges to fulfilling the mutuality principle, as unlike permanent employees, they do not have the same access to company benefits such as training (Kustin et al. 2018).

The importance of permanent or long-term business relationships was also salient for the micro-entrepreneurs working in Project Maua, who sought not the autonomy and self-sufficiency conventionally associated with entrepreneurship but an enduring inter-dependent relationship. They hoped that their efforts would eventually lead to permanent employment so that they could be brought more fully into the sphere of protection and patronage the company represented for them: 'They are good people. They told us that we put effort in the work and they can employ us; when an opportunity comes, they will give [it to] us. That is why we are working hard.' When actors in the value chain—such as micro-entrepreneurs—are not fully incorporated as associates, mutuality is less likely to work as a way to connect strategic and business concerns to a shared identity or corporate culture—and this has implications for how 'enduring shared benefits' may be conceived (Dolan nd). The difference in the contractual relationships between senior leaders and some Mars associates, as well as between Mars/Wrigley managers and Maua micro-entrepreneurs, means that the kinds of relationships and benefits that each would consider mutual and would like to see 'endure' differs. As Kustin et al. observe, while the more expansive timeframe enabled by family ownership may facilitate enduring business relationships, it does not, in and of itself, carry the potential for ethical possibility.

Conclusion

This chapter has examined some of the means through which one of Mars' core principles—mutuality—is constructed and diffused as a framework for interpretation and action. Mutuality is a central organizing principle of corporate practice, working to cohere and diffuse organizational identity internally as well as externally. Yet, as our analysis of the content of mutuality suggests, the concept connotes multiple meanings and actions. There are significant differences in the way that senior leaders and Mars/Wrigley associates interpreted mutuality, and the way that micro-entrepreneurs participating in the Maua programme spoke about it—and key terms like 'just profit', 'shared benefits', and 'growth'. This ambiguity, however, worked to conceal the contradictory nature of these different forms of economic action (for example, from CSR and shared value to charitable action and patronage) and how they were represented, drawing together people with multiple agendas and coalescing seemingly incompatible perspectives. Indeed, it is precisely mutuality's lack of specificity that appeared to sustain its presence across the company and afforded adaptability in different contexts.

Drawing on the multiple meanings and organizational interpretations of mutuality in the Mars ecosystem, we made visible *six underlying attributes of mutuality in business that enable* its coherence as a principle. Mutuality carries diverse meanings and strengthens organizational identity; focuses on growth for all actors in the company; is neither charity, amoral profit maximization, nor a model of CSR or shared value; it is embedded within the business model; it accommodates contradictions and allows for contextual adaptation; and it has a long-term orientation predicated on enduring relationships. These attributes reflect the wide-ranging and strategic position of mutuality at Mars, and how the principle retains its productive capacity to forge a form of ethical capitalism that endures through time.

Notes

1. This includes interviews with senior leaders at Mars; new and longer-tenured employees who attended the Mars onboarding process; and associates and contractors involved in Mars' Maua programme in Kenya.
2. The Maua pilot was launched in 2013 in Dandora, a slum of Nairobi, in collaboration with Wrigley East Africa.

3. These attributes were identified by our analysis of interviews, as well as by Mars associates themselves.
4. This was particularly visible when Mars associates reflected on their Essence of Mars training. The Mars family emerged as one of the key artifacts, i.e. the embodiment of mutuality and family ownership.

6

Mutuality and Concepts of Responsible Business

Alastair Colin-Jones and Sudhir Rama Murthy

Introduction

The core tenets of financial capitalism—shareholder primacy and profit maximization—are being criticized and reimagined. Since 2008 we have heard about many different forms of capitalism—from conscious capitalism to inclusive capitalism, Capitalism 2.0, creating shared value, and, of course, the subject of this volume, the Economics of Mutuality (EoM).

Each of these concepts can be described as a type of capitalism, as it exists within a system based on free markets and private ownership. But each offers a significantly different vision of the purpose of business compared with that presented by financial capitalism. As Michael Porter and Mark Kramer write of Creating Shared Value, 'The purpose of the corporation must be redefined as creating shared value, not just profit per se' (2011: 64). Nevertheless, while all of the concepts listed above can legitimately be understood to share the common goal of 'redefining' the purpose of the corporation, they offer solutions, approaches and alternatives at quite different levels, from the highly conceptual (e.g. values, principles and logics) to the very technical (e.g. practices and processes).

This chapter aims to compare the differences and similarities between these various 'responsible business capitalisms' (RBCs).

It begins by presenting a framework for classification that provides a basis for comparison and helps to structure and organize the contributions

Alastair Colin-Jones and Sudhir Rama Murthy, Mutuality and Concepts of Responsible Business In *Putting Purpose Into Practice: The Economics of Mutuality.* Edited by: Colin Mayer and Bruno Roche, Oxford University Press (2021). DOI: 10.1093/oso/9780198870708.003.0006

of each RBC concept. The second part of the chapter will discuss what the classification framework tells us about the contribution of EoM in particular.

Responsible Business Capitalisms: Classifications and Paradigms

Conscious capitalism describes its goal as offering 'a new paradigm' for business: 'Business needs to become holistic and integral with deeper comprehensive purposes. Corporations must rethink why they exist' (Strong 2009: 103). Such a statement clearly adheres to the general goal of RBCs—but what makes it a new paradigm? Does rethinking the purpose of business constitute a new paradigm? Would instituting new practices of 'servant-leadership' (Mackey and Sisodia 2013), integrated strategies and triple bottom line accounting (Elkington 1998) amount to a new paradigm? Gladwin et al. (1995), also drawing on the language of paradigms, suggests that all of the above would be required: 'new fundamentals, new languages, and new lenses' (877). This is not because RBCs must be complete concepts, but because they must *compete* to displace those existing ideas that are dominant—at least this is what the paradigm approach would suggest.

The 'paradigm-view'[1]—a concept identified by the physicist and philosopher Thomas Kuhn—has been highly influential in both the social and natural sciences, but its application in the former has been somewhat loose.[2] Indeed, the economist John Kay said that 'paradigm' is 'the most overworked and abused term in the study of management'. Nevertheless, the use of a paradigm-view is appropriate given both the ambitions of RBCs to challenge the *fundamentals* of financial capitalism and the present context of socio-political crises facing the broader economic and business world. Indeed, Kuhn argues that challenges to the fundamental philosophy of a dominant paradigm indicate the potential for paradigm-change to occur.

A paradigm is more than a synonym for 'model'. As the philosopher Margaret Masterman argued, Kuhn's ideas involve three main meanings

Table 6.1. Paradigms within the capitalist worldview

Capitalist worldview		
Metaparadigm	**Sociological paradigm**	**Construct paradigm**
The core assumptions and epistemological positions relating to the interaction between business, society, and planet.For example, shareholder primacy in financial capitalism.	The habits, frameworks, and principles that drive and frame the activities of businesses and behaviours of managers.For example, profit-maximization and short-termism.	The specific business models, practices, and tools that enable the actual work of businesses, for example, accounting standards and quarterly reporting.
Low concreteness		*High*

of paradigm: metaparadigms, sociological paradigms, and artefact paradigms:

- *Metaparadigms* are of a philosophical nature, dealing with a 'new way of seeing', focusing on knowledge and assumptions.
- *Sociological paradigms* are accepted approaches and habits; in business these would equate to corporate cultures, strategies, or business models.
- *Artefact/Construct paradigms* are the most 'concrete', offering specific tools, practices, and textbooks.

In other words, a paradigm is composed of all of these meanings, which together constitute a whole worldview.

It is 'the constellations of beliefs, values and concepts that give shape and meaning to the world a person experiences and acts within' (Norton, 1991: 75) as well as the artefacts and constructs which form the apparatus required for work to be done. Table 6.1 shows how these paradigms relate to the capitalist worldview.

Applying the Paradigm View Classification

So what happens when we apply this paradigm-view to the major types of Responsible Business Capitalisms?

Corporate Social Responsibility

Any discussion of responsible business cannot ignore the concept of corporate social responsibility (CSR). These ideas have been around for some time, emerging from the belief that corporations have an obligation to work for social betterment, and have influenced research, discussions, and action at the intersections of business and society.

However, it is a broad field, loosely defined. It incorporates (at worst) cynical PR-driven greenwashing as well as some valuable and serious concepts that could be justifiably included in our definition of responsible business capitalism. There is not sufficient space here to examine the contribution of CSR as whole. Nevertheless, stakeholder theory is one particular idea, discussed in detail below, that as an early offshoot of CSR provides an important starting point for understanding more recent RBCs.

Stakeholder Theory and Conscious Capitalism

The philosopher and management scholar R. Edward Freeman calls stakeholder theory a 'new narrative' for capitalism. It is based on adopting the relationships between business and the groups and individuals who can affect or are affected by the business's activities as the key 'unit of analysis'. In our classification, taking stakeholders rather than shareholders as the central unit of analysis is a fundamental re-examination of the old assumptions of financial capitalism at the metaparadigm level. Indeed, it strikes at the heart of the question: what is the purpose of the firm? Is it to serve shareholders by making as much profit as possible? Or is it broader, as stakeholder theory argues, so that shareholders are included amongst other relevant stakeholders to whom the firm must also deliver value?

Stakeholder theory therefore is underpinned by a 'normative core': it engages substantively with questions on the purpose of business and its obligations to society and the planet. In other words, it challenges the most basic assumptions of the dominant paradigm.

However, stakeholder theory is not just a set of primarily philosophical questions. It can also be considered in terms of the sociological paradigm.

Stakeholder theory applied at the sociological level is called stakeholder engagement. It requires executives to think beyond a transaction-by-transaction or contract-centred basis for its strategic operations. Instead, executives must engage and strategize by considering a far more complex picture of connected multiple stakeholder[3] interests—whether employees, customers, suppliers, communities, government, or shareholders. All these stakeholders are affected by the activities of business in some way, and so business must actively manage the effects of its activities across the whole 'ecosystem of stakeholder relationships'. More recently, scholars have discussed the importance of stakeholder engagement being two-way: in other words, that executives must be thoughtful listeners and that those outside the firm are highly influential on firm performance itself.

When it comes to the construct paradigm, however, stakeholder theory seems to have contributed few specific tools and artefacts—with the exception of accounting and marketing. In accounting, the theory has influenced developments such as value-added statements, environmental impact and sustainability reporting, and corporate social disclosure. In marketing, the use of various stakeholder scorecards is a good example of a tool for companies to track and measure the level of satisfaction of its key stakeholders.

Closely related to stakeholder theory is the increasingly high-profile conscious capitalism movement founded by the CEO and co-founder of Whole Foods Market John Mackey. Conscious capitalism builds quite explicitly on the normative assumptions of stakeholder theory that take the firm beyond profit maximization alone—to what is termed a 'higher purpose'—and emphasizes the need for cultivating virtuous corporate cultures and heroic leadership. Therefore, similarly to stakeholder theory, conscious capitalism contributes constructively to thinking at the meta and sociological paradigm levels by highlighting the role of purpose, culture, and leadership in driving positive transformation in business. However, it contributes no further tools for managers and employees below the C-suite or senior leaders to actually implement the tenets of conscious capitalism whilst navigating the complexities of day-to-day decision-making. Ultimately, the concrete practicability of conscious capitalism does not extend beyond a reliance on the strength of corporate culture, CEO's leadership, and generally managing stakeholder interests.

Creating Shared Value (CSV)

CSV is perhaps the RBC that has gained most attention since its introduction in a 2011 *Harvard Business Review* article by Michael E. Porter and Mark R. Kramer.

The core ideas of CSV emerge from C. K. Prahalad's well-known base of the pyramid theory (BoP) and pockets of the strategic CSR literature that argue social programming ought to be included at the core of business strategy: 'Business and society have been pitted against each other for too long' (Porter and Kramer 2011: 64). By shifting these concerns from the periphery to the core, a firm can generate both social and economic value in three ways:

1. By reconceiving products and markets
2. Redefining productivity in the value chain
3. Building up supportive industry clusters in the company's locations.

Porter and Kramer describe CSV as 'policies and operating practices that enhance the competitiveness of a company while simultaneously advancing the economic and social conditions in the communities in which it operates' (2011: 66). So the thrust of CSV as 'policies and operating practices' is at the sociological level, where a paradigm develops its core models, strategies, and habits. Importantly, however, Porter and Kramer couch CSV as the way to 'reinvent capitalism' and answer the widespread demand for a 'new conception of capitalism' (64), an ambition that would require a more thorough reformulation at the metaparadigm level. In this sense, the classification reveals an important conceptual sleight of hand that requires some attention.

A typical CSV example would be of a large multinational firm, with its headquarters in the developed world, entering the developing world seeking the win–win of profitability and social value. In order to achieve this, the firm reformulates its products and business model to meet the requirements of the local context. Common reformulations of products would include single-use packets for beauty products and smaller sizes, creating lower, more affordable price points. In parallel, the firm will re-think its approach to supply chains by building a local cluster through infrastructure development that most improves the value-creation opportunities. Lastly, the firm might partner with an NGO to recruit local underprivileged entrepreneurs to distribute the products and in the process give them additional training and income-generating opportunities.

In such an example, the firm is certainly re-thinking its business strategies and practices, but has there been a change in the fundamental assumptions of business activities? At first glance, it would appear that the profit-maximization motive has been replaced by the goal of creating shared value. However, a closer examination shows that two crucial assumptions of financial capitalism remain unchanged—firm-centricity and financial priority.

This can be seen clearly in Porter and Kramer's articulation of local cluster development: 'Then the task is to focus on the weaknesses that represent greatest constraints to the company's own productivity and growth, and distinguish those areas that the company is best equipped to influence directly from those in which collaboration is more cost effective. Here is where the shared value opportunities will be greatest' (2011: 75). So they suggest that the firm should participate in cluster development only on those issues that most affect its own productivity and growth, and that it should unashamedly prioritize cost-effectiveness. Ultimately, when it comes to the relationship between business and society, apart from those few occasions where the respective interests of firm and society align perfectly, business still wins in CSV. Society is a legitimate stakeholder, but also a secondary citizen subservient to the traditional financial, firm-centric goals of the corporation.

A similar example is Nestlé's Nespresso business that buys premium coffee beans from smallholders in Africa and Latin America. The supply chain interventions described by Porter and Kramer, such as productivity training groups and bank loan guarantees, are reasonable practices. But they remain activities that prioritize the interests of the company. In other words, CSV may help firms create shared value strategies and business models, but it does not do so on the basis of altering the fundamental relationship between business and society. These CSV opportunities comply with existing assumptions and constraints of financial capitalism.

At the construct level, CSV offers little additional detail on any specific new practices. There are broad suggestions on how to do local cluster development, the use of technology to create logistic efficiencies and lower resource consumption. While societal value is integral to business model creation, its performance is still fundamentally reliant on traditional measures of success focused on profit, growth, and sometimes sustainability scorecards. None of these suggested practices is unique to CSV or indeed is explicitly connected to a way of doing business that flows from a more responsible capitalism.

Our classification shows that the main contribution of CSV is at the sociological level, offering a compelling conceptualization of shared value strategies able to generate social and economic value for a firm where market opportunities present an aligned set of stakeholder interests. CSV is an additional corporate 'habit', that enables the firm to address CSR-type problems in profitable ways; but despite its claims, it falls short of changing the purpose of the corporation in any substantive, metaparadigmatic sense. Indeed, an additional explanation of its popularity as a concept could be that its implementation does not require a fundamental transformation of the business, simply a recasting of business strategy to be profitable in a new era, but not substantively more.

Economics of Mutuality

Since 2007, EoM has been researched, developed and piloted by Mars Catalyst—the internal think-tank of Mars, Inc.—and a number of academic partners from leading universities and business schools (see Chapters 3 and 4). EoM, despite the centrality of the word 'mutuality', is not directly related to ideas such as mutual ownership, mutual funds, or the similar sounding 'economy of mutuality'.[4] Mutuality has a distinctive history and meaning within Mars that informs EoM in important ways.

Although EoM was initially conceived through a question of deep philosophical and pragmatic business consequence—what is the right level of profit for the corporation?—the actual birth of EoM was at the artefact-level: namely in the creation of alternative non-financial management metrics (see Chapters 9–12).[5] EoM began developing the tools for puzzle-solving before defining exactly what the puzzle was: 'an artefact, becomes a "research vehicle", and at the same moment, if successful, it becomes a paradigm, by being used to apply to new material, and in a non-obvious way' (Masterman 1970: 78).

Since 2014, building on the creation of these new non-financial management metrics, Catalyst and scholars at Saïd Business School, University of Oxford, and ESSEC Business School have developed EoM further, evolving additional practices and frameworks in the model. These have been important developments at the sociological level and discussed elsewhere in this volume are ecosystem orchestration (Chapter 6) and cross-sector partnering (Chapter 8). Interestingly, at this level there is significant overlap and similarities between EoM, CSV, and stakeholder theory. At the construct level, the mutual P&L (Chapter 13) is a new accounting practice designed to incentivize more responsible management behaviour by bringing non-financial capitals into the management accounts.

Ultimately, however, it is at the metaparadigm-level that the concept of mutuality offers EoM a unique ethic both to confront the dominance of financial capitalism and draw together models (sociological-level) and tools (construct-level) to construct a pragmatic alternative. In other words, EoM is not, by virtue of any single tool or strategy, going to shift a paradigm. However, taken together across the three paradigm-levels, there is a greater consistency and coherence to EoM than to other RBCs. Therefore, while there are undoubtedly similarities between EoM and other RBCs at the sociological and construct levels, there remain important differences. For example, ecosystem orchestration, as in CSV strategy, demands that a firm reconceive products and markets as well as value chains. However, in CSV the re-conception process does not also demand a fundamental decentring of itself. The firm will consider the interests of a wider community and its environmental impact, but it ultimately remains self-interested and profit-driven, albeit more deliberate and strategic in identifying shared value opportunities. The ethic of mutuality is the crucial differentiator as the core ethic (metaparadigm) of EoM. In ecosystem orchestration, mutuality demands not only that the firm place itself as one of many players in a system, but also that a purpose *not specific* to the firm take its place. Furthermore, the practice of ecosystem mapping is explicitly about understanding the system and its problems from the perspective of other stakeholders. Therefore, the purpose of the firm in EoM is to develop solutions to pain points experienced by other stakeholders; the overall business model must be profitable but not every activity is directly income-generating. EoM claims the problems of others as the firm's central purpose, and its unique contribution as a business is to develop profitable, sustainable ways of addressing the problems.

Conclusion

Assessing these RBCs against Kuhn's three paradigm levels suggests that most are still in what he would call a 'pre-paradigmatic state'. They have a growing number of adherents; they are developing their respective philosophies, models and tools; but they still lack the coherence across the three paradigm-levels that would offer a genuine, practicable alternative to financial capitalism. This is a challenge EoM is well placed to take on as it is further researched and practiced as a whole.

The paradigm-view also reveals that some caution is required in assessing models, strategies, and tools such as CSV and some CSR-type initiatives as easily comparable ideas. While they may purport to adhere to the RBC metaparadigm, they are better understood as evolutions *within* financial capitalism. As shown with CSV in particular, the strategies ultimately fail to challenge the core assumptions and epistemologies of financial capitalism.

The task of paradigm-shifting is a complex and painful process on the part of practitioners and scholars, communally and individually.

It requires changing our entrenched way of doing and way of seeing, which ultimately is a challenge that demands a change to the very foundations of our understanding of what it means 'to do' and 'to see' in business. It involves new behaviours, new language, and new models.

Notes

1. Margret Masterman's phrase in 'The Nature of a Paradigm' (1970: 67).
2. Cf. Friedrichs (1970).
3. Freeman defines a stakeholder as 'any group or individual who can affect or is affected by the achievement of the organization's objectives'.
4. Jackson (2016).
5. Beginning at this level is unique amongst RBC concepts, arguably with the exception of triple-bottom-line accounting, although such a method was originally more related to the sustainability agenda rather than the RBC discourse.

7

Purposeful Ecosystem Orchestration

Sylvain Remy, Julie Kolokotsa, Jan Ondrus, Yassine El Ouarzazi, and Nicolas Glady

Introduction

A corporate purpose is usually understood to be a 'higher' objective to improve social welfare, rather than just to maximize profit. This emphasis on 'doing good' is not intended to replace the company's aim of 'doing well' financially, but to support it. In most organizations, the corporate purpose seems mainly to have been developed with an internal focus, seeking to engage employees by investing them with a more meaningful objective than profit. Yet corporate purpose is first and foremost about making a positive social impact on communities outside rather than inside the corporation. This chapter proposes the strategic activity of *business ecosystem orchestration* (BEO) as a means of enabling a corporation to carry out its higher purpose while also capturing new opportunities for value creation and profit.

A business ecosystem is a network of organizations that are involved (through collaboration but also sometimes through competition) in the delivery of a product or service. Essentially, businesses have always worked within ecosystems that include their suppliers, customers, competitors, and other stakeholders. However, increasing digitization has led to a more deliberate pooling of resources to allow the different stakeholders to face change and access new business opportunities. In other words, the stakeholders within the ecosystem are actively co-creating value.

A broad corporate purpose—i.e. one that has an impact beyond the boundaries of the firm itself—will by definition touch organizations other than the traditional primary stakeholders that include shareholders, employees, customers, and suppliers. It can involve non-profits, for example, or affect communities. Similarly, business ecosystems bring together stakeholders from different industries or of a different type, in addition to primary stakeholders. The purposeful corporation can potentially engage with these new stakeholders and orchestrate the business ecosystem both to deliver its purpose and co-create shared value.

This chapter explores how a corporate purpose is typically meant to empower organizations internally yet can fail to do so if the purpose does not achieve social impact externally. In addition, we explain why business ecosystems are useful to better understand how the many different stakeholders involved and co-creation interact. We conclude by discussing how business ecosystem orchestration (BEO) supports a corporate purpose concretely and thereby achieves a real social impact without compromising profit.

Corporate Purpose Inside and Outside the Organization

As Colin Mayer and Bruno Roche discuss in the Introduction to this book, profit maximization is traditionally thought of as the alpha and the omega of doing business, but a corporate purpose comes from a broader understanding of how business engages with society. A single-minded focus on profit, i.e. doing well, does not address people's need to feel inspired by higher social objectives, i.e. doing good. An organization that fails to inspire employees and other stakeholders can end up underperforming. In contrast, an organization with a broader purpose is more likely to inspire its workforce to contribute significantly and creatively to its development.

An effective corporate purpose articulates a company's ambition to contribute positively to society. For example, pharmaceutical company Sanofi's stated purpose is 'to understand and solve healthcare needs of people across the world'. The focus of this statement is not Sanofi itself, but a much broader segment of society. It is also not concentrated on financial performance, but on the fulfilment of more fundamental human needs. Contrast this with auto-manufacturer Nissan, which, while it does not claim to be preoccupied with profit, nevertheless appears to concentrate only on improving its own products: 'Nissan provides unique and innovative automotive products and services that deliver superior measurable values to all stakeholders in alliance with Renault'. Such an inward-looking purpose means that its power to inspire employees is likely to be limited.

One of the perceived benefits of an ambitious corporate purpose is that it motivates employees with the prospect of making a positive contribution to a broader community than just the organization they work for. This motivation is linked to employees' personal affinities with social communities and higher ideals outside work. Once they are united by a common purpose, employees may feel more affinity with the company and with colleagues too.

In addition, they are likely to feel empowered to take initiatives that are aligned with their employer's overarching objectives. A focus on profit can often lead to a rather mechanical style of organization that confines employees to the roles they have been assigned. In contrast, a corporate purpose engages employees and gives them greater scope for responsively addressing new challenges by themselves: they are liberated to create more value.

Articulating and implementing a broad, positive social purpose is not without its challenges, however. Firstly, it is considerably more ambitious than the traditional business activity of efficiently producing and selling goods and services. In addition, social objectives can sometimes run directly counter to traditional business aims. For example, Sanofi's purpose to improve the world's health is not only a tall order, but, if pursued fully, it could entail actually selling less pharmaceuticals.

Secondly, a broad purpose aims to achieve social impact primarily *outside* the corporation, and only incidentally *inside* it. But, ironically, because so many organizations have embraced a social purpose primarily to inspire and galvanize employees, their managerial practices have mostly faced inwards. Yet if purpose is not authentically pursued on the outside, then it may fail to inspire and transform on the inside.

Therefore, the priorities derived from corporate purpose should shift from the inside to the outside and from boosting the corporation first to boosting social impact first. Only once a company has a valid outward approach for pursuing purpose should it turn inward to aligning the organization with this approach.

What kind of outward-facing managerial practices might advance a broader purpose? Traditionally, businesses used to interact with the world through simple market transactions (buy-and-sell contracts) and competition. For this, a business would need to rely only on its primary stakeholders (suppliers, employees, customers, and shareholders). A broader corporate purpose (than profit) implies an expansion, perhaps a transformation, of the ways in which business engages with the outside world. It requires looking beyond simple business transactions, primary stakeholders, and competitors, to other types of interaction and to other types of stakeholders.

External Transformation Starts with a Business Ecosystem

Business ecosystems embrace a broader scope of stakeholders and interactions than the traditional group of primary stakeholders, which are directly involved with an organization. Additional stakeholders tend to be organizations with aligned goals or complementary resources. They may share the same customers or users, but not as competitors. For example, aircraft manufacturers and airports both serve airlines, yet do not compete with each other. This is because aircrafts and airport services are complementary resources for airlines.

This wider network of stakeholders means that ecosystems can cut across traditional industries and sectors. Businesses, non-profits, communities, and governments can have related objectives, so these different sectors can overlap within a given ecosystem. For example, pharmaceutical companies are heavily involved with government health agencies, hospitals, and patient organizations, but not just in the role of supplier, customer, or competitor. At the same time, ecosystems still include suppliers, customers, and competitors alongside these new types of stakeholders, so that ecosystems present a broader view of the business environment.

These new types of stakeholders come into the picture because new types of interactions come into play, in addition to market transactions. Digitization has improved communications, which enable better coordination, so that value chains can be broken down into smaller pieces controlled by more numerous stakeholders. Digital goods and services are particularly amenable to splitting, recombining, and bundling, and thus can involve numerous stakeholders.

As value chains sub-divide ever more finely, stakeholders increasingly need to co-create competitive bundles of products and services. Stakeholders who co-create put assets in common in order to develop joint solutions, which can take the form of marketable products and services. This differs from the classical approach, where value is created independently by and for each stakeholder, who then exchanges products and services (i.e. created value) with others. Value co-creation takes place interdependently across stakeholders, before products and services are exchanged. Co-creation often takes the form of the exchange of knowledge or the joint development of new knowledge or solutions (i.e. co-innovation). For example, in order to drive electric mobility innovation, auto manufacturers need to work hand in hand with a slew of stakeholders, such as new technology providers, power utilities, city governments, and auto insurers, in addition to their traditional parts suppliers and sales partners.

Ecosystems also encompass value exchange through market transactions. For example, an aircraft manufacturer traditionally exchanges products or services with (upstream) component suppliers and (downstream) airlines, who are among its primary stakeholders. However, in order to remain competitive, it now needs also to co-create *laterally* with airports, airport industry associations, and providers of systems and services to airports and airlines (for aircraft and flight servicing), who are not primary stakeholders of aircraft manufacturers. Co-creation can also take place *in addition to* market transactions when corporations co-create with their own suppliers or customers. For example, it is quite common for software user communities to actively contribute to the improvement of software products, as in Microsoft's beta-user programme.

From a corporation's perspective, business ecosystems encompass more stakeholders because they include different types of interactions between different types of stakeholders (Figure 7.1). By definition, independent value creation involves only stakeholders within the corporation of focus (closed loop in the centre of Figure 7.1). Exchange of value (i.e. products and services) may take place only between the focal corporation and its primary stakeholders.[1] Interdependent value co-creation is the *only* type of interaction which bridges the focal corporation with non-primary stakeholders (darker arrow in Figure 7.1), in addition to primary stakeholders. Thus, the ecosystem view extends the scope of value creation from independent (with primary stakeholders only) to interdependent (potentially with non-primary stakeholders).

Crucially, business ecosystems can extend to even more stakeholders if *opportunities* for co-creation are also considered. Some organizations can have aligned goals or complementary resources, even though they do not (yet) interact in any way. These affinities can form the basis of new opportunities for value co-creation. Furthermore, even initially weak affinities could lead to interesting opportunities if organizations strategically decide to work together. In other words, organizations can actively align their respective goals and resources. The same principle applies to stakeholders who already interact in some way and pursue

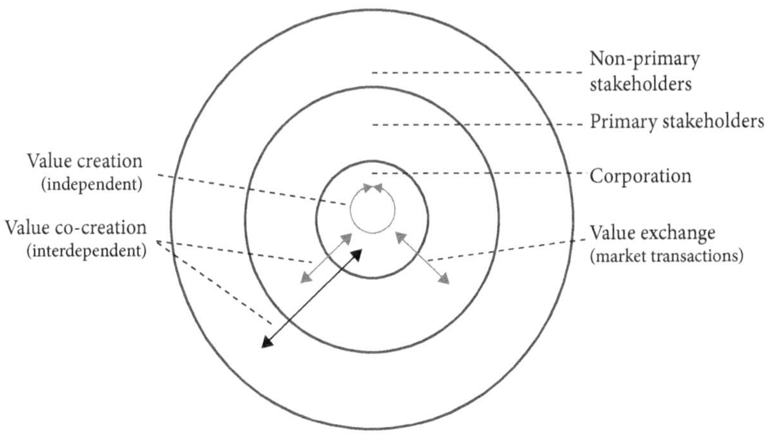

Figure 7.1. Scope of business ecosystem stakeholders and interactions

further opportunities to interact even more. Moreover, business ecosystems also include classical opportunities for independent value creation.

In a nutshell, business ecosystems describe the potential for further alignment among stakeholders, in addition to their existing alignment (Adner 2017). This potential for change means ecosystem stakeholders collectively respond and adapt to threats and opportunities. It also means that ecosystems change shape when and as stakeholders drop in and out of alignment because their respective goals and resources evolve.

Matching Business Ecosystem Stakeholders with Purpose Stakeholders

Co-creation opportunities are where business ecosystems and corporate purpose meet. However, ecosystem stakeholders are not necessarily the same as purpose stakeholders. How can they be matched?

Almost limitless numbers of actors might claim a 'stake' in a corporate purpose, especially a broad one. A purpose stakeholder is anyone who could affect or be affected by the purpose. For example, Sanofi's claim 'to understand and solve healthcare needs of people across the world', taken at face value, touches myriads of organizations and people. Purpose is insufficient to prioritize among them. Indeed, the mere possibility of being affected by or affecting the corporate purpose is not enough to justify an interaction between the corporation and a stakeholder.

Very few purpose stakeholders present the opportunity to contribute to the purpose *jointly* with the corporation. This could be either because their respective goals diverge too much or because their resources have low complementarity with those of the purposeful corporation. Purpose stakeholders may be uncooperative because they consider corporate operations to be socially harmful. Resources might be located too far apart, for example in distant countries. Again, strategic decision-making can play a role in this. Stakeholders with low alignment might still decide, for strategic reasons, to work on reconciling their goals or developing more complementary resources.

Business ecosystems, however, comprise stakeholders with aligned goals and complementary resources. In fact, resources (e.g. aircrafts and airports) only appear complementary in the light of aligned goals (e.g. enabling air transport). More precisely, ecosystems emerge only where there is a need or an opportunity for co-creation between the organizations who control the resources. Certain resources can be complementary (e.g. pen and paper) yet not require co-creation between their respective producers. This what a 'stake' means in the context of business ecosystems. Ecosystem stakes are the stakeholders' respective motivations to collaborate in order to combine their resources and co-create. So aligned goals are at the heart of business ecosystems. And goal and purpose are closely related concepts.

The business ecosystem view is a useful way to discriminate in practice between countless purpose stakeholders by evaluating opportunities for value co-creation with them. By definition, primary stakeholders are already engaged in independent value creation by the corporation, but non-primary stakeholders are not. The ecosystem alternative for non-primary stakeholders is interdependent value co-creation. At the same time, these co-creation opportunities should align with corporate purpose. Alignment is conceivable because non-primary stakeholders also have a stake in the purpose.

In summary, all ecosystem stakeholders should be purpose stakeholders, but the reverse is not true. Only some purpose stakeholders offer opportunities for value co-creation. Some of those are non-primary stakeholders, i.e. they are connected to the corporation only by opportunities for value co-creation. The others are the primary stakeholders who are joined with the corporation's core of independent value creation but may also offer opportunities for value co-creation.

Purposeful Orchestration of Business Ecosystem Stakeholders

Business ecosystem stakeholders may each have a different corporate purpose[2] to push. In turn, each one of those corporate purposes may determine a different ecosystem. So how can differently purposed stakeholders team up in a single unified ecosystem? The first answer is that corporate purpose and ecosystem stakeholder goals are not the same thing, and the second answer is business ecosystem orchestration (BEO).

The difference between purpose and goals explains how ecosystem stakeholders with potentially different corporate purposes can still find common ground for co-creation. Goal alignment is key to co-creation. In the world of market transactions, goal alignment is *not* required, as it is enough for a buyer and a seller to agree on an object and a price. However, in the world of co-creation, stakeholders need to agree to put resources in common and collaborate. This is even more true if the outcome is very uncertain, as in the case of co-innovation. Ecosystem stakeholders might have weakly overlapping corporate purposes at high level, but they should have some aligned goals at a lower level in order to reach that agreement.[3] Thanks to goal alignment, stakeholders can all agree on a value co-creation opportunity.

Corporate purpose is by definition at the level of a corporation, but the size of ecosystem stakeholders can vary widely. Organizations could be of any size, from the nascent start-up to the mega-corporation (or the equivalent in the non-profit or government sectors). Furthermore, a stakeholder could be an entire organization (e.g. a corporation) or just one of its sub-units (e.g. a business unit). The relevant size corresponds with the relevant level of decision-making with regard to co-creation opportunities. This level varies from one stakeholder to another. For example, a business unit of a mega-corporation could decide to co-create with a relatively small start-up. In this case, the start-up might be driven to participate by its full corporate purpose, whereas the business unit participates to pursue lower-level goals aligned with the mega-corporation's higher-level purpose.

Ecosystem stakeholders' respective goals may be aligned already, but an agreement can just as well be reached through negotiation and mutual influence between stakeholders. This is where BEO plays a role, which is another way to reconcile ecosystem stakeholders. BEO is the coordination of multiple stakeholders in order to co-create, alongside more traditional buy-and-sell activities.

The coordination of value creation ordinarily requires leadership in order to prevent or to resolve disputes (Williamson 1991). In the contractual world of market transactions, disputes can be resolved through formal arbitration, e.g. by courts, but it is not so in the more informal world of value creation. Value creation necessarily entails some form of hierarchy in order to enforce myriads of unplanned choices about how to allocate resources along the way. This hierarchy is usually confined to the boundaries of organizations. In fact, the make-up of organizations can be defined as the result of a series of 'make or buy' decisions which depend on the desirability or undesirability of external arbitration. Some activities can be contracted out, and therefore resolved by formal arbitration in the event of a disagreement. Other activities need to be kept in-house (and therefore uncontracted as such), because external arbitration would be impossible or too costly. The latter commonly happens when the expected outcomes of the activity are difficult to define or highly uncertain, as is the case of innovation. It can also be because it is difficult or costly to safekeep the outcomes from outsiders, as is the case of most intellectual property.

The novelty of co-creation is to bring this decision-making outside any single organization and to make it happen across multiple organizations. It starts with two, as in 'co-opetitive' alliances between competing firms. The alliance between Renault and Nissan led to co-developing shared vehicle platforms which can compose models of either make. Co-creation comes more easily between non-competitors, increasing the potential for multiple organizations to co-create. Before the launch of a new Airbus aircraft, all major world airports make adjustments in coordination with Airbus, in order to ensure optimal interoperability. More formal co-creation allows many more co-creators to come together. For example, great technology platforms such as Apple's iOS and Google's Android make specific resources (e.g. computer code) available to independent app developers and publishers. As a result, thousands co-create together with the platform.

As with value creation inside organizations, some form of hierarchy is required amongst co-creating organizations so that leadership can manifest and disagreements can be resolved at a low cost. Renault was the orchestrator in the Renault–Nissan alliance. Airbus takes the lead in coordinating with airports. The limit to this line of reasoning is the sheer number of co-creators and the consequent need for a degree of formality in interactions. Relations between Apple or Android and their app developers are regulated by formal contracts which are litigated in the judicial system. Even if Apple and Android can still be said to be orchestrators, the point is that coordination among co-creators is no longer informal in these cases.

How does an orchestrator emerge? Since an ecosystem of co-creators is a kind of informal organization, the orchestrator is not officially appointed by anyone. One of the stakeholders needs to rise to the occasion and play the role of orchestrator. How does the would-be orchestrator wield the requisite authority over other stakeholders? Within organizations, authority is propped up by the formality of employment contracts. Employees obey bosses within a formal hierarchy. A key difference of co-creation is that any authority among stakeholders is informal (except when co-creation itself becomes formalized as in the cases of iOS and Android). Orchestrators can draw informal authority from unique resources which they control (Gulati, Puranam, and Tushman 2012). Such resources could be tangible (e.g. a key technology) or intangible (e.g. reputation). For example, large firms can establish ecosystem leadership thanks to abundant assets or thanks to market dominance. However, even such resource-poor organizations as start-ups typically orchestrate new, albeit limited, ecosystems thanks to a key innovation or unique knowledge of a market or an industry. Precisely, it is because start-ups lack resources that they need to orchestrate stakeholders who control complementary resources.

Hence, orchestration does not imply continuous, overarching control over one's partners and the totality of their resources, but a sporadic, opportunity-oriented form of control, in order to mobilize or develop specific, complementary resources. Beyond *authority*, the crux of the matter is whether a purposeful orchestrator is able concretely to exert *influence* over other ecosystem stakeholders to adjust their goals and align them with her own (Figure 7.2). Influence can come in many forms, e.g. through social connections, by lobbying authorities, by sharing high-value knowledge, by framing ideas. For example, Edison was able to build the momentum for deploying a large-scale electricity network by framing it as an analogue of the gas-lighting network. Mutual influence and coordinated adaptation are easier in the context of developing new co-creation opportunities. The inherent newness of opportunities means

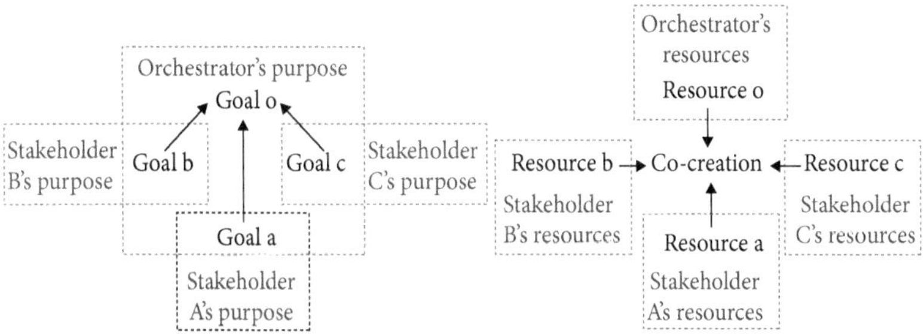

Figure 7.2. Orchestrated alignment of stakeholders' goals and resources

that participants are relatively unfettered by existing resources and set ways of doing things. This frees them to design their respective contributions, in coordination with others and under the leadership of an orchestrator. In turn, this can lead to the coordinated development by stakeholders of highly complementary resources for exploiting the opportunity (Figure 7.2). All in all, orchestration is a way for the corporation to align stakeholders with its purpose.

Earlier in the process, an orchestrator also has to decide who among *purpose* stakeholders are the best *ecosystem* stakeholders for pursuing a purposeful co-creation opportunity. This decision is based on how well stakeholders' (including the orchestrator's) initial resources complement each other. It can also be based on the stakeholders' motivation to contribute to the corporate purpose. High motivation can compensate for inadequate resources to an extent. By selecting stakeholders or not, the orchestrator shapes the ecosystem to her purpose. Thus, an orchestrator can reconcile differently purposed ecosystem stakeholders through skilful selection and alignment. However, this depends on the quality of the leadership, so a less skilful orchestrator might instead disrupt stakeholders.

In summary, stakeholders' respective corporate purposes can be broken down into goals which are better tailored to a given ecosystem. In turn, purposeful and skilful orchestration by a central stakeholder can make other stakeholders' goals align even further into a unified ecosystem. Accordingly, 'purposeful orchestration' itself may not necessarily be pursuing the corporate purpose to its full extent, but only more specific goals aligned with the purpose.

Purposeful Orchestration Advances Corporate Purpose One Co-Creation Opportunity at a Time

As we have seen, co-creation is a way to integrate non-primary stakeholders into a system of value creation (the 'ecosystem') orchestrated by the purposeful corporation. Indeed, co-creation is the *most* effective way for a corporation to interact with unconventional stakeholders, because, at heart, a corporation's role is to create value. Certain types of organizations, e.g. non-profits or communities, may not be in a position to act as (upstream) suppliers or (downstream) customers of the corporation. Instead, they can be engaged *laterally* through value co-creation.

Co-creation is a way to ensure that the broader purpose is *concretely* advanced. This is not just because co-creating stakeholders' interests and goals are aligned with the corporate purpose. It is above all because co-creation provides the opportunity for stakeholders to keep some of the co-created value for themselves. Any value captured by stakeholders represents an actual *piece* of the social impact that corporate purpose intends. Ecosystem orchestration does not automatically generate positive social impact but is a credible approach for fulfilling a broader purpose authentically.

For example, pharmaceutical firm Novo Nordisk (see Chapter 33) was able to enrol multiple stakeholders in its global campaign against diabetes. Although just a medium-sized pharma by global standards, Novo Nordisk is successfully bringing the managers of major cities of the world (Copenhagen, Mexico City, Houston, Shanghai, etc.) on board thanks to judicious framing of its approach. Firstly, it has credibly clarified its corporate purpose as being victory over diabetes, even at the expense of selling more drugs. Authenticity of purpose is key to enlisting non-profit, social-issue-oriented stakeholders. Secondly, it has framed the urban scale as the most relevant to address diabetes, because cities combine population density, diabetes-promoting lifestyles, and unitary political governance. Once city management is mobilized, many more local stakeholders can be persuaded to follow suit, such as local social and health institutions with the requisite knowledge and reach to engage populations at risk. Novo Nordisk then participates in local co-creation initiatives by leveraging its leadership under its global campaign, and its expert knowledge on diabetes and its treatment, including a toolkit it provides cities to help identify cultural determinants and social factors to focus their initiatives on. Each new city partnership can use data frameworks and disaster relief models to do 'vulnerability assessments' for identifying individuals most in danger of diabetes in each location. Then the partnership organizations work to determine the most effective way to reach them, whether for example providing active lifestyle training through faith-based organizations or screening by discreet mobile units. Depending on the city, Novo Nordisk then facilitates wider activities than already planned or in the case of Shanghai, promotes achievement of existing goals through stronger cooperation between organizations.

Ecosystem orchestration does not imply that Novo Nordisk is the nominal leader in all these initiatives. In many cases, it could be more expedient for local governments to lead, as this strengthens the local ownership of the various activities. Ecosystem orchestration implies that Novo Nordisk successfully influences stakeholders and their resources to achieve its corporate purpose.

Conclusion

In conclusion, purposeful ecosystem orchestration presents many advantages by reconciling a broad corporate purpose with value creation, and thus ultimately also profit. It values stakeholders' respective goals and resources by considering them as partners in co-creation in their own right. It empowers unconventional stakeholders to also take part in value creation alongside corporations. This role makes them active partners of the purposeful corporation rather than passive beneficiaries of CSR. It redefines a stakeholder's 'stake' in the corporate purpose as a forward-looking opportunity to co-create value, instead of a backward-looking opportunity to capture value created by the corporation on its own. The co-created value captured by stakeholders embodies a piece of the social impact which the corporate purpose aims for.

Last but not least, ecosystem orchestration is a practical way for businesses to evaluate stakeholders according to value co-creation opportunities. Such opportunities are aligned with the purpose, yet can also be profitable. Purposeful ecosystem orchestration is an approach for advancing purpose one co-creation opportunity at a time. Ecosystem orchestration slices and dices the high ambition of a broad purpose into manageable steps. A broader purpose than profit can appear like a quasi-utopian vision for corporations more accustomed to shareholder value maximization and to traditional business goals. However, purposeful orchestration provides a realistic managerial practice for carrying out a broad purpose.

Notes

1. If a non-primary stakeholder exchanges value with the focal corporation, it then becomes a primary stakeholder.
2. Or the equivalent of a corporate purpose for non-profits, government agencies, etc.
3. High or low level refers to the level of strategic decision-making.

8

Delivering on Purpose

Business Ecosystem Orchestration in Practice

Yassine El Ouarzazi

Introduction

An EY Beacon Institute study on purpose in business found that 'the public discourse about "corporate/ organizational purpose" has increased fivefold since 1994, [and is] now trending at an exponential rate that surpasses the rate of public discourse about sustainability.' Yet, while the discussion on purpose increases, there remains a distinct lack of practical approaches to implementing and ultimately delivering on corporate purpose.

There can be little doubt that this implementation gap is partly explained by the fact that delivering a purpose, like solving a social or environmental problem, is inherently complex. Many external stakeholders and natural factors may have a strong influence on the key targeted outcomes. Consequently, any methodology that claims to help an organization deliver its purpose needs to acknowledge and address this complexity. It should provide a way not only to understand the ecosystem of stakeholders, their objectives, capabilities, relationships, and challenges but also to propose a meaningful way to engage them through means that can help to deliver the organization's purpose. In other words, if traditional companies can afford to keep a firm-focused perspective, purpose-driven organizations have no choice but to adopt an ecosystem-focused perspective, with purpose at the centre of their ecosystem.

Yassine El Ouarzazi, Delivering on Purpose: Business Ecosystem Orchestration in Practice In *Putting Purpose Into Practice: The Economics of Mutuality.* Edited by: Colin Mayer and Bruno Roche, Oxford University Press (2021).

DOI: 10.1093/oso/9780198870708.003.0008

Chapter 6 explored the relationship between corporate purpose and business ecosystems. This chapter will focus on the practitioner's perspective and outline a concrete methodology for organizations genuinely seeking to implement and deliver on a meaningful purpose by putting it at the centre of their value-creation model. We call this methodology 'ecosystem orchestration'. It is important to note that this methodology is not a peripheral sustainability or corporate social responsibility framework: it is an approach to business model design and implementation. It may lead to questioning the organization's current business model and practices. Therefore, it is likely to generate some level of discomfort, as would be expected of any significant collective transformation. On the other hand, it creates a unique opportunity for the organization to clarify its purpose, which can be used to identify and orchestrate collective growth opportunities within its business ecosystem.

The methodology relies on an eight-step iterative process and this chapter will cover each one of them with the objective of providing the key ideas and tools to implement them in practice.

1. Establish your *purpose*
2. Design your *purpose metrics*
3. Identify the *stakeholders* relevant to your purpose
4. Map their objectives, capabilities, relationships, and *pain points*
5. *Select* the key strategic pain points in this ecosystem that your organization wants to address
6. Measure the *baseline performance metrics*: design and implement the performance metrics to track your impact on the key strategic pain points
7. Identify, test, and implement *interventions* addressing these pain points
8. *Measure the impact* of your interventions on both the purpose and performance metrics.

The process is not as linear as this list of steps might seem to indicate. It allows and encourages multiple interactive feedback loops between the different steps, which is to be expected of any dynamic design process.

Establish your Purpose

The objective of this first step is for an organization to crystallize a purpose statement that will be a powerful asset in driving their business model. To do that they need to specify a meaningful problem to be solved.

The term 'organization' in this case refers to any business unit or group of business units that can undertake to solve the same challenges. In some cases, market contexts can be so different that a range of purpose statements are needed for business units in different countries. In other cases, the same company operates in very different product and service categories and cannot reasonably be expected to have the same purpose statement for all of them. Mars Inc., for example, has both a confectionery business and a petcare business that have understandably distinct purpose statements.

A purpose statement should not be confused with other corporate statements, such as corporate values, mission, vision, or brand positioning, although there may be some overlap. Indeed, it is not impossible to build a purposeful business based on a mission-style positive description of existing activities ('Science and industry for a better life', for example) or a restatement of shared values ('Become the most mutual company in the world'). However, a purpose that is framed as a meaningful challenge—one that specifies a problem to solve and implicitly or explicitly defines a target population ('To bring effective proposals to the problems of nutrition / malnutrition')—better provides the level of clarity and tension needed to build a purpose-driven business model.

As the discussion of purpose in Chapter 6 also suggests, such a purpose statement can be effective because it is based on a proper understanding of the challenge from the perspective of the target population ('outside-in perspective'). In addition, the outcomes it aims to improve could theoretically also be measured by external stakeholders ('objective purpose metrics'). It also provides a constructive role for the organization's financial profits: delivering this type of purpose sustainably and at scale can only happen if the key activities are profitable; otherwise it becomes merely another cosmetic charity stunt that gets terminated at the first financial difficulty. This means that financial performance plays the role of a 'sustainability' metric rather than that of main performance metric.

Table 8.1. Purpose archetypes

Purpose archetype	Descriptive	Values	Meaningful challenge
Internal / External focus	Usually internal	Usually internal	Has to be external
Strengths	Easy to link with what we do	Makes tough decisions easier	Opens growth opportunities
Challenges	Tolerant of status quo / small or selective impact	Tolerant of status quo / small or selective impact	Disruptive, may bring some complexity
Profit is	Usually the main goal / constraint	A validation of company values	A scalability and sustainability metric

Table 8.1 captures some of the key differences between a purpose framed as a meaningful challenge and other types of corporate statement.

Design the Purpose Metrics

Once an organization has crystallized its intent to solve a meaningful challenge, it requires the proper metrics to track its performance against this objective. The most important criterion that purpose metrics should fulfill is the following: *measure outcomes, not inputs.*

While it is understandably essential for an organization to track the input resources (e.g. budget, people, equipment, and material) mobilized for a given activity, progress against a purpose can only be adequately measured *as an outcome from the perspective of the target populations* (e.g. for malnutrition: percentage of protein- or iron-deficient children; for healthcare: disease incidence, number of healthy years of life, etc.). Good purpose metrics measure external phenomena, not internal resources.

A more comprehensive resource to measure purpose metrics can be found in the EVPA's Impact Measurement (EVPA 2019). The *Practical Guide to Measuring and Managing Impact* (EVPA 2019) is a recommended reading to explore the topic in more detail. Figure 8.1 illustrates the key distinction between inadequate internally focused and proper externally focused metrics. For this chapter, and more generally within

	1. Inputs	2. Activities	3. Outputs	4. Outcomes	5. Impact
Definition	Resources invested	Co-create actions/ interventions	Tangible products from the activities	Changes resulting from the activities	Outcome adjusted for counterfactuals and knock-on effects
What it means	$, # of people, etc. (*Human, social, natural, financial capital used*)	Development and implementation of programmes/assets	People reached, items sold, etc.	Effects on target population (*Human, social, natural, financial capital created*)	1- Counterfactuals: would have happened anyway (control group, alternative programs) 2 - knock on effects: (un)intended or consequences
Example 1	X$, Y people, relationship with local authorities	Buy land, get authorization, build school	New school with 32 places	8 students with increased access to education	2 students with access who would not have had an alternative (e.g. open-air classes)
Example 2	X$, Y people, relationship with local authorities	Build soap factory and RTM/ad campaign on hand-washing	Ad reached X million Y soap units sold	X% of target population wash their hands 3x daily	Prevalence of infectious disease reduced by X% vs. control

Internal (Inputs → Activities) — *Self-focused* (Outputs) — *Purpose-focused* (Outcomes → Impact)

Figure 8.1. The impact value-chain

Source: Derived from *Shaping the Future*, European Venture Philanthropy Association, 2015.

the Economics of Mutuality, only the last two levels, outcomes and impact, are acceptable purpose metrics.

Identify the Stakeholders

Once an organization has established its purpose, it needs to build a working knowledge of the key stakeholders that have a relationship with and can have an influence on the given purpose. These are all the external organizations, institutions, and communities who either can have an impact on or be impacted by the challenge the organization has chosen to tackle.

The link between purpose and an ecosystem of stakeholders has already been explored in Chapter 6. This link is fundamental for this step in the process: *the purpose defines the boundaries of the ecosystem*. It allows the organization to determine who should be considered as part of the ecosystem of stakeholders, i.e. who should be considered a potential target or partner for possible future interventions.

For example, a fictive pharmaceutical company without a true purpose beyond becoming or staying the leader in its category of products (diabetes-care medicine, for example), may decide that only doctors and insurance companies should be targets for their activities as they are the main decision-makers influencing their commercial success. On the other hand, an organization such as Novo Nordisk's Cities Changing Diabetes®, aimed at holistically addressing the impact of diabetes on the population, has to consider all factors and influencers of the disease's incidence, its management, and the patients' quality of life. This requires them to consider many additional stakeholders as part of the ecosystem defined by their purpose (Figure 8.2). As type 2 diabetes is strongly linked to diet and lifestyle factors, any stakeholder with a meaningful influence on lifestyle or food environment is relevant to the purpose, which includes actors in the following areas: nutritional labelling laws, transportation infrastructure and its influence on exercise, retail, food manufacture, restaurants and cafés, tap water quality and its influence on sugary drinks consumption, the cultural barriers to healthcare access that may be disproportionately affecting certain communities, etc.

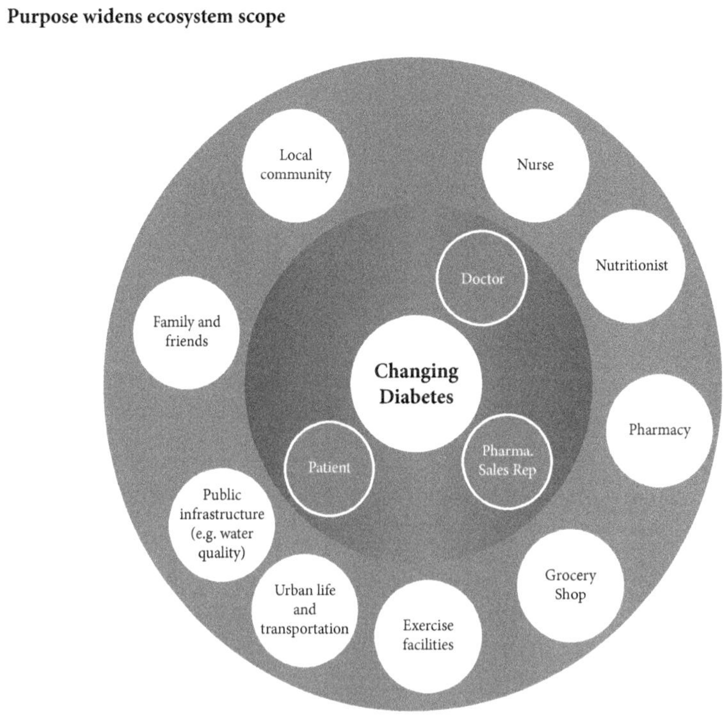

Figure 8.2. An example of an ecosystem
Source: Novo Nordisk's 'Cities Changing Diabetes'

Map Stakeholders' Objectives, Capabilities, Relationships, and Pain Points

Once the ecosystem of stakeholders has been identified, the next step is to conduct appropriate field research in order to collect the following information for each one of them:

1. *Objectives* What role do they see for themselves in the ecosystem? What are they trying to achieve? What are their aspirations? How do they measure their own success?
2. *Capabilities* What are the skills and assets that each stakeholder has access to?

3. *Relationships* Whom does this stakeholder meaningfully interact with? Who is important to them? Who are they important to?
4. *Pain points* What are the biggest challenges, fears, concerns, and frustrations that this stakeholder experiences while trying achieve their objectives and play their role(s) in the ecosystem?

The outcome of this strategic research stage is called an ecosystem map, laying out the purpose, the stakeholders, and their characteristics.

The ecosystem map is the primary input to the next phases of the process where the organization will (co-)design and test specific interventions aiming at improving the relevant outcomes in the ecosystem by addressing strategically selected pain points.

The key objective of the ecosystem mapping step in the process is to build an *'outside-in' perspective* by using research techniques that are designed to identify and understand the stakeholder's objectives and challenges *exclusively from their perspective*, with as little contamination from prior internal 'knowledge' and assumptions as possible. This can be surprisingly difficult for companies to achieve because their internal expertise and market research capabilities tend to be understandably focused on the firm's current business model and activities. For example, a pet-food manufacturer, whose historical research was focused on pet-owners' shopping and feeding behaviour, may find it surprising when ethnographic research identifies separation guilt (i.e. their pet stays indoors the whole workday or is left behind during holidays) as the biggest pet-owner pain point. The manager may find it even more surprising that pet-food access, quality, and choice are practically never cited as pain points for pet owners in most developed markets. That by no means invalidates their business model of course, but it strongly suggests further growth opportunities outside the strict perimeter of food manufacturing and distribution that deserve to be explored.

The easiest way for most organizations to build a good quality ecosystem map is to partner with an agency with strong social sciences capabilities (e.g. anthropology, sociology, behavioural sciences) who have experience in conducting clinical interviews or ethnographic research. These skills can usually be found in qualitative research agencies, universities, or design firms. The key selection criteria for the research partner is its ability to provide an unbiased view of the stakeholders' pain points, independent of the firm's current products or services.

In short, pain points are subjective expressions of frustrations, concerns, fears, or challenges. They are revealed through careful stakeholder-centric qualitative research, not through rational analysis in a meeting room. They are usually best summarized by sentences starting with 'I' or 'we' from a stakeholder's perspective. They can be thought of as symptoms of underlying breakdowns, typically in some kind of infrastructure or in relationships among or between stakeholders.

Let's take an example from a recent malnutrition project in rural India.

- A mother living in a rural village in India says: 'It is very hard to see a doctor, I have to get my husband or brother to drive me to the neighbouring public hospital, then I have to wait for more than six hours while everyone there is ignoring me.' This fits the quality requirements for a pain point. It expresses clearly the difficulties and frustrations from the perspective of the mother, and is a telling symptom of potential underlying breakdowns (from healthcare and transportation infrastructure to relationship with doctors, nurses, and administrative staff).
- In contrast, the insight that 'Mothers are not aware they or their children are malnourished; they are not properly educated on this important health aspect', while it concerns directly the stakeholder 'mothers', is by no means a pain point *of* the mothers. It is not viewed from the mothers' perspective. In this case it is a pain point shared by local and national public services, as well as NGOs trying to tackle malnutrition.

To complete the ecosystem map, once all the pain points are identified, it can be useful to classify them according to the following categories. (These are covered in more detail in Chapters 9, 10, 11, and 12):

1. *Human capital related* These are all the pain points related to the health, well-being, skills, and education of the stakeholder. For example, a key pain point expressed by veterinarians in a petcare

project was, 'I was trained to heal animals, not run a business. I really hate the administrative part of my job, and it takes more and more of my time.'

2. *Social capital related* These pain points reflect degraded relationships and trust breakdowns. In the same petcare study, veterinarians have complained that 'customers (pet owners) do not trust me like they used to; they come with loads of bad information from Google or from their breeder or friend, and they question my recommendations.' Similarly, breeders have complained that 'pet owners do not trust me and do not understand why I have to charge hundreds or thousands of euros for a purebred puppy or kitten.'
3. *Financial capital related* These are the pain points directly related to income, purchasing power, and economic value repartition. To keep the veterinarian example, one such pain point was expressed as, 'Given the years of study and the amount of hard work I put in this job, I really don't earn enough to make it worth my while. If could start over, I would not be a vet and I would not recommend this career to anyone. Better to open a car repair shop, you would make more money.' Sometimes a complaint about a financial issue (e.g. price) might reflect a different type of tension in the relationship between stakeholders. When, for example, pet owners ask, 'Why do I have to pay 70€ here but the same intervention is 45€ at a different vet?' it is directly linked to a financial transaction, but it may better reflect a frustration with price and quality transparency, and was confirmed by our research to be a symptom of a significant trust deficit between pet owners and healthcare providers, eventually classified as a social capital pain point.
4. *Natural capital related* The mapping and understanding environmental challenges linked to any activity in the ecosystem will be better covered in Chapters 9 and 12. In the meantime, if a stakeholder expresses concerns about environmental challenges or access to a raw material, we can easily classify the related pain points in this category. For example, in our Petcare study, many pet-food manufacturers have expressed concerns about the future of protein-sourcing.

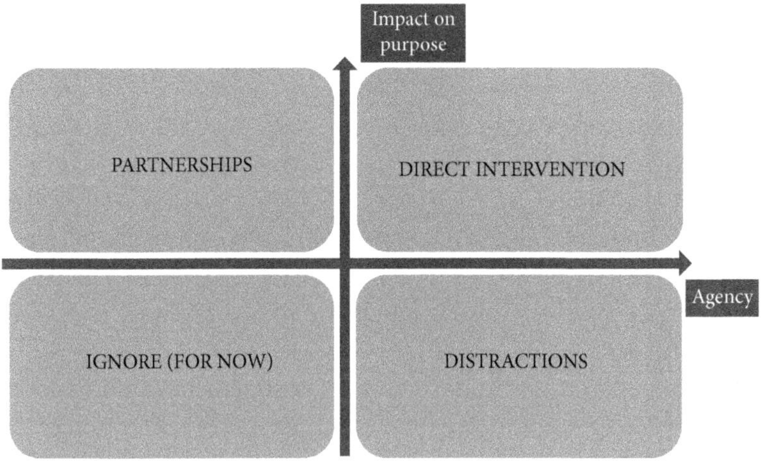

Figure 8.3. Impact x Agency

Select Strategic Pain Points

Typical ecosystem maps have a dozen stakeholders and more than a hundred pain points. One single organization is not likely to be able to coordinate action across all of them. Therefore, it is essential to select a *strategic subset of pain points to address as a priority*. Depending on the organization's context, culture, and leadership structure, this selection can be made as a top-down management decision, voted for collectively, or as a bottom-up process. In our experience, the third option enables a higher level of engagement from the rest of the organization.

Once a strategic subset of pain points has been selected, we have found it very useful to map them on a simple impact x agency matrix. See Figure 8.3.

- *Impact* How important is each pain point for the overall purpose? Pain points are usually symptoms of underlying breakdowns in the ecosystem (inadequate infrastructure, adverse cultural factors, degraded relationships, etc.). How much do these underlying breakdowns contribute to the overall challenge the organization is trying to address (the purpose)? The 'impact' dimension must be assessed independently of the organization's assets, it is a purely externally focused exercise.

- *Agency* How relevant are the organization's assets and capability relevant in tackling each selected pain point? How much can the organization do about it? The 'agency' dimension describes the distance between the external pain points and the organization's internal assets and capabilities.

1. High-impact, high-agency pain points are opportunities for direct intervention by the organization. These are important pain points (high impact) and the organization can do something about them (high agency).
2. High-impact, low-agency pain points should not be ignored or de-prioritized (high impact), but since the organization cannot act alone on them (low agency), they constitute important partnership opportunities. The organization should then look within the eco-system map for stakeholders with relevant capabilities.
3. Low-impact, high-agency pain points are best described as distractions. It is tempting for the organization to try to address them as they can do something about them (high agency), but it is where discipline should be applied in focusing on the high-impact pain points in order to allocate resources to solving the problems most relevant to the purpose.
4. Low-impact, low-agency pain points can naturally be de-prioritized.

Measure Baseline Purpose and Performance Metrics

The notion of purpose metrics was introduced earlier in this chapter. It is critical to establish a baseline by measuring them before any specific intervention is put in place. This will allow for proper tracking of progress against the stated purpose of the organization.

The same baseline needs to be established for what we call performance metrics, which are the second family of metrics involved in this methodology. While purpose metrics are independent of the activities of the organization and are measured exclusively on the target population(s) related to the purpose, the performance metrics are linked to the subset of strategic pain points selected in Step 5 and to the related interventions (Step 7). They can be measured anywhere in the ecosystem and reflect the financial, human, social, and natural resources that may be created, used, and transformed in the ecosystem. They will be covered in detail in Chapters 9, 10, 11, and 12, including practical guidelines on how to deploy these measurement capabilities.

The key idea behind these metrics is that performance has multiple dimensions and is not limited to financial aspects. Each pain point has been classified in one of the four capitals (human, financial, social, natural) and can therefore be measured using the principles and techniques covered in Chapters 9, 10, 11, and 12.

One of the critical, often overlooked, requirements for a proper impact measurement framework is the use of control groups that would be included in the baseline and follow-up metrics assessment but would not receive the interventions.

Design Ecosystem Interventions

Once the priority pain points have been identified, the organization is ready to start (co-)designing and testing interventions.

By intervention, we mean anything the organization starts doing, stops doing, or does differently with the express purpose of addressing the prioritized pain points. Since these pain points have been prioritized with their impact on the organization's purpose as the main criterion, addressing them will naturally contribute to delivering the purpose.

Designing an intervention means answering the following questions:

1. What pain points is it addressing and how?
2. What relationships is it mediating and improving?
3. What capabilities and partnerships does it require?
4. How does it contribute to the economic sustainability of the ecosystem?

The actual design process will differ from one organization to the other, from one culture to another. We are sharing some our team's best practices below:

- Include both internal and external stakeholders in designing and testing potential interventions
- Use design thinking facilitation methods
- Use the ecosystem map as the key source of inspiration, and include the research agency that built it in the ideation workshops
- Expect your initial intervention designs to fail. Identify quick, cheap in-market experiments that can be conducted to verify/falsify the key hypotheses behind each intervention as fast as possible so you can improve them iteratively and quickly. The Lean Startup® approach is a useful one for this aspect.

We will use the used-car company case study[1] (henceforth referred to as UCC) to illustrate some key characteristics of successful ecosystem interventions. Please refer to the detailed case study in chapter X.

1. It can be a simple product of service: having identified the trust deficit between the buyer and the seller, specifically around the condition of the car, they have created a car inspection service that acts as a trusted third party and creates transparency for the buyer on the condition and quality of the car.
2. It can be a more indirect value creation: through their car-dealer franchise, UCC has been able to collect a large enough sample of transactions to be able to create a used-car price benchmarking service, which then addresses the trust deficit between buyers and sellers, leading to a larger number of transactions.
3. It improves one or more relationships: the transparency created by the car inspection service and the car-price benchmarking have improved both the buyer–seller interaction but also the buyer–banker relationship. The banker, having a more reliable estimate of the value of the collateral, can lower its risk and grant loans more easily to the buyer.

4. Each intervention does not have to be monetized, but the combination of interventions needs to be economically sustainable: the car-price benchmarking service was offered for free, but it also removed a significant barrier to the growth of the whole ecosystem (trust deficit), leading to a positive economic outcome for many stakeholders: the dealers (more transactions), the banks (more loans), and UCC (more franchise royalties).
5. It is critical to identify and engage with partners to address the high-impact, low-agency pain points. UCC did not have the dealership management system it needed to support its franchisees and collect the necessary data to create the price benchmarking system. They engaged with a small, agile IT company that was looking to improve and sell their own point-of-sales system, and entered a mutually beneficial partnership where UCC was able to access an effective cloud-based point-of-sales system while being an extremely valuable stepping stone for their IT partner who could through their relationship with UCC improve the quality and relevance of their features and fund their growth. The cost stem map can be instrumental in identifying the kind of partnerships that would be valuable as it not only maps pain points but also capabilities, so when the orchestrator identifies high-impact, low-agency pain points, they can look for potential partners who have higher agency on these pain points and find a mutually beneficial way to engage them, as UCC did with their IT partners. This emphasizes the value of including external stakeholders in the design and testing of interventions.

The key message from this section is that addressing the right pain points in the ecosystem is the way to deliver both the organization's purpose and sustainable economic value simultaneously.

Measure Impact on Purpose and Performance Metrics

This last step consists of tracking the purpose and performance metrics over time to assess the impact of the interventions and the progress against the purpose.

It is worth reiterating the importance of setting up control groups when measuring the baseline metrics. Only if we have proper control groups can we confidently attribute any impact to the interventions we put in place.

Conclusion

This chapter has outlined the specific methodology used in EoM to deliver on corporate purpose. It has shown how beginning with a meaningful purpose is the crucial starting point for both defining the ecosystem the business is part of and the development of interventions that address the problems and pain points of stakeholders. It has shown how an 'outside-in' perspective nurtured through the creation of an ecosystem map is a foundation for the development of strategic business interventions able to drive innovative value creation. Lastly, it has re-emphasized the importance of metrics both to measure impact and drive the performance of interventions. Without quantified knowledge of impact and progress, a corporate purpose will find its way into the implementation gap. Underlying the deployment of such a methodology, however, are some fundamental mind-sets that have been alluded to throughout the chapter but must now also be made explicit.

The first is that this methodology requires a firm to consciously de-centre itself from the system, so that it does not de facto—essentially out of habit—place its own version of reality, problems, and performance at the centre of the ecosystem. Second, the firm must embrace an ethic that seeks to create a mutuality of benefits for many based not on enlightened self-interest, but out of a commitment to delivering on the purpose. This means that a firm adopts the posture of an orchestrator not a dictator, leading on the basis of trust rather than fear or power. Third, when delivering on a purpose, complexity is unavoidable and should not be reduced, but it can be collectively managed through developing the right tools and partnerships. Once managed, that complexity can also become a source of inspiration, innovation, and the impetus for firms developing their purpose to solve meaningful challenges.

Note

1. Disclaimer: the UCC business case is a very powerful example of ecosystem orchestration and building a business model by addressing ecosystem pain points. We must also recognize that the natural capital dimension was not specifically addressed in our report of the case study, only human, social and shared financial capitals were. Please refer to Chapter 9 for more specific illustration on how to address this dimension and integrate natural capital in your organization's performance metrics.

9

Creating Cross-Sector Partnerships

Sudhir Rama Murthy and Alastair Colin-Jones

Introduction

As the previous chapters have indicated, the complexity and scale of societal concerns are too great for any one institution or sector to tackle independently. The future flourishing of society fundamentally depends on establishing effective partnerships among business, civil society, and government. The UN Sustainable Development Goals specifically call out in Goal 17 the need for, 'global partnerships for sustainable development' (UN 2015). Goal 17 proposes crossing institutional boundaries to address the other sixteen Goals such as poverty, food shortage, clean water, climate change, and inequality. These partnerships extend beyond vertical integration and horizontal integration in the supply chain. These are partnerships with institutions from other sectors such as non-profits, social enterprises, and governments. As highlighted in Chapter 6, the ecosystem of stakeholders is rich and diverse. The business–non-profit partnerships discussed in this chapter are one possible implementation of ecosystem orchestration practice. Here, we elaborate on how businesses can build and manage business–non-profit partnerships to address the societal and environmental concerns of communities.

A key issue in managing a partnership is sustaining the participation of all partners over extended periods of time. We explore how partnerships can be managed to deliver long-term success to the corporation, the non-profit, and to the community. These discussions are based on a

Sudhir Rama Murthy and Alastair Colin-Jones, Creating Cross-Sector Partnerships In *Putting Purpose Into Practice: The Economics of Mutuality.* Edited by: Colin Mayer and Bruno Roche, Oxford University Press (2021).
 DOI: 10.1093/oso/9780198870708.003.0009

qualitative research study in which we interviewed partnership managers from corporations, non-profit organizations, and social enterprises.

Corporations and non-profits have different expectations from their partnerships. We find that these expectations change as the partnership stages change. Even within the same institution, managers on the ground work to different goals than do the managers at corporate headquarters. We offer managerial recommendations for using different sets of key performance indicators (KPIs) to clarify and manage these different expectations. Impact measurement remains an incomplete component in partnership management.

Context and Theory

Since the 1990s two powerful trends have converged, both elevating and extending the importance of collaborations between corporations and civil society. The first is the effect of globalization on the power and scope of multi-national corporations (MNCs) to influence and reach people. Today, not only are many MNCs larger (in monetary terms) than nation states, their extended value-chains cut across countries around the globe.

The second is a deep distrust in shareholder capitalism—or, put positively, the widespread acceptance that corporations have a social as well as an economic purpose and are responsible for more than profit maximization for distribution to shareholders. Indeed, as Colin Mayer and Bruno Roche argue in Chapter 1, the debate about *whether* it is the responsibility of business to address social and environmental challenges is over. The question now is *how*.

Together, these trends have sparked a substantial change in the nature of the relationship between corporations and civil society. This is shifting from a primarily adversarial posture—civil society seeking to challenge and hold corporations to account for their poor behaviours—to collaboration. Now, both parties primarily see each other as key contributors in tackling complex global social and environmental challenges. This is what Bradley Googins and Steven Rochlin (2000) dubbed the 'partnership society' and Pieter Glasbergen (2007) the 'partnership paradigm'. For this chapter, we will use an inclusive definition of cross-sector partnerships set out by John W. Selsky and Barbara Parker (2005) and will focus on partnerships between the private and not-for-profit sectors. Cross-sector partnerships are collaborations between organizations from different sectors, designed to achieve a common overarching social or environmental goal.

Business–Non-profit Partnerships

There has been an undeniable increase in academic attention devoted to partnerships, particularly since 2010. Similarly, on the practitioner front, there is grey literature of successful case studies (e.g. Acumen Fund) and best practices. However, reality at the implementation level and the degree of impact achieved are often sobering. John Elkington (1998) leans in favour of corporations and non-profits complementing each other in win–win strategies in which the non-profit discerns outlier corporations within an industrial sector for partnerships.

Business–non-profit partnerships can draw on the relative strengths of each partner and on diverse resources to tackle societal and environmental problems in unfamiliar markets. They evolve through multiple stages along what the business academics James E. Austin and Maria May Seitanidi called a *collaboration continuum—philanthropic stage, transactional stage, integrative stage* and *transformational stage* (Austin and Seitanidi 2012a, 2012b).

In the *philanthropic stage*, the corporation is a charitable donor channelling a unilateral transfer of financial resources to the non-profit. In the *transactional stage*, there is a reciprocal exchange between the two partners, with a functional relationship pertaining to specified activities such as employee engagement opportunities. In the *integrative stage*, there is an organizational integration of values or the mission of the two partners based on what they have learnt from their partnership experience. In the *transformational stage*, the emphasis is on value created at the societal level or the community level, rather than for either of the partner organizations. This stage looks at the transformational changes to the local community whose problem was placed at the centre of the partnership. As these partnerships evolve through different stages, the relationships among the partners and stakeholders are revised, and the benefits accruing to each partner alter accordingly. Partnerships can terminate at any of the stages along this continuum, with repercussions for the local community which had been the recipient of those products or services. Further, cross-sector partnerships have been analysed at three levels: the macro, meso, and micro levels (Vock, van Dolen, and Kolk 2014) focusing on implementation effectiveness, formation and outcomes of the collaboration, and on individuals and their interactions, respectively. The micro-level is perhaps the least developed, with further questions remaining on the linkages among these levels.

Inter-Managerial Relations

The relationship between individuals is an important yet underexplored aspect of partnership management. Different stages of partnerships pose different considerations for the partnership managers. One NGO Manager in our study explained:

> There are all sorts of assumptions about what it means to work with someone from another economic segment of society and . . . often our people think they (corporations) have tons of money and are secretly evil, they (corporations) think we're (NGOs are) sort of hippy-dippy and not serious.

By intent these partnerships are convened to deliver win–win relationships to the three primary stakeholders—the corporation, the non-profit, and the community:

> It's when there are two entities that have mutual benefit of working together where there's a win/win and that, you know, both are doing something to get to something in the end.

Value Proposition

Whether formally or informally, all firms operate on a business model that creates value, delivers value, and captures value in its transactions with its customers. The value proposition by a firm to its customers has been at the heart of business thinking and business modelling. Conventionally, value has pertained to economic benefit. However, with approaches such as business–non-profit partnerships, we are seeking ways to make it profitable for the firm to solve societal and environmental problems. As the number of stakeholders increases, value takes various forms encompassing economic benefits, societal benefits, and environmental benefits because different stakeholders seek different benefits from their value transactions with each other. Value proposition can guide managerial decision-making. Value proposition is therefore applicable not only to corporations, but to non-profits and partnerships too.

To address this gap in partnership management, we explore how business–non-profit partnerships can be structured to deliver success to the corporation, the non-profit, and the community.

The Research Study

This chapter is based on a research study that explored partnership success from the perspective of partnership managers who described their experiences and managerial decisions over various stages of those partnerships.

We spoke to twenty-one partnership managers, drawn from eight multinational corporations, five non-profit organizations, and four social enterprises. The corporations spanned multiple industries—food, fast-moving consumer goods, beverages, pharmaceuticals, and textile furniture. The smallest firm we considered has about $1bn in revenues (2017) with operations in three continents; the larger firms have up to $100bn in revenue (2017) and up to 250,000 employees worldwide. The non-profits in the study are also large organizations: the smallest was operating in over twenty countries with about $50m in revenues; the larger non-profits were operating in over ninety countries, managing about a thousand projects with revenues touching $1bn. The social enterprises were expectedly smaller in size, revenue, and geographic reach.

Interviewees were responsible for the relationships with their counterparts in partner organizations, and for delivering results to their own organizations from those partnerships. Within their parent organization, they were usually part of a team that managed both philanthropic and partnering engagements.

Defining Partnership Success

Partnerships need to be beneficial to each stakeholder in order to ensure continued participation, and therefore survival of the partnership itself. But not only do different partners interpret success differently: our study also found that partners' expectations and priorities change as the partnerships move from one stage to the next. To add to the complexity, individual managers at different levels in the hierarchy also have different performance measures. As a manager in an NGO told us:

> I think everybody comes to the table with various different agendas and expectations...it's really working out how closely the two different agendas can be aligned together to make a partnership work...it's really reviewing that at the very beginning, planning it.

These different expectations and benefits can be interpreted as key performance indicators (KPIs)—a separate set for each partner (Figure 9.1). The corporation may measure the number of bars of soap distributed, for example, while the non-profit may measure the number of people reached through a hygiene awareness campaign. As a manager in an MNC described it:

> What do you (from the NGO-side) have to do, what I (from the MNC-side) have to do, what we have to do together, what's the governance, what are the KPIs that we're going to measure if it's successful, like all that, to be clear with it and put it in a legal document (is how I manage my partnerships).

Meanwhile, the partnership itself would be better served by measuring societal impact in a corresponding manner. Impact measurement helps track project success and to persuade future partners to participate. An NGO manager explained how one project adopted KPIs at the

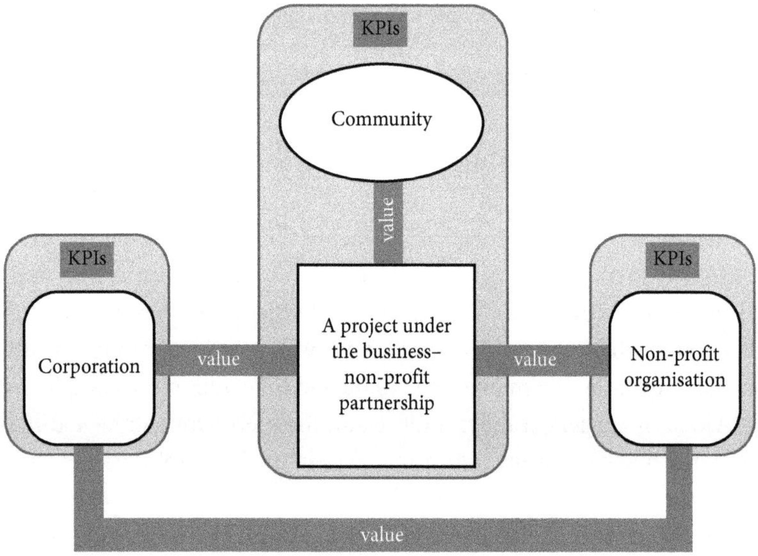

Figure 9.1. Performance indicators across partnerships

MNC-level as well as at the partnership level, through measuring the effect of the project on the community:

> You could...have very physical (KPIs), so number of insecticide-treated nets distributed, number of toilets built, number of bars of soap distributed, those kinds of things, but ultimately we find that the health impact on the DALY [Disability-Adjusted Life Year] is most effective and that's where we will always go to in terms of indicators of success.

The above discussion on KPIs pertains to the operation of a partnership within one stage. However, the partnership itself may shift from one stage to the next if deemed agreeable to the partners. As a manager in an NGO described it:

> So the conversation will start with compliance, human rights potentially and maybe traditional CSR, but then it's getting operationalized completely and moving into the commercial, which is great for the partnership really because it gives it real legs.

By combining the above two insights—the use of sets of KPIs to characterize performance of a partnership stage, and the partnership itself changing from one stage to the next—we argue that the accruing benefits for a partner would be revised as the partnership changes from one stage to the next. Partnership managers would need to manage their projects either as philanthropic or commercial, each with its own set of KPIs. An NGO manager illustrated this as:

> At (my NGO) we have a Partnerships Team . . . within the Fundraising Division but increasingly . . . we're closest to . . . our Private Sector and Campaigning Team . . . on influencing and working with companies on key issues in their supply chains . . . which is . . . part of our corporate partnership work which is interesting. So we seem to sit across the teams now and we manage a number of partnerships with companies . . . So some of our work is strategic, some is more philanthropic, some is more marketing-driven. So our partnerships really range across the spectrum of different partnership models.

The micro-level of partnership management pertains to inter-managerial relationships. As a generic structure (Figure 9.2), we identified that each institution—corporation or non-profit—had people filling possibly three roles. The operations were managed by the designated partnership managers. These partnership managers also had supervisors and administrative support personnel. While the bulk of the communication was between the two partnership managers, all six people were aware of each other and familiar with the roles that they all held. The cross-linkages were activated under two circumstances. Firstly, when partnership success was to be demonstrated to the boss of one partnership manager, they would work closely with their counterpart to present results. As a result, the other boss would also notice what was happening. Secondly, for escalation of issues—if the two partnership managers were unable to resolve an issue in the partnership, then the two bosses would discuss the issue.

Different managers have different performance metrics depending on their position within the hierarchy of their own organization. For example, within the same corporation for the same partnership, the

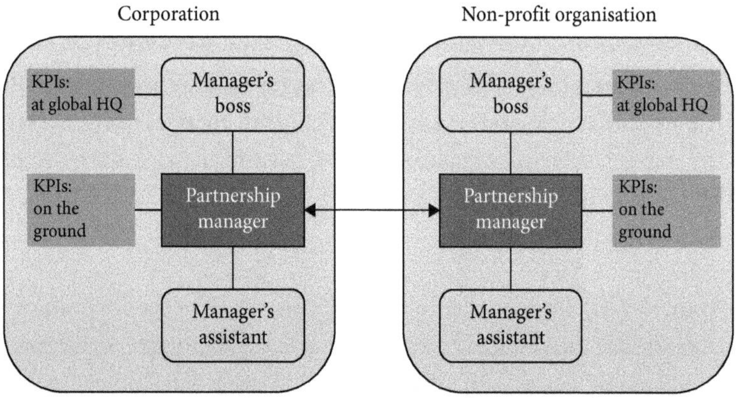

Figure 9.2. Inter-organizational managerial linkages

local manager on the ground level and the manager at global headquarters would have two different metrics for partnership success. As a regional manager in an NGO told us:

> 'The project I'm working on . . . is being implemented in one of the countries in Africa . . . It's being handed over to local management for implementation and . . . the person on the ground in Africa who's being asked to implement this has got different levels of motivation, different targets, is working on multiple other projects, you know, he's being pulled in different directions by different people I'm sure.

The managerial relationship can become a key factor in developing successful partnerships. One NGO manager described how these relationships can develop:

> We have been engaging more with professionals from our partners . . . coming and spending . . . three to six months with us . . . And then you end up with ten, fifteen advocates for your organization sitting in (the corporation's) headquarters. One of them sits on the board now. These guys are sort of like, you know, whenever anything's coming up and it's like, 'Oh we've got a market that needs creating, we should talk to (my NGO).' So, so many of our partnerships have either started in that

place or have been expanded from actually having their people sitting in our offices and spending time with us.

The different KPIs emerge because of the varied managerial expectations. We find that there can be two types of KPI-mismatches (as shown in Figure 9.2). A *horizontal mismatch* of KPIs is between the MNC manager and the NGO manager on the same partnership, as discussed earlier. A *vertical mismatch* of KPIs is between managers within the hierarchy of the same organization. Organizational studies have concentrated on the roles and relationships between managers in a common hierarchy, within the same organization. However, we find that understanding these inter-organizational linkages among managers is needed to manage partnerships, since they belong to dissimilar institutions. Our findings bridge the meso-level considerations of partnership organization to micro-level considerations pertaining to inter-managerial relations. We explain how interactions at the individual level underpin partnership management.

Conclusion

Cross-sector partnering is inherently challenging. There is nothing simple about managing across different interests, motivations, incentives, cultures, and ways of working, often across time-zones and virtually, in institutional arrangements that lack trust. We find that these expectations change as the partnership moves from one stage to the next. Even within the same institution, different managers work to different priorities on the same partnership. This chapter not only elucidates these horizontal and vertical mismatches in priorities but also proposes how to manage for these different motivations in partnering. Successfully meeting the expectations of each partner is needed for continued participation. We offer managerial recommendations to use multiple sets of KPIs to clarify and to manage these different expectations. These KPIs would be different but aligned for the community's benefit. Further, they would be redrawn for every stage of the partnership. In essence, we are proposing a lifecycle view for partnership management, based on evolving KPIs.

Multi-level impact measurement remains an incomplete component in partnership management. When successful, partnerships build social spaces for solving community-level problems. This chapter proposes how to sustain the necessary interest at various levels simultaneously.

10
Measuring Non-Financial Forms of Capital

Francesco Cordaro, Alain Desdoigts, Justus von Geibler, and Claudia Senik

Introduction

The previous chapters have given a general idea of how a company can and, we think, should move beyond the Friedman doctrine and adopt a holistic vision of creating value that is more than financial value. This vision requires redefining the raison d'être of a company as the pursuit of a purpose; orchestrating an entire ecosystem that places this purpose as its centre; and knowing how to identify and alleviate the pain points that constitute a barrier to the fulfilment of the purpose. These pain points can be of various kinds. They may relate to difficulties of a relational type between two or more stakeholders, such as a trust deficiency in their transactions (social capital pain points); they may be personal in nature and related to working conditions (human capital pain points); or they may relate to environmental conditions, such as unsustainable exploitation of natural resources (natural capital pain points). The pain points may even be purely financial—but in this case we at least know how to measure them and how to monitor interventions aimed at alleviating them. There is considerably less agreement about how to measure pain points relating to human, social, or natural capital.

Measuring these non-financial forms of capital corresponds to identifying those performance metrics of Chapter 7 that, when properly managed,

Francesco Cordaro, Alain Desdoigts, Justus von Geibler, and Claudia Senik, Measuring Non-Financial Forms of Capital In *Putting Purpose Into Practice: The Economics of Mutuality.* Edited by: Colin Mayer and Bruno Roche, Oxford University Press (2021). DOI: 10.1093/oso/9780198870708.003.0010

have a positive impact on the outcome. In this chapter, we describe our attempts to do this, largely based on our experience of analysing parts of the Mars ecosystem. A more in-depth exploration of each of these non-financial forms of capital is left to Chapters 10, 11, and 12.

Measuring Natural Capital

Natural resources are an essential input for every production in the value chain, as well as for services and the infrastructure of economic systems in general. From a global perspective, an efficient use of natural resources is important, especially if we bear in mind that their availability is limited and shrinking per person due to the increasing world population. The Sustainable Development Goals (SDGs) have assigned an important position to resource efficiency, being directly reflected in SDG Goal 12: Ensure Responsible Consumption and Production Patterns. Therefore it is necessary to better evaluate and economize on the use of these resources.

From a single business perspective resource efficiency is highly relevant. Maximizing material and energy efficiency has been identified as an archetype of a sustainable business model. Improving resource efficiency could lead to considerable cost savings. In many industry sectors, raw material costs represent more than 50 per cent of total costs (B20 Germany 2017); European industry could achieve overall savings of €630 billion per year (Greenovate Europe 2012). Companies can also benefit from circular economy strategies: for example, from reduced dependency on scarce natural resources and hedging against future price volatility (Circle Economy et al. 2018). Many companies have started to analyse and reduce the environmental impacts of their processes, products, and services, which has led to the development of various tools and instruments.

Measuring Inputs for Products and Services in a Coffee Value-Chain within Mars

In the logic of the industrial metabolism, all industrial processes require natural resources as an input (e.g. raw materials) and, from those, produce outputs (e.g. products, emissions, or waste). Following a model of causal chain analysis, 'input' refers to all resources that are used for a specific activity and 'outputs' are all direct and indirect effects of the activity. 'Outcomes' are the short- to mid-term effects caused by the outputs, while 'impacts' are defined as long-term effects of the outcomes. To generate electricity, for example, fossil energy carriers are used as an input. A direct output of the electricity generation activity is CO_2 emissions. An outcome of the CO_2 emission is the accelerated greenhouse effect in the earth's atmosphere, while the impact of this enhanced greenhouse effect is global warming.

Outcome and impact are difficult to measure. Companies should therefore focus on analysing inputs since this information is easy to obtain (see Figure 10.1). For example, the quantity of energy carriers needed to produce one kWh of electricity is easy to measure and known to the electricity company. Since some outputs and impacts are not yet known, reducing the inputs can be much more effective in reducing the overall environmental burden than individual measures on the output side. By reducing the natural resources used in the manufacturing processes, environmental issues can be addressed at source.

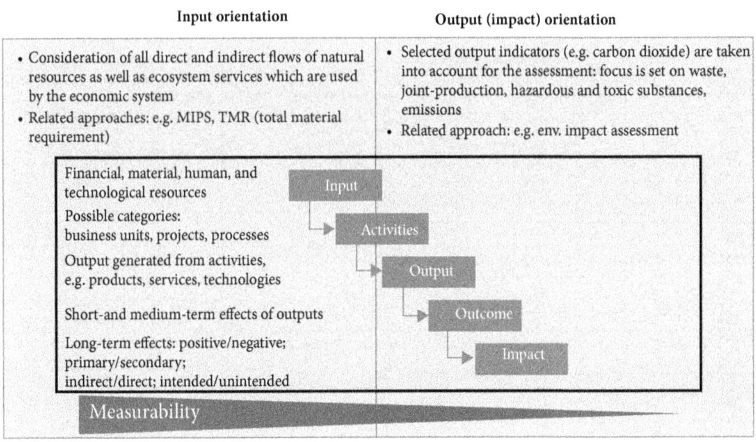

Figure 10.1. Relationship between input and output orientation alongside the representation of the casual chain from input to impact with a decrease in measurability

Source: Geibler et al. (2016).

Quantified and semi-quantified approaches can be used to enable the assessment of the products and services. In both cases, it is essential to specify the different phases of the product life cycle (Figure 10.2).

The quantified MIPS (material input per unit of service) approach, for example, has been developed as a material flow-based indicator for assessing product life cycles at the micro-economic level (Schmidt-Bleek 1994; Ritthoff et al. 2002; Liedtke et al. 2014). MIPS can estimate the potential environmental impact of a product used for providing a specific service or benefit (e.g. drinking 200 ml of coffee), and thus provides a measure of eco-efficiency.

Semi-quantitative approaches include hot spot analysis (HSA), developed as a screening method to identify key ecological challenges along the entire value chain in a quick and but reliable way. The results

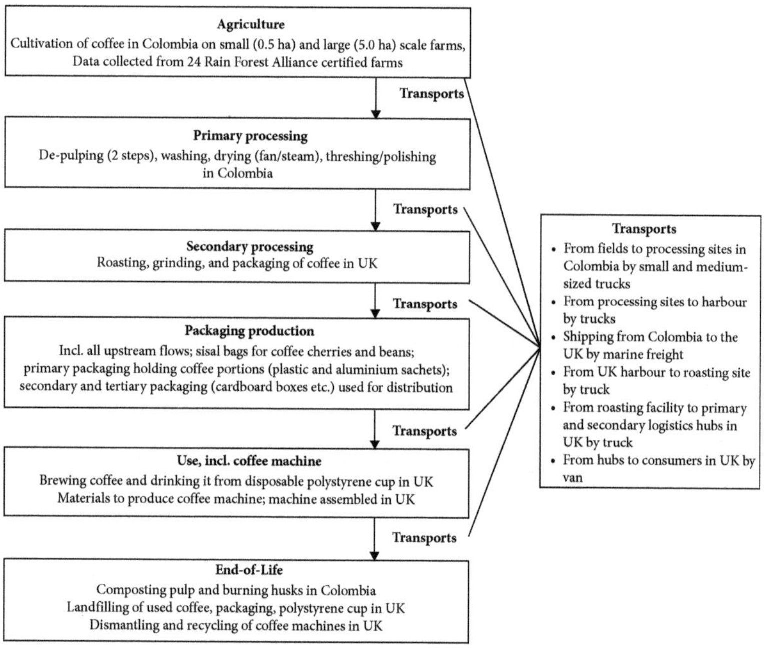

Figure 10.2. Product life cycle for coffee
Source: Geibler et al. (2016).

highlight so-called 'hot spots' as aspects along the life cycle of a product with highly relevant resource use and environmental impact, which can be starting points for making improvements. Table 10.1 summarizes the steps needed to perform MIPS and HSA analyses.

Both MIPS and HSA have been applied in a mixed-method approach to a specific coffee value chain within Mars Inc., both highlighting the same relevant life-cycle stages (Geibler et al. 2016). The MIPS approach outlines the distributions of abiotic and biotic resources, water, air, and erosion. It helps to identify the critical phases in the life cycle of the cup of coffee: agriculture, usage, and packaging (see Table 10.2 below).

The results of the HSA for the cup of coffee also show relevant environmental impacts in the agriculture, packaging, and use phases. In the agriculture phase, raw materials, air emissions, impacts on biodiversity and land use are highly relevant. In the use phase, the raw materials, energy, and air emissions are critical (these impacts are related to energy consumption, which is used to heat water to brew the coffee) as well as water use and waste production. The packaging phase shows hot spots in the raw materials, water, and air emissions categories.

Table 10.1. Steps to perform MIPS and HSA analyses

Assessment elements	Methodological steps of MIPS	Methodological steps of HSA
Scope definition	1. Defining system boundaries, scope and service unit (life-cycle phases, resource categories, service unit)	1. Defining system boundaries and scope (incl. life-cycle phases, categories, product unit)
Data gathering and inventory	2. Data gathering 3. Calculating material input 4. From material input to MIPS	2. Data gathering 3. Category significance assessment 4. Life-cycle phase significance weighting
Interpretation of results	5. Interpretation and evaluation of results	5. Identification of hot spots 6. Stakeholder verification (optional)

Source: Geibler et al. (2016).

Table 10.2. Results of a MIPS analysis for a single-serve coffee (200ml) and most relevant life-cycle phases

Metrics	Input	Percentage of metric	Form
Abiotic	146 grams	75%	Packaging, distribution, drinking
Biotic	41 grams	96%	Agriculture
Water	3,4 liters	85%	Packaging, processing, drinking
Air	69 grams	68%	Agriculture, usage
Topsoil erosion	12 grams	100%	Agriculture

Source: Geibler et al. (2016).

Measuring Social Capital

A comprehensive definition of social capital is given by S. Bowles and H. Gintis (2002):[1]

> Social capital generally refers to trust, concern for one's associates, a willingness to live by the norms of one's community and to punish those who do not. These behaviours were recognized as essential ingredients of good governance among classical thinkers from Aristotle to Thomas Aquinas and Edmund Burke. However, political theorists and constitutional thinkers since the late eighteenth century have taken Homo œconomicus as a starting point and partly for this reason have stressed other desiderata, notably competitive markets, well-defined property rights, and efficient, well-intentioned states. Good rules of the game thus came to displace good citizens as the sine qua none of good government.

Like physical and human capital, social capital can be accumulated, earns a return, and requires maintenance because of depreciation. However, it is more like a public good, i.e. non-rival (if you are using it other people still can use it) or, more precisely, a club good, because it is partially excludable (you can prevent others from having access to it). Moreover, it yields externalities to members of the club through transfers of knowledge and technologies as well as by facilitating collective actions, which may be achieved, for instance, by shared trust, norms, and values.[2]

Questionnaires based on the World Bank's Social Capital Assessment Tool can be used effectively for measuring social capital. A multiple correspondence analysis can then be applied to questionnaire responses in order to create a social capital 'map': that is, the distribution of social capital, including where the survey distinguishes between structural (horizontal organizational density, decision-making processes, leadership, exclusion or acceptance of diversity, and collective action) and cognitive (trust-based relationships, solidarity, behaviour, and attitudes) social capital.

Social Capital in Small-Scale Tropical Agriculture

A study of social capital in the context of impoverished and highly vulnerable farming communities yields some useful insights. The project aimed to develop a quantitative instrument to measure social capital across coffee and cocoa producers in the tropics. It investigated the relationship between smallholders' socio-demographic characteristics and social capital, and considered whether social capital is a key resource for higher agricultural productivity, looking at the low propensity to adopt more efficient agrarian practices and the obstacles to their diffusion. To address these questions, the researchers used the assessment tool to build a map of social capital in which farmers were located relative to one another according to the way they perceive the other members of the community in terms of shared understanding and the nature and quality of relationships.

The questionnaires were administered among coffee and cocoa smallholder households living in small communities in Ivory Coast, Papua New Guinea, Tanzania, and Indonesia over the period from 2011 to 2015. Unpacking the relationship between smallholders' individual characteristics and their social capital made it possible to differentiate sub-groups of smallholders according to their individual socio-demographic variables: kinship, natives versus outsiders, gender, age, religion, land rights, etc.[3]

Three dimensions emerged systematically: i) inclusion and cohesion; ii) trust, solidarity, and reciprocity; and iii) collective action and cooperation. Within each country, however, social capital varies substantially from one community (village) to another; and even within a community it varies greatly from one smallholder to another.[4]

The study shows that productivity (kg/ha) is positively correlated to social capital, in particular with the dimension reflecting trust/solidarity and reciprocity. On average, individual productivity is higher for farmers who are connected to their community through group membership or networks and trust-based relationships.[5] More specifically, the findings demonstrate something happening in cooperatives tending to favour the economic performance of a farmer (e.g. exchange of information, access to inputs). The performance is even higher when he is also a member of a family association or diaspora (e.g. access to credit). Additionally, the trust farmers place in their peers and compliance with values such as individual responsibility, altruism, and the solidarity farmers have with their peers, tend to make them more productive.

The results also suggest that, all other things being equal, there is a positive correlation between a farmer's social capital and his propensity to revise his farming practices. Through the process of social interaction, farmers adopt their organizations' values and practices. Having a network of diverse weak ties (bridges) through the participation in cooperatives or economic interest groups (versus clan or religious group) is highly beneficial to exchanging key information on agronomic practices and learning, eventually leading to a revision and improvement of agronomic practices.

To conclude, it turns out that where people are connected to their community through group membership and to each other through trust-based relationships, individual productivity is higher. Furthermore, a rather optimistic belief about community members' trustworthiness (relative to pessimistic beliefs) leads a farmer to be more proactive in seeking information and trusting those in possession of it like, for instance, representatives of agricultural organizations, family members, neighbours, and friends.

Measuring Human Capital

As explained in Chapter 11, in the classical definition, human capital is the stock of skills and experience that an employee accumulates through education, or on the job at a company. However, well-being at work can be seen as a form of *specific capital* that pertains to the relationship between the firm and the employee and includes the working conditions that are of value to the employee. These features of the work relationship, in turn, have a clear return for the employer, as they potentially generate non-negligible returns in terms of commitment, productivity, and retention of employees.

Well-being at work has become a primary-order concern for employers, notably in view of the excessive turnover of workers, especially the 'Y generation', who are looking for good progression and learning prospects, and meaningful activities on the job. Promoting well-being at work is certainly instrumental in retaining the most dynamic employees. As illustrated by an abundant literature in social sciences, the experience of happiness stimulates productivity, creativity and cooperation, and reduces absenteeism. But what makes people feel happy at work?

A clear lesson of research is that workers' well-being involves more than the traditional factors of wage and working hours. Workers are concerned by the degree of hierarchical 'steepness' in their firm, by the management style, by the dispersion of wages, their prospects for upward mobility, the corporate identity of their firm, and its social responsibility, among other things. These sources of well-being at work can be seen as human capital.

Drivers of Well-being at Work for Mars

As part of a research study, researchers ran several tailored surveys, and used the Gallup Q12 survey, in different segments of Mars (drinks, petcare, chocolate, and Wrigley) in different geographies, and matched this information with Human Resources data. At the same time they analysed the impact of an empowerment programme for a population of entrepreneurs in Kenya (Maua).

Well-being at work is measured in several dimensions, including job satisfaction (based on Maslow's pyramid of needs and satisfaction), attitudes to wage inequality, prospect of upwards mobility, hierarchy and status, the intensity of corporate identity, the composition of corporate identity (values, beliefs), including PiA (social responsibility of the firm), and social capital (trust, networks).

Drivers of well-being at work in Mars could be divided into two groups: self-centred and group-centred.

In the self-centred category it is no surprise that wages are linked to well-being at work. However, the 'prospect of upward mobility' (POUM) motive (see Chapter XX) appears to be just as powerful a factor. In many of the surveys, employees display a strong preference for increasing wage profile over time, especially workers who stand lower in the formal hierarchy. In some emerging Asian countries, as well as China, it was clear that workers' job satisfaction was only affected by the progression of their pay and not by their current level of wage, suggesting that they were essentially interested in the dynamics of their wage profile. In several cases, the POUM motive also led Mars associates to accept a greater differentiation of wages inside the firm as long as they hoped to progress upward in the distribution.

On top of monetary compensation, status—that is, the symbolic part of a job, including power and prestige—is also important. Before it changed its organization, Mars had a formal system of hierarchy ('zones') that gave employees a manager status or not. The surveys revealed that being or becoming a manager was associated with higher job satisfaction. As expected (because status is about symbolic values), the impact of status was much stronger on 'higher' satisfaction domains (values, flourishing, and progress) than on basic needs satisfaction.

Of course, wage and status are overlapping concepts. In terms of magnitude, between one third and one half of the effect of having a manager status was (statistically) explained by the level of wages associated with that status. Employees appeared more sensitive to wages when they work in a division that, as Royal Canin, did not adopt the zone system. This points to the fact that status and wages are partly substitutes.

Other aspects of organization also proved to matter, including the strong impact of the line manager's personality on the well-being at work of his or her subordinates. The mobility of line managers seems to be detrimental to respondents' well-being.

Small divisions seem to be preferred: the larger the size of the division where people work, the lower their satisfaction and engagement scores. This observation comes from comparing individuals who work in different divisions (cross-section analysis), and individuals who change division over time (panel analysis).

Finally, feedback is a primary-order condition of well-being at work. For instance, within Mars, the regular engagement survey creates expectations that should not be disappointed. Workers who declare that the feedback session was not followed through by action score very low in terms of job satisfaction.

Group-centred drivers depend on the collective aspects of the work organization. Among those, trust, corporate identity, corporate culture, and wage distribution seemed to matter most.

One of the main findings of the study is the relevance of corporate identity measures. Identity was scored based on employees' degree of knowledge of Mars' specific language and property structure as a family firm. Unsurprisingly, those who scored high on the corporate identity scale were also more satisfied with their job and had higher levels of within-firm trust.

This indicator of intensity of corporate identity could then be used for a further exploration of the firm's corporate culture. At Mars, those with higher corporate identity scores responded more favourably to group incentives and group performance indicators than to individualistic management practices. They had a preference for clear and explicit rules and guidelines, and respect for hierarchies and managerial authority, as opposed to more informal and horizontal governance structures. Surprisingly, in some countries, such as China, the stress put on collective functioning went hand in hand with a wide acceptance of competition and wage differentiation based on performance, as well as a strong demand for the possibility to learn and grow from their job. Those with higher corporate identity scores cared more about their firm's socially responsible behaviour and were more likely to adopt socially responsible practices as consumers. Moreover, they seemed to see no contradiction between social responsibility and corporate performance.

Choice experiments were used to elicit workers' attitudes to wage distribution within the firm. These consisted of asking employees to choose several times between two projects that yielded more or less unequal bonuses. They first chose 'behind the veil of ignorance', i.e. not knowing what their own bonus would be. Then they chose again knowing what their own pay would be.

In China, most people chose projects that could yield a higher pay-off and a higher total amount of bonuses, even if the bonuses were less equally distributed. This was all the more likely as employees:

- Declared a higher job satisfaction
- Expected a promotion or a wage rise
- Agreed that their job gives them opportunities to learn new skills
- Thought they had valuable skills
- Believed that large income differences are useful to incentivize individual effort
- Thought that competition is useful
- Believed that groups are more efficient than individuals
- Had a high level of firm-specific trust and social capital.

Conclusion

Measuring forms of non-financial capital is a complex undertaking. Unlike financial capital, for which there are international standards for measurement and use in accounting, for non-financial capitals, consensus has not yet been reached either on their definition or on the methods for their measurement. In this chapter we set out to contribute to this endeavour by capitalizing on the countless studies done on the ground over the last ten years, based on data collected on several thousand participants in surveys in rural areas in the tropics, among the workforce within of Mars and among the entrepreneurs employed in the micro-distribution project in Kenya. We aimed to show that measuring natural, social, and human capital is possible and pragmatic:

1. In a parsimonious way: through a limited number of basic indicators that cover at least 80 per cent of the variance observed in the data collected
2. With stable and comparable results across different production sectors and different geographical areas
3. In direct relation to the economic outcome, whether it relates to agricultural productivity in cocoa farming communities or to productivity generated by an increase in well-being at work or as a direct result of a more efficient use of natural resources.

At the time of writing this book, we are undertaking further analysis of human and social capital on a larger scale that involves numerous actors within the same ecosystem. The results obtained so far confirm the above: alongside financial, human and social capitals emerge as essential components in the orchestration of an ecosystem in addressing the various pain points observed and to fulfil a pre-established purpose.

Notes

1. 'Social Capital and Community Governance', *Economic Journal*, 112: F419–36.
2. The collection of articles compiled in *Foundations of Social Capital* (2003) edited by E. Ostrom and T. K. Ahn provide an insightful overview of the concept of social capital.
3. We highlight the importance of embeddedness (i.e. the insertion of the economic sphere into the social sphere) of land transactions in tropical rural areas, which crucially depend on the social relations between smallholder households within the community in which they live.
4. Interestingly enough, and similarly to inequality, intra-community variability is greater than inter-community variability.
5. These correlations are robust to differences in individual characteristics (gender, age, education, administration rights, risk of expropriation, born in village), and plot characteristics (tree life cycle, size, plantation material, origin of material). Quantitative results of our studies conducted in the various countries and in the associated communities are available upon request.

11
Building Social Capital

Marcel Fafchamps

Introduction

The concept of 'social capital' describes the quality of the social context in which exchange and teamwork take place: does the social context promote efficiency and coordination, or is it an impediment to trade and a source of distrust? In this chapter we answer the following questions: What is social capital? How is social capital created? What are the determinants of social capital and how are they measured? What is the relation of social capital to the performance of firms? We also endeavour to relate the concept of social capital to that of mutuality.

Social Capital as a Mechanism for Trust and Cooperation

As noted by the sociologist Mark Granovetter (1985) and others, economic exchange does not take place in a vacuum: it happens within a social context. This is because exchange involves interpersonal interactions and triggers a wide range of human emotions, from satisfaction at having reached a good deal or outsmarted a competitor, to the guilt of having betrayed a business acquaintance, or outrage at having been cheated by a trading partner. Even if trade is conducted in an impersonal manner, the human mind is quick to realize or imagine that another person is involved, thereby triggering the emotions associated with promises and betrayal.

Marcel Fafchamps, Building Social Capital In *Putting Purpose Into Practice: The Economics of Mutuality.* Edited by: Colin Mayer and Bruno Roche, Oxford University Press (2021).
DOI: 10.1093/oso/9780198870708.003.0011

Social interactions also activate various cognitive processes—such as inferring someone's type or motives. Unfortunately, however, most people are poor at drawing inferences: they jump to conclusions based on limited evidence (e.g. Kahneman 2011); they misjudge the precision given by small and large samples (e.g. Rabin 2002, Griffin and Tversky 1992); and they underestimate echo-chamber effects in rumours and gossip (e.g. Jackson 2009). Furthermore, expectations about the future behaviour of others are often shaped by shared norms and identity, meaning that people can misinterpret the actions of those from a different culture or background. As a result of all these processes, people often have erroneous beliefs, a feature that, combined with statistical discrimination, leads to prejudice and distrust.

Taken together, these biases and the emotions associated with them form the social context in which human exchange takes place. They affect how economic agents interact with each other—for example, in transactions with clients, workers, and suppliers—and in teamwork within firms and other hierarchical organizations. When people do not trust each other, trade and cooperation are impeded. Because information is by nature imperfectly distributed and unforeseen shocks occur constantly, opportunities abound for things to go wrong in economic transactions and within teams. And when something goes wrong, misperformance may be interpreted as a sign of incompetence or mischief. This creates distrust, and distrust makes trade difficult and renders organizations dysfunctional. Hence in the absence of a mechanism to alleviate or mitigate naturally arising distrust, economic exchange within and across organizations is bound to be inefficient.

Laws and courts are often seen to provide the required mechanism. While they are clearly important, there are many aspects of human behaviour that they cannot affect, such as when stakes are small, or when taking legal action would be futile or too costly. Formal institutions must be supplemented by informal mechanisms for trust and cooperation. Social capital is one such mechanism, loosely defined as a combination of interpersonal links, shared beliefs and identities, and norms that together reduce the incidence of distrust in economic exchange and teamwork. Creating social capital to reduce distrust and support mutually beneficial exchange is at the core of the idea of mutuality, which aims to promote a mutuality of service and benefits between a company, its employees and shareholders, and its consumers, suppliers, and other commercial partners.

Creating Social Capital

Trust is essentially an expectation of behaviour: trusting means expecting someone to behave in a predictable and beneficial way. This expectation comes partly from our understanding of that person's private interest. But in trade or teamwork situations, private interests are typically opposed: theoretically the client prefers to avoid paying; the supplier can save money by delivering bad quality; and the team member would benefit from free-riding. People can be encouraged to act against their private interest by the social penalties involved in not doing so: non-paying clients are blacklisted; unreliable suppliers are dropped; and shirking workers are laid off. These kinds of penalties are stronger when interpersonal links are hard to replace, serve many functions, and are part of someone's identity or group membership. Groups that are cohesive and have a strong identity are better able to discipline members for violating norms of cooperative behaviour. When this social capital is used to support market exchange and firm performance, it can enhance efficiency. But it can also be used to pervert exchange—for example, by favouring kith and kin—and to undermine organizations, perhaps by diverting time and resources away from the goals of the organization.

One way of creating social capital is thus to form a group identity that supports the economic goals of an organization or market. Because group identities are typically persistent, they are not necessarily amenable to rapid change—and can even become a force against change. Creating this type of group identity requires leaders able either to generate it from scratch or to channel an existing identity to serve a new purpose. Many firms and organizations rely on devices such as team sports or happy hour drinks to create a sense of conviviality that hopefully fosters group cooperation. Some business organizations engage in similar types of group bonding activities, with the view of encouraging more ethical and group-minded business practices. In other cases, the leadership comes from existing group structures that are repurposed for an organizational or market-support role.

Another approach to social capital consists of cultivating norms of individual behaviour that support the good operations of markets and organizations. The human mind comes equipped with a moral sense, and there are many human emotions associated with the respect and violation of norms, such as conformism, pride, guilt, shame, moral outrage, and self-righteousness. Norms associated with pro-sociality, redistribution, and fairness generate their own set of additional emotions, including altruism, envy, ambition, and competition. All these emotions are strong motivators of human behaviour, suggesting that deliberately cultivated social norms can be harnessed to support trustworthy behaviour in markets and firms.

Social norms can also evolve following the introduction of new legislation or through interventions directly intended to change social norms, such as educational campaigns and other awareness-raising activities. Firms too can influence social norms, particularly by setting standards of fairness in the way they deal with clients, suppliers, and workers. Early efforts in that direction include 'paternalistic' employers who vow to treat their employees as they would treat relatives. More recent expressions of this approach include corporate social responsibility initiatives and mutuality, which is arguably its most evolved and satisfying manifestation.

By identifying the key dimensions of social capital, the above discussion helps us identify the levers upon which to act in order to create it. But it does not clarify how this is done in practice. What distinguishes mutuality from other forms of social capital formation is the determination to construct social capital through mutual investment by the parties involved. This approach resonates with the observations we made at the start of this chapter: economic relationships take place in a social context, and this context triggers a wide range of human emotions that can either support or hinder exchange. Mutuality relies on what is essentially a modern version of reciprocal exchange[1] to trigger a virtuous cycle of reinforcing trust between economic partners. Reciprocal gift exchange has long been an effective way of building strong human ties between strangers, as it triggers a wide range of emotions conducive to trust and empathy. Mutuality borrows from this timeless wisdom.

Measuring Trust and Trustworthy Behaviour

Now that we have a better understanding of what social capital is and of the factors that determine it, how can we measure it? More precisely, how can we assess the extent to which the social context is conducive to market efficiency and to cooperation in large organizations and firms?

The most direct measure of social capital is its key output: the expectation of trustworthy behaviour. This expectation can be measured with respect to an unspecified stranger, or towards a member of a specific group to which the respondent does or does not belong—for example, in a caste-based society, towards a member of the same caste or a member of a different caste. Expectations can also be measured differentially towards trust in market transactions versus trust in teams of co-workers. It is possible also to ascertain the extent of trust: for example, would you entrust this person with amount of money *X* for a friend?

Trust may be misguided, however, and if destroyed can undermine performance and pull people apart. Hence measures of trust should be complemented by measures of trustworthiness. One way of achieving this is through an experiment in which respondents are entrusted with money and asked to forward it to a specified stranger. By varying the amount of money and the type of stranger, it is possible to ascertain the extent and directed nature of trustworthiness in a population. If respondents are equally trustworthy irrespective of stranger type, we can talk of generalized morality: people can be trusted to act reliably with all strangers. In contrast, if they treat strangers differently according to their type, this indicates in-group bias.

More can be learned by assessing trustworthiness in different types of market interaction (for example, as client, supplier, employee, or borrower) and towards different contractual parties: towards a corporate seller or a street vendor; towards a co-worker or manager; or towards a bank or MFI. People from different cultures or backgrounds may have different views of what constitutes acceptable behaviour in market transactions and in employer–employee relations.

Next the researcher may want to know whether the social capital is based on group membership or social norms. In order to measure this, questions should be asked about the respondent's different identities (gender, ethnicity, religion, caste where relevant, and place of origin) and about membership and engagement in associations and other relevant social groupings. The purpose is to examine whether in-group bias in trust and trustworthiness correlates with group identity or membership. If it does, this suggests social capital based on group membership. This type of social capital may reflect strong within-group bonds, but may be insufficient to support efficient exchange and collaboration between members of different groups or identities; it could even be counter-productive. It may also be useful to examine the extent to which respondents participate in group activities organized by economic agents (e.g. firms) compared to those organized by non-economic ones (e.g. churches, extended family, sporting groups).

If engagement with mutual investment activities correlates with trustworthy behaviour towards co-workers and managers, this constitutes suggestive evidence that mutuality can create social capital. A similar observation applies to engagement in mutual investments between the firm and its clients, suppliers, and investors. The question is whether a firm can compensate fractured identities and group membership by creating a corporate culture of mutuality that fosters trustworthiness and cooperation within the firm. This leaves open the question of whether the social capital created by one firm would benefit or hurt other firms. Ultimately, however, truly convincing evidence that firms can create social capital requires experimenting with various corporate culture interventions—including mutuality—and submitting the observed outcomes to rigorous statistical analysis, preferably based on the randomization of treatment across plants or establishments. (See Chapter 15 for a description of a randomized controlled trial of a reciprocal investment intervention involving a Mars company and its distributors in Kenya.)

Social norms are another important source of social capital. In some societies, for example, it is acceptable to display distrust towards strangers—perhaps refusing to talk to them, or to eat with them. In Western societies, we are supposed to be polite and courteous even with strangers, and we are not expected to cheat strangers just because they are strangers. In other words, being trusting or trustworthy can simply be 'the right thing to do'. Information about norms can be collected by eliciting respondents' attitudes towards normative statements, such as 'it is acceptable not to pay a supplier in order to take a child to the clinic' or 'it is acceptable for an employer to dismiss a worker for unjustified absence', with responses following a Likert scale (i.e. on a continuum from 'strongly disagree' to 'strongly agree'). While normative questions are informative, though, they may capture what respondents believe others expect them to say. Stronger evidence can be obtained using incentivized methods, such as experimentally putting the respondent in a specific situation and observing their actual behaviour. By comparing behaviour with responses to normative statements, it is possible to gain a sense of how strongly people adhere to specific norms. For instance, people may deviate from the norms they hold in response to behaviours perceived as insulting or disrespectful.

Norms are delicate determinants of human behaviour and should be approached as such. One particular issue that affects firms is how individuals respond to incentives. Economists are strong believers in the usefulness and legitimacy of material incentives—so much so that they often cannot imagine others might think differently.

However, fostering a culture of unconditional cooperation may succeed better than hard incentives if conditional cooperation is perceived as illegitimate. For instance, in countries where people face many problems at home, dismissing a worker for missing work is often seen as unacceptably harsh. Instead of reducing absenteeism, applying this punishment to a worker as an example for others may create a backlash: seen as inherently unfair, the employer loses the moral high ground and employer loyalty suffers, triggering a loss of morale and an increase in turnover and, possibly, pilferage. Seen in this light, mutuality may better serve the long-term interest of the firm than a policy of harsh conditional penalties.

The appeal of the social capital approach is that it covers many of the ways in which social context affects markets and organizations within a single framework. It also brings to the fore both the bright and dark aspects of social capital: while it enhances group cohesion and boosts trust, it can also turn parochial, as when members of a particular ethnic group or gender discriminate against outsiders, or when loyalty towards a commercial enterprise fosters potentially destructive competition (so-called corporate warfare).

Social Capital and Firm Performance

What lessons can we learn from this rapid overview regarding the relationship between social capital and firm performance? Social capital can benefit or hurt firm performance depending on the types of group loyalties and social norms that are activated by it. If economic partners of the firm—i.e. workers, investors, suppliers, clients—identify with the firm and share similar norms of behaviour, strong social capital among these partners should help the firm perform better. On the other hand, if the main allegiance of economic partners is to groups outside the firm and/or shared social norms that are contrary to those of the firms, then strong social capital among them will hurt the firm. For instance, corruption is often associated with collusion among employees (and some managers) to work against the interests of the organization. The ability to collude successfully is helped by strong social capital among workers. Similarly, investors, suppliers, and clients can collude, either explicitly or implicitly, to discriminate against the firm. The stronger the ties they have between them, the easier collusion is.

To counteract these forces, the firm needs to be informed about relevant social groupings and prevalent social norms among its main economic partners. Failure to do so can lead to a loss of performance—especially when the firm operates cross-culturally (e.g. Chu et al. 2018). The next step is for the firm to identify the most problematic rifts and to experiment with ways of creating unifying social capital—for example, by emphasizing a shared identity and a commonality of interests, by creating opportunities for enjoyable and memorable social contact across divisions, and by gradually shifting norms of behaviour. The latter requires the firm to understand precisely which penalties and reward systems are seen as morally and socially acceptable. I have offered ideas above on how to collect the necessary information.

Conclusion

Mutuality can be seen as promoting a humanist approach to business, one in which the firm seeks to create a sense of common purpose and values with its economic partners, rather than adopting an exploitative approach or pandering to local norms and allegiances. Based on analysis, the ability to pursue this strategy effectively depends on the absence of local social capital operating against the firm's mutuality principles. It is nonetheless important to recognize that fostering mutual investment in reciprocal relationships has been practiced by human societies since time immemorial to build social capital and achieve mutually beneficial exchange. The difference is that the approach is applied to the market realm, which is known to be such a powerful mobilizer of human dynamism and ingenuity. It is this combination of old and new that makes mutuality such a promising avenue to joint prosperity.

Note

1. Also called gift exchange in the anthropological and sociological literature (e.g. Polanyi 1944, Platteau 1994a, b).

12

Well-Being at Work as Human Capital

Claudia Senik

Introduction

Research in social science has demonstrated forcefully that workers' well-being encompasses more than the traditional factors of wage and working hours. As discussed in Chapter 9, workers are also concerned with the 'steepness' of the hierarchy in their firm, by the management style, by wage differences within the firm, by the prospects for upward mobility, by the corporate identity of their firm, its social responsibility, and more. These unconventional sources of well-being at work can be seen as a form of human capital, as they potentially generate non-negligible returns in terms of commitment, productivity, and retention of employees.

In the classical definition, human capital is based on the stock of skills and experience that an employee accumulates through education, or on the job at a company. But in this chapter, we focus on those other factors of human capital that relate to their well-being. Obviously, well-being at work is not of a form of *general capital*, but rather a type of *specific capital* that represents a unique fit between the employee and the firm. It pertains directly to the relationship between the firm and the employee and includes the working conditions that are of value to the employee.

These features of the work relationship, in turn, have a clear return for the employer. Employees who feel better and happier at work are more engaged, more productive, more creative, more flexible, and better negotiators on behalf of their employers. On a broader level, workers'

DOI: 10.1093/oso/9780198870708.003.0012

attachment to the firm creates a competitive advantage for the company, by reducing turnover.

This chapter is devoted to describing the drivers of well-being at work that constitute such firm-specific human capital.

Sources of Well-being within the Organization

The main source of procedural well-being at work is related to the organization of the firm. This includes, inter alia, the degree of verticality of the hierarchy, status and career concerns, and, more generally, the mutual feedback between employees and managers.

Verticality

Usually, vertical hierarchies—those with many layers in them—are detrimental to well-being at work. A hierarchy generally restricts the potential for people's innate need for self-determination, autonomy, and the experience of competence.

The reason that employees enjoy more horizontal organizations, and dislike long chains of command, is the notion of *locus of control*. Locus of control refers to the sense of autonomy, the feeling that an individual can decide how to organize themselves, when and how they perform their tasks and pursue their objectives. Understanding the entire process that one is engaged in, from the starting point to completion is essential, as discussed by Matthew Crawford (2009). This is also the condition for being able to acknowledge whether one's undertaking was successful or not. Hence, in general, well-being at work depends on this sense of responsibility and autonomy. By contrast, a situation where employees are given clear objectives without the means or the resources to achieve them is extremely detrimental to well-being.

Feedback is important as a means of giving employees a complete view of their actions and their respective consequences. It is also important that employees feel that they are valued for their accomplishments. This is more easily done in small organizations, with a short authority chain. Note that performance feedback, given at the level of working units or divisions, is another important aspect of the governance of the firm. This is because it creates a disciplining device by diffusing the information about workers' and managers' outcomes. It also provides opportunities for improvement of the organization.

Another issue in a hierarchy is the way people are promoted into more senior positions within the firm. The degree to which this allocation is transparent and open plays an important role in workers' satisfaction.

All these organizational aspects are embedded in the concept of *procedural utility*, in other words, the share of well-being that depends on *how* an outcome is achieved, rather than on the outcome alone.

Status

Status reflects the non-monetary aspect of a job, including the symbolic value of the work. It often corresponds to a rank in the firm's organization, giving power, prestige, or tenure. It is associated with occupations, responsibilities, skills, and other means of differentiation of jobs. It is also related to hierarchical power inside the firm.

Status thus comes with a non-wage, administrative, or symbolic payoff, and is likely to have an impact on workers' well-being. Therefore, it potentially plays the role of a 'job amenity'. In his theory of 'compensating differences', Adam Smith predicted that workers enjoying more positive amenities in their workplace would accept lower wages (or would be forced to do so by competition for these jobs). Status could be one of these amenities that workers are ready to trade for wages. In fact, several studies have shown that workers with status reached the same level of well-being at work as those with a higher wage and no status. It is thus of interest to know and measure the extent to which status is causal to well-being at work and can be a substitute for pay.

Line Managers

The economic literature has stressed the role of the manager in terms of leadership, trust, governance, and capacity to solve coordination problems in a context of uncertainty and imperfect information. In the data that we collected at Mars, this *line manager fixed-effect* was crucial: the personality of the line manager had an important impact on the well-being of the employees. The data also demonstrated that employees suffered when line managers changed roles. This creates a trade-off for the firm, as career progression (of managers) almost always entails mobility.

Career Progression

An important contributor to well-being at work is the possibility of learning and growing in the firm. This includes career progression. In our field study in China, this turned out to be the main criterion of attraction and retention of workers by the firm.

Inclusiveness

Organizations may be more or less inclusive, in the sense of making all sub-groups feel part of the same group. This can be measured by asking about how different types of employees are consulted about decisions, about their awareness of the ongoing discussions and decisions. How often are different types of workers asked for help by colleagues, and whom can they ask for help themselves? Measuring the degree of inclusion can help detect whether some groups are more fragile and less included, thus helping to make an ongoing diagnosis of human capital and well-being at work.

The Role of Corporate Culture and Identity in Well-being

A further, less visible, feature of the organization concerns *corporate identity* and *corporate culture*. In a general sense, culture may be defined as the body of shared beliefs, understanding, values, goals, and practices that characterizes a group in a persistent way, due to the fact that it is transmitted by older group members to younger ones. The importance of culture in shaping preferences, choices, and behaviour is now the object of an abundant literature, even in economics.

Economists have described corporate culture as an instrumental device used to reduce uncertainty and transaction costs in firms and organizations, and allow the coordination of individual expectations and decisions. Workers who need to interact frequently and solve a variety of problems repeatedly often unintentionally develop their own specific system of conventions, understanding, and knowledge. This shared culture then substitutes for explicit communication. But corporate culture also shapes workers' preferences, attitudes, and modes of thinking. Thus it affects their ability to work productively and autonomously, and feel included. In other words, the culture may have a positive or negative effect on well-being.

Measuring the Dimensions of Corporate Culture

The most famous typology of corporate culture has been proposed by the Dutch social psychologist Geert Hofstede (2001). His work suggests a classification of cultures that help describe the differences between countries, firms, organizations, and even families, based on a standardized questionnaire.

In the context of the firm, some elements of Hofstede's classification are particularly relevant, for example:

- Power distance. This refers to the attitudes of employees to inequality, authority, and hierarchy; preferences for centralized or decentralized structures, for directive versus democratic managers.
- Uncertainty avoidance. This captures the notion of stress and anxiety in the face of unknown futures, aversion to imprecise rules, preferences for completely explicit procedures, preferences for long tenure, strong loyalty to the employer, preferences for larger organizations, innovation versus rules, etc.

- Individualism versus collectivism (group). This addresses the importance of individual (rather than group) performance and incentives, of individual decision-making; of wage-equality versus acceptance of competition and wage-differentiation, etc. Linked with this classification is the type of group thinking that takes place. How are collective decisions taken? Is it expected that meetings will lead to a consensus, or is a person in charge of choosing between different conflicting options that are proposed during the meeting?
- Social responsibility. Social responsibility potentially constitutes an important element of the specific corporate culture of the company. To capture this, it is possible to introduce questions about the perceptions of employees concerning the socially responsible behaviour of their company, as well as the behaviour of employees themselves as consumers. An additional consideration is whether social responsibility is seen as an intrinsic motivation on behalf of the firm's management, or as an extrinsic motivation, i.e. a profit-maximizing device. It is often believed that extrinsic motivations tend to crowd out intrinsic motivations. However, in the case of SR, this needs not necessarily be the case, if employees understand that SR is now embedded in the core of the business model instead of something that comes later, after profit-maximization.

Measuring the Intensity of Corporate Identity

In order to measure the intensity of corporate identity—the degree to which employees adhere to the firm's style and identify with it—we developed a system based on the idea that identity is mediated through language. When people live together, work together, and interact frequently, they start developing communications shortcuts that are specific to what they do, otherwise known as jargon. This is in line with the view of corporate culture as a set of conventions and language elements that save on the costs associated with explicit coordination.

The more people master the specific corporate jargon, the higher their degree of corporate identity. In the case of Mars for instance, the metrics capture workers' degree of knowledge of the specific terms relevant to the firm, as well as their awareness of the specific ownership structure of the firm.

Using the Measures of Corporate Culture and Identity

After having measured the intensity and dimensions of corporate culture, the next step is to look at how these correlate with well-being at work. It is expected that people who share a greater intensity of corporate culture are happier in the firm. This measurement can thus be used as a tool to evaluate the fit between employees and firms. For instance, if corporate identity is associated with a culture of hierarchy and clear rules, a person coming into that community with different values will not fit, and will probably not reach a high level of well-being at work.

Well-being, Social Capital, and Trust

'Man is by nature a social animal', wrote Aristotle (*Politics, I*). More recently, in Maslow's (1943) pyramid of human needs, love and belonging come just after basic physiological and safety needs. The World Happiness Report, prepared at Yale University under the auspices of the United Nations, finds that having someone to rely on is one of the most powerful drivers of happiness. Clearly, the sources of individual well-being cannot be circumscribed to individual circumstances. They also include the set of social interactions through which individuals are interconnected. Since the seminal work of Robert Putnam (2000), social capital is generally defined as the quantity and quality of social relations in a community.

It is defined as a 'capital' because people's social networks are accumulated over time (like financial capital) and yield benefits (inclusion and cooperation). As a network, social capital also includes a notion of externality, i.e. mutually reinforcing benefits for all members.

Importantly, social capital has a local dimension and is by nature restricted to a community, i.e. a sub-group of the population whose members interact directly and frequently, share common norms and a sense of common identity. De facto, it has been shown that staying rooted in the same neighbourhood for a longer time is associated with higher levels of all types of trust, especially neighbourhood trust (Helliwell and Wang, 2011); conversely people who live in districts where the population is dense and highly mobile are less likely to trust their neighbours. It is likely that the same rule applies to firms: social capital is lower where the turnover of workers is higher. Because of this local-norm-enforcing nature, social capital can constitute an alternative or an addition to market allocation and explicit rules, and is welfare-increasing.

Measuring Trust

Trust plays a crucial role in social capital. The notion of trust is very much related to the framework of the game theory, which analyses strategic interactions between interdependent agents. Trust, understood in this way, promotes cooperation by reducing uncertainty about the behaviour of others, in particular the risk of moral hazard (cheating). Accordingly, in surveys, social capital is often measured by questions about trust and confidence that others (neighbours, co-workers, etc.) will behave in a cooperative way.

Social capital is also measured by the frequency of cooperative behaviour (in laboratory and field experiments). One famous experiment is the 'lost wallet' experiment, first conducted by the *Reader's Digest Europe* in 1996 and designed to indicate interpersonal trust in a number of countries. Since then, a question about the likelihood that a lost wallet, if found by a stranger, would be returned to the police was introduced in international surveys, such as the World Values Survey and the World Gallup Poll, as well as certain national surveys (e.g. in Canada and the United States) to elicit social trust. The question can be adapted to measure trust at the workplace the firm ('If you lost your wallet in the premises of the firm how likely is it that someone would return it?').

Finally, other measures of social capital within the firm also include the number and frequency of contact between workers, i.e. the social density of the social network within the firm, as well as how easy it is to ask for help and information from colleagues when needed.

The Returns on Social Capital and Trust

The relationship between happiness and concepts of social capital has then been tested, thanks to survey data containing self-declared happiness, trust, and social connectedness questions. The result is that trust, self-stated social connections, and social identities are associated with higher life satisfaction and happiness, in all countries off the world where the relationship has been evaluated. It is important to underline that it is trust in colleagues, trust in management, and other measures of social capital in the workplace that appear to be most highly correlated with well-being at work (Helliwell and Huang, 2009).

Social capital can be favourable to performance. In their real-life experiments, Bandiera, Barankay, and Rasul (2010) observed that, everything else equal, performance is higher in teams of socially connected workers, where a higher effort norm enforcement within the group exists. For instance, people will be willing to take more risk to innovate in a corporate environment where they trust their colleagues and management.

Well-being and Wage Distribution

Wage distribution within the firm constitutes one of the most widely recognized drivers of well-being at work. The idea is that workers do not only care about the level of their own wage, but, most of the time, are also concerned by the pay of others, and the general degree of wage inequality within the firm. They have preferences about the way wages are set and about the resulting wage distribution within their firm.

These concerns are based on different potential motives. Some are 'self-regarding', when employees just seek to improve their own situation, and some are 'other-regarding', in the sense that employees may care about other people's pay even if it does not affect their own situation.

One self-regarding motive has received particular attention from researchers and seems to be widespread: the prospect for upward mobility (POUM, an acronym coined by Benabou and Ok, 2001). POUM implies that inequality is interpreted as a ladder that can be climbed. Hence, employees will accept a greater differentiation of wages inside their firm as long as they hope to progress upwards in its wage distribution. Whenever POUM is an important concern, this means that the dynamic aspect of workers' pay, i.e. the prospective wage profile that they can expect, matters as much as the static level of wage at a given period.

Research also shows that people are very sensitive to the floor wage. They may not care about the general degree of wage inequality within the firm, but still feel bad if they are aware that some people are earning a very low wage.

Eliciting Preferences for Wage Distributions

Depending on their views and preferences, employees may feel satisfied or dissatisfied with the distribution of pay within the firm. For management to measure this dimension of well-being at work they can either use simple survey questions or implement choice experiments in the lab or 'in the field'.

Conclusion

The drivers of well-being at work and the metrics that we have presented can be considered as part of the value of a firm. Of course, there are many things that were not covered in this chapter. Working at distance, co-working spaces, platform and mission-based contracting instead of employer–employee wage contracts take an increasing importance in work life. Technological innovations transform the modalities of work and the working relationships. The more we are able to measure the impact of these transformations, the better we can harness them to the benefit of workers' well-being. Ultimately, the objective is to make these metrics part of the dashboard of managers at par with financial indicators, to measure the value of the firm.

13
Accounting for Natural Capital

Richard Barker

Introduction

The argument in this chapter is that the concept of mutuality has important implications for corporate accounting for natural capital. Such an accounting must respect the preservation of natural resources as an end in itself, and not as something that is secondary to shareholder interests. Mutual accounting should seek to reflect the full impact of a company on natural capital, and in so doing it should recognize how the distinctive properties of ecosystems and other natural resources raise distinctive challenges for accounting. Finally, a mutual accounting system must be deployed alongside a corporate purpose that incorporates the intrinsic benefits of natural capital, because there is otherwise an unavoidable conflict between the objective of natural capital maintenance and other objectives of the business; in this regard, accounting can be understood as a measurement system, a window on corporate performance, but it can only be truly mutual if the business being measured is itself pursuing an objective of mutuality.

Natural Capital and Accounting

The resources of nature ('natural capital') feature prominently in the 2018 World Economic Forum's annual Global Risks Report (WEF, 2018). With global risk defined as 'an uncertain event or condition that, if it occurs,

Richard Barker, Accounting for Natural Capital In *Putting Purpose Into Practice: The Economics of Mutuality.* Edited by: Colin Mayer and Bruno Roche, Oxford University Press (2021).
DOI: 10.1093/oso/9780198870708.003.0013

can cause significant negative impact for several countries or industries within the next ten years', the report compiled survey evidence from World Economic Forum (WEF) multi-stakeholder communities, members of the Institute of Risk Management and the professional networks of the World Economic Forum Advisory Board Members. Nine global risk factors, from a list of thirty, were assigned higher-than-average perceptions of both likelihood and impact. Of those, six were specifically concerned with natural capital. In descending order of overall rating, these were: extreme weather events (e.g. floods, storms, etc.), leading to major property, infrastructure, and/or environmental damage, as well as loss of human life; natural disasters; the failure of governments and businesses to enforce or enact effective measures to mitigate climate change, protect populations, and help businesses impacted by climate change to adapt; water crises, whereby a significant decline in the available quality and quantity of fresh water harms human health and/or economic activity; human-caused environmental damage and disasters (e.g. oil spills, radioactive contamination, etc.); and major biodiversity loss and ecosystem collapse (terrestrial or marine), with irreversible consequences for the environment, resulting in severely depleted resources for humankind as well as industries.[1] In addition, the report notes that 'truly systemic challenge here rests in the depth of the interconnectedness that exists both among these environmental risks and between them and risks in other categories—such as water crises and involuntary migration. And as the impact of Hurricane Maria on Puerto Rico has starkly illustrated, environmental risks can also lead to serious disruption of critical infrastructure.'

In contrast, and as recently as 2010, not a single issue concerned with natural capital was ranked in WEF's top five global risks, for either impact or likelihood.

The point here is stark and simple: human impact on natural capital has become an overwhelmingly pressing concern for business and society (Wilson, 2016). The point is made here with data from WEF (2018). It could equally well be made with, for example, authoritative evaluations of the existential threats posed by climate change (IPCC, 2018) and of the current, unprecedented and unsustainable rate of loss of biodiversity (WWF, 2018).

This is not a time for the corporate sector to offer an uncritical assertion that it is somehow the solution to the challenges faced by the natural world. On the contrary, the very effectiveness of corporate growth has 'enabled' our unprecedented rate of natural capital consumption and depletion, such that the corporation has historically been the problem rather than the solution (Mayer, 2013). The need for fundamental change is, to say the least, pressing.

Enter mutuality. If nature is regarded as a stakeholder in corporate activity, and if that activity can be regarded as benign only if all stakeholders are reasonably respected and rewarded, then there is the hope of avoiding the current, unsustainable trade-off between economic growth and adverse impact on the natural world. Moreover, there is an important sense in which this is not an option. If there is not mutuality between the natural world and other stakeholders in the corporation, then we are headed for disaster.

Of course, a mutual business is more easily imagined than realized. An important practical challenge in the realization of mutuality lies in the design of an appropriate system of accounting, because measures of corporate performance provide a means of directing and evaluating corporate activity, while also enabling a system of reporting and so of external accountability. Accordingly, this chapter concerns the role of accounting in the context of corporate responsibility with respect to the natural world.

Importantly, the preservation of natural capital must be regarded as an end in itself. It cannot—in the context of mutuality—be regarded as something to be traded off against growth in financial capital. This is because a mutual business is not one in which the benefits to one category of stakeholder are achieved at the expense of another. It would not, for example, be 'acceptable' to regard shareholders' financial capital as available for depletion for the benefit of other stakeholders. A more subtle and negotiable question is how much financial capital should be allowed to grow in relation to growth in other stakeholder investments, but the basic principle of financial capital maintenance is 'non-negotiable'.

Challenges for Accounting

Enacting mutuality in the context of natural capital raises four distinct challenges for the measurement of corporate performance, and thereby for accounting.

The first challenge arises if there is a conflict in corporate objectives with respect to financial capital and natural capital, and a conflict therefore in the notion of what constitutes performance. Specifically, it is widely understood and accepted that (in the typical case) financial returns for shareholders provide the primary basis for understanding how well a company has performed. All other metrics are secondary, they are instrumental to the ultimate purpose of financial return. If, therefore, performance with respect to the preservation of natural capital stands in conflict with performance with respect to financial returns, then the conventional resolution is that the latter 'wins'. Clearly, if the preservation of natural capital is an end in itself, then the conventional solution is problematic. The challenge here is that the accountant is not currently called upon to measure a bottom line other than financial profit for shareholders. Providing an alternative bottom line would not solve the problem of preserving natural capital, but what it would do is give the problem appropriate salience.

The second challenge—which relates closely to the first—is one of framing. The issue here is the context within which natural capital is said to be preserved. Is the focus of concern the natural capital on which the corporation depends in order to sustain its activities? Or is the focus instead the natural capital which is affected by the activities of the corporation? In other words, is the concern with dependency or impact? In both cases, there is also a secondary question, namely whether and how natural capital can be specified and measured in order that its preservation (or otherwise) can be understood. It will be argued that impact is 'what matters' and that—to the extent possible—impact measurement should not be partial. The link to the first challenge above is that the primacy of financial returns for shareholders leads instead to the opposite conclusion, that dependency should be the focus. This second challenge is in effect an extension of the first; it is a call for the accountant to understand and measure the bottom line in terms of corporate impact on natural capital.

The third challenge is to recognize a critical difference between accounting for financial capital and accounting for natural capital. There is something dangerously beguiling in the shared language of 'capital', along with the appropriation of an economic logic in conceptualizing the natural world. This approach invites us to view as analogous performance measurement with respect to financial capital and to natural capital. In particular, it appears that depreciation in financial accounting is analogous to depreciation in natural capital accounting. Yet it is not. The challenge here is to 'see through' the accounting and to guard against the misrepresentation of underlying phenomena.

While the first three challenges can be understood as conceptual (alternatively as normative, or ethical)—what *should* a corporation focus on in order to preserve natural capital?—the fourth and final challenge raises a more practical question, grounded in the law and in conventional business practice, which is what *can* a corporation do in order to preserve natural capital? Historically, economic growth has been achieved at the expense of natural capital (IPCC, 2018; WWF, 2018). In part, this is because laws and conventions have allowed this to be the case (Barker, 2019). An implication is that—historically at least—the 'obligation' to make good consumption of natural capital is not actually an obligation at all. The challenge here is the practicality of 'doing the right thing'. The challenge is to identify the mechanism by which accounting can have practical consequences. As will be argued, this can ultimately be achieved only if the purpose of the corporation does not entertain the consumption of natural capital in the service of the growth of financial capital (Mayer, 2018).

Overall, the argument here is that the meaningful application of 'mutuality' to the preservation of natural capital calls for all four of the above challenges to be addressed.

The Dominance of Financial Returns

The problem of a conflict in corporate objectives can be illustrated with an example. In selecting such an example, it is worth keeping in mind that, within any given industry, there are leaders and laggards with respect to corporate responsibility towards the natural world. The example is provided here of a leader, within the context of the chemicals industry. The reason for choosing a leader is to illustrate a core problem that plagues even best practice. The example ('ChemCo') is anonymized because the purpose is not to vilify the company in question; after all, it is leading the way and should be encouraged for so doing. But the data are real because this makes the message more powerful.

ChemCo defines sustainability according to the Vision 2050 of the World Business Council for Sustainable Development (WBCSD), that 'people live well and within the resource limits of the planet'. This is very much the language of mutuality. ChemCo asserts its commitment to a leadership role with respect to sustainability, which it notes is deeply embedded in its corporate values. Very much in line with the language of mutuality, ChemCo seeks to maintain a balance between economic success, protection of the environment, and social responsibility, which it argues has been fundamental to its way of doing business for decades.

ChemCo backs up its broad statement of commitment with a very specific, and very impressive, target. By the year 2030, its commitment is that all of its products and processes should be three times as efficient as they are today. Moreover, its performance with respect to enhancing efficiency is starting to head towards satisfying this ambition. Over the time period 2013–17, energy consumption per unit of output has reduced by 9 per cent and carbon dioxide emissions per unit have likewise reduced by 8 per cent.

Meanwhile, ChemCo's business has been growing, and so lower environmental impact has not obviously been at the expense of financial performance. Sales were just over €16bn in 2013, growing to €20bn in 2017. Operating profit has likewise grown over this period, from €2.5bn to €3.5bn.

So far, so good. Consider, however, the ecological indicators presented in Table 13.1, noting that these are reported as absolute amounts rather than on a per unit basis. The simple observation to make here is that environmental performance has deteriorated. This decline would be greater in the absence of the efficiency gains that ChemCo has realized, yet those gains are insufficient to offset the effects of growth. Moreover,

Table 13.1. ChemCo ecological indicators

	2013	2014	2015	2016	2017
Amount of production in thousand metric tons	7,690	7,867	7,940	8,456	9,392
Energy consumption in thousand megawatt hours	2,291	2,221	2,300	2,376	2,538
Carbon dioxide emissions in thousand metric tons	654	634	654	685	734
Water consumption in thousand cubic meters	7,642	7,438	7,190	7,658	8,431
Waste for recycling and disposal in thousand metric tons	128	118	112	120	124

the 'headline' in ChemCo's reporting of corporate performance is the growth in sales and in profit; it is not the growth in ecological impact.

The message here is that a commitment to improving efficiency with respect to ecological impact is not a commitment to preserving natural capital. Instead, the enactment of mutuality requires—at a minimum—capital maintenance with respect to all stakeholders. A business is not mutual if it records a financial profit while also depleting natural capital. There is, in principle, a very simple challenge here for accounting, which is to keep track not just of financial performance but also of natural capital performance, and to judge both against the benchmark of capital maintenance.

Framing Natural Capital

In order to measure the maintenance of natural capital, it is necessary to consider carefully what is actually being maintained (Barker and Mayer, 2017).

Following a logic of the primacy of the shareholder, natural capital maintenance is relevant only indirectly to corporate activity, to the extent that it is required in order for the economic value creation of the business to be sustainable.[2] This is the logic of a dependency upon natural capital. So, for example, a company's land use might cause both a degradation in soil quality and also a loss of biodiversity. If, for the sake of argument, the loss of soil quality caused a decline in crop yield, and so in revenue for the company, then a reversal of that decline—and, so, the maintenance of natural capital—would be called for. Yet this would not be to treat natural capital maintenance as an end in itself, but instead as instrumental to the primary goal of maintaining shareholder returns (Gray, 1992 and 1994; Bebbington and Gray, 2001; Milne and Gray, 2013; Helm, 2015). This can be seen if, again for the sake of argument, the biodiversity loss had no direct economic consequences for the company, in which case natural capital maintenance would not be desirable from a shareholders' perspective.

The alternative—implied by the concept of mutuality—is, so to speak, to ask not what natural capital can do for the company, but ask what the company can do for natural capital. This is to be concerned with impact rather than dependency. It is to regard the maintenance of natural capital as an end in itself. It is a perspective that would make no distinction between the loss of soil quality and the loss of biodiversity, because both are depletions of natural capital.[3] Critically, it is an approach that defines materiality with respect to impact on natural capital itself, and not selectively with respect to aspects of natural capital that serve shareholder returns. It is important to be clear on this point. To illustrate, the 'selection of material issues' in Chapter 13 calls for 'the organization to select a limited number of material issues that are most relevant and significant to the achievement of its purpose'. If the purpose is mutuality, then those factors must include adverse impacts that remain external to the economics of shareholder returns.

In a practical sense, specifying this concern for impact on natural capital is very far from straightforward. It requires that appropriate natural capital impacts are identified, measured, and reported. In this sense, the selection of material issues in Chapter 13 is simply a practical measure whereby only a limited number of material issues can realistically be identified and tracked. In practice, such efforts are increasingly attempted by some form of adoption of frameworks and other guidelines, such as the Natural Capital Protocol (NCC, 2016), the Global Reporting Initiative (Boiral, 2016; Boiral and Heras-Saizarbitoria, 2017; GRI, 2016), or the Greenhouse Gas Protocol (GHG, 2015).

It is difficult, however, to capture all effects on nature, not least because of the complexity and inter-dependence in ecosystems. The risk here is of being partial, and of excluding from financial calculation impacts that are either difficult to measure or that are 'convenient' to ignore because they do not materially affect business operations (RSPB, 2018: 12). Biodiversity is particularly problematic in this regard. The Convention on Biological Diversity defines biological diversity as 'variability among living organisms from all sources including, inter alia, terrestrial, marine and other aquatic ecosystems and the ecological complexes of which they are part; this includes diversity within species, between species,

and of ecosystems' (CBD, 2017). The measurement challenges here are complex and considerable (Addison et al., 2019; Adler et al., 2017; Boiral, 2016; Mace, 2019). In addition, it is of course problematic to define the boundaries of the accounting entity, which arise throughout the value chain for impact on natural capital, from original supply to final consumption, whereas for financial capital, the concern for capital maintenance concerns only economic resources controlled directly by the reporting entity (CDSB, 2018; eftec et al., 2015).

As argued in Chapters 10 and 14, mutual profit must be given appropriate salience for the concept of mutuality to be enacted. Salience is not, of course, a sufficient condition for the practice of mutuality. After all, a company could report negative impact on natural capital. Salience is, however, a necessary condition. In addition, and as will now be discussed, it is important that the financial measurement bears a meaningful relationship to the physical reality, with respect to which 'capital' has an important difference in meaning in its financial and its natural form.

Different Meanings of 'Capital'

Financial capital and natural capital are less alike than their common nomenclature might suggest.

Manufactured assets wear out and can be replaced. If the revenue from usage of an asset exceeds the depreciation charge, then value has been created, and replacement is itself likely to be value-creating. In contrast, a distinctive property of many natural assets is that they do not 'wear out' but instead are an inherently sustainable source of goods and services. If the natural capital stock declines, then this is not simply a depreciation charge, in the sense of being a measure of the consumption of an asset that is used up and then replaced. It is instead a warning signal. This is unlike manufactured assets, which are inherently transient, with a construction cost that for accounting purposes is allocated, or consumed, over the asset's useful life. Instead, natural capital assets are 'given by nature', rather than the product of costly investment, and they can be viewed as permanent, not transient, just so long as they remain healthy. 'Depreciation' in this context is an indicator of the risk of permanent damage, rather than a simple economic indicator of the cost of replacement. This is not least because there are commonly critical levels of biodiversity below which ecological function is disrupted, making replacement either economically infeasible or ecologically implausible. In the words a leading ecological conservation charity, 'if biodiversity declines beyond a certain point, the natural functioning of the system can change in the short or long term in unpredictable, non-linear, and non-marginal ways' (RSPB, 2018). In short, while the notion of financial capital maintenance is similar to that of the maintenance of natural capital, there is also a critical sense in which it is fundamentally different. While the depreciation of manufactured capital is unproblematic, the same is not true for natural capital that is allowed to depreciate below a critical, sustainable threshold.

The Obligation to Do the Right Thing

There is an important practical concern to guard against. Specifically, the concept of mutuality must not be appropriated so that, in substance, it means little more than (financially) sustainable shareholder returns (Milne and Gray, 2013; Deegan, 2013). The need here is to ensure that the business is itself pursuing a mutual purpose. No system of accounting can itself direct corporate behaviour. While an effective accounting system is indispensable for understanding and communicating corporate performance, and for enabling the corporation's directors to be held to account for that performance, if the corporation is pulling in one direction, then the accounting cannot in itself pull it back. In short, mutuality in corporate purpose is a necessary prerequisite for mutual natural capital accounting to be effective.

To illustrate this point, consider the EU Non-Financial Reporting Directive (EU, 2014), which calls for 'a non-financial statement containing information relating to at least environmental matters . . . (to) include a description of the policies, outcomes and risks related to those matters' and 'details of the current and foreseeable impacts of the undertaking's operations on the environment, and, as appropriate . . . the use of renewable and/or non-renewable energy, greenhouse gas emissions, water use and air pollution' and, in addition, 'adequate information' concerning 'principal risks of severe impacts, along with those that have already materialized . . . (which) may stem from the undertaking's own activities or may be linked to its operations.' This seems more than comprehensive. It seems to be a legal requirement to take responsibility for natural capital impact seriously.

In practice, however, a 'requirement' such as this is problematic because it is inherently vague, and therefore subsumable to competing priorities. To illustrate, companies required to apply the EU Non-Financial Reporting Directive (EU, 2014: Section 9) 'may rely on national frameworks . . . (or) the Global Reporting Initiative, or other recognized international frameworks'. In other words, there are no specific requirements. Indeed, even the selection of one framework over another allows significant room for management judgement. More problematically, there is actually nothing in the Directive that calls for the maintenance of natural capital, if such is not in the shareholder economic interest. The Directive can be interpreted simply as a rebottling of a conventional logic of shareholder value creation, in which a new form of environmentally aware legitimacy is called for in both product markets and capital markets, yet where responding to that call is grounded in economic self-interest rather than in environmental responsibility per se (Dowling and Pfeffer, 1975; Suchman, 1995; Deegan, 2014).

The message here is to be realistic about the alignment of corporate activity with mutuality. If there is not a 'win–win' in sustaining both financial capital and natural capital, then the corporation is not acting mutually. This is a question of corporate purpose (Mayer, 2018). Highlighting this point in a set of accounts will not in itself make the problem go away, and—in the absence of mutuality in corporate purpose—the risk is that sustainability reporting gives a false appearance, that the corporation is 'taking seriously' a commitment to natural capital when it is actually predisposed to its subordination. There is a clear need here for rigour and honesty in accounting, to ensure that mutual profit is reported in a way that is in itself true to the concept of mutuality, and that surfaces rather than hides difficult questions about the activities in which a business is engaged.

Conclusion

The argument in this chapter can be stated simply. The concept of mutuality requires that the maintenance of natural capital is an end in itself. This requires four things with respect to accounting. First is recognizing that natural capital maintenance cannot in principle be 'trumped' by shareholder primacy; mutuality implies that natural capital has primacy in its own right. Second is that natural capital maintenance must be defined, which requires a framing around impact rather than dependency, and a complete rather than partial view of impact. Third is recognizing that the maintenance of natural capital raises conceptual and practical challenges that are distinct from the maintenance of financial capital; this applies in particular to notions of depreciation and replacement. Fourth is acknowledging the institutional challenges of corporate purpose that set the scene for points one to three: stating the problem of how to do natural capital accounting is one thing, making it possible by means of mutual corporate purpose is another.

Notes

1. The other three leading global risks were cyberattacks, large-scale involuntary migration, and interstate conflict.

2. See, for example, the approach of the Task Force on Climate-Related Financial Disclosures (TCFD), which was set up by the G20 to make investor-oriented recommendations for voluntary climate-related financial disclosures, in mainstream reporting, that are positioned as consistent, comparable, reliable, clear, and efficient (2016).
3. See, for example, 'corporate natural capital accounting' (CNCA), which is designed to enable organizations to gather natural capital information in a coherent and (financially) comparable format, to help both companies and policymakers make better informed decisions about the management of natural capital (2018).

14

Implementing a Mutual Profit and Loss

Robert G. Eccles and François Laurent

Introduction

Putting Economics of Mutuality into practice involves adopting a new type of business model and requires a new type of management practice that puts much greater emphasis on certain non-financial performance indicators in the categories of human, social, and natural capital. It also requires these non-financial indicators to be linked strongly to financial performance indicators in the company's system for performance measurement, performance management, and, ultimately, compensation.

Traditionally, the backbone of the performance measurement and performance management in business is financial accounting, and the primary success indicator is financial profit as it appears in the profit and loss statement (P&L). To effectively support the transformation of the business from one main dimension (financial) to multiple dimensions (financial, human, social, and natural) we need to challenge our traditional ways of constructing and measuring profit and explore ways of transforming the *financial* P&L into a *mutual* P&L.

The mutual P&L will be a powerful force for change to help put the Economics of Mutuality (EoM) into practice, by:

- Signalling clearly to the organization that performance in terms of human, social, and natural capital impacts is at the same level of importance as financial performance

Robert G. Eccles and François Laurent, Implementing a Mutual Profit and Loss In *Putting Purpose Into Practice: The Economics of Mutuality.* Edited by: Colin Mayer and Bruno Roche, Oxford University Press (2021).

DOI: 10.1093/oso/9780198870708.003.0014

- Ensuring rigorous performance management in non-financial dimensions (e.g. robustness of metrics, frequency of review, and decisions to drive performance)
- Creating a stronger alignment in the organization between purpose and the management system (including, ideally, the incentive system).

Conceptual Framework

To create a mutual P&L framework, we need first to understand some fundamental conceptual differences that exist between financial accounting and the measurement of human, social, and natural capitals. For simplicity we can focus on the three most important issues:

- *Internality and externality*: Financial accounting is focused on elements (equity, assets, liabilities, income, and expenses) that belong to the reporting entity based on legal or contractual rights and obligations (in that sense, considered 'internal' to the company). However, a company often mobilizes (and affects) the human, social, and natural capitals of its ecosystem in a way that is not limited to legal or contractual rights and obligations (thus considered 'externalities'). For example, a business may cause damage to environmental assets that it does not own, without having any legal obligation to pay a compensation for it. This type of externality would be 'internalized' in the mutual P&L.
- *Exhaustivity*: Financial accounting must be exhaustive in all material aspects to be considered exact. Failing to recognize a significant income or expense is in no way acceptable in the construction of the financial P&L. In contrast, human, social, and natural capitals, by nature, may have multiple and subjective dimensions, with potentially complex interdependencies between them. Therefore, it does not appear realistic to define exhaustively the externalities of a given company. The mutual P&L will take into account the externalities selectively, and not exhaustively.
- *Monetary value*: All elements in financial accounting are captured in terms of monetary value. In many cases it is a challenge to

evaluate or describe human, social, and natural capital issues in terms of monetary value (e.g. the dollar value of well-being at work and employee training, the direct and indirect cost implications of plastic in the oceans, and the cost of child labour in the supply chain). It is important to keep in mind that not all elements of human, social, and natural capitals can be (nor should be) 'monetized' and the process of translating a non-financial externality into a dollar value is simply necessary to create a connection with the concept of profit in the mutual P&L. Arguably, the basis for valuation in this case will be the valuation 'at cost' because it does not require making any assumption on a 'market value' or intrinsic value of the non-financial capitals.

These considerations are important to develop a concept of mutual P&L that is both technically feasible and meaningful. Because of them, we cannot entertain the idea of an all-inclusive accounting framework that would capture all elements of human, social, and natural capital used in a given business and show the dollar value of their stock and flow. These limitations lead us to approach the concept of mutual P&L as follows: the mutual P&L is an extension of the financial P&L that takes *into account selected* human, social, and environmental issues that are *relevant* for the organization and its ecosystem, towards a stated *purpose*.

The idea of *extending* the financial P&L comes from the fact that the P&L is a cornerstone of a company's operating system and yet is *incomplete* from the standpoint of EoM. The financial P&L does not reflect any of the deep interactions that exist between the company and the human, social, and natural capitals present in its ecosystem—although these interactions are often essential to the achievement of the purpose, or simply to the sustainability of the company over time.

By analogy with financial capital, we can think of these interactions in terms of capital usage (i.e. consumption and depreciation) or capital creation (i.e. appreciation). For instance, a company that *employs* large amounts of a certain form of human capital *depends* on that human capital. If this company, as the result of its operations, has a positive impact ('pay back' or 'dividends') on the human capital present in its

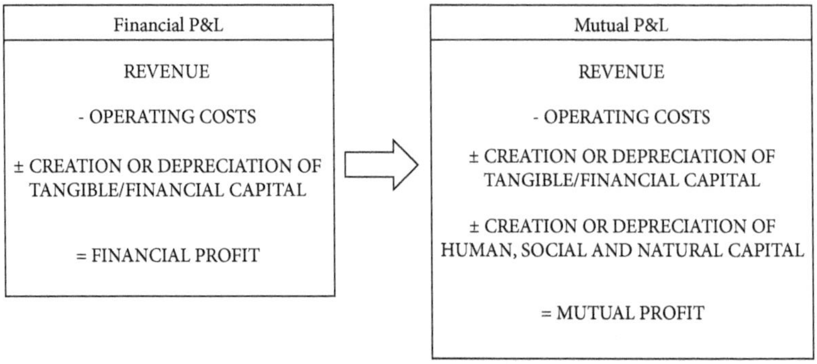

Figure 14.1. What is included in the mutual P&L

ecosystem, it improves its own prospects of prosperity. Conversely, if this business has a negative impact on the human capital as a result of its operations, it is limiting its own potential of further profitable growth. This is the type of impact (positive or negative) that we want to capture in the mutual P&L—to the extent that it is relevant and significant to the organization's purpose and strategy.

Schematically, to transform the P&L into a management tool that is effectively aligned to a company that has purpose and supports the implementation of EoM, it is necessary to include in its scope (in a meaningful and practical manner) the impact of the business on not only one form of capital (financial) but multiple forms of capital, as shown in Figure 14.1.

Constructing the Mutual P&L

The construction of the mutual P&L requires four distinct phases that are discussed below. The first phase is to select the right issues to be taken into account in the mutual P&L. The second phase is to ensure that each issue is clearly defined and has adequate performance measurement and management. The third phase is about translating the non-financial impacts into P&L entries with a dollar value. The final phase is about integration and presentation of the mutual P&L.

Phase 1: Selection of Material Issues

The fact that human, social, and natural capital issues by essence cannot be apprehended exhaustively will lead the organization to select a limited number of material issues that are most relevant and significant to the achievement of its purpose, with its ecosystem and the idea of mutuality in mind. This selection process is the result of the ecosystem-mapping and the pain-point analysis as discussed in Chapters 6 and 7.

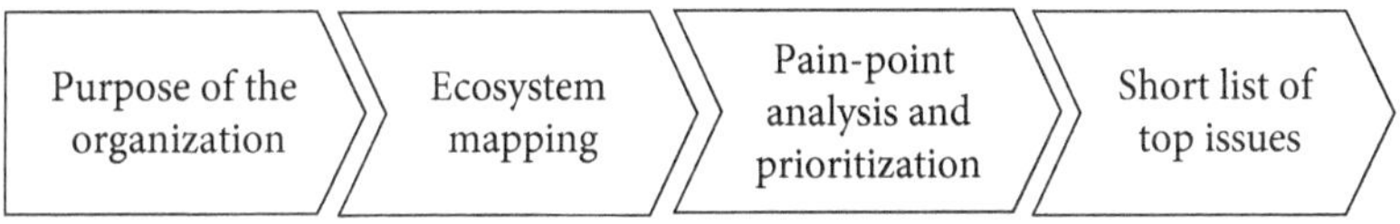

The number of material issues to be considered for the mutual P&L needs to be carefully calibrated to have the right balance between coverage and focus. Focusing the organization on a small number of issues can drive better performance, increase the clarity of the mutual P&L, and keep the process from becoming a burdensome bureaucratic exercise. Trying to cover too many issues could result in resource dispersion, unclear performance assessment, and excessive paperwork. The selection of top issues is a phase where the involvement and judgement of the organization's leadership is of paramount importance. The selected issues need to be truly and deeply connected to the purpose and strategy of the business and, as such, stay relevant in the medium or long term. On this condition, the mutual P&L will be stable in its construction and comparable across the years.

Which human, social, and natural capital issues are material is a function of a company's industry and strategy. For example, carbon emissions are material for an electric utility company but not for a pharmaceutical company where access to medicine is. Stakeholder engagement is a key element in determining a company's material issues. General guidance, with an emphasis on externalities, is available from Global Reporting Initiative (GRI), and industry-specific guidance with an emphasis on what is of interest to investors is available from the Sustainability Accounting Standards Board (SASB).

Phase 2: Business Initiatives, Performance Measurement and Management

The human, social, and environmental issues that are selected in Phase 1 are critical to the organization's purpose, strategy, and business model. As such, they need to be monitored and managed with the same attention and rigour as the (more traditional) commercial or financial operations in the business. The organization will drive initiatives to address those issues and create the conditions to manage and measure performance for each of them:

- Clear definition of the issue, the objective of the intervention, and the link to purpose
- Defined resource allocation to meet the objective (budget)
- Performance criteria (non-financial metrics as discussed in Chapters 9 to 12) and targets
- Empowerment and responsibilities in the organization.

A precise articulation of these elements for each selected EoM issue is a condition to develop a mutual P&L that is credible and based on robust data, especially for resource allocation, metrics, and their targets. At this point, it is necessary to make a distinction between two types of priority issues that may arise from the pain-point analysis:

- *Capital creation initiatives*: When the company identifies a critical pain point in the ecosystem that is not resulting from its own operations, but can be positively addressed by it with mutuality in mind (i.e. with a shared benefit for the company and its ecosystem). For this type of situation, it is necessary to have a clear measurement of the resources allocated (budget) and whether the initiative is effective in addressing the external pain points (metrics showing actual impact vs. targets).
- *Capital depletion issues*: When in the ordinary course of business the organization has a negative impact on the human, social, or natural capitals causing a threat to the ecosystem and ultimately the achievement of its purpose. The issue is not visible in the financial

P&L because the company is not paying for it. Typically, this would be the type of issue facing a company that depends on the massive consumption of a scarce natural resource or causing a form of pollution that has substantial negative externalities. For this type of situation, it is necessary to measure the (negative) impact and to create an incentive to find a remedy (at least to stop the negative impact or to repair the consequences).

Phase 3: Valuation of Impacts

As we mentioned earlier, items need to be expressed in terms of monetary value to be included in a P&L. At first glance, this poses a problem as human, social, and environmental issues are difficult to value in monetary terms. However, in accounting there are various valuation methods and the one that can apply to the issues defined in Phase 2 is the valuation *at cost*. With this method, it is not necessary to make an assumption on the intrinsic value of the human, social, or natural capital at stake (depleted or created). We can translate these issues into accounting language by focusing on the *cost* implication for the company.

1. For capital creation initiatives: treat the spend as investment, not expense

When a business initiative results in the creation (or positive reinforcement) of human, social, and natural capitals that are external to the company but crucial to its strategy and its ecosystem, the resources allocated to that initiative are considered as an investment and not as an operating expense in the mutual P&L. The P&L adjustment in this case is an increase of the profit shown in the P&L.

Conceptually, this consists of recognizing that the human, social, or natural capital creation is similar to the creation of an asset that—although it is not owned by the company in this case—will contribute to the company's profitable growth in the future. By way of analogy, the logic is similar to the treatment of internal software development costs, that can be capitalized both in US GAAP and IFRS if certain criteria are met.

One important idea is that the spend should be considered an investment only on the condition that the initiative has an actual impact on the external capitals, that can be measured and considered successful. Due to the particular essence of human, social, and natural capitals, the measurement of impact relies on the specific set of metrics developed for EoM (Chapters 9 to 12) and the criteria for success is the achievement of pre-defined targets for these metrics. Without these criteria (defined in Phase 2), the mutual P&L would lack the necessary robustness and credibility.

Treating the expenditure as an investment and not an operating cost can be a powerful enabler to build an EoM business model because it removes the conflict that often exists between, on one hand, the need to allocate resource in line with the company's long-term purpose or strategy (which is typically defined over a medium to long-term horizon), and, on the other hand, the need to deliver the short-term profit target (as measured in the P&L). Changing the accounting treatment does not change the fact that the money is spent as a matter of fact (in cash). However, the access to budget will be generally easier if the spending does not have a full immediate negative impact on the profit measurement, and the decision can be made with the long term in mind (as it is the case typically for fixed assets investment budgets).

Table 14.1 gives an illustration of an initiative with different levels of success (actual impact vs. targets) across the years, as measured by EoM metrics. The spend is considered an investment only to the extent that it drives effective results, in line with a pre-defined target. When the spend does not entail successful results, it is considered an operating cost (following the same logic as the write-off of an asset that has no value).

Table 14.1. Capital creation initiative

Capital creation initiative	Year 1	Year 2	Year 3	Year 4	Year 5
Budget allocated	$50	$50	$50	$100	$100
EoM metric target (index variation)	+5	+5	+10	+10	+10
EoM metric actual measurement (index variation)	0	+5	+5	+10	+15
Success rate	0%	100%	50%	100%	100%
Mutual P&L adjustment (profit up)	$0	$50	$25	$100	$100

2. For capital depletion issues: internalize hypothetical replenishment costs

The company measures the capital depletion using the appropriate non-financial metrics (Chapters 9 to 12), then identifies a *hypothetical replenishment cost* corresponding to the investment (in dollar terms) that *would be* necessary for the company to replace the depleted capital. This requires it to analyse the options available to replenish the capital in the specific context of the business (location, access to resources and technology, etc.), understand the cost of these options, and retain the one that would be preferred by the company (in terms of practicality and affordability).

The impact of internalizing the hypothetical cost in the P&L is a decrease of profit shown in that P&L. The cost of replenishing the external capitals is hypothetical as long as the company does not actually spend it (in which case the cost will be already included in the financial P&L). There are many reasons why companies don't spend this money in the first place including lack of legal obligation, lack of awareness, lack of social and environmental responsibility, lack of long-term thinking, and lack of resources. By internalizing into the P&L the hypothetical replenishment costs related to material capital depletion issues, the leaders of an organization can change its context in a profound way as they:

- Create awareness, make the issues highly visible internally so they can be managed
- Create an incentive for the organization to mitigate or solve the issues (drive change)
- Better understand what part of the financial profit is sustainable over the long term and what part of the profit is being generated in the short term at the expense of the future.

Table 14.2 gives an illustration in the case of a company that measures a capital depletion issue consistently over time and creates a situation where the P&L will evolve positively when the issue is addressed or mitigated (years 4 and 5).

Table 14.2. Capital depletion issue

Capital depletion issue	Year 1	Year 2	Year 3	Year 4	Year 5
EoM metric—measured impact (units)	20	25	30	15	10
Hypothetical replenishment cost per unit	$5	$5	$5	$5	$5
Mutual P&L adjustment (profit down)	-$100	-$125	-$150	-$75	-$50

Phase 4: Integration and Presentation of the Mutual P&L

The P&L adjustments determined in Phase 3 can complement and modify the financial P&L to form the mutual P&L as shown in Table 14.3 below.

By taking into account selected non-financial material issues as explained above, the mutual P&L becomes a management tool that is not dramatically different from the traditional financial accounting, but sufficiently different to tell a different story about a company's profit performance and drive different decisions and actions.

The mutual P&L does not replace, nor challenge, traditional financial reporting because it serves a different objective. External financial reporting '*provides financial information about the reporting entity that is useful to existing and potential investors, lenders, and other creditors in making decisions about providing resources to the entity*' (definition from the IFRS Conceptual Framework). The mutual P&L is a new form of internal management accounts that provides information that is distinct and additional to the external financial reporting for the organization itself to drive performance toward its purpose and with

Table 14.3. Mutual P&L statement

	Year 1	Year 2	Year 3	Year 4	Year 5
Financial profit	$400	$410	$420	$430	$440
EoM—material issues					
#1. Initiative A (capital creation)	$0	$50	$25	$100	$100
#2. Issue B (capital depletion)	-$100	-$125	-$150	-$75	-$50
Total mutual P&L adjustments	-$100	-$75	-$125	$25	$50
Mutual profit	$300	$335	$295	$455	$490

EoM in mind. The above table shows that the two sets of accounts, although different, can always be reconciled easily.

Conclusion

To be meaningful and effective, the mutual P&L relies on the right selection of material issues and initiatives, the right metrics, and a certain degree of stability over time. The mutual P&L will be a powerful tool to drive change if the mutual profit becomes the basis of financial incentives for the organization's leadership and staff, in place of the traditional financial profit.

While we believe this to be a promising idea, we are also well aware of the challenges in implementing and achieving the benefits of a mutual P&L. The measurement issues are obvious and have been discussed. These technical issues, while difficult, are the easiest to resolve. Much harder are the organizational ones, such as the issue of how the different 'realities' of the financial and mutual P&L will co-exist. Will one become dominant or will each be used for its intended different purpose? For the mutual P&L to be successful in contributing to the company's purpose, senior management needs to clearly explain its purpose. Senior management needs to hear and respond to concerns raised by those implementing it. Everyone needs to recognize that the mutual P&L is a new idea whose proof in practice remains to be seen. Its success will depend on an appreciation of this fact and the goodwill of everyone involved.

Finally, this chapter focuses on the mutual P&L and does not discuss the notion of a mutual balance sheet. This is the result of a conscious choice. Indeed, the P&L describes flows, operations, and their impact in terms of net value creation over a period of time, and is the primary measurement of business performance in a majority of companies. Proposing a different mode of P&L construction supporting the EoM principles will achieve the maximum impact in terms of changing decisions and actions with the minimum complexity. A condition, though, is to always consider the P&L with the long-term in mind (i.e. the history of P&L over multiple years as shown in the illustrative tables above). Conversely, the construction of a mutual balance sheet raises a number of problematic technical questions (e.g. the notion of hypothetical assets and liabilities, risk of confusion between hypothetical and real liabilities, amortization of capitalized costs, opening balance sheet, etc.) with little or no additional benefits, in the sense that in most industries' management decisions are much more driven by the financial P&L than the financial balance sheet.

For this reason, we believe that, for now, the concept of mutual P&L (with no need of a mutual balance sheet) will be the most powerful and accessible tool to help guide a company to achieve its purpose in a profitable way over the long term through the resource allocation decisions made by management. Accomplishing this will require the implementation of the mutual P&L throughout the entire organization and at every level where P&Ls are currently being produced.

15
The Impact of Mutual Profit on Business Behaviour

Robert Eccles and Judith C. Stroehle

Introduction

To appreciate the ambition of a project such as the mutual profit and loss statement (mutual P&L) at Mars, one needs to reflect on the role of accounting systems in society. Financial accounting systems are highly formalized. They follow strict guidelines, such as the International Financial Reporting Standards (IFRS) of the International Accounting Standards Board (IASB) or the Generally Accepted Accounting Principles (GAAP) of the US Financial Accounting Standards Board (FASB), and make use of universally implemented concepts such as double-entry bookkeeping. In fact, there is nothing as well defined and consistent across companies as financial accounting, where the book of operations serves as the ultimate determination of performance for all organizations.

But accounting is much more than just the numbers that companies record at the end of the day. A company's accounting system forms the bedrock of corporate strategy and action. More fundamentally, it defines the 'reality' that exists within a company. In an early reflection on the roles of accounting in organizations and society, a group of important accounting researchers echoed this:

> What is accounted for can shape organizational participants' views of what is important, with the categories of dominant economic discourse

Robert Eccles and Judith C. Stroehle, The Impact of Mutual Profit on Business Behaviour In *Putting Purpose Into Practice: The Economics of Mutuality.* Edited by: Colin Mayer and Bruno Roche, Oxford University Press (2021).

DOI: 10.1093/oso/9780198870708.003.0015

> and organizational functioning that are implicit within the accounting framework helping to create a particular conception of organizational reality. (Burchell, et al. 1980: 5)

It is important to recognize that these realities are neither given by nature, nor are they completely neutral. They are socially constructed and self-perpetuated by the people who use them and the institutions that legitimize them. Once adopted through national legislation, they become the reality of entire economies rather than just organizations, affecting issues well beyond the corporate borders, such as wealth distribution, social justice, and environmental degradation (Baker and Bettner, 1997). Adjusting the principles of accounting can therefore not only alter the reality of organizations, but, by its extension, also that of the society in which they are embedded.

The Growing Importance of Purpose

Over the last few decades, we have seen the transformation of the corporation from an organization predominantly focused on tangible assets (such as land and labour) to one that is increasingly concerned with intangible assets, such as intellectual capital and reputation, and the conservation of resources whose supply is finite (e.g. natural resources) (Barker and Mayer, 2017). This shift has been accompanied by a call for a new understanding of value and profit, away from a sole focus on the financial to one that is inclusive of environmental and social dimensions (important books in this area include Mazzucato, 2018; Mayer, 2018; Roche and Jakub, 2017; Eccles and Krzus, 2010, 2014). In addressing these issues, financial accounting is intrinsically limited and therefore incomplete in capturing what really matters for corporations, and essentially for society. The idea of extending the traditional P&L to a more inclusive, mutual P&L is directly linked to this.

By designing a management account inclusive of social, human, and environmental capital, the so-called mutual P&L (see Chapter 13 for detailed description), Mars Catalyst and the business units they work with enter a process of social construction themselves as they decide which issues are material, and therefore to be tracked in the mutual P&L. To arrive at this selection of issues, an extensive ecosystem map (see Chapters 6 and 7 for description) is drawn, which identifies the company's main stakeholders and the challenges they face. From this list, first the key stakeholders and then material issues are chosen and prioritized by the company in view of which role they play in helping the business to achieve its self-declared purpose. The purpose is a statement defined at the corporate level which functions as a guide for action and decision-making for everyone working in the business. In the Mars petcare sector, for example, this purpose reads 'creating a better world for pets'. Only issues material to this purpose are included in the mutual P&L. With this definition of materiality, the mutual P&L differs, for example, from the Sustainability Accounting Standards Board's (SASB) definition of materiality, which is commonly used for impact-investing strategies and identifies material issues at the industry level according to their relevance for firm financial performance.

The Research Study

To study not only the construction but also the impact of this mutual P&L, we are accompanying one of the first pilots to implement it as a management accounting tool in a chosen business unit of Mars. As a pilot site, corporate leadership decided on the pet nutrition business in one of the Eastern European markets. The market that was chosen is one of the smallest in terms of revenues within the European market. However, it displays a comparatively high growth, which has repeatedly outperformed the growth of the same segment in other European markets in the last few years. Due to both, the market was deemed a 'safe environment' to test the mutual P&L. In the format of a longitudinal, ethnographic research, data will include interviews with the seven members of the local management team, regular attendance of meetings and document reviews before, throughout, and after the construction and implementation of this tool. The management team consists of the board (including the GM, CFO, the head of PNO, and plant managers), as well as the directors of sales, consumer market intelligence, corporate affairs, and operations. Through this, we seek to understand how this 'alteration of reality' at the business unit affects internal processes and operations, as well as the reasoning and decision-making of managers.

So far, we have attended introductory meetings with the pilot site's director and CFO, and have completed a first visit to the business unit to conduct 'benchmark' observations and interviews with the rest of the management team that will be working with the mutual P&L. Our observations and interviews up to now show that expectations are high. The management team seems not only open and excited about the project, they also express a sense of pride in having been chosen by corporate leadership to serve as a pilot for this tool. Most interviewed members of the management team say that their interest in the project is driven by the expectation that they will be able to gather new insights about their ecosystem and their market. The possibility of using these insights to improve the so-called 'calorie conversion' in the market—one of the industry's key performance indicators that describes how many pets are fed with pet food as opposed to human food scraps—was mentioned particularly often. However, beyond the excitement about the potential insights provided by an ecosystem map, it is so far unclear to us whether and how much the management team is aware of the changes a mutual P&L as management account can have for their business. Are they aware that their reality is going to change? At this early stage, we estimate that the project is still perceived as a philosophical exercise for management that will potentially lead to exploration of new market potentials, rather than as a fundamental accounting issue that has the power to transform the organization's reality.

Changing the Definition of Profit

This observation speaks directly to our research interest: how will the mutual P&L be embedded within the company? And is there danger of a gap between the perceived and the intended purpose of the mutual P&L? The intended purpose of a mutual P&L is to have business operate under the account of 'the right' level of profit, as defined by Bruno Roche and Jay Jakub (2017) from Mars Catalyst, where the 'right' level of profit is that which also accounts for social, human, and environmental capital, in addition to the traditional measure of financial capital. In other words: 'The main point of expanding the basket of metrics available to business managers to include non-financial forms of capital is to give them tools to manage hitherto unrecognized (squandered) assets available to them' (Roche and Jakub, 2017: 132). To achieve this vision, the mutual P&L has to be implemented fully, as a prioritized management accounting tool, and with all the related managerial and operational consequences that management accounting traditionally implies. This includes the consideration of this tool for a wide variety of decisions, such as those of capital allocation, budgeting, incentives (pay), career development, market strategy, product portfolios, and more.

Since the intended purpose of a mutual P&L is that of an internal management accounting system, it does not replace the external side of financial accounting, such as the IFRS in public companies. If we think forward to a world in which the idea of mutual P&L could be scaled to public companies, this may lead to tension between internal and external definitions of performance. However, the information included in the mutual P&L would certainly also be of interest to investors, and therefore potentially turn external. In fact, reporting on non-financial information has already become increasingly important over the last three decades, especially with disclosure on the so-called environmental, social, and governance (ESG) issues. The attempt to seriously account for material non-financial issues in relation to a company's level of profit has only recently seen a spark of interest in public companies. However, these attempts are diverse, somewhat experimental and, as far as we can tell, are usually used for reporting and disclosure rather than for management accounting. Examples of such tools include the environmental P&L at Kering,[1] the so-called four-dimensional P&L (including financial and natural capital) at AkzoNobel,[2] the calculation of 'true earnings' (earning adjusted by socio-economic and environmental values) at Samsung,[3] and the 'value-to-society' measurements of BASF[4] (who are, incidentally, currently developing an 'integrated profit and loss statement'). These examples show that the idea of accounting for non-financial information is gaining momentum, especially in the context of increased interest in the topic from investors in the capital market. The implementation of the mutual P&L as a management accounting system in a private company (and thus without the external pressures of investors), however, is, as far as we know, unique to Mars. That is why the question of how the mutual P&L is embedded within this company, and with which consequences, is so important.

The Consequences of a Mutual P&L

When we think about the potential impacts of the mutual P&L in a private company like Mars (or any company for that matter), we can think about two key areas in which consequences are likely: first, the external environment of accounting systems, by which we mean the operations and formal processes in place; and second, the internal dynamics of an organization, addressing questions of leadership capability, reasoning, and decision-making. Furthermore, it is important to consider the conditions under which these impacts are likely or unlikely to occur.

In the external environment to accounting systems, such as operations, the mutual P&L has the potential for widespread impact, which is, however, subject to the degree of its implementation as a full management accounting tool. Used to optimize processes according to shifting priorities, a mutual P&L would affect a wide range of processes from capital allocation, budgeting, and purchasing to human resources and marketing. For example, the formal requirements for choosing suppliers could change from dimensions primarily focused on cost and quality, to including a range of other (i.e. social, environmental, and human) criteria. Similarly, guidelines about practicalities such as the logistics of sourcing, packaging, and storage could be affected. For example, the use of large cooling systems in mid-term storage units could be deemed unsustainable, leading to an increased use of just-in-time sourcing for short-life food and chemical products. These are just hypothetical scenarios, but they exemplify how scaling up a tool like the mutual P&L has the potential to lead to significant changes in business operations. Because of this, the full implementation of this tool is likely to bear several initial costs for a company until all processes are adjusted as necessary. For example, contracts with suppliers usually run for a certain number of years and the cost of finding new ones can be high. Although the mutual P&L allows for declaring these initial costs as investments, questions of how far and how fast an organization implements this new management accounting tool remain important, as rash execution may lead to disruption instead of transformation. A successful, full implementation of the mutual P&L would therefore, by our estimation, be a mid- to long-term, rather than a short-term objective.

Regarding internal dynamics, the mutual P&L will create a new framework for leadership to assess the organization. Managerial accounting has, by definition, the goal to provide performance information to managers on which they subsequently base their decisions. The mutual P&L as a management accounting tool therefore affects the prioritization of issues and frames a new organizational reality for them. This is not to be underestimated, as often managers have been educated and socialized in a way—learning the traditional definition of financial performance—that is quite different from what the mutual P&L measures for them. It cannot be assumed that all managers will have the immediate cognitive abilities that are needed to successfully translate findings of the mutual P&L into corporate decision-making. Whether or not leaders of a company accept this new reality can, however, play an important role in the implementation of the mutual P&L. If accepted, the potential for transformation and disruption—as elaborated above—is high. If not accepted, the consequence could be the creation of 'alternate realities' in which managers choose to use the mutual P&L only for some processes, such as human resource allocation, while continuing to use the financial P&L for other, more complex or costly processes, such as capital allocation and sourcing practices, to avoid the costs and other potentially unintended consequences associated with a full implementation. To avoid the creation of these alternate realities, incentivizing the use of the mutual P&L through compensation and career development perspectives can therefore be an important piece of the puzzle.

Since traditional notions of profit are deeply embedded in corporate decision-making, the new modes of profit also need to follow this model. However, just as the measurement of financial profit can have unintended consequences (for example, frequent measurement of performance can induce short-termism), this may also occur for the mutual P&L. Careful considerations of timelines and frequency in performance measurement can help to anticipate and manage such challenges. Decisions on how the new tool will relate to traditional management accounting practices, and where the mutual instead of the financial calculation of profit applies, could offer a sensible start for evaluation. Consequently, by deciding how to measure, for example, the internal rates of returns (IRR), what a cost volume profit analysis would look like and what the relation to already exiting balance scorecards would be, a company could take first steps in understanding what the new reality, created by the Mutual P&L, would look like.

Conditions of Effective Mutual Accounting

The above discussion suggests that the possible impact of the mutual P&L on an organization is conditioned both by the external environment of accounting (how easily are operations transformed?) and by the internal dynamics of an organization (how willing and capable are leaders to transform?). Empirical evidence in the literature on management accounting supports these expected limitations. For example, Naranjo-Gil et al. (2009) show how both management accounting changes and the implementation of innovations are highly dependent on the willingness and capability of leaders within an organization. The structure of an organization will hereby play an important role as well. In the case of the mutual P&L at Mars this topic also arises, as many strategic corporate issues are decided on a centralized, European level. The implementation of a mutual P&L, however, happens at the level of the business unit. This raises the question whether working with measures of mutual profit at the level of the business unit is inhibited insofar as decisions made at the European headquarters, who, at least for the moment, still work with a financial P&L, cannot be altered. In other words, if management considerations based on a mutual P&L challenge those considering a purely financial P&L, then the former can probably only trump the latter if the governance structure of the firm allows it. It is of course possible that a successful, gradual implementation of the mutual P&L at the pilot site leads to a firm-wide spill-over, eventually removing this conflict. However, if the mutual P&L is to be a tool with ambitions of scale beyond Mars, it is important not to underestimate the importance of corporate governance structures and the potential conflicts of interests that can arise if a mutual profit is implemented bottom-up, at the business-unit level, rather than top-down, at the firm level.

Studies which examine the implementation of innovation in management accounting further discuss timelines as an important factor in the implementation of management accounting tools. Kasurinen (2002) points out that management accounting tools can have relatively short life cycles, making them susceptible to incomplete implementation. This would suggest that only if tools are fully implemented will their lifetime be extended. However, the most important accounting innovations have taken a long time to be adopted and institutionalized, with up to ten years for techniques such as activity-based costing and balanced scorecards (Bhimani and Bromwhich 2010). For the mutual P&L, this indicates that a full and, as we suggest, gradual implementation of this tool may need a much longer time than managers may expect. Key changes in business and market environments, economic or natural crises, and technological advancements are all factors which may in the meantime have an influence on the implementation of this new tool. Willingness for change is often, for example, significantly influenced by moments of crises. Complementing a medium- with a long-term implementation plan for the mutual P&L may be a helpful tool for managers piloting mutual profit to not lose sight of their progress in the long run.

Conclusion

In conclusion, we repeat our point from above: there is nothing as well defined and consistent across companies as financial accounting. The most significant questions surrounding the impact of the mutual P&L will therefore be what a change in this consistent reality will imply for Mars. We find that the list of issues that the mutual P&L will encounter is large and the road will be a long one to travel. Nevertheless, we think it is a worthy and important challenge for Mars to face. We discussed how the consequences of the mutual P&L as a management accounting tool will likely affect both the external environment of accounting and the internal dynamics of organizations, specifically leadership. We therefore do not see the full implementation of the mutual P&L as a short-term objective. The transition from one management account to another must rather begin with the practical transformation of familiar accounting concepts and a gradual integration of the extended definitions of profit into mid- and long-term decision-making, in order to avoid disruption. Whether and how the definition of reality will effectively be changed is conditioned by the willingness and capability of leadership to understand and accept both the potential disruption and the opportunities which the mutual P&L can bring to Mars.

C-Suite Personal Leadership Coach for Major Corporations

Robert Krenza, Founder & CEO, BlackWolf Consultants

Across the world many of the planet's finest minds are beginning to align on the challenges facing today's leaders.

As I said recently, while chairing the Master Class on Leadership at the 2017 Responsible Business Forum at Saïd Business School in Oxford, UK, 'Business has never experienced a more demanding and disruptive, volatile, uncertain, complex, and ambiguous environment.'

Executing a vision of mutuality requires unprecedented leadership to navigate today's rapidly changing business environment; that is, leadership that is focused on shifting the mindset of entire organizations, and measuring success from an ethos of sustainability, thereby having a positive impact on future generations.

In my opinion, the responsibility of today's business leaders is to initiate a global mindset shift, and a radical change in the measurement of success. This is even more pressing due to the urgency of the task, and the way contemporary organizations are currently being designed and developed.

What I am writing will, by intention, create a tension in the thoughts and minds of the reader. This tension is fundamentally created by the awareness of the necessity of shifting from a mindset of 'causality', to 'self-authoring', and the resistance to take the 'actions' that need to be taken.

Leadership and the Urgency of a Global Mindset Shift

Beliefs and mindset are synonymous. Beliefs drive behaviour. They always have and always will. To shift our behaviour we must shift our beliefs. It is impossible to change our behaviours and our behaviour-based systems until we recognize that the source of our behaviours is our beliefs. This is fundamentally the meaning of transformation, which is: 'Seeing and believing in a possibility that we have not considered before.'

Today's leaders must shift from a 'causality mindset', where we react from a belief that others cause us to think, feel and behave the way we do, to a 'self-authoring mindset', where we respond from a belief of, 'I am able to choose how I think, feel, and behave, and I can create whatever I believe or imagine.'

The question asked by those stuck in a consciousness of causality or reactivity is: 'Is it too little too late?' The consciousness of choosing to be the author and creator of your reality asks, as George Bernard Shaw said: 'There are those that look at things the way they are, and ask why? I dream of things that never were, and ask why not?'

At present, we are in the middle of a perfect storm, and I use that phrase both figuratively and literally. Leaders are choosing to be in a causality or fear-based mindset by allowing themselves to be bullied into reactive behaviours.

Economics of Mutuality: The Urgency to Shift the Measurements of Success

Today's leaders must courageously ask themselves, 'How do I choose to live as a human being on this planet?' 'What impact do I want to have?' 'What legacy do I want to leave behind for future generations?'

For the sake of the planet and humanity, a radical change in the way we measure success must take place. In the business world, this means creating organizations that measure success against other forms of capital in addition to financial, which includes human, social, and environmental capital. Metrics that measure not only financial growth, but also the positive or negative impact we are having on the environment and humans need to be created and implemented.

If we see growth as the only financial goal, we must examine what the beliefs are that we are articulating as growth? If we believe that 'the sole responsibility of corporations is to maximize shareholder return', then we will act according to that belief. If we believe that measuring profit and growth against environmental, human, social, and financial metrics is imperative, then we will act according to that belief.

The factors that will create radical change involve consulting with organizations, with leadership teams, and with individual leaders.

Yet many corporations are still looking at the world through a lens that has been applied from post-World War II to the present. These leaders are using an old model, a model that was never comprehensive or inclusive; a model that is focused solely on growth. Ask yourself, 'What is the belief that drives growth for growth's sake?'

When it comes right down to it, if we ask business leaders what they really value in a business, it is to make a contribution and to leave a better world behind for their children and grandchildren.

As Albert Einstein so accurately declared, 'No problem can be solved from the same level of consciousness that created it.'

Notes

1. http://www.kering.com/en/sustainability/whatisepl, last accessed September 2018.
2. http://report.akzonobel.com/2014/ar/case-studies/sustainable-business/measuring-our-impact-in-4d.html, last accessed September 2018.
3. https://www.samsung.com/uk/aboutsamsung/sustainability/strategy/, last accessed September 2018.
4. https://www.basf.com/en/company/sustainability/management-and-instruments/quantifying-sustainability/we-create-value/impact-categories.html and https://www.basf.com/en/company/sustainability/management-and-instruments/quantifying-sustainability/we-create-value.html, last accessed September 2018.

16
Mutuality and the Potential of Microequity

Muhammad Meki, Kate Roll, and Simon Quinn

Introduction

Work on building more mutual business practices is under way in busy streets and rural markets across Kenya. Through Mars-Wrigley Confectionery's Maua Business, initiated in 2013 by Mars Catalyst, over six hundred micro-distributors take part in a route-to-market programme selling Wrigley chewing gum products alongside other goods. These sellers purchase bags or boxes of gum at a small discount from local wholesalers and then sell either directly to consumers or to small shops, where the packets are sold to consumers. Pursuing joint goals, the programme enables the company to access areas of the country that it had been unable to reach with conventional distribution practices, as well as providing a new source of sales and training for low-income sellers. In explicitly bringing together social and business goals, the programme is a site of social innovation at Mars, and encourages those who manage the programme to think in new ways about the relationship between sales and the social and human capital of sellers. For Mars, the Maua programme is an opportunity to try out new ideas around mutuality and expand the boundaries of their business.

The Maua Business is also the site of academic research into mutual business practices. This research, which is being led by a team of economists and social scientists at the University of Oxford, empirically

Muhammad Meki, Kate Roll, and Simon Quinn, Mutuality and the Potential of Microequity In *Putting Purpose Into Practice: The Economics of Mutuality.* Edited by: Colin Mayer and Bruno Roche, Oxford University Press (2021).
 DOI: 10.1093/oso/9780198870708.003.0016

tests the performance of a novel mutuality-driven instrument against conventional practices. This is important for providing an empirical basis to work on mutuality in business as well as potentially bringing greater nuance to our understanding of how individuals with different measured levels of social and human capital respond to such interventions. To do so, we are focusing on providing microequity to sellers interested in purchasing a productive asset—in this case a bicycle suited for carrying cargo. We view microequity as embodying core ideas of mutuality, specifically the focus on joint flourishing and the interdependence of a firm's stakeholders. Microequity, as compared to dominant forms of microcredit, better shares the risks and rewards of the investment. So, does this lead to better outcomes? Along what measures? And for whom? These are the questions that we are investigating in this ongoing research.

The concept for the microequity study arose through qualitative interviews with Maua sellers in 2014 and 2015, as well as surveys on human and social capital conducted by Mars Catalyst. This work revealed that micro-distributors considered transportation to be a key constraint to productivity; surveys showed lower satisfaction with 'materials and equipment', which at the time primarily consisted of backpacks for carrying the goods and promotional materials. Indeed, micro-distributors who were walking complained of long days and back pains, for example, and aspired to carry their goods either on bicycles or motorbikes. Sellers who were able to buy such vehicles reported significant increases in income. Vehicles have the potential to reduce the sellers' fatigue and dramatically increase their range—essential for increasing the number of small shops or *dukkas* that they serve—and allow them to offer a wider range of products.

The expressed need for better access to transport created the opportunity for our team to work closely with Mars Catalyst, the Mars-Wrigley business, and microfinance partners to develop and test a new, more mutual way of financing these assets. As noted above, mutuality demands attention to the extent to which benefits and costs are shared equitably. In order to translate mutuality into a business practice, we focused on the distribution of risk and reward within microfinance contracts. For the study, we have designed multiple types of contracts—both conventional and microequity driven—which we are able to offer to interested participants, for whom we will then track a range of different outcomes in order to rigorously measure impact. A pilot in 2017 with thirty-two participants showed that the mutuality-inspired microequity product is viable; we are currently testing the effects of this product in a larger study that is under way and includes just under a hundred participants at the time of writing.

This study is novel in its use of field experiments to identify the causal effect of more mutual practice on performance. However, rather than presenting the technical aspects of the study, this chapter instead discusses our work conceptualizing and testing the new, more mutual, approach to microfinance. We examine two core questions that emerge from the case: What are the prospects for scaling the microequity model? What have we learned about conducting field experiments in the context of a corporate programme? The chapter concludes by discussing how the effort to capture and test the idea of mutuality enabled us to engage more deeply with the concept itself.

The Evolution of Microcredit

Microcredit, which is often defined as the provision of small-scale loans to low-income individuals in developing countries, had been heralded as a key poverty-alleviation tool with the potential to stimulate the growth of credit-constrained microentrepreneurs. For the purposes of this discussion, we define microentrepreneurs as individuals who engage in non-agricultural commercial activity, with the majority working alone or hiring at most one other employee. These individuals pose particular challenges to lenders, as they often lack collateral and credit histories, and the loan amounts that they require are often too small to justify the effort and administrative costs for a large bank. The question of how to overcome this challenge has been the subject of intense study and experimentation over the last two decades.

In 2006, Muhammad Yunus was awarded the Nobel Peace Prize for his contributions to microcredit through Grameen Bank. The success of the original Grameen model—with its very high repayment rates—can be attributed to a number of features that instilled discipine and leveraged local knowledge and peer pressure, including joint-liability group lending, high-frequency repayments with group meetings in public, and dynamic incentives through graduated loans. The bank also focused on women. The Nobel Prize Committee stated that 'Yunus and Grameen Bank have shown that even the poorest of the poor can work to bring about their own development... in the continuing efforts to [eliminate poverty], micro-credit must play a major part.'

Initial reporting based on success stories and studies based on observational data suggested that microcredit created large positive social and financial effects for borrowers.[1] However, more rigorous recent research has revealed a different story. A number of large-scale RCTs have shown that microcredit has not, in general, had a transformative effect on poverty. Across a number of settings, these studies reveal low demand for microcredit and no substantial increases in household income, educational outcomes, or female empowerment (Banerjee, Karlan, and Zinman, 2015). While most of the studies do show expanded business activity, these investments rarely resulted in increased profits. This may reflect the fact that many of the small business owners are likely to be in subsistence-level entrepreneurship and are not 'growth-oriented', or reluctant entrepreneurs who would prefer to have a wage job (Banerjee and Duflo, 2011; De Mel, McKenzie, and Woodruff, 2010; Schoar, 2010).[2]

While these results have disappointed many practitioners and led to a lively debate over the benefits of microcredit, recent academic work on microenterprises has shown more promising results. In particular, scholars have seen positive results from the provision of cash or capital grants to microentrepreneurs (De Mel, McKenzie, and Woodruff, 2008; Fafchamps, McKenzie, Quinn, and Woodruff, 2014) and when introducing more flexible microcredit products that allow repayment grace periods (Field, Pande, Papp, and Rigol, 2013).

While the investigation of flexible credit products has certainly provided promising results, and recent progress in mobile banking now allows lenders to assess creditworthiness by observing transaction behaviour, concerns with the underlying model remain. One hypothesis for the failure of microcredit to lead to microenterprise growth relates to the debt-based structure of microcredit. Microcredit contracts tyically feature a very rigid repayment structure and high interest rates. Requiring a fixed repayment amount regardless of the performance of the business may not be the optimal financing method to stimulate the investments of high-potential but risky microenterprises. A more mutual way of financing may be to provide the implicit insurance of performance-contingent payments, which can better allow microentrepreneurs to make the higher-risk, higher-reward investments that are necessary to accelerate the growth of their businesses. Recent work has shown the potential for equity financing to stimulate investments with a greater expected return, using a 'laboratory in the field' experiment (Fischer, 2013).

Mutuality Meets Microequity

Equity-based contracts have the potential to provide a more mutual form of financing. Rather than requiring a fixed rate of return regardless of the performance of the business, microequity contains implicit insurance through performance-contingent payments. A performance-contingent payment simply means that repayment is linked to earnings; a borrower repays more when her business is performing well and repays less when business is slow. Equity-based contracts explicitly allow for loss-sharing in the case of lower incomes; concomitantly, in return for the capital provider taking greater risk, they require higher payments when business incomes are high. Such contracts may be particularly valued by more risk-averse entrepreneurs, who may be concerned about losing their wealth under a debt contract when their business receives a negative shock.

Reflecting the idea of growing businessess through creating mutual benefits, microequity contracts seek to align the incentives of capital providers and users. With debt contracts, microcredit loan officers may be incentivised to lend to lower-risk, lower-reward entrepreneurs who repay their loans. They also may be less interested in financing higher-risk entrepreneurs who may make a lot of profit but may also make some losses before that, because loan officers are exposed to the downside risk and do not share any of the upside. In microequity, the more successful the entrepreneur, the better the result for the capital provider.

In this study we are interested in whether a more mutual contract, in this case microequity, can out-perform a conventional contract—for example in terms of repayment rates—as well as if microequity can produce better outcomes across multiple capitals, one of the central concerns of Mars' economics of mutuality approach. In examining outcomes, we could imagine contract A and contract B performing identically as finance instruments; however, if we could observe greater gains in social or human capital in contract B, we could also think about that contract as having more holistic, mutual effects. Similarly, as we used baseline surveys to capture elements of participants' human and social capital, we will be able to see how these endowments affect performance in a contract, all else being equal.

One of the major challenges in implementing equity-based contracts is access to accurate information on performance, on the basis of which income-sharing payments are linked. In the unique context of the Maua Business, in which uplifters directly purchase the stock from Maua-approved stockpoints, and we are able to estimate incomes based on the price sold to customers, we can credibly link repayments to performance. We can then use a careful experimental design to investigate the preference for equity contracts of entrepreneurs with different levels of income and risk aversion, with the ultimate question of interest being the impact of such contracts on the lives of entrepreneurs.

The Maua Study

A pilot study, conducted as a randomized controlled trial (RCT), was launched in January 2017, involving thirty-two participants; the RCT design allows researchers to measure causal impact. Five of the uplifters from the pilot received a bicycle financed by a fixed-repayment loan contract, while thirteen received bicycles using our mutuality-inspired microequity contracts, where repayments were linked to uplifters' sales. The rest formed a control group. Administrative data from the pilot revealed that the microequity contracts significantly outperformed the fixed-repayment debt contract in terms of repayment performance, with very few missed payments compared to a relatively large number of missed payments for the debt contracts, although we are careful not to put too much interpretation into the results from such a small sample.

Nonetheless, the viability of such contracts was demonstrated, and we are now testing them in our larger ongoing study. In January 2018, after delays due to post-election violence, we returned to Nairobi to launch the roll-out of the full-scale RCT, which is ongoing, with just under a hundred microentrepreneurs admitted into the programme at the time of writing. Looking at data from our (pre-intervention) baseline survey, 90 per cent of entrepreneurs are male, and the median entrepreneur is aged 30, married, and comes from a household containing four members, typically with only one member of the household earning any income. Median business profits are approximately 65 GBP per month, and median monthly household income and expenditure from all sources is 137 GBP and 130 GBP respectively. This low level of net household income is reflected in relatively low levels of savings at the household level (approximately 280 GBP for the median household, which indicates that a bike costing 90 GBP would constitute a very large share of total household savings).

We are currently expanding the programme (and have recently included entrepreneurs from the coastal area of Kenya, Mumbasa), and are collecting follow-up data for all entrepreneurs. Preliminary data reveals a high take-up rate for all of our contracts, in the region of 82–92 per cent, which compares very favourably with take-up rates from all other prominent microcredit studies (where take-up ranges from 13 per cent to 31 per cent). As yet, there is no statistically significant difference in take-up rates between most of our contracts, but we expect this to change as our sample size increases. One exception to this is that take-up does seem to be lower for our income-sharing contract that has a fixed duration, which is unsurprising since such a contract requires entrepreneurs who are very successful to share a very large amount of money in comparison to other contracts. We look forward to investigating take-up patterns in more detail as our sample increases, for example exploring the correlation between contract preference and risk aversion. As mentioned, we also intend to test the hypothesis that more mutual contracts can more effectively help entrepreneurs grow their business, by measuring the impact of our contracts on a range of difference outcomes including human and social capital indicators; for example, we hypothesize that providing more mutual contracts that share in risk and reward with entrepreneurs could lead them to better identify with the values of mutuality and increase their reported levels of trust in their business and other relationships.

The conceptualization and design of the Maua microequity RCT raises a series of important questions about the positive potential for this type of microfinance product and randomised evaluations more generally. But can either contribute on a wider scale? As discussed above, a core challenge for the implementation of a microequity contract is securing credible information on income. A particular advantage of working with the Maua programme has been the availability of reliable, high-frequency sales data, as the business records micro-distributors' sales in order to calculate bonus payments. By contrast, many micro-distributors are not part of similar programmes and there is not a system to ensure reliable, centralized, frequent sales collection. This includes workers in small shops, for example, who may or may not keep accurate records of their earnings.

But is this something that will soon change? Innovations in financial technology and digital payment systems mean that it may be more common for entrepreneurs to have detailed and accurate records of their earnings, which would allow models such as ours to scale. As more workers and entrepreneurs use digital platforms to transact, thus producing accurate records of their activities and sales, the potential sites for offering microequity—and more mutual ways of doing business—appear large. The ability to measure performance, given progress in financial technology, can therefore allow the design of more mutual sharing arrangements in the future.

Conclusion

At the centre of the concept of mutuality are relationships. In the business context, this challenges us to re-imagine business practices as a means of creating shared and sustained benefits for consumers, workers, suppliers, and investors. This demands attention to the conditions that allow for flourishing in the long term, as well as reflection regarding the extent to which benefits and costs are shared equitably. Mutuality distils a relational, embedded view of the firm that stands in sharp contrast to the model of business as a zero-sum game. In a system in which corporations shape markets, this question of what a more mutual way of distributing the costs and benefits of business activities gains urgency.

This experimental study gives us an opportunity to test both whether a more mutual approach, in this case microequity, can out-perform conventional approaches in terms of performance, as well as drive more mutual outcomes for Maua sellers in terms of their human and social capital. The comparison of microequity and conventional debt contracts will help us better understand the optimal financing structures to help micro-distributors grow. This is an important question, as microfinance is an increasingly common feature of the lives of low-income individuals, and yet it continues to leave expectations for transformation unmet. More broadly, this study also speaks to big-picture questions about how the balance of risk and reward influences behaviour and how best to design products or practices with sensitivity to the needs and concerns of mutliple parties. These questions touch on the key intuitions behind work on mutuality in business.

The challenge of translating the complex and multi-faceted concept of mutuality into an intervention that could be tested in a 'fair horserace' against conventional practice has been, in and of itself, an important exercise in thinking about what mutuality means at the practical level. Indeed, asking, 'How can microfinance be made more mutual?' demands the distillation of the charactistics of a mutual relationship. This needed to go beyond simple benefit—the provision of at least a marginal benefit is the theoretical basis of any non-coerced transaction—and to engage with the idea of joint, even interdependent, prosperity over the long term. How can this be baked into a microfinance product? We focused on the sharing of risk and reward in the relationship between the lender and borrower (or investor and investee), hypothesizing that a more mutual sharing of risk could enable sellers to do more to grow their businesses. Microequity captures these key features. We are confindent that the results of this reserach will help to shed light both on the performance of microequity contracts as well as, more broadly, the potential for creating more mutual relationships between corporations and workers within their supply and distribution systems.

Notes

1. See Roodman and Morduch (2014) and Banerjee, Duflo, Glennerster, and Kinnan (2015) for a discussion.
2. These empirical studies have been complemented by anthropological work that has examined the way in which peer lending functions, with some authors raising concerns about intense social pressure being placed on borrowers (Karim, 2008; Montgomery, 1996; Rahman, 1999).

17
The Impact of Mutuality on Ownership

Jonathan Michie

Introduction

The terms 'mutuality' and 'mutuals' have been used variously over the decades and between countries. As indicated in Chapter 3, a common usage of mutuals as a corporate form has been in relation to financial mutuals, meaning companies owned by their 'members', which in these cases have generally been the customers. Financial mutuals include credit unions, co-operative banks, and building societies, the last being the type of company which in Britain provided the overwhelming majority of home loans (or mortgages) for many decades, until the demutualization process transferred many (comprising the majority of the sector's assets) into shareholder-owned banks. The term 'mutual' is also used to describe any company owned by its members, as opposed to being owned by a private individual or family, by external shareholders, or by the state. This more general definition would include co-operatives and employee-owned firms, and while for many of these the member-owners are the customers, for others the member-owners will be the employees, and there may be other member-owners such as producers, or representatives of national or local government; and hybrid mutuals have a combination of more than one such category of member-owner.

The motivation for structuring ownership in this fashion, rather than via the more usual external shareholder model, has generally been the belief that if the organization is owned by, for example, its customers, it is more likely to prioritize the interests of those customers. Thus, any

DOI: 10.1093/oso/9780198870708.003.0017

financial surplus or gain (for example from the overall value of the organization's growing) will belong to the member-owners, and should be returned to them in some form, whether this is a financial dividend, or being charged a lower price (for example a lower interest rate on a loan or mortgage), or being provided with a better service than might otherwise be the case. Mutuality thus refers not only to the ownership and governance of companies, but also to their aims and objectives; corporate culture, incentives, and decision-making; policies and practices; and outcomes in the sense of the quality and price of the goods or services delivered. Thus, even if the term mutuality is considered to refer primarily to ownership (with a 'mutual' meaning a member-owned company), it still makes sense—and is important—to consider such issues as the relationship between 'the economics of mutuality' and ownership, as there is no automatic link between ownership and behaviours. A member-owned organization might be poorly managed and thus fail to deliver improved outcomes for its members. Conversely, while a shareholder-owned company may have a duty to prioritize the interests of its shareholders, if it is well managed it may be able to give due regard to the interests of its other stakeholders—customers, employees, suppliers, and the local communities in which it operates.

In this wider context, 'mutuality' implies a commitment by a company to share success with its stakeholders, so there is a mutual sharing of benefits—and more generally a commitment to respecting the interests and well-being of stakeholders, so if it is a question of losses, these will not be passed on to stakeholders opportunistically, without regard to the mutual interest.

Such behaviour will be costly, in that resources will be devoted to these stakeholders that could alternatively have been retained, or some share of losses may be absorbed rather than passed on. But the company's loyalty to its stakeholders is likely to be reciprocated. For example, suppliers may be less likely to behave opportunistically in exploiting a temporary shortage to their advantage; employees may be more motivated—and prepared—to contribute discretionary effort and innovative ideas; and consumers may display a degree of consumer loyalty, rather than switching to other suppliers for what might be only a temporary opportunity to benefit.

Any such loyalty from suppliers, employees, and customers is likely to have economic benefits over the long term—in effect, returns on the investment in mutuality, so that the value of the company and the level of its profitability may thereby become greater over time than had the commitment to mutuality not been made (albeit there would then be an expectation to share this success, on a continuing basis, for this process to continue).

In short, there is a commitment to the welfare of stakeholders (an investment), with this commitment likely to be reciprocated, to the economic benefit of the company. Whether a company taking a 'mutual' approach will be more successful as measured by levels of profitability will depend on which of these is greater in quantitative terms, the investment or the returns.

This affects ownership for two reasons. First, whether the commitment by the company is reciprocated depends on the confidence stakeholders have in the company's commitment to mutuality, the ability of managers to deliver, and the likelihood these will continue. A way to signal the commitment is mutual ownership. Having at least a degree of mutual ownership (that is, even if the stakeholder ownership stake is less than 100 per cent) will give confidence that the policy of recognizing mutual interests will not be reversed at any moment, but rather is embedded in ownership, with rights of governance and decision-making.

Second, if the owner wishes the principle of mutuality to continue, then introducing mutual ownership is the way. Many companies in the past had commitments to such principles, but have since abandoned them, such as Cadbury's or Barclays Bank. A family-owned company is likely to be converted sooner or later into a shareholder-owned company, and thus follow the Cadbury's and Barclays route. The only way to maintain the mutual ethos is to embed a degree of mutual ownership.

Ownership forms and governance arrangements play a critical role in ensuring the future of mutual practices and outcomes for any company committed to them. Using 'trust' or 'foundation' structures has proved successful at delivering such outcomes in a range of companies across the leading industrialized economies.

High-Commitment Work Systems

Employment contracts can go so far in setting out what employees are expected to contribute during the working day to achieve organizational outcomes and corporate success—but only so far. Work can be monitored, but this is costly. Ultimately, employees have a degree of discretionary effort. High-commitment work systems bring together policies and practices to enable, encourage, motivate, and facilitate employees to contribute such discretionary effort—and on a long-term, sustainable basis.

Such policies aim to achieve three outcomes:

First, ensure employees have the capabilities to deliver the desired discretionary effort.

Secondly, employees need to be afforded the opportunity to contribute the discretionary effort. If they are working on a production line, there may be little opportunity to contribute anything beyond performing the number of tasks the production line speed dictates. So work organization is key. If the discretionary effort is to include devising and proposing product and process innovations then employees need to be well informed and probably involved to some degree in decision-making, so policies around information-sharing, consultation, involvement, and participation may be vital.

Thirdly, motivation: these may include explicitly economic incentives such as profit sharing, including employee share ownership. Here one can see a link from the one definition of mutuality, as sharing in the success of business—whereby information-sharing and participation in decision-making may create the opportunity for enhanced output from which all can benefit—through to the other definition, where employees have a stake, which will be a motivation to contribute discretionary effort on a sustained basis.

Ownership and Governance

The link between ownership and outcomes is governance: there needs to be a mechanism to ensure managers prioritize the interests of the owners, rather than, for example, their own interests. This was the original case for establishing member-owned organizations—to ensure they would operate in the interests of members.

There is a separate question of time-scale—whether the organization will operate in the long-term interests of its members. The short-term interest might be to sell the organization to a shareholder-owned business, with the members enjoying a financial windfall. But that may mean the end of the mutual's existence. If one wishes to safeguard long-term interests, this requires ownership, with the necessary legal framework. With the John Lewis Partnership this is achieved by requiring the trustees to act in the interests of the current *and future* employees of the company.

Unless such governance arrangements are thought through, there is a danger that mutuality might result in member-owners acting in a short-term fashion. This is why the '*Trust*' form of mutual ownership is important.

Ownership and Employee Motivation and Innovation

One incentive to give an ownership stake to employees is to motivate them to prioritize financial outcomes—profitability. Ownership may take the form of individual shares, or ownership being held in trust, with the trustees obliged to act in the interests of the employees. With individual share ownership, higher profits may boost the share price. In the case of shares held in trust, a rise in profits may be distributed to employees as a bonus. These financial incentives may lead to employees being loyal to the organization and motivated to contribute additional discretionary effort, becoming more productive and innovative, with beneficial outcomes including lower staff turnover, higher rates of innovation, increased productivity, higher quality of outputs, and increased profitability.

In the case of innovation, if an employee sees a way to reorganize work that would do away with their job, will the employee volunteer this information? If they think they would be made redundant, they may withhold the idea. If they had confidence the information would improve performance, and the gains would be shared—including through reassigning employees to alternative roles—then such suggestions are more likely to be forthcoming. The confidence that such an approach would be taken may be enhanced by mutuality.

Organizations may seek to enjoy these benefits by promoting mutuality without ownership. The advantages of underpinning such policies with ownership are, first, that this can embed such commitments as long-term. Second, the causal mechanisms depend crucially upon subjective attitudes of trust, loyalty, and commitment, and without the organization committing to the ownership aspect of mutualism, the other aspects are likely to be that much weaker. So, it is a matter of degree, and of time horizons.

Using Mutualism to Promote Corporate Diversity

In addition to the benefits of mutuality for companies, there's a benefit to the economy from corporate diversity. Economies have a range of ownership forms, including family ownership, shareholder ownership, state ownership, and mutual ownership (including financial mutuals, co-operatives, employee-owned businesses, and other member-owned companies). The balance between these varies—across economies and over time.

The United Kingdom is peculiarly dominated by shareholder-owned companies, exacerbated by the privatizations and demutualizations from the 1980s onwards. In response to the global financial crisis of 2007–08, the United Kingdom's 2010–15 government pledged to boost corporate diversity across the financial services sector, and to support mutuals to deliver on this pledge (which was not achieved, as documented by Michie and Oughton, 2013, 2014). The point is not that one corporate form is preferable to others: some may be preferable for some purposes, and others for others. The aim is to keep options open, and to promote 'biodiversity' across the economy (Michie, 2011, 2017; Ownership Commission, 2012).

Thus, for example, in Denmark many of the largest companies are controlled by non-profit foundations. Carlsberg is majority-owned by a foundation that uses its profits to fund scientific research. The shipping company Maersk is majority-controlled by a foundation. The Lundbeck pharmaceutical company is majority-owned by a foundation that funds around $75m worth of medical research and educational programmes a year. Novozymes has 69 per cent of its voting stock owned by a foundation. These foundation-owned companies deliver similar financial returns to their competitors (Thomsen and Rose, 2004). Firms owned partially by a foundation comprise a quarter of the largest 100 Danish corporations and their market value represents around half the market value of the Danish stock exchange (Hansmann and Thomsen, 2013). In Sweden, IKEA is foundation-owned.

In Germany many companies are fully or partially owned by foundations, including Bertelsmann, Bosch, Korber, Mahle, ThyssenKrupp, ZF Friedrichshafen, Aldi, and Lidl. The median return on assets of such foundation-owned firms was found by Gunter and Matthias (2015) to be about 6.7 per cent, compared to 7.5 per cent for matching firms; foundation-owned firms also tend to follow a more conservative financing policy, which stabilizes their long-term existence.

There are many other companies across the globe with varying ownership and governance structures, seeking mutual sharing of success. The Mahindra Group was ranked by Forbes in 2009 as among the top 200 most reputable companies in the world; in 2011 it launched a new corporate brand Mahindra Rise, which seeks to unify Mahindra's image and brand as aspirational, supporting customers' ambitions to 'rise'. The Group is involved extensively in philanthropy and social responsibility. This includes supporting the Mahindra United World College (UWC), one of the seventeen UWC colleges globally.[1]

The LEGO Group was founded in Denmark in 1932 and remains family-owned; in 1986 25 per cent of the company was constituted as a foundation whose 'activities are based on the belief that all children should have access to quality play and learning experiences'. Thus, 25 per cent of the company's dividends go to the foundation, to further these aims. There are two aspects: first, it's a mechanism for the company to put into practice their values; second, it makes this outcome more sustainable. Without the foundation, if the management changed, the practice might cease—and it almost certainly would do so were the company to be floated on the stock exchange, with shareholders wanting maximum returns on their shares. Having 25 per cent of the company protected by its foundation status makes it less likely that the company would be taken over by owners seeking maximum financial returns; and even if it were, the foundation status ensures that funds would continue to be dedicated to the charitable purposes.

The John Lewis Partnership and the Rule against Perpetuity

Sustaining mutuality requires permanent ownership structures. In the United Kingdom, employee benefit trusts (EBTs) are governed by the 'rule against perpetuity', which limits EBTs in England and Wales to 125 years. The law 'has its origins in seventeenth-century common law and was developed to restrict a person's power to control perpetually the ownership and possession of his property after death and to ensure the transferability of property.'[2]

In the case of John Lewis, an EBT has held all the shares of the company on behalf of employees, current and future, since 1950. The trust is governed by three trustees and the John Lewis chairperson; the trustees hold 60 per cent of the shares, the chairperson the remaining 40 per cent. Trustees are elected through a system of representative councils (Pendleton, 2001: 26–9).[3]

The John Lewis trust uses a version of the perpetuity rule 'dating back to the era of the Crusades' that fixes the longevity of the EBT at 'twenty-one years after the death of the last survivor of the descendants then living of the British monarch at the time—King George V' (Erdal, 2011: 212). This means the John Lewis trust shall continue until 'twenty-one years after the death of the Queen or, if the seventh Earl of Harewood lives longer, twenty-one years after his death' (Erdal, 2011: 212). This creates a problem for John Lewis, with its legal team looking for alternatives to the projected dissolution of the trust. One example of circumventing the rule against perpetuity comes from the Baxi Partnership, which successfully pursued an Act of Parliament to allow for the Baxi trust to last as long as the company lasts. This solution, however, remains ad hoc and has not been codified in law.

The 2012 Nuttall Review[4] recommended the rule against perpetuities be re-evaluated in relation to EBTs; such a change has been made in both Jersey and Guernsey. The Department for Business, Innovation and Skills (BIS) began this review in 2013; the John Lewis Partnership made a submission complaining that 'banks may also be less willing to lend to companies approaching the end of their term, so stultifying growth.'[5] Despite such arguments, the review concluded in 2014 against changing the rule.

In the United States, the Tax Reform Act of 1969 has virtually eliminated trust ownership by restricting how much of a for-profit business a private foundation can own. This effect appears to have been deliberate, to prevent foundations such as Rockefeller or Carnegie from wielding corporate power over current firms.

So, to protect and enshrine the principles of mutuality within a company in perpetuity is certainly possible, but the mechanisms available will vary across jurisdictions.

Conclusion

One motivation for the creation of mutuals—in the sense of member-owned organizations—has been in response to the problem of succession for family-owned businesses. The next generation may not wish to take on the running of the company, but the family may not wish to see the company lost, which will be the eventual outcome of either a trade sale or a flotation (Davies and Michie, 2012). In this case the employees, or a combination of stakeholders, can ensure the company's continued existence. Another motivation for the creation of mutuals is to encourage positive employee behaviours, such as innovation and commitment, and to align the interests of employees and the firm by sharing benefits.

Mutuality as a business practice can enhance organizational outcomes and corporate performance through a range of mechanisms, including employee motivation and discretionary effort, customer loyalty, and the ability to work with suppliers on a long-term basis. Underpinning such practices with mutual ownership can enhance the positive impact through reinforcing the belief that such policies will be maintained, so that it becomes worthwhile for stakeholders to invest in this mutual relationship.

Notes

1. Disclosure: the author is a member of the UWC Council, and chair of governors for UWC Atlantic College. Bosch, above, also supports the UWC in Germany.
2. http://www.fieldfisher.com/publications/2014/01/employee-ownership-one-year-on.
3. See John Lewis case study: http://cets.coop/moodle/pluginfile.php/43/mod_folder/content/0/Cases/John%20Lewis%20Partnership.pdf?forcedownload=1.
4. https://www.gov.uk/government/uploads/system/uploads/attachment_data/file/31706/12-933-sharing-success-nuttall-review-employee-ownership.pdf.
5. BIS findings here, John Lewis comment on page 11: https://www.gov.uk/government/uploads/system/uploads/attachment_data/file/337988/bis_14_963_bis_response_to_call_on_amending_the_rule_against_perpetuities_2.pdf.

18

The Influence of Large Investment Funds

Helen Campbell Pickford

Introduction

Of all the mechanisms of traditional capitalism, few are blamed as harshly for the collapse in values, or seen as exploiting workers to benefit a self-serving elite than large investment funds. Divorcing the investor from any contact with, or even knowledge of, where her money is being invested, they have a legal obligation—a fiduciary duty—to make the best possible profits on their investors' capital. For decades, this has been interpreted as a licence to buy and sell shares as rapidly as profit maximizing will allow. Investment was regulated to benefit one stakeholder only in the investment: the one with the capital.

Profit maximization does not mean just that the investor wants to make a good return. It means that the fund has to try to return more than all the others, or, usually, the investor can move her money. Competition between funds forced all of them into ever more rapid turnover of share ownership as quarterly or even monthly figures were compared. Where share ownership is measured in days, or fractions of days, any sense of the investor having any responsibility to the company—to help it grow, to improve, using the money invested in it—is lost. The only stakeholder in the transaction whose profit matters is the investor. As events have shown, short-term profit maximization drives businesses into serving their shareholders at the cost of their employees, and even of their customers or clients. In this chapter, we look at the ways some investment funds have started to try to rebalance transactions so that the

DOI: 10.1093/oso/9780198870708.003.0018

benefit is not limited to one side—so that not only those providing the capital, but the investee companies, and those affected by their behaviour also start to benefit. Clearly the Economics of Mutuality cannot operate unless large investment funds are willing and able to become responsible partners to responsible businesses. This chapter shows that promoting the Economics of Mutuality need not damage profitability, but indeed can help funds to grow over the long term.

Why the Ownership of the Fund Is Important

This chapter looks at examples of very large funds—private equity funds, pension funds, and sovereign wealth funds (SWFs)[1]—which have thousands, or even millions of investors as their owners. Sovereign wealth funds do not have a single agreed definition, but share several characteristics. The OECD describes them as, 'a fund set up to diversify and improve the return on foreign exchange reserves or commodity (typically oil) revenue, and sometimes to shield the domestic economy from (cycle inducing) fluctuations in commodity prices. As such most invest in foreign assets' (Blundell-Wignall et al. 2008). For countries such as Norway, setting up a SWF is a way to manage an influx of wealth from a commodity—in Norway's case, oil—so that it is less vulnerable to a drop in the price of that asset, and to avoid a sudden glut of cash destabilizing the economy. Many SWFs are designed to provide an income for the country after the original source of the income—oil, diamonds, copper, or any finite commodity—has run out. The Sovereign Wealth Fund Institute (SWFI) describes these as 'future generation funds'.[2] Typically, they aim for a very diverse portfolio, spreading the risk amongst different sectors and regions. Some SWFs buy controlling stakes in companies, but many, including Norway's, buy smaller stakes in large numbers of companies. The SWFs in this chapter are protected from too much political influence, including the temptation to spend windfalls from non-renewable resources, by the government of the day being kept at arm's length through independent managers. Some, including Singapore's GIC, only invest overseas, avoiding domestic investments and their potential for political influence. Any estimate of the total size of SWF assets under management is subject to rapid changes, but for up-to-date information, the Sovereign Wealth Fund Institute's Wealth Fund Rankings webpage[3] gives the current size, and date of origin. At time of writing, the SWFI listed over USD 8109 billion held by various countries, over half derived from oil and gas.

Public pension reserve funds finance pensions, usually by pay-as-you-go schemes, where the employees, and often the employers, contribute over long periods. Pension funds are usually thought of as being owned by the contributors, but they may be set up as part of a social security system, possibly managed in the public sector, such as the Japanese Government Pension Investment Fund, or the Danish Social Security Fund. Others are managed by the government separately from any social security system, such as New Zealand's Superannuation Fund. While SWFs typically invest overseas, public pension reserve funds (PPRFs) often come under pressure to invest domestically: the Japanese GPIF and Korean National Pension Fund are invested entirely in government securities (Blundell-Wignell et al. 2008). They have one clearly defined aim, paying pensions, where SWFs may be attempting to avoid 'resource curses', shield against inflation, plan for resources diminishing, and export national values through 'soft power'. Since many pension funds were established over a century ago, whereas most SWFs were established within the last fifteen years, it is unsurprising that the structures that had been developed in pension funds to ensure independence from political influence and the security of the fund have influenced similar structures in SWFs. Pension funds have had independent boards with strict criteria for the eligibility of trustees, including professional qualifications and experience of managing investment funds, for decades. Many SWFs have adopted similar strategies. Their sources of income are different, they have different liabilities, and they invest in different regions, but the aspect they have in common is the need for independence from raids by short-term, often politically motivated governments.

Raids by governments, on capital or profits, are not the only temptation towards short-term aims. However they are managed, pensions are 'owned' by everyone who contributes to them, often for decades, and SWFs are owned by all the citizens of the country that holds the fund. With so many owners, organizations are set up to manage the day-to-day transactions of buying and selling the shares. These managers have a fiduciary duty to maximize the profit they make on behalf of those who own or contribute to the fund, and this is where the temptation to short-term profiteering comes in. Under current legislation, investors who buy shares in companies have no responsibility to grow the company, to add to its value, let alone develop the employees' capacity or consider the relationship between the business and communities around the sites where it operates. Investment managers may consider the business's use of natural resources if they are concerned that exploitation constitutes a risk, and they may be wary of negative publicity about unfair treatment of workers, but a quick turnaround on buying and selling is one way to reduce these risks. It takes a more imaginative, as well as a more responsible approach to make an investment *mutually* profitable to investor and company.

The funds we examine here *could* behave like typical, profit-maximization funds, since few of the pension contributors or citizens who contribute to them or 'own' them have any knowledge of the investments made for their benefit. They *could* buy and sell with no sense of ownership of the companies they invest in. What makes the funds discussed here different—and important—is that they are innovating to make the investment relationship mutually beneficial both to those providing the capital, and the company—and therefore the employees, customers, and communities where they operate. To be clear, these funds are not 'social impact' funds, designed to benefit a struggling community, nor are they philanthropic funds demanding only social benefit in return, nor are they running non-profit corporate social responsibility projects in parallel to making a profit on their main investments. Like other funds, they have a fiduciary duty to make a profit for their contributors. The critical difference is that these funds have realized that they can maximize their profit not through ever faster turnover, but through investing in the long term, building mutual relationships with the companies they invest in. By behaving like owners who want to see their return continue past the next monthly report, they aim to develop the companies to be profitable—but sustainably.

Why Long-Term Investment Is Critical

The change of mindset from short-term shareholder profit maximization, to a mutually beneficial investment in which the profit derives from the sustainable growth of the company, depends critically on the investment being long term. The shareholding fund becomes a steward, or 'guardian', of the companies it invests in. It requires a mindset where the portfolio is not a set of speculations, to be ditched if they are not working, but a search for companies which can survive short-term difficulties and grow sustainably. Sustainability becomes not a fashionable buzzword, but a crucial feature of a company which can manage resources over decades, or generations.

Building a relationship between investor and investee needs a set of skills missing from short-term ownership. The necessity of building long-term partnerships affects every aspect of the funds' structure, culture, and governance.[4] Learning to be the stewards of their investments has required innovations which go much deeper than holding shares for a minimum length of time. Many funds around the world are innovating in ways which refocus on the long term, meaning that there are currently many models being tried out, and a whole new vocabulary to go with them. One example is Australia's Future Fund, where managers are known as Guardians of the Fund, intended to benefit future generations of Australians. As the director of Oxford University's Smith School of Enterprise and the Environment, Professor Gordon L. Clark notes, 'being appointed a "Guardian" is to stand guard against short-term political interests, a mandate for behaviour that... goes well beyond the requirements of simply being a professional.'[5] Managers who regard themselves as stewards, or guardians, of the investments they make, need to think strategically over the long term about how to build the value of the company. Many different strategies have been tried in recent decades, and models for business responsibility are still rapidly evolving, giving rise to a variety of terms—ethical, sustainable, long-term, triple-bottom-line—to capture what makes them responsible.

Classifying Responsibility: Ethical, Sustainable, or 'Green' Investing and ESG

Because the whole field of responsible investment is in flux, many overlapping terms are used to describe practices which have similar aims in making investment sustainable and mutually beneficial to the investor and company—but slightly different strategies for achieving them. Terms are still evolving; most funds have moved on from 'corporate responsibility' (which aimed at little more than not breaking the law), and even from 'ethical investing', since many of the funds aim for more than ethical compliance. 'Green' investment obviously focuses on environmental sustainability, and 'triple-bottom-line' investing includes ways of measuring profit beyond purely financial measures, sometimes including measurements of environmental or human capital. 'Sustainability' was defined as long ago as 1972 by the United Nations' Brundtland Commission[6] as 'development that meets the needs of the current generation without compromising the ability of future generations to meet their own needs'. It's a useful definition, as it demonstrates the link between current responsibility and future sustainability.

The investment strategies which are most often seen as responsible are the ways they consider ESG (environmental, social, and governance) factors. This term recognizes the connection between the ways in which a company is governed and its impact on the environment and society. At first sight, putting the internal governance of a company together with its external impact on the environment and society to assess risk in investing might seem to be counter-intuitive, conflating different metrics. However, the point of ESG measures is that they recognize that the internal governance determines the external impact. A company run on short-term horizons with no long-term plan for growth is high risk, and likely to impact negatively on society and environment. As with so many aspects of research into long-term investment by large funds, the measures for ESG are undecided, and several systems are used to assess companies. Amongst practitioners, the SWFI uses the Linaburg–Maduell transparency index, and the *Financial Times* developed its own ESG ratings; the Global Reporting Index offers sustainability reporting standards to analyse impact for climate change, gender equality, supply chains, and transparency; and taking an academic approach, Clark and Urwin (2008) analysed best practices globally to publish their governance scoring system diagnostic tool, and a proposed framework for governance in the *Journal of Asset Management*; while Cambridge University's Judge Business School produced the S&P Long Term Value Creation Global Index. At present, this means that no one standard measure for ESG factors has been universally adopted, and funds are able to use the metric that displays them to advantage.

Without a universally recognized standard, it is difficult to compare levels of responsibility and their success in building mutually advantageous relationships with businesses round the globe. However, there are some initial research findings by the GSIA showing areas of strength which could be expanded to other areas of the world through sharing best practices across networks which share codes of conduct or guidelines. GSIA showed that community-level investing and sustainability reporting are practiced by investors in Asia and Australia; Europe and Canada are strong in screening for compliance with international human rights law. There are several organizations working to develop and disseminate strategies for responsible investing, including the United Nations Principles of Responsible Investment's Academy, UNEP offering training for businesses, and (of the funds analysed for this chapter) Generation Investment's seed funding and advocacy for responsible investors.

Of course, governance is vitally important not only in the companies that funds invest in, but in the funds themselves—it's difficult to imagine a fund where staff are recruited and promoted with short-term incentives somehow growing long-term value in the companies in their portfolio. Here, we examine firstly, the ways in which funds are screening for companies with sustainable growth potential; and secondly, how the funds themselves are developing governance structures allied to long-term investing.

Investment Strategies

Funds have always had strategies for selecting their portfolios, but with responsible investment these have evolved from short-term profit to seeking companies in which they can grow value. Ownership Capital are unusual in actively managing 100 per cent of their shareholdings; their declaration 'Being an owner means knowing what you own' requires a highly skilled specialist investment team 'dedicated to understanding every facet of each portfolio company's business through an in-depth, hands-on research process... we actively engage with all portfolio companies on a continuous basis'.[7] It would be hard to imagine a mindset more different from the short-term turnover of traditional funds. However, different funds have different capacities to develop such relationships with all their investees. Norway's SWF actively manages around 6 per cent of its shares, prioritizing those in the highest risk areas; the Ontario Teachers' Pension Fund actively manages around 80 per cent. Many large funds are seeking to increase their in-house management capacity through employing more skilled staff, or (in some cases, including GIC) building longer-term relationships with external managers.

Among the earliest strategies for building knowledge of companies into the portfolio was 'negative screening', initially rejecting companies profiting from such products as gambling, alcohol, tobacco, weapons, or pornography. Funds which own shares in companies conducting a lot of different activities may also disinvest if they move into such areas. Other funds screen for very specific practices: for example, Australians can opt for an 'ethical investment' pension fund[8] which screens for 'the dignity and well-being of non-human animals'. Others screen out businesses involved in fracking, or laying pipelines across indigenous-owned land (see, for example, ING's statement on their divestment from the Dakota Access Pipeline in March 2017).[9] These show how some large investors can respond to local cultures and their concerns.

Negative screening, however, provides only a minimum of responsibility, by avoiding the worst investments. (It is also ineffective where shares are simply bought by a different investor.) Critically, for a long-term partnership between investment fund and company, the risks inherent in commodities or products subject to regulation are often too great. Ownership Capital's CIO, Alex van der Velden,[10] emphasizes that their negative screening for fossil fuels is not for ethical reasons, but because over a long-term investment horizon, they will become a high financial risk. For van der Velden, initial negative screening is not an ethical precaution, but a necessity for long-term profit.

'Norms-based' screening is a short step up from negative screening and divestment, seeking companies compliant with minimum standards set by agencies such as UNHRC (United Nations Human Rights Convention), the ILO (International Labour Organization) or agencies with more specialized remits, such as the ICMM[11] (International Council on Mining and Metals). Again, mere compliance could be seen as unambitious for reforming the sector.

'Positive' or 'best-in-class' investing seeks companies with good ESG factors—not just avoiding exploitation of people and damage to the environment, but seeking innovative ways to prevent these practices. The Forum for Sustainable and Responsible Investment[12] describes positive screening as 'investment in sectors, companies or projects selected for positive ESG performance relative to industry peers. This also includes avoiding companies that do not meet certain ESG performance thresholds.' Investors are constantly developing new metrics enabling them to identify companies' best ESG performance. The Canadian Coalition for Good Governance (CCGG) represents institutional investors by 'promot[ing] good governance practices in Canadian public companies and the improvement of the regulatory environment to best align the interests of boards and management with those of their shareholders.'[13] An obvious difference between negative screening, divestment, and norms-based screening versus seeking the best-in-class is that organizations such as CCGG aim actively to influence not only the companies they invest in, fostering good practice, but even the wider regulatory environment.

'Active' share ownership is increasingly seen as essential to developing good ESG practices. Funds leading innovation to make investment more responsible aim to engage with companies, either directly through attending shareholder meetings, or by employing external agents chosen to align with the fund's values. The Ontario Teachers' Pension Fund actively manages 100 per cent of its infrastructure investment fund; Ownership Capital actively manages 100 per cent of its shares through visits to investee businesses. For the very largest funds, developing the capacity to manage all their shares actively is difficult, but they employ external managers selected for their shared values. Norway's SWF holds shares in 9,000 companies; with so many, it prioritizes directly managing the 6 per cent of its shares in the highest risk areas, and its largest investments.[14] CPPIB emphasizes that its external managers are partners, and that they use feedback from their partners to develop their own capabilities. Because active management (directly or indirectly) by shareowners takes time and significant expertise from the fund's employees, it only makes sense in a long-term relationship—in other words, learning requires a partnership.

While voting on all their shares is assumed to be an essential part of active management (by instructing external agents how to vote where necessary), some funds have evolved more advanced ways of using voting. Norway's SWF holds a minority share in all its companies, but publishes its voting intentions in advance and files shareholder proposals, aiming to influence other shareholders. Generation Investment Management regards proxy voting as 'an opportunity for analysts to gain additional insight into companies', and report to their clients on how their proxies voted.[15] Several funds make it clear that their voting is to a consistent set of values, including OTPP, who publish their corporate governance principles, seeing them as in shareholders' best long-term interests,[16] and NBIM, who invite collaboration with their 'predictable', 'transparent' strategy.[17]

Voting contributes to the maintenance of relationships between investor and company through regular reading of proposals, contact at meetings, and the use of voting to establish guidelines embodying the values determining how investors vote. In addition, funds have developed further strategies for direct management. Ownership Capital proposes changes in compensation or even to replace the compensation committee. NBIM is one of the funds which use 'flags of warning', which lead to divestment if ignored. Litigation is rare, because funds find sustaining partnerships through communication more effective. Funds building longer-term relationships are finding that having a transparent set of values and frequent communication are more effective than threats or divestment.

Building Values into the Structure of the Organization

Moving from short-term to long-term investment relationships doesn't just take a change of mind-set: funds have to change their own governance and practices. Instead of bonuses for maximizing profit by whatever means, they must provide incentives to invest responsibly. The challenge for funds aiming to be more responsible is finding ways to innovate towards long-term horizons while operating within the existing law.

Funds have found ways to encourage longer-term horizons in their boards of directors, and across their employees more widely. Singapore's SWF, GIC, sets an ethics quiz for employees annually, and provides a confidential platform to enable whistle-blowers to raise concerns.[18] Other funds have pensioner or employee representation at board level; the Netherlands' pension fund, PGGM, has a Members' Council, in which fifteen current employees and fifteen pensioners are represented, enabling them to influence board decisions. PGGM treats pay as a vital aspect of governance; rewarding responsible investing affects every aspect of managing the organization, from recruiting staff with the right motivation, to the stability of a management aiming for a horizon of up to ten years.

Ensuring that managers and the board are incentivized to invest responsibly is vital. Ownership Capital consider non-financial as well as financial measures in setting bonuses, and pays them only when the investments outperform the market—pay by long-term performance. Norway's SWF bases bonuses on performance, limits them to a percentage of salary, and instead of paying them at once, pays half immediately and the rest over three years. The Ontario Teachers' Pension Fund lists several measures to ensure that pay is based on performance, combined with full disclosure on pay and benefits. It has introduced say-on-pay voting, banned 'one-off discretionary awards', and states its intention of paying senior and middle managers linked to the long- and short-term objectives of the company. Employees must keep equity awards for a minimum of a year after retirement, preventing their immediate sale and motivating employees to consider the value of the award even after their retirement. Increases in salary must be approved by an independent assessor, based on performance. Finally, it uses clawback provisions, 'allowing the company to recoup compensation already paid in the event of financial restatements or misconduct'.[19]

As well as adopting such measures themselves, responsible funds ask the companies they invest in to adopt them too. CPPIB explains how it cooperates with other organizations in order to extend its influence on both governance practices and legislation. Alongside active management of their shareholdings, funds need to be actively involved in making sure their innovations are more widely adopted. Making them mainstream will need changes in the regulatory environment before short-term investors are likely to change.

Conclusion

It is always difficult to draw conclusions from a field in which innovation is at the experimental stage, and practices are still evolving before being widely accepted. However, these funds provide several crucial lessons. Firstly, far from innovation being stifled by complying with more ethical or responsible standards, this is driving the development of research within the funds into balancing pay and bonuses, experimenting with employee representation, and finding new ways of leveraging their influence as shareholders. Having learned from their experiments, funds are actively seeking ways to encourage others to share this knowledge across regulatory networks.

Secondly, the time factor required to build partnerships with investee companies is crucial. Developing knowledge of a company's current operations, the structures it has in place to manage future risks, the ways it is ensuring effective governance through planning successions: all of these new kinds of knowledge are essential to a stewardship role. In order to tolerate regular questioning about its plans, a company must focus on its own long-term horizons, but must also want a long-term relationship with the investor.

The skill set needed to build and maintain such partnerships is profoundly changing the ways in which funds recruit, compensate, and retain staff aligned with their values. Balancing the need to be transparent and responsible about pay at every level with the need to retain knowledgeable staff who are building relationships with companies which could last decades is also driving innovation. Only those funds whose governance structures enable them to innovate in areas such as employee representation, partnering businesses, and sharing the knowledge from their innovations will be able to influence other funds, the businesses they invest in, and the regulatory environment.

Notes

1. For this chapter, around thirty funds were screened for innovative practices allowing for more mutual relationships with the businesses they invest in. The funds included as a focus of best practices are three Sovereign Wealth Funds, Singapore's GIC, Norway's NBIM, and Australia's Futures Fund; three pension funds, the Ontario Teachers' Pension Fund, the Canadian Pension Plan Investment Board, and the Netherlands' PGGM; and two private investors' funds, Ownership Capital and Generation Investment Management. They therefore represent different classes of owners: sovereign states, pension contributors, and private investors, but all are large funds seeking responsible ways to invest.
2. http://www.swfinstitute.org/sovereign-wealth-fund/.
3. https://www.swfinstitute.org/sovereign-wealth-fund-rankings/.
4. For a more detailed outline of the 'Guiding Principles' and investment strategies over the long term, the 'Long-Term Portfolio Guide' (FCLT March 2015) is a useful resource, developed by the Canadian Pension Plan Investment Board and McKinsey and Company.
5. Clark and Knight (2010).
6. The Brundtland Commission's report for the United Nations, *Our Common Future,* defines a sustainable company as 'one whose current earnings do not borrow from its future earnings; whose sustainability practices . . . drive profitability and competitive positioning, and . . . provide goods and services consistent with a low-carbon, prosperous, equitable, healthy and safe society' (http://www.un-documents.net/our-common-future.pdf).
7. https://www.ownershipcapital.com/investment-philosophy.
8. https://www.australianethical.com.au/pensions/.
9. https://www.ing.com/Sustainability/ING-and-the-Dakota-Access-pipeline.htm.
10. Johnson (2015).
11. https://www.icmm.com/en-gb/about-us/member-commitments/icmm-10-principles.
12. http://www.ussif.org/esg.
13. https://www.ccgg.ca/.

14. https://WWW.NBIM.no/en/responsibility/ownership/.
15. https://www.generationim.com/media/1141/generation-im-stewardship-code-october-2016.pdf.
16. http://www.cppib.com/en/public-media/headlines/2016/long-term-portfolio-guide/.
17. https://www.nbim.no/en/transparency/news-list/2016/clear-expectations-towards-companies/.
18. http://www.gic.com.sg/about-gic/code-of-ethics.
19. https://www.otpp.com/investments/responsible-investing/governance-and-voting.

19
The Impact of NGO Activism

Andreas G. F. Hoepner and Qian Li

Introduction

Corporations often draw criticism and face demands from non-governmental organizations (NGOs); some typical examples of controversial issues raised by NGOs include climate change, pollution, fracking, GMOs in food, animal welfare, supply-chain issues, and labour standards. The most pressing concern for the majority of corporations is profit maximization; NGOs, however, traditionally only concern themselves with issues related to people, the environment, and society. As such, it is difficult for NGOs and corporations to find common ground in solving problems. In tandem with the increasing demand for firms to look beyond profit and to behave more responsibly and sustainably, the interactions between corporations and NGOs have increased in breadth, intensity, and complexity. For instance, NGOs are now forming partnerships with corporations to address environmental and social concerns. This emerging trend raises some intriguing questions. Why is it important for companies to maintain a mutually beneficial and healthy relationship with NGOs? How can NGOs conduct themselves in such a way as to achieve mutually beneficial outcomes? What are the benefits and drawbacks of these aligned interests for both parties?

This chapter analyses the relationship between NGOs and corporations through the lens of the Economics of Mutuality. In particular, we discuss whether the relationship between the NGO and the corporation itself can be considered as a mutual partnership aimed at achieving

Andreas G. F. Hoepner and Qian Li, The Impact of NGO Activism In *Putting Purpose Into Practice: The Economics of Mutuality.* Edited by: Colin Mayer and Bruno Roche, Oxford University Press (2021).
DOI: 10.1093/oso/9780198870708.003.0019

long-term goals and objectives through effective implementation based on mutual understanding, common interests, and shared values. With the support of examples and cases, we discuss the strategies that NGOs use to change business practices and the direct and indirect impact of NGO advocacy activities on firms' conduct and operations.

The Interactions of NGOs and Mutuality

In essence, mutuality refers to a situation in which businesses achieve long-term reciprocal benefits with regards to sustainable economic, social, and environmental development. NGOs are the most prominent actors advocating for social and environmental issues. Issues such as climate change are so complex that governments as well as businesses have realized the importance of NGO involvement. Consumer and social pressure as reflected in NGO campaigns is an important vehicle by which the interests of customers, communities, and societies are communicated to companies. Since NGOs are not motivated by a desire for profit (although they do face pressures to fund their staff), they are seen by the public as being more trustworthy than other organizations, and they have become increasingly important as they have grown in number and variety. According to the Union of International Associations, approximately twenty thousand international NGOs were registered in 1985; by July 2018, this number had increased to over sixty-seven thousand.[1]

Historically, NGOs have often been regarded as being antagonistic towards companies. More recently, however, there is an increasing appreciation of the fact that NGOs can be very useful to companies in garnering the support of both local communities and specific social groups. NGOs and corporations can form collaborative relationships to address social and environmental issues. As both NGOs and corporations face public scrutiny (e.g. NGOs themselves are monitored by Charity Navigator), collaboration between NGOs and businesses is more likely to produce 'win–win' results:[2] companies can enhance their legitimacy and improve their business practice while NGOs increase their revenue and influence. However, in some rare cases, NGOs also suffer from their partnership with businesses. If NGOs do not choose sponsorship carefully, they end up drawing public criticism just as companies do. For instance, BP and Shell's sponsorship deals with British cultural institutions has drawn criticism from other NGOs and anti-fossil-fuel activists. The ensuing pressure caused BP and Shell to withdraw their annual contributions to these institutions. In other words, NGOs can run the risk of being accused of doing corporate PR work in return for revenue.

In addition, although corporate governance issues are more likely to be influenced by investors, NGOs have also been recognized as important influences on the conduct of firms. NGOs such as ShareAction, which focuses on investment systems and environmental protection, adopt a shareholder-activist campaigning model to participate in corporate governance issues (Ivanova 2016). When collaborating with companies, however, NGOs have to be careful to avoid financial dependencies which can lead to mission drift. Only NGOs that remain sufficiently financially independent of companies can apply the necessary scrutiny to ensure that companies are genuinely attempting to have a positive impact and are not just engaged in greenwashing.

The trade-off between companies' engagement with external pressures and their need to change their policies fits the pattern of maintaining a mutually beneficial and healthy relationship with NGOs. When facing pressure, boycotts, and campaigns from NGOs, companies have to judge how they should respond to and engage with them. From the valuation perspective, how much do changes such as shutting down a pollution unit or investing in new technologies cost companies? By how much does the value of a company increase as a result of gaining consumer confidence, such as when food companies decide to use sustainably sourced ingredients? How much value do companies gain in terms of long-term benefits? Companies must choose how to respond to outbursts of criticism wisely in order to maintain profits and impact positively on society and the environment.

The Influencing Strategies of NGOs on the Mutual Behaviour of Firms

NGOs' engagement with the behaviour of firms can be diverse and complex. There are four types of engagement strategy: direct compromise, direct coercion, indirect compromise, and indirect coercion. Examples of indirect strategies include research reports and policy briefings, while examples of direct strategies include protests, boycotts, disruption, picketing, and occupations (Frooman and Murrell 2005). In this chapter, we narrow our focus to strategies that NGOs can use to form mutually beneficial relationships with corporations in order to emphasize the positive impact of NGO activism on corporations' value-creation and greater levels of environmental and social responsibility. As can be seen in Table 19.1, the strategies used by NGOs are categorized into three forms: 1) advising and consulting; 2) collaboration; 3) shareholder activism.[3]

Advising and Consulting

To engage with companies on certain issues, NGOs often seek out specialized communities, networks, and knowledge. When companies start to interact with NGOs, it marks the beginning of the learning process through which new strategies are formed for achieving economic benefits as well as benefits to society and the environment. Examples of this include the Environmental Defense Fund (EDF), providing knowledge and expertise on energy issues; the Clean Water network, sharing its extensive knowledge on water quality; the WWF, providing help on the sourcing of materials; and Conservation International (CI), providing expertise in food and agriculture. NGOs can serve as consultants and advisors helping companies to become more responsible and sustainable. These characteristics can have positive impacts on companies' business operations, management practices, supply chains, and their reputation in society.

Table 19.1. Evolution and progression of NGO influencing strategies

Source: Modified, based on Guay, Doh, and Sinclair (2004: 133).

The interaction between companies and NGOs provides a learning and knowledge-exchange opportunity for firms that lack expertise in certain innovations and new practices and regulations, or that are not aware of the potential impacts of uncertainties. NGOs often have analytical and technical skills that can help corporations to set standards, generate new ideas, address new issues, and respond to other stakeholders. For instance, the World Resources Institute (WRI) produces and curates datasets as part of their commitment to turning information into action. One of the datasets enables users to explore, compare, and assess the greenhouse-gas mitigation plans in each country's Intended Nationally Determined Contribution (INDC).[4] Another example is the International Union for Conservation of Nature (IUCN). One of the IUCN's key objectives is to share the knowledge gathered by its unique global community of more than ten thousand scientists.[5]

However, there are also concerns regarding NGOs' accountability in their roles as advisors and consultants to multiple stakeholders. Some scandals have been reported in the NGO sector, such as misuse of funding, misconduct, and a lack of transparency in their financial systems. For example, the Red Cross, the world's best-known humanitarian organization, reported in 2017 that more than $5m (£3.8m) of aid money was lost to fraud and corruption during the Ebola epidemic in West Africa. In 2018, Oxfam admitted that some of its members had engaged in sexual misconduct in Haiti. This had severe consequences including loss of credibility in the eyes of the public, reduced funding support, and Haiti's banning Oxfam from operating in the country.

NGOs are at the frontline of the battle to obtain transparency from companies. However, NGOs themselves should not be exempt from transparency requirements. Organizations such as Charity Navigator have now been set up to rate how effectively NGOs manage themselves. NGOs are assessed based on financial efficiency and capacity, and on how they manage accountability and transparency.

Collaboration

NGOs and companies tend to begin the engagement process with different needs and views. Communication helps both parties to balance their needs and expectations so that they can achieve common goals. NGOs and companies can develop mutual forms of collaboration based on their aligned interests and complementary resources. Hoepner, de Aguiar, and Majithia (2013) studied managerial compliance with the International Code of Marketing of Breast-Milk Substitutes over a twenty-year period; their findings suggest that corporations that adhere responsibly to NGOs' international standards are less likely to provoke consumer boycotts and have better reputation risk management while not encountering any shareholder value reduction as result of their responsible behaviour. In addition, NGOs can help with organizational change and increase transparency within global supply chains (e.g. more disclosure on social and environmental information) (Reid and Toffel 2009; Mcdonnell and King 2013). However, any violation of the rights of key stakeholders, such as consumers, employees, suppliers, and governments could have significantly negative impacts on the supply chain, potentially causing business failure.

For NGOs, collaborative relationships offer them the power to steer companies' policies and operations, and therefore to achieve their own goals. However, there are factors that can potentially moderate the influence of NGOs. In contrast to having an antagonistic relationship with the same company, a collaborative relationship may influence the independent standing of NGOs. Doh and Guay (2006) argue that different institutional structures and political legacies can explain the influence of NGOs in the policymaking process. Also, given that NGOs work across borders, their impact is constrained by national and regional contexts.

Shareholder Activism

Although NGOs do not normally invest in shares, in recent years, activist NGOs have begun either to buy shares as their own (in order to participate in proxy meetings and other resolutions) or to find allies among firms' other shareholders in order to address their concerns and pressurize companies to change. Institutional owners often find themselves called upon by NGOs to vote as proxies on a wide range of environmental and social issues—such as those dealing with diversity, climate change, pollution, waste, animal welfare, and others. NGOs can either pressurize investors to invest capital in certain companies or attempt to influence company directors by interacting with them directly and intervening in the annual general meetings (AGMs). The Interfaith Centre on Corporate Responsibility (ICCR) pioneered the use of shareholder advocacy to urge companies to act on environmental, social, and governance (ESG) issues (Goodman et al. 2014; Hebb et al. 2018). For instance, ICCR member initiatives include calling for increased diligence to eliminate forced labour risks in global supply chains, curbing GHG emissions to align with the 2° warming scenario established by the Paris Climate Agreement, and pressing for more sustainable food systems.[6]

Another example is ShareAction's 'Tar Sands—Counting the Cost' campaign aimed to stop BP and Shell extracting oil from tar sands, which incurred severe environmental, social, and financial risks. ShareAction persuaded 100 shareholders to table a resolution at the AGMs of BP and Royal Dutch Shell in 2010, which resulted in Shell's AGM 11 per cent of voting and BP's AGM 15 per cent of voting. While such shareholder activism is unlikely to win majority support, it can increase public awareness and may lead to self-reflection among corporate executives, as shareholder meetings and results are often covered by the media. For future events, NGOs may need to weigh this publicity against the long-term commitment and dedication required for effective shareholder engagement.

The Impact of NGOs on the Mutual Conduct of Firms

As NGOs address the interests of customers, employees, and society, they are considered to be one of the main motivating factors in driving change in corporate conduct. NGO campaigns can be successful in altering corporate conduct and policies by shifting to more socially and environmentally focused managerial practices that also have a positive effect on financial value. For example, companies can save costs by improving energy efficiency and can improve business operations by improving employee well-being. NGOs foster communications and interactions with business which can generate social capital and in return benefit business overall. In addition, NGOs are helpful in embedding values of responsibility and sustainability in the for-profit corporate culture.

NGOs are essential players in helping companies to expand and shape sophisticated networks. NGOs collaborate with other stakeholders of the firm (e.g. customers, suppliers, investors, governments, regulatory bodies, and other NGOs) to shape the norms of corporate policies, culture, and beliefs. There are value potentials for businesses interacting with NGOs with regard to accessing their latent knowledge and networks. With help from NGOs, companies have the potential to discover and expand into new markets. Endorsement from reputable NGOs can help companies to attract more customers.

When companies commit to change, the actions often impact positively on their corporate reputation and public perception. Companies also maintain a level of legitimacy that helps them to gain the trust and acceptance of multiple stakeholders including government, media, employees, customers, suppliers, and investors. In contrast, companies that are unwilling to change may find themselves facing additional pressure and monitoring from activists and the public, or even increased regulatory attention. As a result of activist campaigns, companies make changes to policy, products, and business operations. Companies are requested to disclose more information on social and environmental performance. With more transparency, consumers become more informed about products and the company's performance. As NGOs can motivate corporations to change management practice and increase transparency within global supply chains (Reid and Toffel 2009; Mcdonnell and King 2013), there is great risk-reduction potential for businesses interacting with NGOs in diminishing supply-chain risks.

NGOs can play an important role in promoting sustainable development and embedding societal issues through serving as early warning mechanisms and providing help in monitoring and implementing international agreements. For example, Volkswagen might have spared itself the pain of the 2015 emissions scandal had it paid attention to a 2013 report by the International Council on Clean Transportation (ICCT).

'From Laboratory to Road' showed that the gap between official CO_2 and real CO_2 values was continuing to increase, even using the VW Passat as an example—showing that the gap was more than 30 per cent in 2011.[7]

Collaboration between NGOs and corporations can help to pre-empt conflict and to reduce the amount of criticism drawn from environmental activists and the public. In areas where regulation is increasing, companies that have already made changes in response to NGO activism are well prepared for legislative shocks. This preparedness can serve as a competitive advantage in many industries. For NGOs, cultivating relationships with corporations can help improve the environment while increasing their own publicity and visibility. Building these relationships also helps NGOs to gain additional funding from business and individual donors, thus increasing long-term financial security and stability.

Conclusion

In spite of the increasing interactions between NGOs and corporations on social and environmental issues, there are many dynamics and challenges that should be addressed from the perspective of the Economics of Mutuality. If more companies formed mutually beneficial relationships with the NGO community, the interaction between the two would grow in importance and significance over time. The impact of NGOs' activism on the mutual conduct of firms is dynamic and complex. The effect may differ across different areas of concern, companies, industries, and market environments. Some companies proactively engage with NGOs, while others try their best to avoid any involvement with them; some companies use NGOs to greenwash their damaged reputation, while others are genuinely concerned about environmental and social issues and are fully committed to changing. Corporations and NGOs both evaluate their own situations based on value and return: corporations are more likely to change if there are multiple benefits foreseeable in the near future; meanwhile, NGOs are more likely to select companies as targets if they believe that the impact of doing so will be more significant.

Corporations and NGOs need to formulate better methods to align their mutual interests and achieve common goals. NGOs need to work on improving their communication, strategies, and action. Corporations need to change their perception of their relationships with NGOs and behave more responsively and responsibly. Although NGOs have become prominent stakeholders, corporations must still engage with a wide variety of other stakeholders (e.g. customers, suppliers, investors, governments, and regulatory bodies). How can businesses best manage these complex and dynamic relationships with stakeholders? Do larger companies in consumer-facing industries benefit more from collaborative relationships with NGOs? Are companies that exist in a weaker institutional environment more likely to be targeted by NGOs? Will all mutual interactions and collaborations benefit both NGOs and business or are NGOs at risk of selling their values? Further empirical evidence is needed to answer these questions.

Notes

1. Source: https://uia.org/ybio. 'The Yearbook of International Organizations includes detailed information on over 37,500 active and approximately 38,000 dormant international organisations from 300 countries and territories--including intergovernmental (IGOs) and international non-governmental organisations (INGOs). Approximately 1,200 new organisations are added each year.'
2. Additional details of Charity Navigator: https://www.charitynavigator.org/.
3. As advocating has been considered the main role of NGOs, we only focus on the more specific strategies that NGOs can use to benefit the corporations and themselves.
4. 'Under the U.N. Framework Convention on Climate Change (UNFCCC), countries committed to create a new international climate agreement by the conclusion of the Paris climate summit in December 2015. In order to help facilitate that goal, countries agreed to release public outlines of actions they intend to take. These commitments are known as INDCs' (World Resource Institute). Data sets provided by World Resources Institute can be accessed at: http://datasets.wri.org/dataset. The CAIT Paris Contributions Data can be accessed at: http://datasets.wri.org/dataset/85940e80-d6dd-4978-a2e6-82ca743b0884.
5. Resource provided by International Union for Conservation of Nature (IUCN) can be accessed at: https://www.iucn.org/.

6. More details can be found at: https://www.iccr.org/about-iccr. Each year, ICCR members typically file close to two hundred resolutions and ICCR publishes the full list online. The full list of resolutions can be found at: https://www.iccr.org/iccrs-shareholder-resolutions.
7. More details can be found at: https://www.theicct.org/blogs/staff/trend-that-cant-continue-europes-car-co2-emissions-gap.

PART III
CASE STUDIES

20

Bel Group

Harnessing the Power of an Informal Distribution Network

Alastair Colin-Jones, Alexandra Berreby, Caroline Sorlin, Hannah Radvan, and Justine Esta Ellis

Introduction

Since Bel Group's early years, the family-owned cheese-manufacturing group has been driven by its core values to 'Dare, Care and Commit'. More recently, Bel has increasingly emphasized achieving growth through the pursuit of shared value creation. As family-member and CEO Antoine Fievet puts it, 'Growth must happen through the creation of wealth, not just for the company, but for society as a whole.'[1]

Bel's commitment to these principles led to the creation of Bel Explorer (BE) in 2011 to serve as the Group's idea incubator for inclusive and break-through business model approaches. This dedicated unit aims to increase global access to high-quality nutritional and affordable products by including lower income communities in its value chain.

In November 2011, BE attended the International Convention of Street Vendors organized in New Delhi.[2] At the time, the Group was investigating India as a potential market, and the event sparked a deep interest in how best to engage the informal sector as an alternative distribution method. It also became apparent at this conference that strategies based on mutual interest and needs had the potential to create innovative forms of sustainable business.

Alastair Colin-Jones, Alexandra Berreby, Caroline Sorlin, Hannah Radvan, and Justine Esta Ellis, Bel Group: Harnessing the Power of an Informal Distribution Network In *Putting Purpose Into Practice: The Economics of Mutuality.*
Edited by: Colin Mayer and Bruno Roche, Oxford University Press (2021). DOI: 10.1093/oso/9780198870708.003.0020

One of Bel's five key brands, The Laughing Cow, had a strong presence in Vietnam, accounting for over 90 per cent of the national cheese market. With an effective local subsidiary in place, BE decided to launch its first Sharing Cities (SC) project in Ho Chi Minh City (HCMC). The very first iteration involved a system of door-to-door saleswomen recruited to sell a new affordable nutrition product designed specifically for the market. Problematically, however, the model was loss-making.[3] Sales were insufficient to cover fixed costs and to generate enough income for the vendors.[4]

BE quickly adapted the approach to build on the city's already extensive networks of street vendors instead. According to the International Labour Organization, the informal sector employs 1.8 billion people globally (while the formal sector accounts for 1.2 billion), constituting an 'incredible sales force'.[5] Moreover, street vendors represent the main channel for food purchases for most consumers in the developing world.[6] In HCMC, 80 per cent of the food consumed by low-income families comes from street vendors.[7] BE therefore returned to HCMC in 2012 to test the sustainability of this untapped sales force of over 135,000 street vendors[8] as an alternative distribution network for The Laughing Cow.

Pain Points in the Ecosystem

BE began by investigating the structures and patterns of the existing street vendor network and the needs of the vendors themselves. In accordance with BE's policies, this crucial research stage was not treated separately from the active development of the inclusive business model. The business unit had to share the resource costs required to finance the initial ecosystem analysis. The business unit and BE then agreed together that the research had resulted in a worthwhile opportunity to pilot.

BE ran various research projects to develop a profile for the vendors that highlighted their daily working activity, typical products in their baskets, and their typical margins. BE chose to focus on the community of fruit and vegetable sellers (estimated to be twenty-five thousand individuals),[9] since they acquired all their products from a limited number of large wholesale markets in the city. This diagnosis stage was conducted between March and April 2012 with over three hundred vendors across three fruit and vegetable markets. Significant research, observation, and interaction highlighted the crucial hurdles the business model would need to overcome to strike the right balance between maximum social impact and business viability.

The street vendors in HCMC represent a vulnerable segment of society with low education, and low and uncertain incomes, as well as a lack of access to many social services. Over 65 per cent are women, most of whom are aged between 35 and 50 and typically have children. According to this research, a key aspiration of this group is to pay for their children's education. For 92 per cent of vendors interviewed, selling their entire stock takes over 12 hours per day, during which time they earn the equivalent of €3–10.

Despite their appealing numbers as a sales force, the street vendors in many instances lacked proper education, confidence in their sales ability, and effective sales techniques to acquire new customers. Nevertheless, BE's research found that the majority of these vendors possessed a highly valuable and impressive business tool: their relationship with loyal customers.

The interviews revealed that travelling vendors typically sell 80 per cent of their basket to regular customers, with whom they have a trusted relationship. Moreover, on average, a street vendor has between 100 and 150 regular clients that he or she visits per week, and, when travelling by bicycle, makes roughly forty sales per day. The vendors spend the bulk of their time visiting their network of regular customers and developing friendships with them. Each consumer has his or her own preferred itinerant seller that he or she will support over many years. In fact, 65 per cent of consumers surveyed reported that they bought goods in order to support their seller. Seventy-six per cent of consumers said that they had been buying from the same street vendor for over five years.

The professional and personal development of the vendors was, from the outset, at the heart of the initiative. BE recognized that investing in the vendors' own development would not only attract more vendors, but also would naturally improve business performance through the vendors' improved skills and productivity.

Therefore, during the diagnosis phase, BE conducted focus groups with vendors to understand their main social concerns, as well as their thoughts on the initiative. BE also contacted local NGOs to further their understanding of the key social needs in the wider community. A host of social issues were identified, including access to education, healthcare, and finance. The latter was found to be an obstacle to engaging street vendors in the programme. Most vendors pay in cash and their daily revenues would barely generate enough margin to diversify their basket of products—let alone support the purchase of branded products that initially represent a costly and uncertain investment. Moreover, the usual fruits and vegetables offer better profit margins than conventional branded products. The vendors' legitimate expectations regarding profit margins were therefore higher than what Bel could offer, especially since Bel did not wish to set up a preferential margin system for street vendors and risk undermining their traditional sales network.[10]

Vendor concerns were not only financial, but also psychological. Their apprehensions were rooted in a lack of confidence in their own selling ability, combined with their belief in how consumers perceive them. One street vendor, for example, said that he could not sell branded products because 'nobody buys brand products from a street vendor'. Convincing the street vendors to sell a new product therefore presented a challenge.

Business Strategy

Almost paradoxically, it became clear that the social concerns of the vendors (income levels, healthcare, etc.) could contribute to finding a potential business model solution. BE developed an incentive system based primarily on providing social benefits tailored to the needs of the street vendors in return for high sales performance. Street vendors selling The Laughing Cow would gain access to business training, health insurance, and a bank account. When a street vendor first joins the programme, Bel offers him or her three free boxes of the Laughing Cow to try and sell. At the outset, free goods and immediate cash undoubtedly represent the most attractive incentive for the vendors. However, over time access to health insurance and skills training are as valued as free goods or cash bonuses. In fact, a survey of the best-performing sellers showed that the health insurance was viewed as the most valuable incentive.

In developing the right business model to overcome the identified obstacles and to optimize for the opportunities discovered in the diagnosis stage, BE used the following series of key design principles:

i. Fit the culture of the community. BE set up three hubs in existing wholesale fruit and vegetable markets so that vendors did not have to travel to a different location to stock Bel products. The operational team in HCMC selling to the vendors are Bel employees.[11]
ii. Add to the vendors' baskets, never replace. Bel sales should not represent more than 20 per cent of the vendor's total income so that they do not become dependent on the availability and demand of Bel's products. The main product sold is The Laughing Cow since it is affordable, popular, and its quality and nutritional benefits are preserved even when unrefrigerated.
iii. Simplify the standard business sales process. Bel sells directly to the street vendors who sell directly to their clients. This allows for closer interaction with the sellers and consumers while also simplifying the value chain.
iv. Promote the Bel Group brand. When the street vendors join the programme they receive a brand uniform and can therefore become the brand's ambassadors throughout the city; these elements should be encouraged, rather than enforced.[12]

The social component is equally vital in the functioning of this initiative. Vendors had significant reservations about selling branded products, as well as concerns about receiving lower margins for The Laughing Cow. BE adopted a holistic approach, identifying the vendors' key concerns, as well as carefully selecting the best partners to work with on key areas:

i. Training and skills-building: Partnering with the European Institute for Cooperation and Development (IECD), BE established Business Schools for Vendors in December 2012. This eighteen-hour module offers vocational training, covering topics such as food security, sales techniques, basic bookkeeping, and technical management. Once vendors complete the training, IECD organizes follow-up meetings with the vendors at their respective sales locations.

ii. Access to insurance: BE has partnered with the insurer Groupama to offer a micro-insurance product at $1/month to cover the potential 'cost of hospitalization and children's education in the event of disability'. Rather than charging the vendors, Bel and Groupama co-finance the entire premium for this insurance. The total costs amount to $12 per individual each year. In effect, the insurance incentive acts as an equivalent to cash bonuses, but with a clearer social benefit.

iii. Access to financial services: Bel promotes the purchase of new material and equipment. It also encourages vendors to save through helping them open bank accounts.

iv. Access to the formal sector: Bel supports the vendors with their administrative paperwork and integration into the formal sector by assisting them with taxation, social security access, and migrant registration.

v. Benefiting the whole ecosystem: Bel seeks to improve the vendors' environment through advocacy and lobbying, and contributing to the public debate on street vendors.

These incentives allow BE to deliver widespread social impact while also helping to attract and recruit new sellers. The business training is a particularly powerful incentive since it improves the productivity of the sellers, resulting in increased growth of sales and revenue, for the vendors as well as for Bel.

It is important to note that these social incentives are generally not free, and the vendors gain access to different levels of social benefits relative to their levels of performance. It remains crucial to Bel and the vendors that SC is not perceived to be a philanthropic programme. Therefore only those who have performed the best and have been identified as suitable for prolonged training will be enrolled into the Business Schools for Vendors. Currently, half of the vendors in HCMC receive insurance, while 15 per cent receive the business training.

After designing the social incentives, BE established two sets of performance indicators, which measure business performance and social impact respectively. The major indicators are:

i. Business (this is how the sales team supervisors are assessed): Total volume, sales, investment, and profit; evolution of the sales per street vendor; percentage of the street vendor business vs. traditional trade.
ii. Social: Number of street vendors in the programme, percentage receiving a social incentive (detail on health part/business training/access to financial inclusion), and impact of the business training on the street vendors' global activity. Since the business training aims to achieve holistic goals, the social performance indicators also measure impact on self-esteem, confidence, and aspirations.

During the pilot phase, Bel monitored the business performance and development of the community on a weekly basis in order to analyse results quickly and adjust operations if necessary. In order to facilitate this, in 2015 BE created and implemented a dedicated online Customer Relationship Manager at each kiosk. On a daily basis, the local sales executives register new street vendors and record their sales. The supervisor of each team uses the kiosk to analyse performance, and at the end of each month supervisors can automatically identify the list of street vendors who will receive incentives and what incentives will be offered. Finally, at a global level, Bel is able to monitor global performance indicators, to compare one market/model to another.

Performance

Despite some initial hesitance from the business unit managers, BE launched its first SC initiative in 2013 in HCMC. Although the initial objective was set at forty sellers within six months, only four months later the team celebrated the arrival of their 100th vendor. Furthermore, by December 2013, less than a year after the programme launched, there were nearly 250 vendors active in the SC network in HCMC—a number that has grown ever since.

BE and the local business successfully managed the SC programme to profitability within two years of its launch. By 2016 they had 2,261 street vendors representing 28 per cent of the volume of single-serve portions of The Laughing Cow made in General Trade. In terms of social impact, as of December 2016, 429 of vendors had graduated from micro-entrepreneur courses, 1,000 received health insurance, and 817 opened bank accounts. On average in HCMC, the vendors who had received business training improved their revenue by 30 per cent after twelve months. Today the programme offers the same level of profitability as other sales channels, along with greater social benefits for its wider ecosystem of distributors.

Prognosis

The promising results from the HCMC pilot resulted in the decision to scale up the pilot project and pass the leadership to the business unit managers in 2015. The pilot had reached the important target set by BE for all projects: that it should match—or be forecasted to match in five years—the level of profitability in Bel's traditional route to market within that country.

Since the SC launch in HCMC, BE has successfully implemented this business model in Kinshasa (Democratic Republic of Congo), Antananarivo (Madagascar), Hanoi (Vietnam), and Istanbul (Turkey). The initiative has seen the steady growth of its informal sales network, with 2,100 street vendors in 2013 to 7,500 in 2018, and a targeted 80,000 by 2025.

The SC programme has proven that it is possible to simultaneously identify new business growth opportunities and develop a more inclusive economy in order to improve the welfare of the vulnerable in the ecosystem. Certain emerging countries, such as Vietnam and the countries of sub-Saharan Africa, where these informal networks already exist, will contribute significantly to Bel's business development. By using alternative distribution channels of locally trusted street vendors, the programme is allowing Bel to become firmly established in areas with high population growth. The programme is integrated into Bel's core business strategy for regional inclusion and customer growth. Notably, the Bel Foundation has no involvement in SC because it is considered a business concern alone.

Ultimately, Bel Group has created, tested, and scaled an innovative and inclusive business model, which creates financial value for the company while respecting and ensuring positive benefits for members of its ecosystem. Addressing both marketplace success and social good, Bel's initiative has developed an ecosystem of like-minded partners who are gaining a new perspective on the role of the corporation in society, recognizing that being mutual is not just good for business—it *is* good business. As Antoine Fievet comments, 'the way in which the Group achieves its results is just as important to us as the results themselves. It is possible, and indeed essential, to combine strong management and best practices, profitability and integrity, growth and ethics.'

Notes

1. 'Polaris: Building a Flourishing Family Business,' Family Business Network, Ideas Innovations & Inspiration from our Network & Beyond 2 (Bel Group 2016): 35.
2. J.M. Guesné and D. Ménascé, 1.
3. J.M. Guesné and D. Ménascé, 2.
4. J.M. Guesné and D. Ménascé, 2.
5. Interview with Caroline Sorlin, General Manager, BA, Bel Group, 2013, https://www.youtube.com/watch?v=DwYB0uoaGVg.
6. J.M. Guesné and D. Ménascé, 2.
7. 'Polaris: Building a Flourishing Family Business,' 33.
8. J.M. Guesné and D. Ménascé, 2.
9. J.M. Guesné and D. Ménascé, 3.
10. J.M. Guesné and D. Ménascé, 6.
11. In regions where Bel does not have its own subsidiary, the central stock point is managed by employees of a partner organization, where Bel ensures they receive at least the same level of social benefits as the street vendors themselves.
12. J.M. Guesné and D. Ménascé, 6.

21

Marks & Spencer

Improving Supply-Chain Sustainability

Sudhir Rama Murthy, Mike Barry, and Justine Esta Ellis

Introduction

Over the past decade, Marks & Spencer (M&S)—a major British retailer of household items, food products, and clothing—has increased its focus on fostering sustainability throughout its supply chain. In response to both business needs and a growing customer demand for sustainable practices, M&S has aimed to show leadership in minimizing its environmental impact.

Founded in 1884, M&S is now a public limited company with over a thousand stores across the world, 852 of which are located in the United Kingdom. It has over eighty thousand employees and revenues of over £10 billion. In the United Kingdom, there are 368 firms that supply directly to M&S and employ over 119,000 people. These sites include 302 food factories and thirty-eight drinks factories. With the goal of increasing transparency, product quality, and worker well-being throughout its supply chain, M&S instituted a Sustainability Scorecard system in 2010 to measure impact and incentivize best practices. This metric continues to help M&S achieve positive performance by promoting good relations with suppliers and customers.

Sudhir Rama Murthy, Mike Barry, and Justine Esta Ellis, Marks & Spencer: Improving Supply-Chain Sustainability In *Putting Purpose Into Practice: The Economics of Mutuality.* Edited by: Colin Mayer and Bruno Roche, Oxford University Press (2021).
DOI: 10.1093/oso/9780198870708.003.0021

Ecosystem Pain Point

Over 90 per cent of M&S's social and environmental impact occurs within the supply chain and outside its own operations. Even though 98 per cent of M&S products are sold under its own brand, M&S does not manufacture any products itself and relies instead on its suppliers. For this reason, M&S has to take a special interest in developing relationships with its suppliers and collaborating with them in the area of sustainability.

This collaboration can yield a range of benefits for M&S. For example, sustainability-based innovations such as optimized packaging design, a reduction in transit packaging, and load-sharing during transportation can lower costs. Alternative product designs or formulations can create improved products. Environmental and social risks can be reduced through better sourcing of materials and high labour standards in supplier factories. And supply and reputational risks are lowered when there is greater transparency across the whole supply chain.

However, there are challenges associated with implementing new approaches to supply chain sustainability. As an industry report explains:

> Most companies in the grocery sector initially approached supply-chain sustainability from a need to ensure compliance and to minimize supply and reputational risks from across the supply chain. Whilst some industry-wide initiatives, such as Sedex (Supplier Ethical Data Exchange) have been successful in providing an effective framework for this risk management approach, this can result in defensive behaviour by suppliers and can reinforce relationships that are characterised by a 'tick-box' process for ensuring compliance.[1]

In order to offset potential risk, M&S needed to create new ways in which to align suppliers with M&S's broader sustainability goals.

Business Strategy: The Sustainability Scorecard

The supply chain forms a critical part of the overall M&S Sustainability Programme—which they call Plan A. In 2010, M&S established a

Sustainability Scorecard that aims to align suppliers with the company's sustainability objectives by tracking the progress of their own sustainability activities.[2] This scorecard enables M&S to award Provisional, Silver, Bronze, and Gold ratings to participating suppliers. The scores are calculated based on three pillars: environment, human resources and ethical trade, and lean manufacturing.

> Overall, M&S aims to ensure that there are good working conditions throughout the supply chains and that products are sourced with integrity. Resource efficiency is associated with supply efficiency and reduced costs associated with raw material, energy, and waste. And M&S aims to incentivize and facilitate better and leaner practices amongst suppliers.

At least once a year each of the direct suppliers' sites works through the scorecard's framework and completes self-assessment questionnaires.[3] As a case study by the Financial Reporting Council describes, suppliers take the process of generating and auditing these scorecards seriously:

> A critical part of the process is audit and assurance where it must both satisfy itself that the required standards are being met and avoid alienating its suppliers by being too strict... The company has opted to give a window for when audits will take place, so that the suppliers know that the assurance team will arrive at some point within the space of, say, a month. The period is short enough to limit the disruption but long enough to prevent bad practice being temporarily hidden.[4]

In this way, M&S addresses the need to collect excellent data without overburdening suppliers. The practice of providing suppliers with a 'window' during which the audit will take place helps foster goodwill and promote accountability, without disrupting production.

Buyers take these scores into account. Furthermore, only products from Silver and Gold factories are eligible for recognition as having 'Plan A product attributes' for sale to consumers. By 2020, M&S plans to source 100 per cent of products from sites that are scored Silver or Gold. In recognition of their efforts, Silver and Gold suppliers are awarded certificates at the M&S annual commercial conference.[5]

Environment

The first element of the scorecard considers the environmental measures. These measures focus on energy use, water use, waste, and carbon outputs. This part of the scorecard includes environmental impact assessment, risk assessment of key raw materials. It also shows a sustainable procurement plan and tracks the percentage of renewable energy at site.

M&S has identified waste as a specific issue, both in production and in packaging. The current goal is to source 25 per cent of food from suppliers who operate zero-waste factories. As the company's Plan A Commitments report describes:

> Different parts of M&S supply chain face different challenges on waste. Food supply chains create more waste, but much of this is currently recycled. M&S works with food suppliers to help them recycle their remaining volumes that still go to landfill, by using the most carbon-efficient approach available, for example anaerobic digestion or composting. We'll also work with our suppliers to minimize food packaging write-offs.[6]

As this example of the food supply chain demonstrates, there are many opportunities for increasing sustainable business practices all along the supply chain. Offering increased access to recycling helps M&S align its suppliers with its ongoing sustainability goals by tackling the challenges of food waste.

Human Resources and Ethical Trade

A second key aspect of the scorecard is human resource management and ethical trade. This section includes employee representation, staff turnover, workforce cohesion, and external accreditation for employee bodies. As the company reports: 'We want our food to only come from factories demonstrating leading standards in training, workforce and community engagement, health and safety and employment practices.'[7]

The scorecard system helps advance M&S's human resource and ethical trade goals.

The company's Global Sourcing Principles draw from key international documents and standards, including UN Universal Declaration of Human Rights, the ILO Declaration on Fundamental Principles and Rights at Work, the UN Guiding Principles on Business and Human Rights, the UN Women's Empowerment Principles, the UN Human Right to Water and Sanitation, the Children's Rights and Business Principles, and the UN Global Compact. By aligning the company's requirements with these international standards, M&S is able to encourage engagement and streamline the compliance burden for its suppliers.[8]

Lean Manufacturing

The third element of the scorecard is lean manufacturing. Here, the scorecard tracks whether suppliers use formal tools for cross-functional problem solving, employ value-stream mapping to illustrate and analyse the manufacturing process, and identify key suppliers for improved relationships.

Participatory Approach

M&S seeks to encourage suppliers to take ownership of the sustainability agenda. Rather than imposing targets and monitoring compliance, it has chosen to collaborate with key suppliers and to work with them to create a number of model factories. Although some of the lessons from the model factories initiated supplier changes through Plan A commitments, the larger focus was, and continues to be, demonstrating the business case for action. M&S views this as a powerful incentive for galvanizing change across the supply chain.

In addition, M&S encourages its suppliers to use an online knowledge platform which provides advice, case studies, and toolkits for making practical changes within factories and on farms.[9] These materials also highlight the business benefits of implementing those changes.

The scorecard framework is supported by a Supplier Collaboration Programme. This has three main areas of focus: facilitating supplier exchange meetings, where suppliers can share their learnings; providing skills training and development opportunities for suppliers; and delivering financial benefits and improved ways of working.

There is further encouragement through other incentives and collaborative programmes such as the annual supplier awards programme and networking sessions. The 'awards recognize and showcase suppliers that have made tangible and demonstrable improvements in areas such as process innovation or product sustainability' and the supplier networking sessions take place every two to three months. These sessions focus on areas of the performance scorecard in which suppliers experience difficulties. In these sessions, suppliers that have made progress on specific challenges are encouraged to share experiences and outcomes with their peers, and M&S technical experts are also on hand to share operational knowledge and expertise. M&S also makes a point of not requiring suppliers to share how much they have saved and how much of the savings results from M&S's involvement. This approach stems from the belief that suppliers may be concerned that M&S's buying departments would use the information to negotiate on price. Moreover, since the relationship between supplier engagement and decisions to adjust business practices is not always clear-cut, these sessions function primarily as opportunities to identify best practices. The networking sessions help provide a platform for discussing challenges, free from the concern that such disclosures would have a negative impact on the supplier's relationship with their buyer.

The Benefits of the Scorecard Approach

The scorecard enables M&S to understand and manage its supply chain better. This approach helps incentivize best practices. As summarized by Hazel Culley, Sustainability Manager, the programme brings to the fore many previously unnoticed aspects of the supply chain:

> It's great to be able to see the real change that's happening; for example, when we started out only seventy of our sites had staff surveys—now more than two hundred do. We've also seen great environmental

> improvements including over 40 per cednt of our sites sending no waste to landfill and 25 per cent volume is now from sites that have reduced energy by 20 per cent.[10]

More broadly, through the suppliers' self-reporting M&S gains insights on the energy, material, waste, and carbon performance measurements for those factories; suppliers' risk assessment of their raw materials; suppliers' employee representation, gender ratio, employee turnover, and employee survey results at those supplier sites; and the production capabilities of its suppliers. These insights allow M&S to better select and interact with its suppliers for product innovation and other improvements in its products.

Performance

Overall, the Plan A programme, of which the scorecard is a component, has delivered significant saving through waste reduction and environmental efficiency. In the 2014/15 business year, these savings totalled £160 million. The programme has saved £625 million since 2007.

M&S views the value of the programme as extending beyond these savings. As reported in a case published by the Financial Reporting Council:

> The company does not seek to measure the financial impact of Plan A in terms of margin, corporate earnings, and brand value. It considers this is a number that cannot be calculated, but it believes that the impact of Plan A in terms of the trust it generates with customers, as well as on the morale of its workforce and that of its suppliers, will make the company more resilient and more adaptable, enhancing its sustainability in a rapidly changing world.[11]

As the report indicates, putting an increasingly sustainable supply chain into practice creates benefits for both M&S and its suppliers. The Sustainability Scorecard initiative bolsters brand value by enhancing relationships among the main business, suppliers, and customers.

Examples of Supplier Achievements

As a result of the Sustainability Scorecard programme, M&S created value and savings across its supply chain:

- Through the introduction of vacuum packing for fresh meats, an unnamed company calculates it saved £16.3 million in 2011/12.
- Worldwide Fruit, an M&S food supplier, was named supplier of the year in 2012 for its achievements in reducing electricity consumption by 14 per cent a year and water demand by 75 per cent.
- Brandix, a designated M&S eco-factory, was named clothing supplier of the year in 2012 for reducing carbon emissions by 80 per cent, energy usage by 46 per cent, and water consumption by 58 per cent.
- AMC Grupo Alimentación Fresco y Zumo, a fruit supplier, introduced a closed-loop manufacturing methodology for fruit squeezing. This led to zero fruit waste, with 90 per cent of fruit waste being used elsewhere in the business.
- Courtauld, a clothing supplier, developed a new bra made from 100 per cent recycled polyester, with improved durability and guaranteed non-yellowing.[12]

As these supplier achievements show, the scorecard initiative has the potential to align suppliers with M&S's sustainability goals in mutually beneficial ways.

Prognosis

Looking ahead, M&S aims to source 100 per cent of products from at least Silver-level suppliers by 2020. In addition to meeting its internal standards, the company plans to have a sustainability story for each M&S product. This way, it can demonstrate the origins of its products and highlight the benefits of its new supply-chain model.

Additionally, M&S plans to expand its Plan A initiatives to include a wider range of sustainability programmes. To this end, M&S will launch a five-year, £50 million Plan A innovation fund to support new ideas in the business.[13] An additional future goal will be to help suppliers create 200 Plan A factories and have ten thousand farmers join the initiative.[14] Taken together, these programmes aim to catalyse innovation along M&S's sustainable supply chain and to continue fostering good relations between the company and its suppliers.

Notes

1. Stanley (2013).
2. Bhattacharya (2016).
3. 'Sustainability Scorecard: Capacity Building Initiatives', corporate.marksand-spencer.com, https://corporate.marksandspencer.com/plan-a/our-approach/food-and-household/capacity-buildinginitiatives/sustainability-scorecard.
4. 'Our Plan A Commitments 2010–2015', Marks and Spencer Group, March 2010, http://corporate.marksandspencer.com/plan-a/85488c3c608e4f468d4a403f4ebbd628.
5. Hazel Cully, 'Silver and Beyond--Foods Sustainable Factory Programme', https://corporate.marksandspencer.com/blog/stories/silver-beyond-food-factory.
6. Plan A, corporate.marksandspencer.com, 25, http://corporate.marksandspencer.com/plan-a/85488c3c608e4f468d4a403f4ebbd628j.
7. Plan A, corpororate.marksandspencer.com, 28, http://corporate.marksandspencer.com/plan-a/85488c3c608e4f468d4a403f4ebbd628j.
8. 'Global Sourcing Principles,' Marks and Spencer Corporate, November 2016, https://corporate.marksandspencer.com/documents/plan-a-our-approach/global-sourcing-principles.pdf.
9. Ibid.
10. Hazel Cully, 'Silver and Beyond--Foods Sustainable Factory Programme', https://corporate.marksandspencer.com/blog/stories/silver-beyond-food-factory.
11. 'Case Study: Marks and Spencer--Supply Chain Standards', Financial Reporting Council, https://www.frc.org.uk/Our-Work/Corporate-Governance-Reporting/Corporate-governance/Corporate-Cultureand-the-Role-of-Boards/Case-Study-Marks-and-Spencer-%E2%80%93-Supply-chain-stand.aspx.
12. Stanley (2013).
13. 'Our Plan A Commitments 2010–2015', corporate.marksandspencer.com, March 2010, https://corporate.marksandspencer.com/plan-a/85488c3c608e4f468d4a403f4ebbd628.
14. Ibid.

22

Sabka Dentist

Taking Accessible Dental Care to Scale

Yassine El Ouarzazi, Lionel Khalil, Aida Hadzic, Kate Roll, Judith C. Stroehle, and Vikram Vora

Introduction

Sabka Dentist (SD) is the largest chain of dental clinics in India, with an emphasis on affordable care. Currently SD owns and runs 112 dental clinics in India, with 250 dental chairs, more than five hundred dentists, and one thousand five hundred people. The company is active in Mumbai, Pune, Ahmedabad, Surat, and Bangalore, and it serves approximately three hundred thousand patients every year. The company reports strong revenue growth, increasing from $187 thousand in 2012 to $8.1 million in 2016.[1]

The company's mission is to provide affordable dental care to all people in India, with a special focus on the poorest members of the urban population. This goal was the main driver for creating SD's innovative business model, which uses a low capital expenditure model, exemplified by the small clinic size and focused menu of procedures, to make dental care accessible to everyone.

Pain Points in the Ecosystem

Dental care is important for everyone, yet it tends to be overlooked as a component of overall health and well-being, and it is often expensive and

Yassine El Ouarzazi, Lionel Khalil, Aida Hadzic, Kate Roll, Judith C. Stroehle, and Vikram Vora, Sabka Dentist: Taking Accessible Dental Care to Scale In *Putting Purpose Into Practice: The Economics of Mutuality.* Edited by: Colin Mayer and Bruno Roche, Oxford University Press (2021).
DOI: 10.1093/oso/9780198870708.003.0022

in short supply. With a dentist-to-population ratio of 1:10,000 in urban areas and 1:150,000 in rural areas, most Indians have no access at all to basic oral health services.[2] As a result dental diseases are a significant public health menace across the country, where they have a substantial impact on the quality of life, daily performance, and general life satisfaction A 2016 study on oral health in the country found 50 per cent of school children are suffering from cavities and tooth decay and more than 90 per cent of the adult population is affected by periodontal disease.[3]

Traditionally in India there was little provision between high-priced private treatment or the primitive street-corner tooth-puller. Anyone who could not afford the top-of-the-range treatment had little incentive to visit the dentist and no knowledge of what they could do in the way of preventative care.

To tackle this problem, SD first developed an efficient model that enables dental clinics to offer affordable access to dental services. The company estimates that it has reduced the cost of treatment by 40 per cent compared to competitors, enabling it to lower the price to patients. SD has since made the details of their model publicly available, in order to help other businesses also treat as many people as possible.

Business Strategy

At the heart of SD's approach is creating a high degree of standardization, which enables it to scale operations easily and offer a high-quality service.

The majority of the clinics operate for 12 hours from 9am to 9pm and each clinic is fitted out according to a standard unit model which comprises two chairs in a small clinical area of around 400 sq ft. This means that a new clinic can be fitted out and launched within three weeks. SD also offers free check-ups in clinics and through the use of mobile van units to create a better preventive environment, which enables patients to know about dental problems earlier, making treatment easier and cheaper.

The company provides massive training programmes that cover all dental procedures in detail, enabling consistent care. SD organizes continuous education programmes for their dentists. This also includes a plus-one invitation for each dentist to offer free training to an external colleague. This means that training to improve the quality of dental care is provided to the whole industry and not just the company itself. By offering training not only in-house, but also to dentists outside the clinic, SD tackles low-quality dental care and human capital creation at the same time.

SD has worked to recruit and retain female employees; 95 per cent of employees are now women. In India a high proportion of graduating dentists are female, but they often do not practice. To address this and make the workspace more attractive to women, the company has been built around their preferences for flexibility.

In addition, to making dental care more accessible, the company enables its patients to make payments in twelve interest-free instalments. In these credit arrangements, either SD will pay the interest itself or it will seek partnerships with financial institutions.

The high standards and quality of care in SD clinics have started to attract affluent patients, making it possible to cross-subsidize care for the poorest. SD has added a premium, higher-margin offering (for example, a ceramic crown instead of metal or resin) which is attractive to wealthier patients; the higher margin is used to subsidize lower-margin treatments for the poorer patients. The prices charged to the poorest patients can then be reduced by up to 50 per cent.

When a similar company was started in the North of India, Sabka Dentist's CEO decided to share his entire strategy with them, including procedures, prices, and technology, so that they could benefit from SD's experience and provide affordable dental care better and faster. When asked why he helped a potential competitor, the CEO answered: 'I want all Indians to have access to affordable dental care. What you call competition, I call people working towards my purpose for free so I help them if I can.' He has since created an online platform where all these resources are freely available to the public.

Performance

SD's model contributes to a better distribution of human resources and treatment of patients. Regular check-ups not only decrease the severity of interventions, they also enable SD dentists and employees to save time and treat more patients in shorter appointments, thereby making dental care more available. This is an important factor because of the disproportionate ratio between the number of patients in need of dental care and the number of dentists.

Sabka Dentist has invested in establishing a set of performance indicators that go beyond a focus on financial performance. These are listed below in order of importance:

1. *Purpose*: Number of patients treated
2. *Quality (inside-out)*: In-house surprise audit score (out of 200)
3. *Quality (outside-in)*: Patient satisfaction score (likelihood that patient will recommend clinic to family and friends)
4. *Sustainability*: Average revenue per patient.

These metrics are used to guide management decisions. Both the CEO and the managers' performance and variable pay are indexed on these four measures, with the highest weight on the first (purpose metric).

These indicators inform every management decision at every level: Who to promote? Which clinic to close? Where to allocate resources? When a clinic fails on the first measure, it triggers an immediate audit and intervention. If issues are not sufficiently addressed within nine months, the clinic enters the 'red alert zone' (receiving more marketing and more senior dentists) for three months. If it still does not achieve the target number of patients, it will be closed. The purpose metric (the number of patients treated) is thus used to ensure a responsible allocation of the firm's resources.

As a further example, the third measure reflects a fundamental focus on patient experience and feedback. There is a feedback link on the website which directly emails the CEO. In addition, a random sample of patients get called back by phone, and specially trained personnel tease out negative feedback. This is a challenge in a society where people are culturally reluctant to say bad things about their doctors.

Each strategy deployed by SD essentially addresses these performance metrics. Quality is thus addressed through high levels of standardization, which guarantees high quality and fast scalability of operations. Quality audits are thorough and led by an internal team with specialist training to get patient satisfaction feedback through phone surveys. Transparency is another important factor, which SD addresses by making all prices publicly available on its website.

On the financial side, SD's business model and strategy can be called a success. Firstly, the company witnesses steady growth: in the early stages the company saw an expansion of two clinics per month; now SD has a steady increase of seven additional clinics per month. Secondly, operations are not only a social impact success, but also both profitable and sustainable. Today SD is a lucrative dental care chain with 100 clinics.

Prognosis

There are several explanations for this overall success. SD has sought a high degree of standardization, low capital expenditure and standardized quality in order to make operations scalable. By scaling and increasing affordability, the company hopes to increase the use of regular check-ups across India and decrease the need for complicated surgeries, which are more expensive. In other words, enabling people to have regular access to dental care decreases their need for more complicated interventions and this is financially beneficial for both clients and the company. Thirdly, SD have found a way to further subsidize the dental care for the poorest patients (having dropped prices by 50 per cent), while increasing the offer for their more affluent patients.

SD expects to continue its performance and make dental healthcare affordable to all classes of people. Considering the social scale of the business, governments could also become interested and make a contribution by supporting their model in the future. A major challenge is the access to more people willing to pursue dental studies in order to increase the number of dentists. Despite this challenge, considering the existing evidence, Sabka Dentist expects more growth in the future. Building on the lessons learned throughout careful observations and the patient services at Sabka Dentist clinics, the business is likely to adapt quickly to potential challenges.

Notes

1. https://www.healthcarebusinessinternational.com/awards/samsung-innovative-low-cost-business-%20model-finalist-2017/.
2. Tandon (2004).
3. Gambhir and Gupta (2016).

23

Timberland and the Smallholder Farmers Alliance

Creating a Data-Driven Smallholder Cotton Supply Chain in Haiti

Hugh Locke, Atlanta McIlwraith, Lionel Khalil, and Kate Roll

Introduction

Global outdoor lifestyle brand Timberland has established a partnership with the non-profit Smallholder Farmers Alliance (SFA) in Haiti to completely re-imagine the cotton supply chain and create a new system for producing cotton that maximizes benefits to smallholder farmers and export customers.

Timberland designs, manufactures, and sells premium footwear, apparel, and accessories for the urban outdoor lifestyle. The company's dedication to making quality products is matched by its longstanding commitment to environmental and social responsibility to make it better with respect to responsible products, protecting and restoring the outdoors, and supporting communities around the globe. Timberland has over seven thousand employees worldwide and generated $1.9 billion in revenues in FY 2018. The Smallholder Farmers Alliance is a Haitian non-profit organization co-founded in 2010 by Hugh Locke and Timote Georges with the objective to plant trees in Haiti. The SFA applies business solutions to help feed and reforest a renewed Haiti by establishing market-based farmer cooperatives, building agricultural export markets, creating

Hugh Locke, Atlanta McIlwraith, Lionel Khalil, and Kate Roll, Timberland and the Smallholder Farmers Alliance: Creating a Data-Driven Smallholder Cotton Supply Chain in Haiti In *Putting Purpose Into Practice: The Economics of Mutuality.* Edited by: Colin Mayer and Bruno Roche, Oxford University Press (2021). © Oxford University Press

DOI: 10.1093/oso/9780198870708.003.0023

rural farm businesses, and contributing to community development. The SFA is organized as a foundation under the laws of Haiti.

The new supply chain is built around next-generation data and aims to be blockchain-ready. This will enable the partners to measure the economic, environmental, and social benefits for smallholders—farmers who farm less than two hectares or five acres of land—while at the same time measuring success for potential customers such as Timberland, Vans, and Patagonia in terms of increased transparency and efficiency.

The partnership will ultimately enable a new supply chain for Haitian-grown cotton to come to life through a blend of philanthropy and commercial investment. The partnership is currently incubating a social enterprise, which will deliver both agricultural and community services from profits. The SFA has also built an innovative 'tree currency' approach that allows farmers to reduce their cost of operation by earning agricultural credits for seed, tools, training, and financing in return for planting trees. While the partnership's current focus is to reintroduce organic cotton farming to Haiti, this smallholder supply-chain design and its related data-management system has the potential to be applicable to any smallholder-grown crop anywhere in the world.

Pain Points in the Ecosystem

Haiti is one of the most deforested countries in the world, and the severe lack of tree cover reduces agricultural productivity, raises average temperatures, and makes rural areas more susceptible to flooding. Further complicating the situation, low agricultural productivity means that farmers turn to cutting trees and making charcoal to supplement their low incomes. This locks rural Haiti into a cycle of deforestation, low productivity, and poverty.

Locke and Georges thought the best way to break this cycle was to pay farmers to plant trees. This would make trees worth more in the ground than cut for charcoal. They approached Timberland for funding: the company had a factory in the neighbouring Dominican Republic and a history of sponsoring tree planting in various countries. Timberland agreed to be the SFA's corporate sponsor, but with two conditions.

First, they challenged the organization to plant five million trees in five years to meet a commitment the company made through the Clinton Global Initiative. Second, the SFA had to make the programme self-sustaining. This meant that simply paying the farmers in cash to plant trees would not work, as the project would stop when Timberland's five-year funding commitment was complete and they needed a solution that was not reliant on external funding.

In re-thinking the basic model, Locke and Georges realized there were three things that almost every farmer in Haiti needed but could not access: good quality seed, basic hand tools, and agricultural training. They asked farmers if they would plant trees and accept payment in the form of farm credits that could be exchanged for seed, tools, and training. The farmers agreed, and the SFA created tree nurseries where the farmers could work and earn these agricultural services. The SFA also developed a plan to make the resulting operation self-financing over a period of years through a combination of establishing seed banks and training the farmers from the outset to one day take over the operation.

In 2010 the programme launched. Within weeks, hundreds of farmers had joined, and their numbers rapidly grew to more than a thousand. The SFA created tree nurseries as fast as possible, but finally had to limit the programme to 1,500 farmers. Over the next few years the programme gradually grew to engage some six thousand members on three thousand farms; the SFA recognizes husband-and-wife teams who farm together as separate and equal members. The SFA currently operates thirty-one tree nurseries in six locations throughout Haiti.

The SFA met Timberland's original challenge to plant five million trees in five years. By 2018, the smallholder farmers who work with the SFA had planted close to seven million trees. Farmers grow fruit trees, which they plant on their farms and in small orchards. They plant trees as living fences and to stabilize deforested slopes that contribute to flooding. They have reforested large tracts of community land that will eventually be connected to form the first green belt of its kind in Haiti. All these trees in the ground have earned farmers better seed, tools, and training that have, in turn, resulted in an average 40 per cent increase in their crop yields, all grown using organic principles, and an average increase in household income of between 50 and 100 per cent.

Tree Currency Finances Agriculture

The participating farmers helped Locke and Georges realize that, in designing a model through which planting trees earned agricultural services, they had actually created a form of currency: tree currency. This realization came as the farmers began to ask for additional services in exchange for their farm credits. Some of these requests were directly related to agriculture, such as using credits to buy livestock or improve irrigation. But increasingly the farmers asked to exchange credits for community services including adult literacy classes, basic business training, and a micro-credit bank with loans for women farmers. And it was the farmers themselves, with just a bit of guidance and support from the SFA, who implemented all these services.

Another benefit was the revival of an agrarian tradition which had previously been on the verge of disappearing. *Kombit* is a Haitian creole word that refers to farmers coming together at planting and harvest times to share the workload. One farmer explained *kombit* best when she said, 'We now work together for the common good and I care about the community as I care about my family.' Kombit is also the name Timberland gave to a 2015 documentary film about its tree-planting work with the Smallholder Farmers Alliance in Haiti.

Introducing Export Crops

In early 2015 the SFA published a feasibility study for moringa. The leaves of this fast-growing tree are unusually high in protein. Timberland and the Clinton Foundation helped introduce the SFA to a US company called Kuli Kuli that asked if the SFA's smallholders could grow moringa trees and have women farmers process the leaves into dry powder form. Kuli Kuli's Moringa Green Energy shots, which were developed to incorporate SFA-sourced moringa, are now on shelves at more than four hundred Whole Foods Markets across the United States. This marked an important transition towards producing export crops.

Phase II: Timberland as Customer

Seeing the success of the moringa crop led Timberland to consider how they might move from being an SFA sponsor to a customer of SFA-grown organic cotton.

The first challenge was that although cotton had once been a mainstay of the Haitian economy, it had not been grown in the country commercially for over thirty years. Timberland sponsored an SFA-led feasibility study to determine if it made sense even to consider cotton's possible return. The final study was published in late 2016 and clearly stated that the Haitian cotton industry collapsed because of politics and policies of the time rather than for agricultural or climatic reasons. The study recommended that cotton be reintroduced as a crop for smallholder farmers, who had grown at least 80 per cent of the crop historically.

The next challenge was that there was no seed stock left in the country. In August 2017 the SFA set up a field trial with annual cotton seed varieties from Brazil, India, and the United States, and with one perennial variety still found in Haitian gardens. Six months later the SFA farmers harvested the cotton and published the results. The first commercial planting by 100 farmers was completed in summer 2018 and harvested in the first two months of 2019.

In its new role as a customer of the SFA, Timberland has made a commitment to buy, through its fabric suppliers, up to one third of its entire cotton supply from the SFA. This is on the condition that it is grown organically, and available at the appropriate price, quality, and volume and to ensure it is not overly reliant on one company.

Timberland anticipates having a fabric supplier make a first purchase of ginned cotton in mid-2019. Timberland has also helped to secure interest from the skate and lifestyle brand Vans and outdoor clothing company Patagonia to help ensure a receptive market and increase the project's potential scale. The SFA aims over the next five years to have 14,000 farms growing organic cotton, with an estimated annual output of around 10 million pounds weight for export.

To maintain food security, SFA farmers will be restricted to using only half their land for cotton. The 40 per cent or more increase in crop yield that is expected when farmers are newly introduced to the SFA will offset any impact on food production due to cotton growing. Also, since cotton only takes six months to mature, farmers can plant an additional food crop each year on the cotton half of their land.

And because the basic SFA tree-currency model remains intact—that is, farmers working in nurseries to grow, transplant, and look after trees to earn cotton and food crop seeds, tools, and training—the SFA estimates that the farmers will plant an additional 25 million trees during those five years.

Transitioning SFA to a Business

The original goal of the SFA was to plant trees. It created an agricultural services arm to incentivize farmers to plant those trees. Then it added community services in exchange for tree planting. Finally, it introduced two high-value export crops, moringa and cotton, with inputs still earned by planting trees. While tree-planting has remained a constant, the stakes are now much higher than when the organization began. The whole operation was getting too big to manage as an NGO and so, in 2018, the SFA decided to transform itself into a socially minded business.

The SFA will create a new for-profit company in which the SFA and farmer cooperatives will be minority shareholders. Over the course of the first five years, the non-profit SFA will work alongside the new for-profit company called *Haiti Rekòt*, which translates as Haiti Harvest. During these five years a blend of grants and capital investment will support the combined operation. At the end of five years of blended operation and blended funding, Haiti Rekòt will take over the entire operation and will implement all agricultural and community services entirely from profits and without the need for any further grant funding. It is important to note that the business for the for-profit entity and model is based on commercial prices for cotton and other crops, with no subsidies.

Supply Chains, Redefined

The transition from a grant-based model to that of a financially viable supply chain demands new approaches and more robust data management. The classic definition of an agricultural supply chain is that each step of a product from the farm to the end-consumer is tracked and measured to improve efficiency and manage overall costs. Haiti Rekòt has revised this definition by adding the tracking and measuring of social and environmental impacts.

Initially this new model of a supply chain will focus on cotton and how the growing, selling, and processing of organic cotton can be tracked and measured based on:

i. How it contributes to *smallholder resiliency*
ii. Its effect on *food security*
iii. How it helps in *combating climate change*
iv. How it *supports women's empowerment.*

Supply chains require data-tracking to manage efficiency and costs. And if a supply chain attempts to incorporate the measurable impact of an agricultural product on smallholder resiliency, food security, climate change, and women's empowerment, it needs to determine baseline data, track changes, and quantify that impact.

At the same time, smallholder farmers themselves need access to data. Less than 10 per cent of the farmers in Haiti could tell you what their input costs are, what their sales were last season, or what their net profit is for any given year. Yet they know if their family is well fed, if their household is secure, and if their children are in school in a country where there is almost no state education and most have to pay for schooling, starting in grade one. But to run their farms at maximum efficiency and profitability, farmers need access to better data.

When the SFA was in the early stages of exploring data management, Timberland asked if it was possible to combine the farmer and supply chain needs with the company's interest in using data to improve the efficiency and transparency of the organic cotton.

This meant that the SFA was looking at very simple data needs at the farmer-end and increasingly complex data needs further along the supply chain towards Timberland and its consumers. This seemed a daunting task until a very simple and obvious approach emerged that was, at the same time, profoundly disruptive.

To help create a data system that incorporates what seems to be very disparate goals and modes of operation, the SFA has put together a team that includes Timberland along with two expert organizations—the Better Sourcing Program and RCS Global—that have pioneered the real-time capture and reporting of quality data from small-scale miners. Into this mix, the team added being 'blockchain ready' to determine how to potentially incorporate this, or a similar form of a secure digital ledger.

The data system exploration began by engaging seven graduate students from Columbia University's School of International and Public Affairs, through what they call their Capstone Project. These students canvassed the world to identify every data-management system that is specifically designed—or could be adapted—for use by smallholder farmers and could also accommodate the more complex needs of a supply chain that included blockchain technology or something similar.

After studying forty-four possible systems, the one that showed the most promise was an e-voucher system developed by the Food and Agriculture Organization (FAO) in Mozambique. This is based on each farmer having a unique digital ID that is biometrically accessed rather than requiring a password—an important factor for a sector of the population with historically low levels of literacy.

This was the only system that had been designed with an understanding of the farmers' needs. All the others appeared to have been conceived at a meta-level and then applied down the supply chain until at last reaching smallholder farmers. The designs were too complicated, too expensive, or were incapable of being modified to meet real needs. The team also found that none of the systems was ready to incorporate blockchain properly or efficiently.

These insights led to the next realization that, when it comes to designing a data-management system that can accommodate both smallholder farmers and global corporations, the complexity involved is directly related to the starting point for the design. If you begin at the meta level and work backwards, the complexity and problems seem to increase as you get closer to the farmers. But if you start with the farmers and work your way up, you can begin with something as simple as paper records and Excel spreadsheets and be ready to add anything up to the level of blockchain. The key is to design a data-management system that is both simple and easy to use, and then gradually add layers of complexity as the basic data gets combined in different ways.

In the spring of 2018 the SFA tested an initial beta version of its farmer-level data system that is based on Excel spreadsheets. By mid 2019 the SFA will have completed the technical specifications necessary for a programme developer to design a new unified data-management system that is blockchain-ready. This will be followed with a pilot test focused on organic cotton farming in Haiti.

Prognosis

The implications of blockchain type data tracking are compelling for retailers such as Timberland that imagine a time when consumers can scan a code on a product hang tag to access information about which farmer grew the cotton and where. What organic protocols were involved in growing the cotton? What impact did it have on the farmer and his or her family? How did growing that cotton affect the environment and food security? How did the community benefit? What was the impact on women farmers?

Timberland believes that customers will increasingly want this kind of transparency in the supply chain that brought them a given product and that this information can help inspire people to make more responsible buying decisions.

Currently some 100 million smallholder farms produce 75 per cent of the world's cotton. Adjust the lens to include any kind of crop and the final count is 500 million smallholder farms throughout the developing world. Add up the people who live and work on those farms and that translates to 2.5 billion individuals, which is a third of all humanity. Simply put, with numbers like that, data-driven smallholder supply chains have the potential to change the world.

24
Dell
The Business Case for a Sustainable Supply Chain

Louise Koch, Stephen Roberts, and Justine Esta Ellis

Introduction

Dell is one of the world's largest computer manufacturers and technology companies. The company sells a wide range of IT hardware, software products, and services for enterprise, government, small business, and consumer markets.[1] As a privately held company, Dell has the freedom to pursue a longer time horizon and to commit to changing how it uses its resources. The principle of efficiency is central to the Dell business model and informs the company's approach to resources, sourcing, and waste management.

Pain Points in the Ecosystem

Dell's commitment to efficiency has prompted the company to take on the timely challenge of improving e-waste disposal throughout its business.

E-waste, that is, discarded electrical and electronic equipment, is the world's fastest-growing waste stream.[2] Rapid technology innovation and ever-shortening product lifespans are contributing to the increase of e-waste.[3] According to a United Nations' University report, the amount of global e-waste reached 41.8 million tonnes in 2014.[4] To compound matters, e-waste has a low overall recycling rate, which means that unwanted equipment remains unused.

 DOI: 10.1093/oso/9780198870708.003.0024

Responsible e-waste disposal is not only important from an environmental perspective, but also makes good economic sense.[5] Vast amounts of gold, for example, exit the economy due to low recycling rates, but increasingly there is an opportunity to recapture that value, as a tonne of computer motherboards contains more gold in it than a tonne of gold ore. In terms of scale, the material value of global e-waste was estimated to be €48 billion in 2014 alone.[6] This underutilized resource has a vast 'untapped potential to create a more sustainable, efficient product ecosystem'.[7]

The circular economy takes the traditional, linear model of 'take, make, and dispose'—which moves products from design to factory to consumer to landfill—and bends it into a more efficient closed-loop ecosystem. Unwanted used electronics can be taken back for refurbishment and then resold on the secondary market. Products beyond repair, or those that are no longer economical to repair, are recycled to allow for precious and scarce materials to be recovered. Recycled content can either be incorporated into the design and manufacturing of new products or sold for others to use.

Research shows that approximately 30 per cent of consumers have technology products lying around the house unused, and half of consumers are unsure about what to do with their old electronics.[8] According to Dell, similar situations exist with businesses warehousing old equipment. Take-back options make it easy for a wide variety of customers to dispose of their old electronic products in a responsible manner. This measure ensures that unwanted electronics get reused or, if at the end of life, properly recycled.

Plastic is one of the most useful and important materials in modern society. It is popular in computers due to its durability, ease of fabrication into complex shapes, and electrical insulation qualities.[9] However, plastic recycling remains challenging and, as a result, the material constitutes a major contributor to landfills and to nonpoint source pollution—pollution from many different sources. The production of traditional plastics also uses a substantial amount of fossil fuels. Manufacturing plastics from fuel is resource intensive, requires large amounts of energy, and releases relatively high levels of CO_2 emissions in the process. Recent research has shown that our current use of plastics will become unsustainable if we do not take steps to improve recycling and reduce plastics' usage.

Using secondary, recycled plastic as feedstock for new computers presents one possible solution. With the fast pace of innovation and product upgrades in the ICT sector, recycled content can reduce the environmental toll of manufacturing with virgin materials. The circular economy and the development of secondary raw material markets are high on the European agenda. Nevertheless, it remains challenging to find a sufficient supply of high-quality post-consumer recycled plastics that meets the technical, economic, and aesthetic requirements of ICT products manufacturers.[10]

Business Strategy

In response, Dell is taking steps towards creating a 'circular' supply chain (see also Interface, Chapter 25). In addition to environmental concerns, the increased volatility in commodities and growing pressure on resources have alerted Dell to the business necessity of rethinking materials and energy use.[11] In 2013, Dell committed to putting a total of 50 million pounds weight of recycled materials back into its products by 2020. The company reached this goal at the beginning of 2017 and is continuing to scale its efforts.

For Dell, sourcing post-consumer recycled plastics from the market and building a new, stable closed-loop supply chain for plastics from used electronics collected through take-back programmes present viable and affordable alternatives to using virgin materials. Rather than focusing exclusively on individual challenges, Dell has taken steps to approach their supply chain from a broader, systemic perspective. Most recently, this has included expanding its efforts to also address precious metals, such as gold. Jennifer Allison, director of supply chain sustainability at Dell, summarizes the company's current business strategy:

> We're talking about systems—not just products, programmes, or initiatives. Looking at the whole system is when change begins to make a significant difference. Technology is a great tool for measuring and

analysing systems, understanding processes, and identifying inefficiencies.[12]

In this way, Dell takes a whole ecosystem view of its product life cycles. This approach is transforming the design of products and services. Dell's life-cycle approach aims to keep viable products and parts in circulation for longer periods of time. It also harnesses global efforts to reuse, refurbish, and resell products and parts to extend their lifetimes and to recycle them at the end of life.

Product design emphasizes ease of repair and recyclability from the beginning. Dell also looks continuously for ways to incorporate sustainable materials, such as recycled plastic and reclaimed carbon fibre, into products and packaging.[13]

The Take-Back Programme

Dell has the world's largest electronics take-back programme, which spans more than seventy-five countries and territories. The programme has recovered approximately 800,000 tonnes of electronics since 2008. For commercial customers, Dell offers a full-spectrum of logistics and disposal capabilities via the Asset Resale and Recycling Service. Current capabilities include data security, on-site shredding, recycling, and full traceability reporting. Dell also makes it easy for individual consumers to recycle by partnering with freight companies to provide free mail-back recycling of Dell-branded equipment. In many countries, the programme will even pick up used equipment from a customer's home.[14]

Another programme designed to make the recovery of obsolete electronics easier and more accessible is the Dell Reconnect Partnership with Goodwill, a not-for-profit organization committed to helping people become independent through education and training. The Reconnect Programme allows people to drop off any brand of used electronics to more than two thousand participating Goodwill locations across the United States. Dell Reconnect accepts any brand of computer equipment in any condition from consumers and provides free recycling services.

Dell returns all proceeds to Goodwill in order to help support Goodwill's mission of putting people to work.[15] By participating in this initiative, customers simultaneously help protect the environment, benefit the community, and receive a receipt for tax purposes. In this way, the programme helps both the customers and the business.

The donated equipment has value as a whole system, as parts, and sometimes as raw materials such as metals, plastics, and glass.[16] If the equipment can be refurbished, Goodwill sells it. If not, the end-of-life product is sent to Wistron, one of Dell's recycling partners, for asset recovery in the United States. Metals such as tin, gold,[17] and tungsten are re-sold in the commodities market. To complete the closed loop, plastics are sorted and shipped to China, turned into pellets, and mixed with virgin plastics for use in new Dell products.[18]

Closed-Loop Recycled Plastic Supply Chain

Dell's 2020 'Legacy of Good' sustainability plan set the goal of incorporating 50 million pounds weight of post-consumer recycled-content plastics and other sustainable materials into Dell products by 2020.[19] Dell met this target ahead of schedule in early 2017.

It started with the launch of Dell's closed-loop recycled plastics supply chain in 2014. Since then, the company has used more than 9,750 tonnes of closed-loop plastics in over 125 products. These products include flat-panel monitors, desktops, and all-in-one computers.

Run in conjunction with various supply chain partners, the programme consists of collecting, recycling, and using e-waste to make new Dell products.[20] It begins with sorting plastics out of the various take-back streams, further processing them, and then sending them to a manufacturing partner in Asia. The plastics are then melted down and moulded into new parts and computer components, thereby creating a closed-loop system. The whole process—from the time the equipment is received for recycling to the time the plastics are back in a customer's hands as part of a new product—takes just under six months. The closed-loop system also provides businesses with a price more stable than the cost of virgin materials, which fluctuates with the price of oil. It also reduces the company's dependence on those environmentally costly virgin materials. Furthermore, by reusing plastics already in circulation, Dell cuts down on e-waste, reduces carbon emissions, and helps drive a circular economy for IT. The closed-loop process yields an 11 per cent lower carbon footprint than a process using virgin materials,[21] and creates products that are better for the environment, which is increasingly what Dell customers demand.[22] Dell was also the first PC manufacturer (January 2018) to use recycled gold from e-waste in its products. Working with the data analyst TruCost, it found that this closed-loop process can cause 99 per cent less environmental damage and avoid $1.6 million in natural capital costs per kilogram processed (US$3.68 million for the pilot project alone) when compared to gold mining. The same study showed closed-loop process can avoid 41 times the social impacts of gold mining.

Dell's leadership in recovering and reusing plastic from used computers constitutes an important step in moving the larger electronics industry towards a circular economy. Louise Koch, corporate sustainability director in EMEA for Dell, describes the impetus for initiating a closed-loop system:

> Dell's programme is driven by both an effort to improve efficiency—a principle that goes back to its founding ethos and business model—as well as a commitment to reducing environmental impact.[23]

The use of closed-loop plastics may create a demand for plastic from used computers and thereby increase the level of plastic recycling from electronics. This, in turn, generates new jobs and opportunities for those in the nascent industry, all while staying true to Dell's founding principles.

Challenges in Moving to a Closed-Loop Recycling System

In moving from the traditional take–make–dispose linear supply chain to a circular supply chain, Dell has had to overcome a number of hurdles.

One of the biggest challenges that Dell faced with the closed-loop recycling was identifying which types of plastic can be incorporated back into new products. As Scott O'Connell, director of environmental affairs for Dell, puts it, 'When dealing with plastics, getting the properties equivalent or better to virgin materials isn't easy... But this is a challenge we've been able to overcome with engineering know-how.'[24] Dell worked with partners to test different approaches. Testing revealed that, due to mechanical and aesthetic considerations, a blend of recycled-content with virgin plastic produces the best outcomes.

Another challenge involves establishing a reliable closed-loop supply chain. As O'Connell describes, 'We had to make sure that we had sufficient volume of product coming in to be able to yield enough plastics to put into a mainstream Dell product.'[25] Supply of products and plastic derives from Dell's own sources, which adds a greater degree of insight and security. However, for the closed-loop recycling to work and scale, Dell needs security of supply, which can be difficult to attain with fluctuating numbers of products collected through take-back. Shrinking form factors—the fact that there is less plastic per item recycled as electronics become smaller—further complicate the situation. Hence Dell needs to continue to drive increasing participation in take-back programmes, while at the same time exploring other means of acquiring recycled-content materials.

Transporting materials poses an additional challenge. Dell customers are all over the world, which means that take-back initiatives must accommodate the global scale. While Dell has a small closed-loop plastics supply chain in Europe already and is exploring ways to scale in other geographies, materials need to be collected in sufficiently large amounts to make shipping to a centralized processor worth the economic and environmental costs. This involves logistics, regulations, and other considerations. In some cases, even the definition of the material being moved can affect the viability of closed-loop efforts: is recycled plastic labelled as waste or a raw material, for example?

The final challenge for Dell is to demonstrate the benefits of closed-loop recycling to customers. Ultimately, the products look and perform exactly the same as those made from virgin materials. Dell must communicate the value proposition to customers by highlighting the amount of recycled content in the final product, the closed-loop nature of the materials, and the benefits to the customers' own sustainability goals.

Performance

Since 2008, Dell has taken back more than 1.76 billion pounds (nearly 800,000 tonnes) of used electronics and since mid-2014, when Dell launched the closed-loop plastic recycling programme, it has created nearly 5,000 tonnes of plastics from recycled computer parts. Dell has saved more than $1.8 million from this process, and the carbon footprint of circular plastics is 11 per cent smaller than that associated with the manufacture of virgin plastics. Dell now uses circular plastics in approximately 125 products across millions of units globally.

Together with TruCost, Dell has completed an evaluation to understand the gains from moving away from virgin plastics. One of the most useful ways for companies to assess the risks associated with new initiatives is to quantify the environmental impacts generated by their activities—internal operations, upstream supply chain, and downstream product use and disposal—and then convert those impacts into monetary values.[26] The monetary value helps identify the value not captured in traditional financial markets and incorporates these considerations into decision-making.[27]

Findings showed that Dell's closed-loop plastic has a 44 per cent ($1.3 million annually) greater environmental benefit than virgin ABS plastic.[28] In particular, increased computer recycling lessened environmental impacts. The research found that recovering and recycling the used plastics from computers minimized 'human health and ecotoxicity impacts' and reduced the overall emission of hazardous substances.[29]

Dell has also begun to incorporate social impact metrics into its valuation framework.[30] Emergent strategies such as analysing activities for their use of social and human capital are likely to be an area for further refinement and application in the future.[31] At present, Dell is combining both environmental and social impact metrics into its process in order to help tackle the challenge of responsible e-waste disposal.

Prognosis

- On a global scale, there is still huge potential to scale up circular resource streams in the IT sector and beyond. Only 10 per cent of the plastics produced today are recovered—and more than 50 per cent end up in landfills.
- Dell has increased the use of recycled materials (both closed-loop and traditional post-consumer recycled materials) in new products and plans to continue to scale the programme.
- As Dell continues to scale the current programme, it will look to expand into reclaiming and reusing other materials. Dell has already had success with using reclaimed carbon fibre for products and is currently using recycled ocean plastics ink made from captured diesel emissions for packaging.
- Dell will also look at how ocean plastics or other solutions can be used with products.
- Dell will continue to measure social impact using the same methodology, updating models for collection totals to follow form-factor trends. It will report progress annually, building on this total toward a cumulative 2 billion pounds by 2020.[32]
- Dell continues to lead conversations with governments and industry partners about recycling and circular loops on a global scale. Dell is open to innovative collaborations with even more customers, partners, and governments in the coming years. Dell sees particular opportunities in creating partnerships in developing countries to strengthen this ecosystem.

Dell's take-back programme presents a compelling example of the potential of circular economy and closed-loop systems to contribute to responsible, mutual business practices. Looking towards the future, creating closed-loop recycling programmes in developing countries represents a new frontier. Recycling products in the countries from which they are recovered brings skilled jobs, creates industry, and strengthens the local economy.[33] Using its proven abilities to leverage partnerships and government relationships to create the infrastructure needed for new programmes, Dell can continue driving a culture of recycling in communities around the world.[34] As Dell's programme example highlights, collaborative approaches have the potential to create both financial and environmental savings for corporations and customers on a global scale.

Notes

1. 'Dell Inc. at a Glance,' Company Profile, Vault.com, http://www.vault.com/company-profiles/computer-hardware/dell-inc/company-overview.
2. Center for Security Studies, http://isnblog.ethz.ch.
3. Baldé, C.P., Forti V., Gray, V., Kuehr, R., Stegmann, P. The Global E-waste Monitor – 2017, United Nations University (UNU), International Telecommunication Union (ITU) & International Solid Waste Association (ISWA), Bonn/Geneva/Vienna.
4. Rubin (2015).
5. Kitsara (2014).
6. Baldé et al. (date).
7. Anya Khalamayzer.(2017) "8 Ripple Effects of the Circular Economy in 2017", Greenbiz, https://www.greenbiz.com/article/8-ripple-effects-circular-economy-2017.
8. 'Switched on to Value,' WRAP Report, November 2014, http://www.wrap.org.uk/sites/files/wrap/Switched%20on%20to%20Value%2012%202014.pdf.
9. 'Plastics: Key Materials for Innovation and Productivity in Major Appliances,' American Plastics Council, http://infohouse.p2ric.org/ref/11/10437.pdf.
10. 'Best Practices in Recycled Plastic,' *DigitalEurope*, August 2016, http://www.digitaleurope.org/DesktopModules/Bring2mind/DMX/Download.aspx?Command=CoreDownload&EntryId=2276&language=en-US&PortalId=0&TabId=353.
11. 'Best Practices in Recycled Plastic,' *DigitalEurope*.
12. 'Full Circle', Institute for Supply Management, October 2016—Lisa Arnseth interview with Jennifer Allison.
13. 'Dell on the Circular Economy', March 2016, http://i.dell.com/sites/content/corporate/corp-comm/en/Documents/circular-economy-0316.pdf.
14. 'Dell Recycling,' Dell Inc., http://www.dell.com/learn/us/en/uscorp1/dell-environment-recycling.
15. 'About Us,' Goodwill Industries International, Inc., http://www.goodwill.org/about-us/.
16. 'Dell Reconnect—How It Works', Dell Inc., http://www.dell.com/learn/us/en/uscorp1/corp-comm/how-it-works-reconnect.
17. www.dell.com/gold.

18. Hower (2015).
19. 'Best Practices in Recycled Plastic,' *DigitalEurope*.
20. Hower (2015).
21. 'Dell 2020 Legacy of Good Plan', Dell Inc., http://i.dell.com/sites/doccontent/corporate/corp-comm/en/Documents/2020-plan.pdf.
22. 'Dell's Closed-Loop Recycling Process', Dell Inc., https://www.google.co.uk/url?sa=t&rct=j&q=&esrc=s&source=web&cd=2&cad=rja&uact=8&ved=0ahUKEwjdkPqots7TAhXhKsAKHde7AF0QFggoMAE&url=http%3A%2F%2Fi.dell.com%2Fsites%2Fdoccontent%2Fcorporate%2Fsecure%2Fen%2FDocuments%2FClosed-LoopRecyclingfull.pdf&usg=AFQjCNHzBL-F4ooKUkKnDSbgyHG8CLRzQ&sig2=bKIXDKjRA1YoWSQgh4H5yg.
23. Louise Koch (Corporate Sustainability Lead for Europe, Middle East and Africa), personal communication.
24. Scott O'Connell (Dell, Director of Environmental Affairs), interviewed by Mike Hower (Hower 2015)
25. Ibid.
26. Dell, Dell Inc., http://www.dell.com/en-us/.
27. Ibid.
28. 'Valuing the Net Benefit of Dell's More Sustainable Plastic Use at an Industry-Wide Scale', Trucost, September 2015, http://i.dell.com/sites/content/corporate/corp-comm/en/Documents/circular-economy-net-benefits.pdf.
29. 'Valuing the Net Benefit of Dell's More Sustainable Plastic Use at an Industry-Wide Scale', Trucost, September 2015, http://i.dell.com/sites/content/corporate/corp-comm/en/Documents/circular-economy-net-benefits.pdf.
30. Ibid.
31. Ibid.
32. 'Dell 2020 Legacy of Good Plan,' Dell Inc., http://i.dell.com/sites/doccontent/corporate/corp-comm/en/Documents/2020-plan.pdf
33. Ibid.
34. Ibid.

25

Interface

Turning an Environmental Problem into a Business Opportunity

Jon Khoo, Miriam Turner, and Justine Esta Ellis

Introduction

Since it first opened its doors in 1973, Interface has grown into a billion-dollar corporation and the world's largest manufacturer of commercial carpet tiles.[1] Headquartered in Atlanta, Georgia, it has offices throughout the United States, Canada, Europe, and Asia-Pacific. It has sales in 110 countries and manufacturing facilities on four continents. Interface focuses primarily on business-to-business sales to commercial, institutional, and residential markets.

Mission Zero—the company's promise to eliminate any negative impact it has on the environment by the year 2020—guides Interface's business strategy.[2]

Interface pursues sustainability goals without sacrificing its business objectives. Like Dell (Chapter 23), its ambition is to shift from a linear model to a circular economic model. The linear 'take–make–dispose' economic model relies on large quantities of cheap, easily accessible materials and energy.[3] By contrast, a circular model, which is restorative and regenerative by design, aims to keep materials at their highest utility and value at all times.[4] Through the example of the Net-Works initiative, which connects Interface's yarn manufacturer with a new source of

Jon Khoo, Miriam Turner, and Justine Esta Ellis, Interface: Turning an Environmental Problem into a Business Opportunity In *Putting Purpose Into Practice: The Economics of Mutuality.* Edited by: Colin Mayer and Bruno Roche, Oxford University Press (2021). DOI: 10.1093/oso/9780198870708.003.0025

discarded nylon to re-use, this case study highlights the potential of circular economic models in advancing sustainability and business goals.

Pain Points in the Ecosystem

Nylon yarn production is a key source of environmental impact in carpet manufacturer supply chains. The manufacture of yarn is energy-intensive and uses high-impact, oil-based virgin materials. A life-cycle approach to understanding yarn's impact shows that the environmental footprint of carpeting arises primarily from the point at which raw materials are extracted and processed. In fact, an estimated 68 per cent of the total impact is created at the raw materials stage.[5] Therefore, to reduce its environmental impact and cut its dependency on oil, Interface needed to find diverse ways of sourcing raw materials.

One potential source of material for yarn was discovered to be discarded fishing nets. Fishermen in developing countries often discard their nets on beaches or in the sea, where the nets may remain for centuries. According to the organization World Animal Protection (formerly the World Society for the Protection of Animals), more than 640,000 tonnes of fishing gear, including nylon nets, is dumped into oceans every year, according to a UN Food and Agriculture Organisation study in 2009. This is damaging both to marine life and to communities whose livelihoods are heavily dependent on fishing. Old fishing nets do not break down easily, and these nets can cause what is known as 'ghost fishing', when unattended nets trap and kill fish and no one benefits from the catch. They also cause problems for divers and other harbour users. According to the United Nations Environment Programme, lost and abandoned fishing gear makes up 10 per cent of all marine litter.

Rather than allowing these tonnes of fishing gear to remain abandoned in the oceans, Interface saw an opportunity to work with its yarn manufacturer, Aquafil, to repurpose it and use it as the building blocks to make carpets. The collection of discarded nets serves an additional social purpose: it complements and strengthens local governments' solid waste management programmes.[6]

Moreover, using recycled content in its products has helped Interface respond to the growing market demand for sustainable materials in the building and interior design industry.

According to the International Energy Agency, buildings are responsible for over one third of the world's greenhouse gas emissions. Selecting sustainable materials has therefore become an important strategy to help interior designers and architects meet both their clients' and their own sustainability goals. Indeed, the growth in demand for sustainable materials is such that companies that do not shift to increasingly sustainable business models may soon be pushed out of the market and become uncompetitive. Interface sees its products as an important way to help projects achieve green building certification such as BREEAM, DGNB, HQE, and LEED.

Business and Programme Strategy

As part of its Mission Zero goal, Interface is committed to seeking to use using only recycled or bio-based materials by 2020.

In 2012, Interface joined forces with the Zoological Society of London (ZSL) and Aquafil to create the Net-Works programme, a collaborative effort that addresses the growing problem of discarded fishing nets in some of the world's poorest coastal regions and contributes to achieving Interface's targets for recycled materials.[7] The programme also aligned with ZSL's goals of developing a new model of community-based conservation: one that would bring immediate benefits to local people and break the traditional cycle of donor dependency, which entails relying on external donations to fund conservation work.[8]

Working with local communities in the Philippines and Cameroon, Net-Works incentivizes people to gather and sell discarded fishing nets that litter beaches, pollute the ocean, and threaten marine life. The fishermen who collect the nets are typically living in hardship and are confronted by declining fish stocks. They have few opportunities to break the cycle of poverty and escape environmental degradation.[9] The nets are cleaned, bundled, and compressed, ready to be shipped to yarn supplier Aquafil. Aquafil then uses its regeneration technology to turn the nets into 100 per cent recycled nylon yarn, called ECONYL, which can be used in carpet manufacturing and fashion. Interface buys its nylon from Aquafil at the market rate.

Interface has worked closely with ZSL, Aquafil, and communities on the technical details of the Net-Works project. An example of this cooperation is the development of the baling machine, which is used to compress the gathered nets. As Jon Khoo of Interface explains:

> It was co-designed by Interface engineers, ZSL's conservation team, and local fabricators; refined following local community feedback; and then turned into a sharable blueprint by Interface's design team. It's now being used to successfully bale nets in two continents and is a tangible example of teamwork in action.[10]

The nets are sold to Net-Works for around 14 pesos a kilogramme (kg), which provides supplemental income to the fishing communities.[11] The programme takes a small fee and sells the nets to Aquafil. For every 2.5 kg of nets collected, a family can purchase one kg of rice—this translates into approximately 4,800 extra meals per village annually on the tables of poor families, whose typical monthly household income totals less than $195.[12] By 2018, residents of the Philippines and Cameroon had collected over 208 tonnes of discarded fishing nets. The programme has seen participants earn supplemental income equivalent to over 629,800 additional meals.[13]

Net-Works operates as a social enterprise, with the proceeds of the net sales covering the administration and running costs. The remainder goes to community banks as savings. Community banks, which are at the heart of the Net-Works model, enable local people to save money and take out small loans to invest in education or in new enterprises. The banks also create 'environment funds' through which community members pool a portion of their savings to fund local conservation projects; these offerings enable communities to come together and determine where these funds are allocated.[14] Since 2012, more than 97 community banks have been established, which have supported at least 2,200 families in gaining access to finance.[15]

Performance

The Net-Works programme generates value for Interface, provides a new source of nylon for Aquafil, and creates income for the participating communities. At the same time, it helps reduce the use of non-renewable resources and benefits the marine environment. The project hits a triple bottom line of being good for people, planet, and profit.

In turning these abandoned fishing nets into a valuable resource, Net-Works helps Interface reduce energy use in its supply chain. Aquafil's nylon regeneration technology and use of fishing nets is more energy-efficient, waste-reducing, and better in relation to CO_2 emissions than using virgin materials. By manufacturing yarn from recycled nylon, Interface's supplier Aquafil generates substantial environmental and financial savings. In 2013, it reported that 12,600 tonnes of waste were eliminated, 70,000 barrels of oil saved, 42,000 tons of CO_2 avoided and 865,000 GJoules of energy saved. More broadly, by buying Aquafil's ECONYL yarn, Interface is using its market power to encourage the production of more sustainable materials and manufacturing processes that reduce energy use, waste, and CO_2 emissions. Net-Works contributes to this effort to use more sustainable materials, while also seeking social benefits for fishing communities.

For Interface, the programme brings a number of distinct benefits. Carpets made of recycled nets help to capitalize on the growing demand for green and sustainable interior design in the commercial marketplace. Net-Works also helps to strengthen Interface's relationships with its business customers by providing a platform for both Interface and its customers to share sustainability goals. In some cases, customers are potential future partners for Net-Works in the finance, manufacturing, or retail industries.

In addition, Net-Works has boosted sales and brand reputation. As an example, Interface has won praise for the initiative from the United States Department of State. Net-Works was also featured in *The Economist* and at the Sustainable Brands conference. In 2015, Interface was able to connect Net-Works directly to over $23.5 million of sales; this is based on an investment of less than $1 million. In a business-to-business market, Net-Works has been popular with customers. The company's focus has distinguished Interface from competitors and has allowed buyers to align their purchase decision with their own sustainability goals and vision. According to a survey of Interface's sales team, 83 per cent said that Net-Works had helped initiate or strengthen their relationships with customers. Jon Khoo commented:

> Net-Works has been a great differentiator for us and has been very popular with our customers. There's a growing realization that social and environmental sustainability are intertwined. As companies look to see where they can contribute to the UN Sustainable Development Goals, we have an example to share of a project that combines tackling poverty and empowering communities, with protecting the ocean and taking climate action.[16]

As Khoo's remarks indicate, pursuing sustainability goals has proven successful for building the brand. Based on interviews with participants, Interface has found that Net-Works has inspired local communities to take genuine ownership of their environments. The programme has become a great source of community pride.

Since its establishment in 2012, Net-Works has reached forty communities in the Philippines and Cameroon. Over 208 tonnes of waste nets have been collected for recycling.[17] Through the programme, 2,200 families have received access to finance through community banks and 64,000 people have benefited from a healthier environment.[18]

In addition to tackling the issue of ghost nets, Net-Works provides a platform for ZSL to engage directly with communities. ZSL helps communities implement sustainable fishing practices and protect mangrove and marine habitats. By 2020, Net-Works aims to have preserved 100,000 hectares of our oceans and coastlines through establishing marine protected areas. By nurturing the local natural environment, the communities benefit from a cleaner and healthier marine environment. The initiative also helps generate additional income via community-driven eco-tourism.

From a social perspective, Net-Works empowers local communities and creates a range of social benefits. It helps to establish and support local community banks, providing much-needed access to financial services in a convenient and local way. It brings communities together to manage and protect their marine resources. Finally, it provides opportunities for livelihood diversification. The programme enables fishermen to develop new enterprises, such as seaweed farming. This livelihood diversification will help reduce their reliance on fishing, thereby creating a more secure financial future.

Prognosis

Interface is committed to helping the Net-Works programme scale and to exploring the use of other forms of marine plastic in its products. With 640,000 tonnes of fishing gear dumped annually in the oceans, the company is unlikely to encounter challenges on the supply side.

Through the Net-Works initiative, Interface is able to supply its own supplier Aquafil with discarded fishing nets. Interface and ZSL have had to meet the same requirements as any commercial rival in their work with fishing communities. They work with the communities to collect, sort, clean, and prepare the nets. They also collaborate with local and international authorities on export and waste permits. United by a shared ambition to turn waste into opportunity, Interface, ZSL, and Aquafil created a system of mutual practices that helped further sustainability and business goals.

The project also challenged Interface and ZSL to explore new models as they began working with communities on the ground. They had to find ways to overcome practical and cultural challenges—both geographically and between the worlds of carpet and conservation. As Jon Khoo said:

> In many ways, setting up Net-Works has felt like developing a start-up. Building an inclusive business model has been something new for both Interface and ZSL. Together we've had to explore and innovate on everything from the laws on waste management, to quality control of the nets, to logistics, to different models of community engagement. It's been a real learning curve, but with a shared vision, a diverse skillset, and a strong network to reach out to, we've found answers to every problem we faced; and we will continue to do so.[19]

Looking towards the future, Interface and ZSL are seeking implementation and funding partners to expand Net-Works globally and launch in additional countries. The company views the Fair Trade model in the coffee sector, for example, as a potential model for rethinking supply chains and sourcing for industries that use nylons.

Notes

1. 'Home', *Interface, Inc.*, https://www.interface.com/US/en-US/homepage.
2. 'Mission Zero,' *Interface, Inc.*, https://www.interface.com/US/en-US/about/mission?_ga=2.91552409.225405492.1505403690-515724855.1505403690.
3. 'Circular Economy Overview', *Ellen MacArthur Foundation*, https://www.ellenmacarthurfoundation.org/circular-economy/overview/concept.
4. 'Circular Economy Overview', *Ellen MacArthur Foundation*, https://www.ellenmacarthurfoundation.org/circular-economy/overview/concept
5. Arratia (2014).
6. de Guzman (2017).
7. 'Mission Zero', *Interface, Inc.*
8. 'Home', *Net-Works*, http://net-works.com.
9. 'Mission Zero', *Interface, Inc.*
10. Jon Khoo, Innovation Partner, Interface. Personal communication with SBS team.
11. de Guzman (2017).
12. 'A Filipino family consumed 8.9kg of ordinary rice in a week in 2006', *Philippine Statistics Authority*, December 2010, https://psa.gov.ph/content/filipino-family-consumed-89-kg-ordinary-rice-week-2006-results-2006-familyincome-and.
13. 'Blue Solutions from Africa: Regional Forum on Solutions for Oceans, Coasts, and Human Well-being in Africa,' *Blue Solutions*, 14 January 2016, https://bluesolutions.info/images/Blue-Solutions-from-Africa-2016_en.pdf.
14. 'Empowering Communities by Turning Waste into Opportunity,' *Net-Works*, http://net-works.com/about-net-works/.
15. 'Blue Solutions from Africa: Regional Forum on Solutions for Oceans, Coasts, and Human Well-being in Africa,' Blue Solutions.
16. Jon Khoo, Innovation Partner, Interface. Personal communication with SBS team.
17. 'Home', *Net-Works*, http://net-works.com.
18. 'Home', *Net-Works*, http://net-works.com.
19. Jon Khoo, Innovation Partner, Interface. Personal communication with SBS team.

26

Solvay Chemical

A Tool for Identifying and Planning Sustainable Business Strategies

Justine Esta Ellis, Alastair Colin-Jones, Jean-Marie Solvay, and Michel Washer

Introduction

Established in 1863, Solvay is a global chemical company with its headquarters in Belgium. It employs approximately twenty-five thousand people and operates in sixty-one countries. Revenues in 2017 were €10.1 billion.[1] As part of its stated organizational mission, Solvay is 'committed to developing chemistry that address[es] key societal challenges'.[2] To this end, Solvay produces a range of chemical products with applications in health, agriculture, electronics, aerospace, and automotive, industrial, and consumer goods.[3] The company was founded as a family business, and family members continue to control 80 per cent of the shares of the publicly traded holding company, Solvac. With control of 30 per cent of Solvay shares, Solvac is the main shareholder in Solvay.[4]

In recent years, Solvay has increased its focus on products that provide sustainable solutions. Simply put, Solvay has begun asking fundamental questions about its own impact and ability to continue creating value into the future. Solvay's line of questioning initiated a process of redefining value creation, moving the company towards a long-term strategy of considering how non-financial, or in Solvay's term, 'extra-financial', forms of capital affect the business. How, Solvay asks, can the company

Justine Esta Ellis, Alastair Colin-Jones, Jean-Marie Solvay, and Michel Washer, Solvay Chemical: A Tool for Identifying and Planning Sustainable Business Strategies In *Putting Purpose Into Practice: The Economics of Mutuality.* Edited by: Colin Mayer and Bruno Roche, Oxford University Press (2021). DOI: 10.1093/oso/9780198870708.003.0026

do more *good* and at the same time do less *bad*? Solvay aims in this way to maximize its sustainability practices and minimize its negative environmental impact. By 'asking more from chemistry', Solvay aims to create sustainable solutions and strategies that will carry the company into the future.[5]

In examining Solvay's mutual business strategy, this case study focuses in particular on the company's Sustainable Portfolio Management (SPM) tool, which provides a means of identifying, planning, and operationalizing sustainable business strategies. As the annual report from 2016 states, Solvay takes financial and extra-financial criteria into consideration in operational management and strategy decisions.[6] This initiative helps integrate sustainability strategies holistically into Solvay's strategic decision-making.

Pain Points in the Ecosystem

Aligning with the UN Sustainable Development Goals (SDGs), Solvay is a supporter of sustainability in its daily operations and long-term strategy. It defines sustainable solutions as having 'direct, significant, and measurable social and/or environmental impacts'.[7] Meeting existing (and anticipating future) sustainability challenges has become a key priority for Solvay. Recognizing sustainability as integral rather than secondary to assessing its profit and loss, Solvay has committed to developing its Sustainable Portfolio Management tool and other means of improving product sustainability and performance.

These issues have particular salience for chemical companies looking to remain competitive in the future. Recent industry analysis suggests that the chemicals sector faces a number of critical structural challenges. According to a report by global accountancy firm PwC, demand for chemicals has fallen, with industry sales growth increasing only an 'anaemic' 2.1 per cent in 2016 as the sector faced declining industrial production and 'broad inventory rightsizing by many of its customers'.[8] With growth in the sector appearing unlikely in the coming years, the report authors urged chemical companies to explore strategies that may lead to profitable growth, such as 'value capture, digitization, and smarter portfolio management'.[9] Moreover, across the sector, there is a growing recognition that 'structural weakness in most markets and recycling and reuse, which impact the sale of virgin materials, are combining to substantially reduce demand'.[10] Faced with these challenges, chemical companies are seeking new strategies to keep their businesses competitive in the future.

New approaches, additionally, must acknowledge and take into account the finite nature of the earth's natural resources. For a chemical company, these sustainability considerations carry particular weight. As a result, gaining market share is likely to prove a crucial challenge in the coming years.[11] Future opportunities within this sector are likely to result from developing substantively different strategies from those that were effective previously. The reciprocal nature and interdependency of financial and non-financial forms of capital rest at the core of this new approach.

Solvay, accordingly, has taken a life-cycle approach to its products, looking for ways to ensure that the business is ready to tackle what it describes as the 'planetary issue of resource scarcity'.[12] By identifying and potentially getting ahead of challenges within its product ecosystem, Solvay aims to ensure the sustainability of both the earth's natural resources and its own business. Through 'anticipation, innovation, and agility', Solvay aims to foresee and respond to challenges down the line.

Business Strategy

Confronting challenges within the chemicals sector necessitates not only a change in mindset, but also a new set of skills and tools. Solvay's management aims to tackle these challenges through internal innovation. The company developed its SPM tool to help assess and map its products' strengths and weaknesses (see Figure 26.1). The tool aims to guide the company towards creating products that both provide sustainable solutions in the marketplace and reduce environmental and social risks for the company.

The tool maps all products according to their environment manufacturing footprint and its correlated risks and opportunities. It uses a

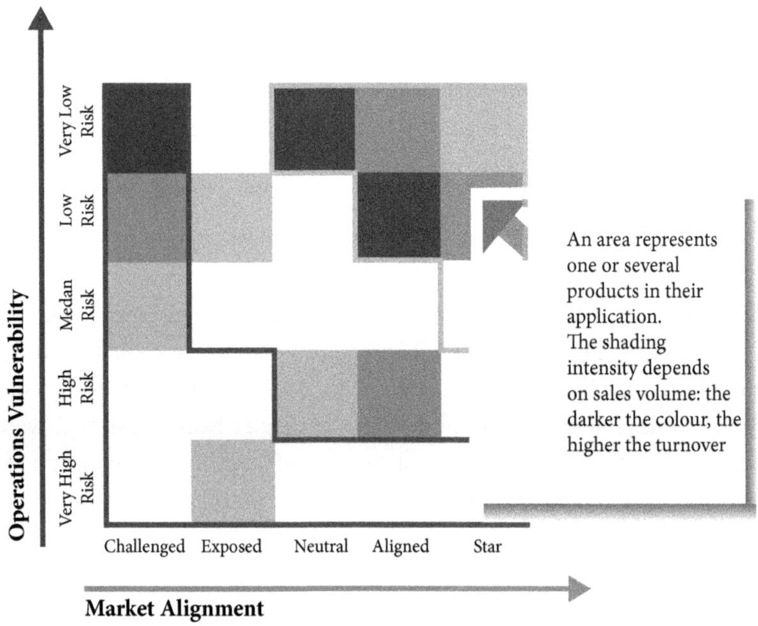

Figure 26.1. Solvay's SPM mapping
Source: Solvay, 'Sustainable Portfolio Management Guide', p. 7.

cradle-to-gate life-cycle assessment, quantifying environmental footprints and using costs, which reflect the cost to society. The total cost to society is then compared to the price of the product. These factors, specifically, help assess operations' vulnerability.

This is then set against the ways in which a product brings 'benefits or faces challenges in a market perspective'.[13] These measures focus especially on market alignment, helping to identify the extent to which 'one product in a given application is part of the sustainable development solution or part of the problem from a consumer and market perspective'.[14] It uses a questionnaire, based on a qualitative, evidence-based collection of sustainability-related market signals. All the sustainability signals assessed using the questionnaire are run through a decision tree. This defines the exact positioning of the product-application combination, or, PAC (see Figure 26.2).

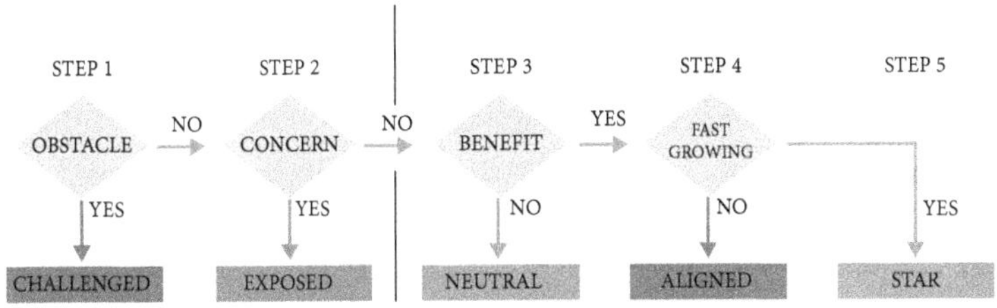

Figure 26.2. Solvay's fast-track market alignment decision tree
Source: Solvay, 'Sustainable Portfolio Management Guide', p. 11.

First Solvay looks at obstacles and concerns. Any obstacle identified will immediately rank the PAC as challenged and anything raising concern as exposed. Solvay then considers the positive signals. If Solvay finds no negative and no particularly positive impacts, the PAC is categorized as neutral. If the PAC analysed demonstrates a direct, significant, and measurable benefit to the market, which has a positive impact on at least one of the sustainability benefits assessed, it is listed as aligned. If, in addition, Solvay registers double-digit growth potential in sales forecasts, the PAC is categorized as star.[15]

SPM gives Solvay a means of assessing the risk profiles of its products and making strategic decisions accordingly. Solvay's sustainable development function manages the SPM methodology. Solvay deploys SPM in close cooperation with its business units and functions in key processes: strategy, research and innovation; capital expenditures; marketing and sales; and mergers and acquisitions. The SPM methodology is part of the Solvay Way framework and helps measure how well global business units and corporate functions have integrated sustainability into their business practices.[16]

Significantly, the SPM profile is an integral part of the strategic discussions between global business units and the Executive Committee. Mergers and acquisition projects are also evaluated using SPM to see if the investment is feasible in the light of sustainable portfolio targets. Investment decisions (capital expenditure above €10 million and acquisitions) made by the Executive Committee or the Board of Directors include a sustainability challenge that encompasses an exhaustive SPM analysis of the potential investment. All research and innovation projects are evaluated using SPM. Finally, in marketing and sales, SPM makes it possible to engage customers on fact-based sustainability topics aimed at creating value for both Solvay and the customer. These areas of mutual interest and concern include climate change action, renewable energy, recycling, and air quality.

Performance

Over the past three years, Solvay's products have experienced greater annual revenue growth rates in areas in which customers and consumers are seeking out Solvay's products to match their unmet social or environmental needs. More specifically, volume annual growth rate per SPM category showed that products in the solutions category grew by +3 per cent, whereas those in the challenges fell by a factor of 2 per cent. As a note, these calculations were based on sales of the same product, same application, and same SPM ranking over the last three years, representing 44 per cent of Group sales (out of which two-thirds came from volume growth).[17]

Prognosis

Although long-term research remains to be done, at present it appears that the SPM tool has been leading to good performance according to environmental, social, and financial metrics. Above all, SPM has become key to strategic decision-making within the company, informing merger and acquisition (M&A) strategy, decisions about investments, and improved customer engagement through marketing and sales.

Signalling its priorities, Solvay debuted its first 'integrated' annual report in 2016. This document differed from a traditional annual report by aiming to show the significance of non-financial or extra-financial forms of capital in furthering Solvay's business objectives. Rather than relying exclusively on financial metrics, Solvay has factored sustainability into an assessment of the company's overall performance. As the report demonstrates, combining various forms of capital represents a strategy that Solvay aims to showcase to the public. Financial and non-financial forms of capital combine to present a holistic picture of Solvay's business. As Solvay looks to the future, it aims to uncover strategies that will sustain the market leadership position for its products. At the same time, and relatedly, Solvay also aims to create sustainable strategies that will benefit the planet and help advance its business goals. By addressing the negative externalities within its ecosystem, Solvay aims to create a series of sustainable practices that will ensure the long-term viability and growth of its business.

Notes

1. 'Annual Integrated Report 2017', Solvay.
2. 'Home', *Solvay*, Solvay.com, https://www.solvay.com/en/index.html.
3. 'Annual Integrated Report 2016', Solvay.
4. 'Annual Integrated Report 2017', Solvay.
5. 'Annual Integrated Report 2016', Solvay.
6. 'Annual Integrated Report 2016', Solvay.
7. 'Annual Integrated Report 2016', Solvay.
8. Bebiak et al. (2017: 3).
9. Bebiak et al. (2017: 11).
10. Bebiak et al. (2017: 8).
11. Bebiak et al. (2017: 8).
12. 'Solvay', *Ellen MacArthur Foundation*, https://www.ellenmacarthurfoundation.org/about/partners/global/solvay.
13. 'Sustainable Portfolio Management Guide: Driving Long-Term Sustainable Growth', *Solvay*, 4, https://www.solvay.com/sites/g/files/srpend221/files/2018-07/Solvay-SPM-Guide.pdf.
14. 'Sustainable Portfolio Management Guide: Driving Long-Term Sustainable Growth,' *Solvay*, 7.
15. 'Sustainable Portfolio Management Guide,' *Solvay*, 10.
16. 'Annual Integrated Report 2017', *Solvay*, http://annualreports.solvay.com/2017/en/extra-financial-statements/sustainability-management/sustainable-portfolio-management.html.
17. 'Annual Integrated Report 2017,' *Solvay*, http://annualreports.solvay.com/2017/en/extra-financial-statements/business-model-and-innovation/sustainable-business-solutions.html#accordion2.

27

Z Zurich Foundation

Building the Case for Effective Insurance in Flood-Prone Areas

Helen Campbell Pickford, David Nash, and Justine Esta Ellis

Introduction

Established in Zurich, Switzerland, in 1872, Zurich is one of the world's leading insurance groups, providing insurance and services to customers in over 170 countries. Zurich's mission is to help its customers 'understand and protect themselves from risks'.

The Z Zurich Foundation contributes to sustainable social and economic development by combining Zurich's global experience and risk-management capabilities with non-profit organizations' local knowledge and development expertise.[1] It takes a long-term cooperative approach to tackling selected global challenges.[2]

The Zurich flood resilience programme is an example of how this cooperative approach can help develop new customer solutions for Zurich, initiate public policy discussions, and create value for communities worldwide.[3]

Ecosystem Pain Points

Insurance companies have observed an upward trend in weather-related insured losses due to the increase in frequency and intensity of extreme

Helen Campbell Pickford, David Nash, and Justine Esta Ellis, Z Zurich Foundation: Building the Case for Effective Insurance in Flood-Prone Areas In *Putting Purpose Into Practice: The Economics of Mutuality.* Edited by: Colin Mayer and Bruno Roche, Oxford University Press (2021).
DOI: 10.1093/oso/9780198870708.003.0027

weather events and the increasing economic cost associated with them.[4] Damage caused by natural catastrophes such as floods have quadrupled in the past thirty years.[5] As David Nash, the Foundation Manager at the Z Zurich Foundation, explains:

> Flood risk is likely to increase in the future due to a combination of socio-economic factors and anticipated increase in the frequency of extreme weather and climate events. It is a global challenge which impacts both developing and developed countries. Despite being a global issue, effective flood risk management is highly complex and there is no one-size-fits-all solution to implement universally.[6]

Extreme weather events of this kind cause large economic, social, and humanitarian losses.[7] Many developing countries are located in high-risk areas, with regular floods affecting large parts of the population. Currently, approximately 800 million people are living in flood-prone areas, of which on average about 70 million actually experience floods each year.[8]

In developing countries severe floods can put at risk past development gains by damaging the natural capital and infrastructure that people rely upon for shelter, transportation, and agriculture, undermining economic development and setting back poverty-reduction efforts. Although total economic losses from floods are higher in developed countries, both the relative economic impact and the number of fatalities are more significant in developing countries.[9] Globally, the rising costs associated with climate change effects pose serious challenges to governments in adopting efficient strategies to manage the increasing economic consequences.[10]

Governments, overseas development agencies, and philanthropic organizations are all involved with efforts to mitigate the effects of floods. However, the vast majority of investment in this area is reactive—it focuses on disaster relief rather than on pre-event planning. In fact, only 13 per cent of disaster-related funding currently targets resilience-building, while 87 per cent goes into activities after the losses have occurred.

This is where the insurance sector comes in. Insurance is a risk-transfer mechanism; transferring risk to the private sector could provide efficient and cost-effective solutions that relieve already strained public-sector budgets. However, unless you tackle the circumstances that lead to or create the risk, it can be too expensive to insure against or, in extreme situations, not worth insuring at all.

There needed to be a greater focus on flood prevention or flood resilience. As Nash describes:

> Should a flood occur, taking action beforehand which reduces the potential losses is more cost-effective than providing post-disaster relief. The more resilience that is built, the more insurance can be brought in to play its part in strengthening resilience by providing reliable and swift pre-determined financial compensation.[11]

Business Strategy

In 2013, Zurich launched a global programme to enhance flood resilience. Flood risk is the result of many factors in a dynamic, complex system. As a Zurich brief outlines, 'a system-wide approach to resilience needs to capture a range of activities, actors, and processes that are part of a resilience building system.' Therefore, in the first phase, the Zurich flood resilience programme worked in partnership with four core partners: International Federation of the Red Cross and Red Crescent Societies (IFRC), Practical Action, the International Institute for Applied Systems Analysis (IIASA), and the Wharton Business School's Risk Management and Decision Processes Centre (Wharton).

Through these partnerships, Zurich created an alliance—the Zurich Flood Resilience Alliance—which has developed processes and tools that can be applied to increase flood resilience at the community level. One such innovation to emerge from these collaborations is a flood resilience measurement framework.

By building resilience, Zurich aims to create an environment in which insurance and other risk-transfer mechanisms can help to address the problems of climate-change-induced disasters such as floods.[12] Zurich has found that it is well placed to educate communities about risk-prevention measures; and this process has helped to increase insurability. It is thus in Zurich's business interest to support public policies that reduce and make risks more predictable. Moreover, Zurich's model shows the potential of private industry to help communities bolster their resilience to flood risk.

The flood resilience programme tests solutions and ideas for replication and scale. Expertise and knowledge from Zurich contributes to these ideas and, in turn, the insights generated from the community experience can be used to refine and tailor insurance solutions and risk management processes.

Research and knowledge is also generated and refined by academic institutions in the flood resilience alliance. The insights gained allow Zurich to develop new technologies and innovations to prevent flood damage.

This interdisciplinary approach broadens the scope of current flood resilience research and offers opportunities to advance understanding of the impact of floods. The knowledge and tools generated are intended for a wider audience and will be made available in an open source format, through a portal and the development of an academy.

Performance

The Zurich programme runs interventions with communities in flood-prone areas in Mexico, Indonesia, Nepal, Peru, and Bangladesh,[13] using slightly different interventions according to the context in which they operate. For example, in Nepal, access to efficient early warning systems, alternative livelihoods, and strengthened collaboration with local decision-makers are key to enhancing resilience.[14] In Mexico, there is also a livelihoods component, but the focus remains on developing local support mechanisms within communities.

In Indonesia, the Zurich Flood Resilience Alliance has found ways to help communities in the river basin of the Bengawan Solo, the longest river on the island of Java, which frequently floods during the rainy season. The programme has proven so successful that local authorities are now using Zurich's approach to help more communities across Java.

Together with the Indonesian Red Cross, Zurich identified the communities that are most likely to benefit from its resilience approach. In the village of Tulungrejo, for example, the community has access to an emergency shelter that the government has provided. However, the shelter is too far for some people to reach. As a first step, the Zurich programme has provided funds to build a raised evacuation site nearer to the village that can accommodate several hundred people. Safe routes were created across the village to the new shelter and local volunteers were trained as first-responders to form a community-based action team, or SIBAT.

Beyond these initial steps, the Flood Resilience Alliance is developing a better early warning system in Tulungrejo and has built a command post, POSCO, that can serve as a crisis centre for emergency response teams during floods. Once established, it will be equipped with technology to provide early warning bulletins, weather reports, and other important public announcements.

To increase the impact of the measure, when not in use during floods, the community volunteers' action team (SIBAT) will conduct flood simulation exercises from the centre. As part of the programme, the Indonesian Red Cross has also introduced activities to raise community awareness, particularly in schools.

The local government in the Bojonegoro district values this volunteer approach, which has been formally endorsed by the district administration. Local administrators have already provided funds to similar projects in another village in Bojonegoro district to set up SIBATs, and are recommending that the model used in Tulungrejo be adopted and implemented in all at-risk communities in the province. District officials believe the programmes could even be adopted nationwide. The intervention has enhanced physical capital through the new evacuation site and better early warning systems. These additions have reduced the time needed to react to floods. In addition, by increasing local knowledge, complementing SIBAT's efforts to increase knowledge and capabilities on a sustainable basis, the programme also enhances human capital.[15]

The programme, moreover, has had a positive impact on Zurich's business. Internally, 93 per cent of staff are proud of Zurich's work in this area, and almost half have volunteered to be part of programme activities. In fact, Zurich has also been able to engage local brokers in the activities. Brand awareness has noticeably increased, with Zurich winning a local insurance industry award for its efforts. The work has helped engage corporate customers and their employees. Taken together, these initiatives strengthen relationships among a variety of key stakeholders.

Other outputs of the alliance have included the community-based flood resilience measurement tool, currently being deployed by Zurich's community partners in more than 110 communities on a trial basis. It is also being scientifically validated through the research partnership with Wharton and IIASA (International Institute of Applied Systems Analysis).[16] The aim is to understand what helps a community build resilience to flood disasters, and thereby identify possible resilience-building actions. This tool is used across all country programmes. This is cutting-edge applied research that will fill a gap, as there is no other measurement framework for disaster resilience available, according to UNDP.[17]

It also provides objective evidence that can influence policymakers' decisions in shaping responses to other climate-change-related risks. Demonstrating the business case for its flood resilience programme to policymakers, Zurich studies show that for every dollar spent on selected flood risk reduction measures, an average of five dollars is saved through avoided and reduced losses. Although climate change is one factor driving floods, policymakers' responses to climate change risks can help manage these impacts.

Prognosis

The topic of floods remains important to Zurich. In July 2018 they launched a second phase of the work for an additional five-year period. The core focus will be to strengthen the evidence base around the resilience measurement approach, through community programmes, and use it to push for more investment from other actors into pre-event work.

Notes

1. 'Z Zurich Foundation Annual Report 2014', Zurich Insurance Group.
2. 'Z Zurich Foundation Annual Report 2014', Zurich Insurance Group.
3. 'Z Zurich Flood Resilience Programme', *Zurich Insurance Group*, https://zurich.com/en/corporate-responsibility/creating-value-for-zurich-and-society Z Zurich Flood Resilience Programme.
4. The ClimateWise, 'Thought Leaderships Series' Issue Two, Cambridge Institute for Sustainability Leadership, 2012, http://www.cisl.cam.ac.uk/publications/publication-pdfs/climatewise-thought-leadership-series-2012-issue-t.pdf.
5. Surminski and Oramas-Dorta (2013).
6. David Nash, the Foundation Manager at the Z Zurich Foundation. Personal communication with SBS team.
7. 'Information about Zurich', *Zurich Insurance Group*, https://www.zurich.com/.
8. Fankhauser and Thomas (2016).
9. Surminski and Oramas-Dorta (2013).
10. Business Perspectives LLC., https://businessperspectives.org.
11. David Nash, the Foundation Manager at the Z Zurich Foundation. Personal communication with SBS team.
12. 'Information about Zurich', *Zurich Insurance Group*, https://www.zurich.com/.
13. Zurich North America—Insurance and Risk Management', *Zurich North America*, https://www.zurichna.com.
14. 'Information about Zurich', *Zurich Insurance Group*, https://www.zurich.com/.
15. Freiner (2016).
16. International Institute for Supplied Systems Analysis, http://www.iiasa.ac.at/.
17. Winderl (2014).

28

Divine Chocolate

Creating Sustainable Value in the Cocoa Sector through Mutual Ownership

Justine Esta Ellis, Alastair Colin-Jones, and Jamie Hartzell

Introduction

Founded in 1998 and designed as a social enterprise driven by a social mission, Divine Chocolate is a UK-based Fairtrade confectionery company that also operates in the United States. With offices in London and Washington DC, the business maintains strong partnerships with a variety of NGOs, and in 2017–18 brought in an annual revenue of £15 million.[1] Well-known companies including the Body Shop have supported Divine Chocolate and its organizational mission. Divine Chocolate has approximately twenty UK employees and twelve US employees.

The company, which began selling its chocolate bars within the UK market but now sells globally, is known for its distinctive ownership model. The Ghanaian farmer-owned co-operative Kuapa Kokoo supplies the cocoa and owns 44 per cent of the Divine Chocolate business. Crucially, the smallholder farmers, as co-owners of the business 'get a share in the distributed profits, a say in the company, and a voice in the global marketplace'.[2] This joint-ownership model between cocoa growers and retailers enables farmers to earn more for their cocoa and to see their interests reflected higher up the value chain.

Justine Esta Ellis, Alastair Colin-Jones, and Jamie Hartzell, Divine Chocolate: Creating Sustainable Value in the Cocoa Sector through Mutual Ownership In *Putting Purpose Into Practice: The Economics of Mutuality.* Edited by: Colin Mayer and Bruno Roche, Oxford University Press (2021).
DOI: 10.1093/oso/9780198870708.003.0028

Significant environmental, social, and commercial challenges face the cocoa sector. Deforestation, child labour, and low farmer incomes all threaten the world's cocoa supply. With a host of issues facing the entire sector, questions remain as to whether confectionery businesses will be equipped to address the reputational challenges and supply pressures associated with cocoa farming. Threats to the cocoa sector's long-term viability and production require multi-pronged solutions to ensure the sustainability of cocoa production.[3]

Pain Points in the Ecosystem

The significant and complex problems facing the cocoa value chain are well known. Every year, multilateral initiatives invest huge amounts of time and resources into tackling the key issues of farmer income, low productivity, price instability, child labour, and deforestation. Multi-stakeholder groups such as the World Cocoa Foundation and the International Cocoa Initiative work to promote cocoa sustainability and to protect children from the abuses of child labour.[4]

To compound matters, cocoa is grown by highly vulnerable smallholder farmers, many of whom live below the poverty line. Given their position, farmers have little or no ability to invest in their farms and to improve their livelihoods. The challenge of sustainable livelihoods persists throughout cocoa-growing communities and, in many cases, farmers receive less than 6 per cent of the price paid by consumers.[5] Cocoa-growing communities, as a result, struggle with the difficulty of boosting farmer incomes. This makes Fairtrade's decision to provide cocoa farmers with a living income all the more important.

Perhaps unsurprisingly given these myriad challenges, the next generation of potential cocoa growers do not wish to work as smallholder farmers. This lack of incentive to continue to farm represents a significant obstacle in the way of meeting the world's ever-growing demand for chocolate. Media coverage of this issue has sounded the alarm as limited supply struggles to keep pace with global demand. With the growth of consumer markets in India and China, coupled with 'the remarkable and still growing Western taste for chocolate with everything', research suggested that the world might face a 'global shortage' of cocoa by the year 2020.[6] But a cocoa glut and lower demand from China, as seen recently in 2017, in fact led to a fall in price. This inability to predict demand accurately makes it especially urgent to identify sustainable solutions across the cocoa value chain.

Naturally, confectionery businesses, many of which rely on cocoa as the primary ingredient in their products, also want to address the challenges facing the sector.[7] Divine Chocolate's ownership structure may present one model to address widespread and persistent problems within the cocoa supply chain. The social enterprise has set its business strategy to engage alternative governance and ownership models, which aim to empower the weakest in the ecosystem so that they are able to share in a greater proportion of the benefits. Divine Chocolate believes that it has developed a prototype for organizing more equitable cocoa supply chains that deliver not only better livelihoods for farmers, but also tackle problems seemingly endemic to the sector.

Business Strategy

Integral to Divine's mutual business strategy was creating the platform for the farmers themselves to be represented higher up the value chain. Divine's story begins with Kuapa Kokoo, a Ghanaian Fairtrade co-operative set up in 1993. In order to sell and distribute its cocoa the co-operative voted to set up its own Fairtrade chocolate company. With the help of Comic Relief, Twin Trading, the Body Shop, and Christian Aid, Divine Chocolate was launched in 1998 and now reaches multiple international markets.

Today, Kuapa Kokoo owns 44 per cent of Divine, with the remaining shares held by Oikocredit, Twin Trading, and three other smaller social investors. Profits are simply distributed according to shareholding and Kuapa Kokoo has full voting rights. Kuapa Kokoo is able to determine the use of the Fairtrade premium, and Divine dividends democratically align spending with its own principles at the co-op level. In terms of governance structure, two co-operative members sit on the board of Divine Chocolate and are involved in all decision-making.[8] There is also a shareholder agreement and other policies that align the interests of all shareholders. Divine's ownership model gives the cocoa farmers the opportunity to be more involved in management decision-making than a usual governance structure would allow.[9] These leadership roles and representation at the highest levels of the company ensure that smallholder farmers play a substantive and determinative role in making business decisions for Divine.

In practical terms, Divine purchases its cocoa directly from Kuapa Kokoo via Cocobod, the Ghanaian government-controlled institution that fixes the buying price for cocoa in local currency, at the guaranteed minimum Fairtrade price of $2,000 per tonne and pays an additional premium of $200 per tonne (NB at the time of writing the Fairtrade price and premium are about to be increased).[10] Divine, moreover, re-invests 2 per cent of its turnover back into its traceable supply chain, which it manages in its entirety.[11] This is in addition to the amount Kuapa Kokoo receives from cocoa sales, Fairtrade premiums, and dividends. For example, Divine has funded a series of Kuapa Kokoo radio programmes which help the co-operative reach its eighty-five thousand members, who live across a vast geographical area. Listening to the radio is very popular in Ghana, and the programme discusses cocoa news, farming techniques, pest-control issues, and democratic decision-making techniques. Divine shares are also an asset on the balance sheet of Kuapa Kokoo, which can then act as security for borrowing, such as for pre-finance, historically a big issue for farmers.

Furthermore, to advance the goal of gender equality, the enterprise has initiated several key practices; and Kuapa Kokoo helps deliver women's empowerment through training and mentoring.[12] For example, introducing quotas (two out of five farmers on the village committee have to be women) has resulted in 35 per cent female membership of the Kuapa Kokoo co-operative.[13] Moreover, the success of the co-operative ownership structure and re-investment strategies has enabled capacity-building initiatives designed to improve women's well-being, particularly in terms of education and equal access to resources. Fairtrade contributions have also helped advance community-building initiatives. Beginning in 2014, with funding from Divine, Kuapa Kokoo initiated several literacy and numeracy programmes, which help women become full participants in business activities. Nearly 70 per cent of all programme participants are female and have had little to no previous access to schooling. Building participants' confidence through training aims to help overcome barriers to positions of leadership and responsibility that many women face.[14]

In addition to leadership skills, the co-operative also offers workshops to help farmers develop alternative means of livelihood during the off-season. These aim to empower women by providing them with a steady source of income.[15] Taken together, these mutual practices ultimately help bolster women's contribution to household income and increase their ability to participate in the global marketplace. Citing the prominent role of women as a 'key ingredient' in the enterprise's success and reflecting its support of goal five (gender equality) of the UN Sustainable Development Goals (SDGs), Divine Chocolate has instituted practices and marketing strategies that affirm its commitment to women's empowerment.[16] Significantly, women hold key roles throughout the organization, from the very top to the bottom of the value chain.

Divine also helps Kuapa Kokoo to develop further its own governance structures. The farmers' co-operative is made up of the main Kuapa Kokoo Farmers Union, which comprises fifty-seven districts (each with its own committee) and 1,300 village societies. Members are able to stand for election to the village, district, and Union committees every four years. The Union also owns a Licensed Buying Company that purchases some 60,000 tonnes of cocoa from its members each year, representing around 5 per cent of the Ghanaian cocoa market. The Ghanaian cocoa industry is government-controlled, so all cocoa is sold on to the government agency Cocobod, which handles exports. Cocobod also regulates the price paid to farmers for their cocoa.

Performance

Divine Chocolate has generated over £100 million in sales since it started, and during the twelve-month period between June 2016 and June 2017, Divine bought 953 tonnes of cocoa beans from Ghana, 'all with a Fairtrade premium paid to farmers of $200 a tonne'.[17] At the same time, Kuapa Kokoo has seen its membership grow from two thousand at its start to over eighty-five thousand in 2018.[18] Additionally, the co-operative provides 5 per cent of Ghana's cocoa and, as noted previously, 35 per cent of its members are women.

The farmer-ownership model of Divine Chocolate has seen the development of self- governed services that many multinational corporations spend tens of millions each year with suppliers and NGOs to cultivate. For example, Kuapa Kokoo has its own child labour awareness programme. This initiative promotes the policy of not tolerating the worst forms of child labour, emphasizes the need for children to attend school, and educates co-operative members on ways to help their children avoid any hazards on the farm. Additionally, an outreach team is responsible for spreading news and disseminating the latest techniques and farming practice. To help ensure that a variety of voices are included in the business, there are regular meetings at village, district, regional, and national levels, as well as at Divine Chocolate's annual general meeting.

Prognosis

Divine Chocolate is not immune to the logistical and cultural challenges inherent to the cocoa supply chain. Promisingly, however, the social enterprise's mutual practices have seen success, which opens up possible avenues for expansion. As it reinvests in the local community, Divine Chocolate increases its ability to improve its operation and grow its business.

The social enterprise remains committed to its founding principles, believing that positive performance stems from cultivating social capital in the form of collective and transparent decision-making. From its start, Divine Chocolate factored community well-being, collective action, and trust into its business model.

Some may question whether the business will be able to retain its ethos of mutual practices and reach a truly transformational scale. However, others argue that the purpose of a social business is growth and profit that maximizes social impact. As a business, Divine has had significant social impact on the cocoa sector as a whole, and while growth could lead to greater social impact, growth should not be an objective if social impact would be reduced.

Notes

1. 'Annual Report 2016–2017', *Divine Chocolate.*
2. 'About Us', *Divine Chocolate*, http://www.divinechocolate.com/us/about-us.
3. Houston and Wyer (2012).
4. For additional information, see: 'Mission & Vision', *World Cocoa Foundation*, http://www.worldcocoafoundation.org/about-wcf/history-mission/; 'About Us', *International Cocoa Initiative*, http://www.cocoainitiative.org/about-ici/about-us/.
5. 'Commodity Briefing: Cocoa,' Fairtrade Foundation, April 2016, https://www.fairtrade.org.uk/wp-content/uploads/legacy/Cocoa-commodity-briefing-6May16.pdf
6. Ford et al. (2014).
7. Saldinger (2014).
8. 'The Divine Story,' *Divine Chocolate*, http://www.divinechocolate.com/uk/about-us/research-resources/divine-story.
9. Wanyama (2014).
10. 'FAQ', *Divine Chocolate*, http://www.divinechocolate.com/us/about-us/frequently-asked-questions.
11. Jamie Hartzell (chair, Divine Chocolate), personal communication with the authors, 23 April 2018.
12. Slavin and Ley (2017).
13. Slavin and Ley (2017).
14. 'Annual Report 2015–2016', *Divine Chocolate.*
15. 'Kuapa Kokoo, Ghana', *Fairtrade Foundation*, https://www.fairtrade.org.uk/Farmers-and-Workers/Cocoa/Kuapa-Kokoo.
16. Slavin and Ley (2017).
17. 'Annual Report 2015–2016', *Divine Chocolate.*
18. Slavin and Ley (2017).

29

Mondragon

Maintaining Resilience through Cooperative Strategies

Justine Esta Ellis, Alastair Colin-Jones, and Ibon Zugasti

Introduction

When the Spanish priest Father José María Arizmendiarreta started a small workers' cooperative in his local community, he can hardly have predicted that his humble venture would grow into a business of global scale. Founded in 1959, Mondragon today is a federation of industrial cooperative associations with over 260 companies and subsidiaries in thirty-five countries—although it remains close to its roots in Spain's Basque Region. Overall, the federation brings in revenues of approximately $14 billion and employs over seventy-five thousand workers worldwide in the finance, manufacturing, retail, and consultancy sectors.

Mondragon is, in its own words, 'created by and for people' and aims to generate 'wealth in society through business development and job creation'. It derives its strength both from the breadth of its activities and its emphasis on employees' professional development and technological research. The federation funds training and innovation, supporting fifteen of its own research and development centres. This investment has yielded over 460 groups of patents.

Previous research into Mondragon's structure has provided insights into the opportunities and challenges associated with operating member-owned businesses. This case, however, focuses on the relationship between mutuality and resilience in Mondragon's performance.

Resilience, defined here as 'the ability of firms to sustain employment and growth during difficult economic conditions,' is an underappreciated aspect of company performance.[1]

Pain Points in the Ecosystem

From the start, Mondragon's assessment of modern economic systems was that neither capitalism nor socialism offered the right conditions for people to thrive and for businesses to operate competitively. Mondragon concluded that social benefits ought to be inherent to competitiveness and structured its management practices accordingly. In other words, competitive financial performance would be found through purposeful investment in social and human capital. Mondragon, therefore, built its own values-driven system within a modern capitalist context on the core principles of cooperation, participation, social responsibility, and innovation. How these principles have been put into practice has evolved over decades, but Mondragon continues to offer a significant example of how business can deliver social transformation while at the same time remaining financially profitable. Above all, the Mondragon business case highlights the importance of purposeful investment in human and social capital as a safeguard against the challenges of economic crises.

From cooperatives to non-profits, social enterprises to mutual societies, social economy enterprises operate on the principle of serving their members, rather than aiming to maximize returns on investment. In other words, as the economists José Luis Monzón and Rafael Chaves describe, social economy ventures are 'organizations of people who conduct an activity with the main purpose of meeting the needs of persons rather than remunerating capitalist investors'.[2] Monzón and Chaves go on to say that the rise of the social economy 'reflect[s] the need for an economy that reconciles social, economic, and financial dimensions, that is able to create wealth, and that is not measured solely in terms of its financial capital, but also—and above all—by its social capital'.[3] This recognition of the need to take into consideration non-financial forms of capital—human, social, and natural—and the relationship between them and financial performance is at the heart of delivering mutuality.

The history of cooperatives suggests that member-owned business often thrive in times of crisis.[4] From as early as the agricultural depression of 1860s Germany to the comparatively recent collapse of the Soviet Union, cooperatives have tended to weather the worst of the economic climate. This is not, however, to suggest that cooperatives only succeed during crises. Rather, 'it is the strength built up by cooperatives during good times that helps tide them over a recession.'[5] In other words, cooperatives may have structures and practices already in place that help protect them against periods of economic hardship.

According to the International Labour Organization, cooperatives have seven interrelated features: voluntary and open membership; democratic member control; member economic participation; autonomy and independence; education, training, and information; cooperation among cooperatives; and concern for community.[6] Taken together, these features arguably help foster a sense of shared identity, ownership, and investment in both the business and local community. Workers, as stakeholders in the business, recognize that it is in their own best interests to advance the cooperative's aims. Since most cooperative members are also members of the same community, they also have a strong incentive to work towards shared goals. Members have a direct stake in the outcome of business decisions, which often results in 'loyalty, commitment, shared knowledge, member participation, underpinned by strong economic incentives'.[7] Research suggests that these factors play a key role in helping protect member-owned businesses during economic downturns.

Integral to cooperatives' resilience is their focus on job creation and retention through 'employee buyouts and rescues'.[8] Rather than letting employees go in response to challenging economic times, cooperatives have an incentive to retain their workers. Further, cooperatives' longevity in the face of financial crises can be attributed in part to their use of 'member capital rather than bank borrowing to expand the business' and their appeal to 'risk-adverse consumers'.[9] Put differently, instead of turning to external lending and borrowing services, cooperatives rely on their own resources and social capital to sustain their businesses.

In banking, in particular, cooperatives have thrived during financial crises. In the wake of 2008, cooperative credit unions and financial services continued to operate under the same challenging economic conditions that had caused several commercial banks to fail. In 2009, for example, the growth of US credit unions' productive loans reached 11 per cent, against a fall of 15 per cent for conventional banks.[10] During the same period, although several European public and commercial banks failed, no cooperative bank failed.[11]

In the period between 2008 and 2013, Spain's economy experienced an extended double-dip recession. The 2008 global financial crisis affected Mondragon's business, and the industrial sectors within the federation were particularly hard hit. Rather than responding with heavy employee or benefit cuts when confronted with this challenge, Mondragon turned instead to a strategy that reflected its values of mutuality: it invested in human capital at a critical time.

Business Strategy

Mondragon's business practices reflect the commitment to its core values of cooperation, participation, social responsibility, and innovation. Investment in human capital lies at the heart of Mondragon's strategy for maintaining long-term financial performance and resilience. The federation's structure is designed both to safeguard and engender mutual practices.

Membership of the cooperative provides employees with specific benefits: all employees have equal rights to vote and ownership; managing boards consist of a combination of employees from all levels of the organization; the highest managers earn no more than six times the lowest paid worker; the general assembly of worker-owners in each cooperative decides how to distribute 70 per cent of profits after taxes; no more than 20 per cent of workers can be temporary contractors; and re-allocating workers across cooperatives in the federation helps retain jobs and support the weakest performing businesses.[12] Taken together, these mutual strategies may have helped Mondragon weather unfavourable economic conditions.

During times of economic stability, Lagun Aro, a welfare insurance cooperative, plays an important role in the Mondragon federation. During times of crisis, it takes on an additional share of responsibility for the welfare of workers within the federation. Lagun Aro offers insurance to members of the workers' cooperative. It provides workers with benefits such as access to health insurance and a complementary pension system. And when a widespread response to the economic crisis was laying off employees, Lagun Aro helped Mondragon to redeploy workers at risk of redundancy in other parts of the federation.[13] This practice not only helped to maintain high worker morale through providing job security, but also helped strengthen businesses within the cooperative that needed extra help. Managing this redeployment of hundreds of workers, Lagun Aro ensured that workers arrived at their new places of employment with the necessary skills to do their new jobs.[14] It covered both training and transportation costs for workers who were deployed to new sectors or locations.[15] If a worker moved to a cooperative with a lower pay scale, either Lagun Aro or the worker's previous cooperative paid the difference in wage.[16] Finally, if a cooperative was unable to place a worker within one of its many subsidiaries, Lagun Aro had the resources in place to provide workers with redundancy pay for two years.[17]

The efficacy of this strategy comes into sharper focus in the example of Fagor Electrodomésticos. In the aftermath of the economic crisis, Fagor, one of Mondragon's largest cooperatives and Europe's fifth largest white-goods manufacturer, shuttered its doors.[18] Despite efforts to restructure Fagor, the Mondragon federation ultimately arrived at the difficult decision that proposed business plans would not ensure the cooperative's future viability. Fagor subsequently filed for bankruptcy. Research suggests that Fagor's insolvency resulted from a variety of interrelated causes, 'including business cycles, poor conditions in the overall economy, and in the specific market in which Fagor operated' as well as governance issues and 'excessive debt due to risky growth strategies'.[19] Taken together, these factors arguably contributed to Fagor's closing.

Although the federation was unable to save Fagor's business, it called upon its ethos of investing in human capital with the goal of increasing overall social capital at a critical time. With around 1,800 jobs now on the line, Mondragon sprang into action to minimize the loss of employment for its workers, taking a two-pronged approach. It invested in cross-training employees to take on different jobs at other cooperatives across the federation, and adopted a strategy of capital transfers to move cash from financially stable cooperatives to those that were facing potential insolvency. Although the latter strategy was not deemed viable in the case of Fagor, capital transfers helped other cooperatives withstand the worst of the economic crisis.[20] Further, as a result of the cross-training, 1,500 people had been placed into jobs elsewhere in the group within six months of Fagor's closing.[21] This practice of pooling resources, in sum, enabled Mondragon to succeed where others had failed: in retaining workers and maintaining stable profits in the aftermath of the economic crisis.

Performance

The response to Fagor's collapse highlights the strength of Mondragon's group insurance mechanism. This mutual business practice, designed to mitigate challenges, helps ensure that the damage resulting from economic crises is absorbed internally and does not spread to the wider community. For the most part, Fagor's workers faced relocation, but not redundancy. The practice of cross-training and supporting the weakest cooperatives through capital transfers arguably helped minimize the potential negative impact on both the business and the local economy.

Although there have been challenges, in particular those associated with expansion and internal reforms, comparative studies assessing growth and overall performance show the advantages of Mondragon's model. The resilience of Mondragon cooperatives during the 2008 crisis in comparison to other companies is one of the most significant and valuable.[22] Research, moreover, suggests that Mondragon's business activities have helped bolster the local economy by causing a spill-over effect in its native region.[23] Comparatively low levels of income inequality in Mondragon's area of operation within the Basque region may be attributed to the business's positive impact.[24]

Prognosis

As the case highlights, even under challenging circumstances, Mondragon continues to operate by the principle that solidarity leads to innovation and stable profitability. Although the company rarely self-promotes, its model undoubtedly makes it a leader among social economy enterprises.[25] Looking to the future, the business is likely to seek ways of retaining its values of reciprocity and mutual practices as it scales. Mondragon aims to continue expanding and applying its model where circumstances allow, facing internally and externally the challenges of globalization that the business believes are eroding social solidarity and the importance of placing people above profit.[26]

Notes

1. Bhalla, Jha, and Lampell (2010).
2. Monzón and Chaves (2017: 11).
3. Monzón and Chaves (2017: 4).
4. Birchall and Hammond Ketilson (2009: 5).
5. Birchall and Hammond Ketilson (2009: 8).
6. Birchall and Hammond Ketilson (2009: 11).
7. Birchall and Hammond Ketilson (2009: 12).
8. Birchall and Hammond Ketilson (2009: 14).
9. Birchall and Hammond Ketilson (2009: 14).
10. Bajo and Roelants (2011: 111).
11. Bajo and Roelants (2011: 111).
12. Mondragon Internal Documents.
13. Roelents et al. (2012: 48).
14. Roelents et al. (2012: 48).
15. Roelents et al. (2012: 48).
16. Roelents et al. (2012: 48).
17. Roelents et al. (2012: 48).
18. Henderson and Norris (2015).
19. Errasti et al. (2017: 188).
20. Ibon Zugasti (International Projects Manager, Mondragon), personal correspondence with the authors, 24 April 2018.
21. Henderson and Norris (2015).
22. Henderson and Norris (2015).
23. Henderson and Norris (2015).
24. Henderson and Norris (2015).
25. MacLeod (1997).
26. Flecha and Ngai (2014).

30

JD.com

Using E-commerce to Alleviate Rural Poverty in China

Lydia J. Price, Liu Xiaowen, and Ni Jing Hua

Introduction

JD.com is one of China's two dominant e-commerce giants, competing with Alibaba in a B2C market worth $600 billion in 2017.

Alibaba had taken an early lead in online commerce in China with a customer-to-customer platform similar to eBay. The decision to receive buyers' payments into escrow, and then release the funds to vendors only after confirmation that purchased goods were received, triggered a boom in transactions between hundreds of thousands of micro-, small- and medium-sized (MSME) Chinese merchants and hundreds of millions of buyers.

JD.com, launched by Richard Liu in 2004, developed the model further, to secure the confidence of buyers seeking high-priced items such as cell phones, computers, and consumer electronics. It became a first-party business-to-consumer retail platform, selling directly to consumers the branded goods that were bought and held in storage and taking control of 'last mile' delivery to assure a high level of service excellence. By 2008 JD.com's product mix included general merchandise, and the company was working to achieve its vision of becoming 'the most trusted company in the world'.[1]

Lydia J. Price, Liu Xiaowen, and Ni Jing Hua, JD.com: Using E-commerce to Alleviate Rural Poverty in China
In *Putting Purpose Into Practice: The Economics of Mutuality.* Edited by: Colin Mayer and Bruno Roche, Oxford University Press (2021). DOI: 10.1093/oso/9780198870708.003.0030

Ecosystem Pain Point

China's online retail sales as a percentage of total retail was 13.5 per cent in 2016, compared with the global average of 8.6 per cent.[2] Analysts predict China's online penetration will reach as high as 25 per cent of a $1.7 trillion total retail market by 2020.[3] Unlike the early years of explosive growth in prosperous coastal cities, however, the locus of China's future e-tail growth will be the rural interior where incomes are low and infrastructure is poor.

China's central government sees e-commerce as a solution to rural poverty, which it pledged to eradicate under the 13th Five Year Plan launched in 2016. Central and provincial government funding has increased each year to support the pledge, reaching a combined total of nearly ¥100 billion in 2016.[4] In addition, the government designated 158 poverty-stricken counties as rural e-commerce pilot regions where domestic e-commerce companies are encouraged to offer assistance and expertise in targeted economic development programmes. Unlike the general poverty relief programmes of the past thirty years, current programmes are meant to be customized according to local conditions. If these pilots are successful, all poor counties will be included in rural e-commerce programmes by 2019.

China's poverty alleviation projects generally include three key components: government funding, farmer training, and local third-party administration. The third party—which might be a local government office or even a local business owner—is often responsible for distributing funds and helping farmers to improve their productivity and income. In the past, many government projects have failed because none of these stakeholders really understand markets. Despite the abundant financial resources tied to these aid programmes and the modern farming knowledge and skills available, they typically do not address other gaps in the ecosystem, such as:

i. IT/Entrepreneurship/Marketing knowledge and skills
ii. The size of local markets
iii. Logistics infrastructure, which is needed to bring farm goods to urban markets at a reasonable cost.

Business and Programme Strategy

In 2016, JD signed a Memorandum of Understanding with China's State Council Office of Poverty Alleviation with the intention of closing these remaining gaps. A four-pronged programme was established to provide industry upgrades, employment opportunities, entrepreneurship upgrades, and marketing and branding support.[5] JD provides logistics services to more than 400,000 of China's 600,000 rural villages, and also extends agricultural loans on favourable terms to farmer cooperatives making capital purchases and investing in the means of production (e.g. seeds, fertilizers, and livestock). The World Bank, Dupont Pioneer, and a number of local businesses cooperate on these financing programmes. Employment options are offered directly by JD and also by cooperating merchants in the JD e-commerce network. Entrepreneurial training is offered in cooperation with UNDP, China Social Entrepreneur Foundation, and other organizations, with an emphasis on boosting e-commerce skills and knowledge. Finally, marketing support is offered on JD's e-commerce platform, where dedicated sites are set up to sell specially designated poverty-alleviation products. Consumer awareness and interest in buying these goods are boosted through digital communications on the JD e-commerce site, and also by organizing discounted group-buying events.

Running Chicken: Taking the Programme a Million Steps Further

After the first year of operations, JD's four-part programme had created 16,000 direct and 5,000 indirect jobs in rural villages. ¥200 million had been extended in loans; 50,000 people trained in e-commerce; and more than 10,000 products and services sourced from poverty-stricken counties.[6] Despite the impressive aggregate metrics, however, the most tangible gains in poverty reduction came from a single village where a highly tailored pilot programme had run. The pilot was designed to tackle two anticipated barriers to meaningfully raising farmer incomes:

1. Market prices for rurally sourced Chinese agricultural goods are generally low and unstable due to uneven and poor product quality.
2. Smallholder farm yields are too small to amass wealth even if prices are high.

JD's Running Chicken programme had been initiated to test the hypothesis that free-range chickens could be sourced at scale from low-income farming zones and sold on JD Mall at a premium price. The pilot was situated in Wuyi County—one of northern Hebei Province's poorest regions that is nevertheless endowed with sandy soil and a climate that is conducive to raising chickens and growing fresh fruits, vegetables, and grains for chicken feed. JD worked with the local government to establish a 200-Mu[7] fenced-off farming zone that scales and concentrates chicken farming without detracting from the landscape's beauty. The region thereby remains a viable location for tourism as an additional source of future revenue. The land-use decision removed the problem of fragmentation—a persistent problem that arose when China's communal farms were chopped up and doled out to eligible citizens at the launch of economic reforms in the 1970s, and which remains in place due to the slow pace of legal reforms concerning land ownership and transfers. JD's Running Chicken farm is large enough to graze 15,000–16,000 chickens at a time, for an average density of less than 80 chickens per Mu.

A local farmers' cooperative is invited to raise chickens at this central facility (typically equivalent to 100 chickens per family), with a promise that JD will buy them at three times the average market price as long as strict growing standards are followed. Chief among these is a requirement that chickens run a minimum of one million steps before slaughter, and another that they be fed a healthy diet including grains twice a day and fresh fruits and vegetables at least three times per week. The cooperative has hired a third-party organization to run the farm, and that organization employs local farmers as labour. The growing conditions are digitally monitored via electronic pedometers attached to chickens' feet along with video images from cameras installed at the farm. When JD purchases the chickens from the cooperative, the funds are allocated to individual farming families.

In total, the programme engages four principal stakeholders: JD, the local farmers' cooperative, the Chinese government, and the local third-party organization, which in this case is an Internet business owner. JD provides interest-free loans to the cooperative for purchasing chicks and feed, without demanding collateral. The government insures the cooperative loans against catastrophic risks. Chicks and feed are currently sourced from suppliers in JD's network. The aim is to source from local suppliers eventually, although no direct programmes have yet been established to cultivate those sources. Once chickens meet the minimum growing standards they are purchased and sold under the proprietary JD brand name Running Chicken at three times the price of ordinary chickens. JD is monitoring sales and also farming conditions closely to determine the connection between farming methods, supply quality, and market demand.

Performance

Running Chicken is a winning programme for all external stakeholders. Thirty thousand chickens were sold in the first year, and consumers generally were pleased with the meat's health credentials and good taste. More than 600 families joined Running Chicken in 2017, most of them elderly or sickly farmers with little education and few other viable means of earning a living. After deducting loan repayments and growing expenses, a typical farmer included in the programme via the cooperative realized an income increase of ¥2000–3000.[8]

In addition to direct farming income, Wuyi County created part-time jobs for cleaning the chicken farm and slaughtering the chickens at the end of the growing period. Running Chicken farm will in principle also become a buyer for locally grown fruits and vegetables once a reliable local supply chain is established. Finally, the Chinese government gained a new and more efficient poverty-alleviation business model and a tangible reduction in national poverty cases. On the basis of this success, Running Chicken is adding additional Wuyi families in 2018 with the aim of doubling the 2017 overall programme size. Pilots are also underway to replicate the programme in other poverty-stricken counties. If successful, Hebei Province Flying Pigeons and Jiangsu Province Swimming Ducks will join JD's traceable premium poultry product line in 2018.

Prognosis

The benefits to JD are difficult to assess in the short term. For a sustainable long run, JD is working closely with government officials and universities to establish agricultural standards for free-range chicken farming and processing. The standards will be based on deep analysis of what works best for raising the chickens as well as building the market demand. Using these standards, local organizations should in future be able to pull independent farmers into the free-range chicken supply chain without the need of JD's financial, human, and social capital inputs.

For now, JD does not assess the programme's success through the lens of short-term profitability. Like many young Internet businesses, the company is spending investors' cash to build market strength and a network that will later be monetized. A successful New York IPO in 2014, and an ongoing stream of investments from institutional ecosystem partners (chief among them TenCent and Walmart) fuels the expansion of JD's market presence and ecosystem services. The powerful logistics network will help JD reach deep into China's growing rural e-commerce space, boosting the platform's active user base and adding critical sales volume to offset the platform's low average product margins. At the same time, a high quality, traceable source of poultry will help JD capture the growing Chinese market for fresh meat. Already a $159.1 billion market in 2015, it has been growing at an annual rate of 6.5 per cent since 2010.[9] JD's own-company online sales of fresh meat grew by 780 per cent year-on-year in 2017, consistent with the overall trend. The Running Chicken programme ties into an overall push toward achieving the company vision of being the most trusted company in the world.

Notes

1. http://corporate.jd.com/missionValues/.
2. 'China Retail Market Report 2016', Deloitte.
3. http://www.alizila.com/online-shopping-in-china-to-double-by-2020-goldman-report/.
4. Approximately $15.9 billion using 2018 exchange rate of $1=¥6.3.
5. Xiong, Nie, Bi, and Waqar (2017).
6. Xiong, Nie, Bi, and Waqar (2017).
7. Approximately equal to 13 hectares or 32 acres.
8. $317–$476 at 2018 exchange rate of $1=¥6.3
9. http://www.agr.gc.ca/eng/industry-markets-and-trade/international-agri-food-market-intelligence/asia/market-intelligence/sector-trend-analysis-pork-trends-in-china/?id=1481126666257.

31
Kate Spade New York
Integrating Social Purpose into Core Business Operations

Taryn Bird, Aida Hadzic, Kate Roll, and Judith C. Stroehle

Introduction

The Kate Spade New York story began in 1993, when Kate Brosnahan Spade set out to design the perfect handbag.[1] The design and colourful palettes were well received by both clients and fashion editors, and the brand was able to open its first shop in 1996 in New York City. After it was acquired by Liz Claiborne, Inc. in 2007, the brand expanded its product portfolio to include clothing, jewellery, bedding, fragrance, legwear, and more. In 2017, Kate Spade New York was acquired by Tapestry, Inc., and is now part of the Tapestry house of luxury brands. Its designs are sold in more than 450 locations worldwide, with 140 retail shops and outlet stores across the United States, and more than 175 shops internationally.[2]

In 2013, Kate Spade New York founded *on purpose*, an innovative approach designed to integrate Kate Spade New York's social commitment to empowering women into its core business operations. Through the *on purpose* initiative, Kate Spade New York financed to build the for-profit social enterprise Abahizi Dushyigikirane, Ltd. (ADC) in Rwanda.

Taryn Bird, Aida Hadzic, Kate Roll, and Judith C. Stroehle, Kate Spade New York: Integrating Social Purpose into Core Business Operations In *Putting Purpose Into Practice: The Economics of Mutuality*. Edited by: Colin Mayer and Bruno Roche, Oxford University Press (2021).
DOI: 10.1093/oso/9780198870708.003.0031

Pain Points in the Ecosystem

Labour rights have been an increasingly important issue in the global apparel industry. As a result, ethical fashion projects have gained enormous global attention among international organizations, human and labour rights activists, states, and consumers. Prior to founding *on purpose,* Kate Spade New York made an early effort to contribute to this ethical fashion movement by focusing its social impact strategy on female empowerment, while aligning with and sourcing from large-scale non-profits, who in turn worked with women in post-conflict countries. However, this CSR -style project targeting women's economic empowerment largely failed. The support that women received from Kate Spade New York was often strongly dependent on the capacities of another organization's abilities in the ecosystem, making it a very inefficient and financially unsustainable mode.

In order to achieve a longer lasting and self-sustaining model, Kate Spade New York decided to shift its focus away from the common approach of making a donation for each product or partnering with large-scale non-profits towards a social enterprise model of empowerment. By building a new business with female entrepreneurs in Rwanda, Kate Spade New York addressed the pain points of a specific group of women in the global apparel industry.

Women in Rwanda, as in many poverty-affected countries, face many barriers to greater financial autonomy and decision-making power. While they typically lack the financial capacities and leadership skills needed for running a business, they are also affected by other issues, such as the lack of familial support and low confidence. Employment opportunities on the local labour market are frequently unsuitable as they do not allow for these vulnerabilities, and local institutional systems lack the capacity to address them sufficiently.

Business Strategy

The social enterprise Abahizi Dushyigikirane, Ltd. (Abahizi Rwanda) was established by Kate Spade New York in 2013 through the *on purpose* initiative. Started in the Rwandan village of Masoro, the company is employee-owned and governed by a local board of directors. Studies show that shared ownership brings about positive results by creating feelings of responsibility and having a personal stake in the business. The transfer of ownership to women was thus targeted at strengthening their personal impact on the business, encouraging them to participate, and empowering them economically and emotionally—both being equally important.

The mission of Abahizi Rwanda is to produce high-quality products for the global fashion industry while empowering women to carry positive change into their communities. While Kate Spade New York was essential in building capacity in the early years, the business has been designed to be able to take on other clients in the future, and to encourage buyer diversification as a 'sustainable path for long-term financial growth'.[3]

The enterprise is committed to creating a supportive work environment for women and addressing specific needs by investing in employee well-being through empowerment and training programmes. To make the enterprise sustainable and address relevant needs of women, Kate Spade New York, in cooperation with Georgetown University, used its access to assess which additional factors are crucial for women in Rwanda. Their study which ran from 2015–16, found that improving the social status and overall position of women would reduce factors that make women vulnerable to external shocks, such as single motherhood, hunger, and sickness.

Abahizi Rwanda is owned by the workforce in equal shares through their membership of the Masoro Community Vendor Capability Cooperative (MAVIC); membership is restricted to ADC employees.

The world of apparel supply chains involves both low- and high-level skills and capabilities. Low-skill-level firms exercise simple assembly tasks, while high-level tasks, such as design, production planning, and marketing are generally performed elsewhere. While organizations in more advanced markets usually perform 'full-package' activities, those in less developed markets may only perform tasks that add less value, such as assembly, sewing, etc.

The dynamics of global value chains (GVCs) thus play a significant role in the context of Abahizi Rwanda. The ability to leverage the benefits of value chains for developing countries often depends on whether the operations take place at the higher or lower level (of added value) of the value chain.[4] Whereas high-end and intangible production activities, such as marketing in post-fabrication stages, are likely to happen in developed countries, less developed economies tend to engage in low-end and tangible production activities, yielding less value-added to the product and thus lower income. The challenge for global apparel suppliers is to push their activities upwards and distribute more benefits from GVCs to poorer nations.

Most of Kate Spade New York's suppliers are full-package and are thus able to lift Abahizi Rwanda artisans to higher levels within the global value chain. To achieve this shift from simple assembly to higher value-adding processes, additional efforts and investments in training and skills are made. Upward movement might be pushed through direct exposure to multinational corporations to expose artisans to best practices in fields such as logistics, production, and human resources.

Kate Spade New York has retained its quality criteria and expects Abahizi Rwanda-produced handbags to meet the brand's expectations. The active engagement of Abahizi Rwanda in the production process is one method of achieving the improvement in skills required to meet those criteria.

Abahizi Rwanda is primarily focused on 'cut and make' supplier tasks. Abahizi manufactures and embellishes its handbags in accordance with customer specifications, while using buyer-provided materials. The quality principles demand consistent supply of fine leather, fabric, fasteners, and other components that could not be sourced in Africa and are thus being brought in from vendors in China and Korea. By training Abahizi in high-quality trades, the initiative enables the artisans to produce for other fashion suppliers too, making the social enterprise more independent and self-sufficient.

The overall product development and production cycle of mid-luxury handbags can take up to a year. Kate Spade New York involves Abahizi in the design process and sends the 'tech packs'—design specifications and instructions—to Masoro for the artisans to make initial samples.

Once those are reviewed and approved, the designers from New York send the final specifications, which Abahizi uses to create the final samples. Upon approval of the final samples, Kate Spade New York initiates orders for cutting, dyes, and raw materials, and Abahizi then starts the production. About five months after the receipt of the final specifications the bags are ready for sale.

Performance

The *on purpose* initiative contributes to creating human capital in three ways. One is the ownership structure, which establishes the artisans as owners of Abahizi Rwanda, while Kate Spade New York has the roles of social impact investor, client, and mentor.

The second contribution is the attempt to shift the women's contributions up the value chain to make them reach potentially higher added-value and higher benefits from within the supply chains.

Finally, Kate Spade New York also ensures that the empowerment of women has an impact on different areas of the artisans' lives, yielding spill-over effects across a larger spectrum of Masoro society, including improvements in child education and nutrition. For this purpose, the success of empowerment was measured by Georgetown University in 2016 according to financial, economic, social, and psychological metrics.

Financial Empowerment

The financial aspect of empowerment was assessed on the grounds of adequacy of compensation and spending power. The lowest artisan salary at Abahizi Rwanda is considerably higher than the median salary for the private sector—up to 40 per cent of the average compensation in Rwanda (Table 31.1).

Based on the overall living standards in Masoro, this salary enabled a 'decent life' for one adult plus one school-aged child, which included being able to save.

Table 31.1. A comparative analysis of ADC compensation

	Net ($/month)
ADC team leader, sample-making department	103
ADC assistant team leader, sewing department	84
Construction trades (masonry, plumbing, and electrical)	83
ADC sewing-machine operator	78
Nurse	76
ADC base (lowest) artisan salary	72
Primary school teacher	57
Construction labourer	42
Miner (variable piece rate)	42
Agricultural day labour	28

Source: After Soule, Tinsley, and Rivoli (2017).

As intended by Kate Spade New York, the financial empowerment of women through employment at the *on purpose* supplier was shown to have positive spill-over effects on the community of Masoro, where women were able to contribute to their households. Strengthening human capital, as well as designing and supporting institutions, has helped to catalyse further development within poorer societies. Future results from the employment at an '*on purpose*' supplier are thus expected to be seen through overall higher rates of educational attainment and a total growth of social participation of women, not only of those working at ADC.

Social and Psychological Empowerment

The Georgetown University study also found that artisans of Abahizi Rwanda were showing higher levels of self-confidence than others in the Masoro community. In particular, their subjective social status—how they viewed their social standing in comparison with their neighbours and other community members—had been positively affected. The researchers tested the artisans and a group of randomly chosen members of the local community (not associated with ADC) using the MacArthur Scale of Subjective Social Status. All participants evaluated their past social standing as very low. However, artisans ranked their current and future social status considerably higher than did the other members of the community.

Several factors are thought to have contributed to this difference between Abahizi Rwanda workers and other members of the community, amongst the most important being a caring management, the opportunity to learn and progress, and growing self-esteem through economic and social empowerment. In particular, opportunities to progress and for self-development were found to be important in the Rwandan context. The empowerment of women regarding their freedom of decision-making in both personal and family finances was also shown to improve compared with other Masoro women.

Finally, building new networks within the global market and forming relationships with companies in the supply chain of global buyers other than Kate Spade New York was seen as evidence of further social empowerment of the artisans.

Business Performance

As the *on purpose* model was specifically designed as a mutual project, and not just a social impact project, Kate Spade New York expected both good business performance and the self-sustainability of Abahizi Rwanda. And, indeed, the production period for 31 March 2017 was able to generate positive net income results.

To make Abahizi Rwanda even more competitive in the global market without compromising its quality and learning curve has been presented as a high priority for Kate Spade New York in the coming years. The strategy for this is to achieve price competitiveness by increasing the output with a modest increase in headcount. Management aspires to achieve this by relying heavily on the benefits of increased worker experience and continuous staff training.

Prognosis

Over the last five years, Kate Spade New York has put a lot of effort into the *on purpose* initiative, but has also received a lot in return. Since the fashion industry is under strong international scrutiny, involving not only activists and non-profit organizations, but also consumers, programmes such as the one in Rwanda can yield invaluable reputational benefits for a brand.

Abahizi Rwanda has overcome initial challenges and achieved crucial milestones. It has the capacity to improve further and to generate greater positive spill-over effects. This provides lessons for other businesses by showing that holistic human-capital assessments can yield great success in achieving higher employee well-being and work performance efficiency.

In the future, Kate Spade New York aims to make additional improvements to push Abahizi Rwanda's growth and potential further. The brand is confident that it will be able to increase Abahizi Rwanda output to 16,000 units per production period, while decreasing costs through increased training and offering a broader scale of products. With these forecasts, Kate Spade New York aims to achieve the financial viability of Abahizi Rwanda and make the enterprise self-sustainable in the long term.

Abahizi Rwanda has some distinct competitive advantages that will help it realize its future goals. One is that the artisans have demonstrated their ability to be flexible and innovative in meeting the different needs and preferences of suppliers. Rwanda's labour costs remain low compared with other garment-manufacturing countries such as China. And Abahizi Rwanda artisans possess skills in embroidery and sewing, which are closely linked to the local culture and which make Rwanda a strong base for fashion suppliers. Further steps include efforts towards improving Abahizi Rwanda's client base and COACH, another Tapestry brand, producing in Rwanda.

Notes

1. Kate Spade & Company 2018, http://www.katespade.co.uk/uk/about-us/page/aboutus.
2. Kate Spade & Company 2018, http://www.katespade.co.uk/uk/about-us/page/aboutus.
3. http://www.katespade.co.uk/content/ebiz/shop/resources/images/additional-images/2018march/category-landing/onpurpose/impact_report_24.pdf.
4. Baldwin (2014).

32

Mahindra First Choice

Orchestrating the Used-Cars Ecosystem

Ben Jackson and Genevieve Joy

Introduction

Mahindra is an Indian multinational company founded in 1945 that has expanded from steel manufacturing to twenty different industries, including automobile manufacturing. Its stated philosophy is to (i) challenge conventional thinking, (ii) innovate, and (iii) enable positive change for its stakeholders. In 2011, this approach was conveyed through a new brand identity, 'Rise', which seeks to empower everyone connected to Mahindra, both internally and externally.

In 2008, Mahindra ventured into the 'aftermarket', or used-car space, with Mahindra First Choice (MFC) in order to meet rising demand from a growing segment of car owners.[1]

The main considerations when buying a used car in India are cost of service and availability of parts. Yet while the used-car market was equal in size to the new car market in 2012, only 15 per cent of transactions were in the organized sector. Combined with a trend toward consolidation, this left an opportunity for a trustworthy company with capital and access to spare parts to play a major role in the market.[2]

Because most transactions were informal, the used-car space was unorganized, fragmented, and lacked transparency and trust, essentially there was a social capital deficit.[3] Mahindra saw an opportunity to develop a more efficient ecosystem by filling these gaps and creating incentives to formalize the industry. It could use its trusted brand name, financial resources, and data to facilitate easier access to sellers and buyers, replacement parts, service repairs, and information on car value and history.[4]

On its own, Mahindra would not be able to meet the growing needs of the aftermarket industry; it would need to leverage other stakeholders' assets, data, experience, and physical presence. By supporting the growth of the whole ecosystem, however, MFC could also grow.

Pain Points in the Ecosystem

Mahindra had a general understanding of the bottlenecks in the used-car industry, but to resolve them, it needed to know the specific problems faced by the different stakeholders. It therefore began by mapping the stakeholders. It looked at how used-car sales occur and between whom, then widened its scope to look at other processes around used cars: repairs, service, and financing. By placing the used-car industry—rather than Mahindra itself—at the centre, the company was able to form a clearer picture of the larger ecosystem.

Six key actors were identified in the space: consumers (buyers), consumers (sellers), car manufacturers, independent used-car dealers, independent car service workshops, and banks. MFC then built customer profiles to see where the bottlenecks, 'pain points', and needs were and developed solutions together.

Consumers (Buyers)

i. *Fair price*: Potential buyers had trouble knowing whether they were paying a fair price for a used car, especially when purchasing directly from a seller or independent dealer.
ii. *Car condition*: It could be hard for a buyer to know the history of a car including accidents and number of previous owners.
iii. *Legitimate paperwork*: There was no referencing system in place to ensure that the paperwork provided by a direct seller or independent dealer was legitimate.

iv. *Reliable and timely service*: It often took a long time to get spare parts for repairs, especially from independent service workshops in smaller cities.

Consumers (Sellers)

i. *Fair price*: Sellers either did not know the value of their own car or did not have the data to support their proposed price, so could end up selling it for a lower price than the car was worth.
ii. *Upgrade own car*: Often sellers were looking to replace their car with a better one, thus facing the same issues as the buyers. Since they generally wanted to buy the new car at the same time they sold it, this was an additional complication.

Car Manufacturers

i. *Competition*: Manufacturers had to compete with other car manufacturers (including Mahindra) and multi-brand chains that could offer a wider variety of product and pricing.
ii. *Penetration into smaller cities*: Single-brand dealers and workshops were not profitable in smaller cities because of a smaller and fragmented consumer base, yet these were important undersaturated markets.
iii. *Scrutiny from Indian Competition Authority*: This commission aims to avoid domination of industries by enterprises by encouraging competition and a level playing field. As a result, popular car manufacturers sometimes faced pressure from the ICA to demonstrate cooperation.

Independent Used-Car Dealer

- *Profitability*: Independent used-car dealers struggled to attract customers and turn a profit.

Independent Car Servicing Workshop

i. *Spare part availability*: Branded spare parts were restricted in supply, making it difficult for these workshops to deliver services on time, resulting in substandard service.[5]
ii. *Skills gap*: Training employees is time-consuming, especially with high turnover, which led to an overall low standard of technical competence.
iii. *High employee turnover*: Employees were generally paid low wages so there was low company loyalty. The high turnover also exacerbated the training problem.

Bank

i. *Resale value*: Banks lacked information about the history and resale value of repossessed cars. This meant a higher financial risk for the bank, resulting in fewer loans that included cars as collateral—and overall fewer used-car transactions.
ii. *Hard to sell repossessed cars*: Banks were afraid of being stuck with repossessed cars since they did not have a network to sell them.

Designing the Ecosystem

The used-car space did not function optimally because of a lack of trust, information, and transparency, so these were primary concerns for MFC as it began designing solutions. It is important to note that a small team within MFC worked on this issue rather than the parent company Mahindra & Mahindra, enabling a more innovative and agile approach. As a separate entity, MFC was able to develop an agile start-up culture that allowed it to remain brand-agnostic and take risks.

MFC determined to add value to the ecosystem by addressing unmet needs and pain points, professionalizing fragmented parts of the ecosystem, and leveraging assets and transactions owned by other participants in the used-car space.[6]

The team worked directly with the different stakeholders to build products that resolved their pain points, then tested and deployed them. As a result, products and services were created that addressed each stakeholder's needs. Some of these innovations overlapped or required the creation of additional solutions, expanding the scope of the ecosystem:

- *Third-party car inspection service*: MFC developed a standardized inspection service, which looks over a car for approximately US$10 and provides an assessment of the condition. This is especially helpful for consumers who are unsure of the quality of the car, or banks who must sell a repossessed car.[7] The service would only be useful on a large scale, however, so MFC decided to create a multi-brand car-dealer franchise that would roll out the system.[8]
- *Multi-brand car-dealer franchise*: MFC created a franchise model and provided systems and services in exchange for royalties. These services included an IT system for inventory management and customer relationship management (CRM); the car inspection service; quality and process support; a warranty service; and the Mahindra brand name, with the marketing and reputation that came with it.[9]
- *Warranty*: The data collected on transactions through the IT system enabled MFC to price a warranty model and share the profits with the dealers.[10]
- *Indian Blue Book (IBB)*: The data obtained on car transactions and prices were also used to benchmark prices and create the industry's first guide to vehicle valuation in India.[11] The IBB was put online for free, resolving the issue of fair pricing between buyers and sellers and for bankers as well. Although the product was not monetized, it did facilitate many more transactions, which was good for the health of the ecosystem.[12]
- *B2B auction platform*: MFC provided an online auction platform so that the banks could sell repossessed cars to brokers, who then sold fleets of these cars to businesses.[13] Since the banks could more easily collect money on the cars, they became more likely to give loans that included the cars as collateral.[14]

- *MFC repair shop*: Customers were unhappy with the levels of service they received at independent garages, so MFC created its own service workshop. It quickly learned, however, that the problem was not the garages—it was the supply chain for spare parts. As a result, MFC closed down the new repair garages and instead focused on the true issue.[15]
- *Hub and spoke supply chain*: Mahindra developed software to optimize supply and distribution across the country and created small hubs.[16] Once the system functioned well for MFC franchisees, it was intended to be scaled up to other car manufacturers in order to ensure a reliable supply of spare parts. But the car manufacturers were hesitant to work with a competitor, so MFC had to forge a partnership with them.[17]
- *Partnership with car manufacturers*: The only way to convince car manufacturers to work with MFC was to fix a problem or add value to the manufacturers' processes. MFC realized that individual car sellers usually sought to upgrade to a better used car or a new car. They therefore proposed to refer sellers to the car manufacturers. MFC also provided valuable knowledge through the IBB, which enabled the manufacturer to know the trade-in value of other companies' cars; and the B2B auction platform, which helped them sell these cars. Furthermore, partnering with MFC helped the car manufacturers avoid trouble with the Competition Authority by showing that they were cooperating with other companies to generate a supply of spare parts.[18]
- *Multi-brand spare part catalogue*: A catalogue was made available to all garages to provide information about spare part availability and where alternatives might be found. This system began with data from franchises and then expanded through crowd-sourced information.[19]
- *Multi-brand repair shop franchise*: Now that it had ensured a spare parts pipeline, MFC offered existing independent garages the opportunity to become franchise repair shops. After its experience with the car-dealer franchises, MFC was familiar with the franchise model. In addition, having the repair shops as part of the system meant they could execute warranties sold by the car dealers.[20]

- *Car diagnosis and repair system*: MFC developed a system that walked the repair technician through a diagnosis process, reducing the high burden of training on employers by reducing the learning curve for less experienced employees.[21]

Prognosis

There is no template or shortcut for ecosystem orchestrators, but there are essential steps that MFC followed:

1. Clearly define the problem and purpose
2. Map the stakeholders
3. Identify the stakeholders' pain points
4. Develop solutions that directly address stakeholder needs and grow the used-car ecosystem
5. Pilot solutions, dropping failures and scaling up successes.

Openness to failure and the ability to change course were vital aspects of MFC's success. 'Seventy percent of what we tried did not work,' said Nagendra Palle, CEO of MFC Wheels. 'We learned that you need to make measured bets. We are not consensus-driven but listening-driven.' When MFC saw that its company-owned service workshops did not solve a problem, it closed them down and pivoted to a new solution; one that solved many problems at once while also improving relationships and trust in the ecosystem.

As a smaller team within a bigger, established company, MFC benefited from the best of both worlds. It had a dedicated group with an agile, start-up mentality—a critical element for disruptive innovation—while its parent company lent a strong brand reputation to its dealings with partners. The small innovation team could propose 'industry first' products; and manufacturers, dealers, and banks were willing to test these since Mahindra's corporate reputation reduced risk.[22]

From the outside, it could seem counterintuitive for MFC to create a multi-brand chain of dealer and repair franchises that could compete with Mahindra dealerships and garages. It also might have gone against business interests to publish the Blue Book for free. Therein lies the importance of the ecosystem approach: By growing the ecosystem and improving trust and efficiency, MFC benefited disproportionately from this growth even though it did not collect value from every single transaction and connection.[23]

Being an ecosystem orchestrator means that financial transactions are no longer the single focus of business growth. Instead, the focus is on enabling—and sometimes controlling—the exchange and accumulation of multiple forms of capital with the ecosystem. MFC's greatest contribution to the ecosystem was not building physical repair shops but rather creating systems and connections that provided information, which in turn promoted trust. The ecosystem orchestration approach opened up added complexity, but at the same time drove innovation that produced creative and productive solutions for all stakeholders.

It is worth re-emphasizing two clear lessons from this case. First, that by opening themselves up to the needs and capabilities of the other stakeholders, MFC was able to understand the reality of the problems and in so doing, gain knowledge of how they might be addressed from a stakeholder perspective. Second, MFC recognized that their own capabilities were not solely financial and that solving the problems for all the stakeholders would mean success for them too, a mutual benefit. For example, a financial-capital-focused solution would have been to buy out the various players in the system and directly control the activities and then find efficiencies in IT and banking through the wider group of businesses owned by Mahindra. This would not only have been an expensive endeavour, but it would have resulted in the creation of significant on-going costs and pressures to manage more businesses profitably in a system that had significant problems. By contrast, the solution of the Blue Book to address the trust deficit, is an excellent illustration of how ecosystem orchestration can return both financial and social value.

Although MFC did not have EoM at the core of their approach, the lessons for businesses wanting to implement EoM are extensive and noteworthy.

Notes

1. Das et al. (2015). Mahindra First Choice Services: Creating a Value Proposition. *Richard Ivey School of Business Foundation.*
2. Das et al. (2015). Mahindra First Choice Services: Creating a Value Proposition. *Richard Ivey School of Business Foundation.*
3. Interviews with Mahindra employees.
4. Das et al. (2015).
5. Interviews with Mahindra employees.
6. Kyrtatou et al. (2015). Business Models, Ecosystems, Data & Digital: Key insights from the Petcare Pathfinder Journey.
7. Interviews with Mahindra employees.
8. Responsible Business Forum presentation.
9. Responsible Business Forum presentation.
10. Responsible Business Forum presentation.
11. Kyrtatou et al. (2015).
12. Responsible Business Forum presentation.
13. Interviews with Mahindra employees.
14. Responsible Business Forum presentation.
15. Responsible Business Forum presentation.
16. Interviews with Mahindra employees.
17. Responsible Business Forum presentation.
18. Responsible Business Forum presentation.
19. Interviews with Mahindra employees.
20. Responsible Business Forum presentation.
21. Responsible Business Forum presentation.
22. Interviews with Mahindra employees.
23. Responsible Business Forum presentation.

33
Novo Nordisk
An Ecosystem Approach to Preventing Diabetes

Ben Jackson and Yassine El Ouarzazi

Introduction

Novo Nordisk is a global healthcare company that employs 43,200 people and is headquartered in Bagsværd, Denmark. The company has been involved in diabetes care for more than ninety-five years and is also a provider of services and advice for the treatment for haemophilia, growth disorders, obesity, and a number of other serious chronic diseases. It has strategic production sites in five countries, and affiliates or offices in eighty countries. The firm produces around 50 per cent of the world's insulin and also makes several drugs under a variety of brand names and became a corporation after a merger in 1989. It is a member of the European Federation of Pharmaceutical Industries and Associations (EFPIA). In October 2018, Novo Nordisk was ranked the fifth most reputable company for corporate responsibility by the business magazine, *Forbes*, the only pharmaceutical company within the top thirty.

Type 1 Diabetes

Type 1 diabetes is a lifelong disease. People with type 1 diabetes are dependent on insulin treatment for survival. Their condition is caused by the body's inability to produce insulin which results in glucose remaining

 DOI: 10.1093/oso/9780198870708.003.0033

in the blood rather than being absorbed by cells. It is therefore vital that people living with type 1 diabetes receive daily insulin treatment.

Type 2 Diabetes

Type 2 diabetes is a chronic disease. It occurs when your body cannot make enough insulin—the hormone that controls the amount of glucose in your blood—and cannot use the insulin it does make effectively. This is called insulin resistance, and it develops over months, or even years. Diagnosed early, type 2 diabetes can be controlled with diet and exercise. If diet and exercise alone are not enough to control your glucose levels, you may also need to take medication. It's important to be screened for diabetes and to recognize the symptoms early. You are more likely to develop type 2 diabetes if you are middle aged or older, if you are overweight, and if you have a family history. Warning signs include: extreme thirst, excessive urination, tiredness and fatigue, blurry vision, and weight loss. There are different stages of type 2 diabetes. If you have pre-diabetes, your blood sugar levels can be controlled with lifestyle changes, including a healthier balanced diet, and regular physical activity. If the condition progresses, your doctor may recommend medication to help keep your blood sugar controlled.

Novo Nordisk capabilities cover the entire pharmaceutical value chain, from idea exploration and early research, upscaling, clinical testing, and regulatory submission to ultimately bringing new innovative medicines and devices to patients. Throughout the journey from idea to medicine, the aim is to create the perfect conditions for scientists' inventions to become reality.

Ecosystem Pain Points

Around 212 million people have undiagnosed type 2 diabetes worldwide according to International Diabetes Federation estimates in 2017. Many have developed complications by the time they are diagnosed, including damage to their feet, eyes, kidneys, and heart. Four out of five people with diabetes live in low- and middle-income countries, where many lack access to diabetes care, either because it is not available or not affordable. Cities are widely considered the frontline in the fight against diabetes and two-thirds of all people with diabetes live in urban areas.

While many developing countries are increasing the proportion of their wealth spent on health care, across the world urban populations are expanding so quickly that it is difficult for health infrastructure to keep up. Unplanned urban growth is also a major driver of poverty. Currently, 900 million people worldwide live in urban slums. The United Nations estimates that by 2030, roughly 60 per cent of city inhabitants will be under the age of 18. Many city hospitals also become overcrowded because patients recognize that's where to find the best doctors, research, and technology. This means primary care is neglected, which can lead to unregulated, unsafe, and ineffective private services. In some African cities, public primary healthcare has almost disappeared, according to the World Health Organization (WHO). Cities can also influence how people live, travel and eat; factors which all have an impact on health.

Business Strategy

Novo Nordisk has a core purpose of driving change to defeat diabetes and other chronic diseases. Its philosophy has been to 'discover, develop, and manufacture better biological medicines and make them accessible to people with diabetes throughout the world'. However, the firm recognizes that it takes more than medicine for people to live a full and healthy life with diabetes. Today, 425 million people—around 9 per cent of the world's adult population—live with diabetes, the majority with type 2 diabetes, a number that has doubled since 2000 and is expected to reach 629 million by 2045.

In 2014, the company launched Cities Changing Diabetes in response to what it called the 'unsustainable global rise of type 2 diabetes'. This platform created a public–private partnership that was focused on the idea of bringing different stakeholders and expertise together to find common solutions and address a complex public health issue: the rise of diabetes in urban areas. The programme coined this term 'urban diabetes'.

The initiative came at a time when the spotlight was focused on the effects of diabetes. The previous year, Mexico City had become the first in the world to levy a tax on sugary drinks, which was considered a factor in the country having among the world's highest obesity and diabetes rates.

In partnering with patients, policymakers, health-care professionals, and non-governmental organizations, Novo Nordisk hoped to address diabetes risk factors in urban areas and ensure that people with diabetes were diagnosed earlier and that they would have access to adequate care to be able to live their lives with as few limitations as possible. There were three global partners, Steno Diabetes Center Copenhagen, University College London, and Novo Nordisk, working together with more than a hundred local partners across the partner cities.

Its aims included putting urban diabetes at the top of the global health-care agenda. From the group's experience, it has been shown that the greatest impact on potentially devasting diseases can be when health-care systems are mobilized to see it as an urgent priority. The group has estimated that obesity must be reduced by 25 per cent globally in order to hold the rise of diabetes prevalence at 10 per cent globally.

Putting urban diabetes on the agenda of those shaping cities for the future is also important: urban planning has a key role to play in delivering health improvements. The group also set itself a challenge of investigating the challenge, the root causes, and risk factors underlying the burden of diabetes in cities, while driving action to halt the rising prevalence of diabetes and improve health outcomes. Five cities—Copenhagen, Houston, Mexico City, Shanghai, and Tianjin—joined the programme, which was later expanded to include fourteen more—Johannesburg, Rome, Vancouver, Xiamen, Hangzhou, Beijing, Jakarta, Buenos Aires, Milan, Merida, Madrid, Leicester, Koriyama, and Beirut.

Since 2014, the partnership has followed a systematic approach of building evidence by mapping the challenge in partner cities, defining and piloting actions on the ground, and sharing findings and outcomes. It refers to this as the map–share–act framework:

Map: The research conducted within the programme contributes to a holistic and multi-disciplinary approach to tackling diabetes in cities. It supports the understanding of the challenges and enables action to be taken while sharing the learnings through peer-reviewed publications, policy papers, research tools, as well as knowledge sharing within research networks.

Share: The programme aims to break down silos in order to lead to significant gains in efficiency and effectiveness. City government (18 per cent), the research sector (22 per cent), and local NGOs such as community organizations and patient organizations (26 per cent) are the main sectors involved with the programme at city level.

Act: The role of the programme is to promote, facilitate and accelerate major initiatives in diabetes prevention and management. According to Novo Nordisk's 2014-2016 Impact review, the programme initiated 18 projects, across six cities, with the majority concerning community involvement in health (30 per cent), health-promoting policy (38 per cent), and health system strengthening (27 per cent).

An Urban Diabetes Toolbox has also been created to enable cities around the world to create an action plan for tackling the conditions; and partners across nineteen cities are collaborating to generate new knowledge and insights.

The key tools include a Diabetes Vulnerability Assessment, a research tool for identifying city-level factors that make certain groups of people vulnerable; the Diabetes Projection Model, which illustrates how reducing the prevalence of obesity would reduce the burden of diabetes; an Urban Diabetes Risk Assessment tool, which identifies the shared priorities and attitudes towards health and diabetes in a group of participants; and the Quantitative Research Tool, a framework that illustrates where gaps need to be closed to ensure that everyone with diabetes is diagnosed, treated, and has a better outcome.

In late 2015, Novo Nordisk formed a research-based partnership with C40, the Cities Climate Leadership Group which connects more than eighty-five of the world's greatest cities.

Prognosis

Almost three years of research was conducted between 2014 and 2016 into the risk factors for type 2 diabetes, specifically the socio-cultural factors; an internal partnership review was carried out by an impact assessment team at Novo Nordisk, supported by University College London, and Steno Diabetes Center Copenhagen. It included thirty-six partner interviews and externally conducted trend analysis of coverage compared with comparative cities Monterrey, Oslo, Hangzhou, Beijing, Dallas, and Milan. The assessment considered the programme's benefits and impacts, value drivers, challenges, and ideas for the future.

The review found that by the end of 2016, a total of eighteen projects or activities had been initiated collectively across Mexico City, Copenhagen, Houston, Tianjin, Shanghai, and Rome. Although several initiatives apply to more than one action arena, the majority of the actions initiated concern community involvement in health (38 per cent), health-promoting policy (26 per cent), and health-system strengthening (31 per cent). However, according to the impact review urban planning is the action arena with the fewest activities by end of 2016 (5 per cent).

Initiatives have included:

- In Mexico City, the partnership worked to address barriers through the establishment of a specialized diabetes centre with the capacity to treat 8,000 patients annually in Iztapalapa, one of the poorest suburbs of Mexico City.
- In Copenhagen, a peer-to-peer programme helped 'vulnerable' men manage their health, engage in the local community, and potentially rejoin the labour market. There are future plans for the programme to be included in the city's health promotion and prevention activities.
- A presentation of the Tianjin Cities Changing Diabetes programme at a stakeholder dialogue hosted by the World Economic Forum at the request of the WHO's Global ordination Mechanism on NCDs.

Meanwhile Cities Changing Diabetes partners wrote an open letter as a wake-up call for urban health, which was posted in *The New York Times* ahead of the Habitat III, the UN Conference on housing and sustainable urban development.

Looking towards the future, the review found that when speaking about how benefits and impacts have been achieved, the partners listed a range of topics pertaining to how the partnership is managed, with flexibility and openness a key driver of success.

Some interviewees advocated a more standardized and systematic approach to the Cities Changing Diabetes partner selection and partnership management, however most agreed there was no 'one size fits all' approach. Interpersonal connections were cited as very important, even when there is nothing new to report, to continuously nurture and strengthen partner relationships and progress partnership activities. The most frequently mentioned challenge was limited resources.

Several interviewees called for more action on the ground based on existing and emerging research results including evaluating ongoing interventions, and developing and measuring the impact of research-based interventions to identify the most efficient and effective ways of improving diabetes prevention and management. Several of the partners interviewed proposed that a more targeted intervention approach may be a way to maximize the impact.

Examples included targeting programme interventions towards specific target groups, such as young people, or around particular challenges, such as primary prevention, screening, or improved control of people with diagnosed diabetes.

Impact measurement and evaluation were considered necessary by most stakeholders interviewed; however, there is no unified answer regarding how this could be done and at what level. While measuring the impact of targeted interventions at city level is widely considered fairly straightforward, understanding the impact of a portfolio of interventions and, not least, impact across cities and countries is considered to be a greater challenge.

Some argue that measuring changes in health outcomes across cities is the only way that the programme can keep its focus on driving change in the long term, requiring the programme to take a uniform and systematic approach to impact measurement.

One key theme for the future is the enhanced collaboration and partnership expansion. Although some partners were concerned that a focus on onboarding new cities will come at the expense of keeping the attention on continued research and implementing already initiated local actions, the majority supported expansion to more cities at national and international levels. Central to this was a call for increased and enhanced collaboration and sharing of best practices across cities.

PART IV
CONCLUSION

34
Conclusion

Colin Mayer and Bruno Roche

What this book has done is to demonstrate the practicality of putting purpose into practice. It has done this in the context of business taking the lead in doing it for itself and not waiting on others—changes in the law, regulation, or institutional investment—to do it for them. In particular, the book has demonstrated that companies can bring about a fundamental change in their business models away from a preoccupation with profits to putting purpose at their heart. This is not about doing good as an add-on to business as usual or a nice to have, or a charitable activity that offers redemption for the nasty things that firms do to make the profits that allow them to be charitable. It is about moving to a view of the firm that recognizes its reason for being to be to 'produce profitable solutions for the problems of people and planet' and 'not to profit from producing problems for people and planet'.

That is a profound change in the way of thinking about business. It is not about production or 'stacking them high and selling them cheap'. It is about being clear about what problems a firm is seeking to solve, for whom—its customers, employees, suppliers, distributors, communities, environment, and societies—how it is solving the problems, by when, and why the company is particularly well suited to solving the problems. It involves establishing a real understanding of the nature of those problems that different parties face and what is required to solve them.

It requires building strong partnerships with a variety of different organizations and individuals in the private, public, and not-for-profit

Colin Mayer and Bruno Roche, Conclusion In *Putting Purpose Into Practice: The Economics of Mutuality.* Edited by: Colin Mayer and Bruno Roche, Oxford University Press (2021).
DOI: 10.1093/oso/9780198870708.003.0034

sectors and recognizing what is required to promote a common purpose and understanding amongst them. It necessitates expenditures and investments in different parties, in human, natural, and social as well as financial and material capital. And it involves constructing the metrics of the performance of those different types of capital, which capture their key performance indicators.

Finally, an accounting framework is required that duly acknowledges expenditures on human, natural, and social capital as investments as well as current expenditures, and maintenance of capitals as depreciation requirements analogous to those of material capital. The construction of a mutual P&L therefore involves reclassifying expenditures as capital rather than current costs and making appropriate provision for maintenance of the relevant capitals.

The book has not only set out the principles and practice of this new management innovation but has also shown how companies in different sectors, parts of the world, and stages of their development have in practice implemented them. It has therefore demonstrated the practical reality as well as the conceptual theory that underpins putting purpose into practice.

The reason why this matters is that shifting from profit production or even goods and services production to problem solving is the means by which business in the future will re-establish the credibility and status that it should command in society. Once people—be they customers, consumers, employees, suppliers, or societies—believe that business is there to solve their problems then they will have trust in an organization that at present they deeply distrust. This converts profit from being a source of conflict between business and society to one that is a means for sustaining levels of trust that avoid the need for philanthropy or government support.

That trust is then the basis of the reciprocal benefits that firms and their investors derive from this approach to business. Trust is one of, if not the, most important and largely unrecognized asset of business. It is the source of greater customer loyalty, more engaged employees, more reliable suppliers and more supportive shareholders and societies. It therefore creates higher revenues and lower costs and therefore greater profits. But it does not come from the pursuit of those profits but as a by-product of the intrinsic purpose of solving other people's problems.

While the book has provided a powerful demonstration of the practical reality of business transforming its business model to put purpose into practice, it has also revealed how much further we need to go before this becomes the conventionally accepted norm. First, the cases reported in the book demonstrate the widespread adoption of these approaches but in nearly all cases, these are examples of companies adopting the practices in part not all of their businesses. Even in the case of Mars, we have noted the ambiguity surrounding what mutuality means has allowed it to experiment with the concept in different parts of the business. However, it also implies that there is no common uniform adoption of mutuality throughout the organization. It is a series of interesting pilots rather than a guiding star of the whole of the company.

Second, while Mars and other companies have been able to adopt mutuality principles, it is much more feasible in a wholly family-owned firm than one that is exposed to the demands of capital markets and institutional investors. While policymakers increasingly emphasize good stewardship of companies by investors, institutions still have a primary duty to their investors and beneficiaries who, with some notable exceptions in the case of impact investing, are predominantly interested in financial returns and often short-term measures of performance. Companies owned by institutional investors are therefore under pressure to prioritize profits and short-term returns, which undermines their ability to promote other purposes.

Third, while the law in general pays due regard to the responsibility of directors to their stakeholders as well as their shareholders, this is in the context of promoting the (long-term) performance of firms for the benefit of their shareholders. In other words, the law has an extrinsic view of purposes of companies and the promotion of parties other than shareholders rather than an emphasis on their intrinsic interests. This is not an adequate basis for a reformulation of purpose around profitable solutions to problems of people and planet.

Finally, regulation is conventionally viewed in the context of the Friedman Doctrine notion of defining and enforcing the rules of the game by which companies maximize shareholder value. It is not considered as a tool for aligning private purposes of companies with public interests in circumstances in which companies perform public functions in, for example, delivering goods and services as utilities or infrastructure providers.

While the book has therefore demonstrated that it is perfectly feasible for companies to adopt principles of mutuality in the context of the existing ownership, legal, and regulatory framework, there are limitations to the extent to which it will be feasible for them to do so. The book has only touched very briefly on these broader policy issues because they have not been its primary focus. However, this should in no way diminish the importance of policymakers recognizing the need for reform to achieve the fundamental reconceptualization of business that is required to address the increasingly pressing social, political, environmental, and technological issues that confront nations around the world and with which this book began.

Bibliography and Further Reading

Addison, P. F. E., Bull, J. W., and Milner-Gulland, E. J. (2019). 'Using Conservation Science to Advance Corporate Biodiversity Accountability', *Conservation Biology* 32(2).

Adler, R., Mansi, M., Pandey, R., and Stringer, C. (2017). 'United Nations Decade on Biodiversity: A Study of the Reporting Practices of the Australian Mining Industry', *Accounting, Auditing & Accountability Journal* 30: 1711–45.

Adner, R. (2017). 'Ecosystem as Structure: An Actionable Construct for Strategy', *Journal of Management* 43(1): 39–58.

Arratia, Ramon (2014). 'The Environmental Footprint of Carpet Tile,' Cut the Fluff, 30 October, http://www.interfacecutthefluff.com/tag/carpet-tile-environmental-footprint/.

Austin, James E. and Seitanidi, M. May (2012a). 'Collaborative Value Creation: A Review of Partnering between Nonprofits and Businesses: Part I. Value Creation Spectrum and Collaboration Stages', *Nonprofit and Voluntary Sector Quarterly* 41(5): 726–58. https://doi.org/10.1177/0899764012450777.

Austin, James E. and Seitanidi, M. May (2012b. 'Collaborative Value Creation: A Review of Partnering Between Nonprofits and Businesses. Part 2: Partnership Processes and Outcomes', *Nonprofit and Voluntary Sector Quarterly* 41(6): 929–68. https://doi.org/10.1177/0899764012454685.

B20 Germany (2017). 'Shaping an Interconnected World Building Resilience—Improving Sustainability—Assuming Responsibility', B20 policy recommendations to the G20. Available at https://www.b20germany.org/fileadmin/user_upload/documents/B20/b20-summary-doc-en.pdf.

Badger, Stephen M., II. (2014). Editorial. *The Brewery*, January: 2–3.

Bajo, Claudia Sanchez and Roelants, Bruno (2011). *Capital and the Debt Trap: Learning from Cooperatives in Global Crisis*. London: Palgrave Macmillan.

Baldwin, Robert (2014). 'From Regulation To Behaviour Change', Modern Law Review 77(6), https://onlinelibrary.wiley.com/doi/abs/10.1111/1468-2230.12094.

Banerjee, A. V., and Duflo, E. (2011). *Poor Economics: A Radical Rethinking of the Way to Fight Global Poverty*. New York: Public Affairs.

Banerjee, A., Duflo, E., Glennerster, R., and Kinnan, C. (2015). 'The Miracle of Microfinance? Evidence from a Randomized Evaluation', *American Economic Journal: Applied Economics* 7(1), 22–53.

Banerjee, A., Karlan, D., and Zinman, J. (2015). 'Six Randomized Evaluations of Microcredit: Introduction and Further Steps', *American Economic Journal: Applied Economics* 7(1): 1–21.

Bandiera, Oriana, Barankay, Iwan and Rasul, Imran (2010). 'Social incentives in the workplace', *Review of Economic Studies* 77(2), 417–58.

Baker, C.R., Bettner, M. (1997). Interpretative and critical research in accounting: a commentary on its absence from mainstream accounting research. *Critic Perspect Accounting* 8(4): 293–310.

Barker, R. (2019). 'Corporate Natural Capital Accounting', *Oxford Review of Economic Policy* 35(1): 68–87.

Barker, R. and Mayer, C. (2017). 'How Should a "Sustainable Corporation" Account for Natural Capital?' Saïd Business School Working Paper 2017–15.

Bebbington, J., and Gray, R. (2001). 'An Account of Sustainability: Failure, Success and a Reconceptualization', *Critical Perspectives on Accounting* 12: 557–87.

Bebiak, J., Sarathy, V., Morawietz, M., and Gotpagar, J. (2017). '2017 Chemical Industry Trends: Delivering Profitable Growth in a Hypercompetitive, Low-Growth World', Strategy& and PwC, https://www.pwc.com.br/pt/assets/strategyand/2017-Chemicals-Industry-Trends.pdf.

Berry, W. (2003). *The Art of the Commonplace*, ed. Norman Wirzba. Washington DC: Counterpoint.

Bhalla, A., Jha, P., and Lampell, J. (2010). 'Model Growth: Do Employee-Owned Businesses Deliver Sustainable Performance?' Cass Business School, City University London.

Bhattacharya, C. B. (2016). 'How Companies Can Tap Sustainability to Motivate Staff', Knowledge@WhartonPartners, September. http://knowledge.wharton.upenn.edu/article/how-companies-tap-sustainability-to-motivate-staff/.

Bhimani, A. and Bromwhich, M. (2010). *Management Accounting: Retrospect and Prospect*. Kidlington: CIMA/Elsevier.

Birchall, Johnston and Hammond Ketilson, Lou (2009). 'Resilience of the Cooperative Business Model in Times of Crisis', International Labour Organization, Geneva.

Blundell-Wignall, A., Hu, Y., and Yermo, J. (2008). 'Sovereign Wealth and Pension Fund Issues', OECD Working Papers on Insurance and Private Pensions, No. 14, OECD Publishing.

Blundell-Wignall, A.Atkinson, P.E. (2008), 'The subprime crisis: causal distortions and regulatory reform', in Bloxham, P.Kent, C. (eds), *Lessons from the Financial Turmoil of 2007 and 2008*, Reserve Bank of Australia, July.

Boiral, O. (2016). 'Accounting for the Unaccountable: Biodiversity Reporting and Impression Management', *Journal of Business Ethics* 135: 751–68.

Boiral, O. and Heras-Saizarbitoria, I. (2017). 'Corporate Commitment to Biodiversity in Mining and Forestry: Identifying Drivers from GRI Reports', *Journal of Cleaner Production* 162: 153–61.

Bowles, S. and Gintis, H. (2002). 'Social Capital and Community Governance', *The Economic Journal* 112: F419-F436.

Brady, Arlo (2014). 'A Brief History of Business in Society: From Liturgies to Lehman Brothers', *The Brewery*, January: 4–6.

Burchell, S., Clubb, C., Hopwood, A., Hughes, J., and Nahapiet, J. (1980). 'The Roles of Accounting in Organizations and Society', *Accounting, Organizations and Society* 5(1): 5–21.

CBD (2017). Article 2: Use of Terms. Available at: https://www.cbd.int/convention/articles/default.shtml?a=cbd-02].

CDSB (2018). 'Uncharted Waters: How Can Companies Use Financial Accounting Standards to Deliver on the TCFD Recommendations?' London: Climate Disclosure Standards Board.

Chu, J., Fafchamps, M., and Jonason, D. (2018). 'The Importance of Just Process: Mutual Dissatisfaction between Managers and Workers in Foreign-Owned Companies', Stanford University Working Paper.

Circle Economy, PGGM, KPMG EBRD, and WBCSD (2018). 'Lineal Risks'. Online available at: https://www.wbcsd.org/Programs/Energy-Circular-Economy/Factor-10/Resources/Linear-Risks.

Clark, G. and Knight, E. R. W. (2010) 'Temptation and the Virtues of Long-Term Commitment: The Governance of Sovereign Wealth Fund Investment', *Asian Journal of International Law* 1(2). DOI: 10.2139/ssrn.1669281.

Clark, G. and Urwin, R. (2008) 'Best-Practice Pension Fund Governance', *Journal of Asset Management* 9(1): 2–21.

Crawford, Matthew (2009). *Shop Class as Soulcraft: An Inquiry into the Value of Work*. London: Penguin.

Davies, William and Michie, Jonathan (2012). 'Employee Ownership: Defusing the Business Succession Time-Bomb in Wales', The Wales Co-operative Centre, Cardiff.

Day, A. (2017). *The Religious Lives of Older Laywomen*. Oxford: Oxford University Press.

de Guzman, Nickky Faustine P. (2017). 'From Nets to Carpets and Cash', *Business World Online*, 9 August, http://www.bworldonline.com/content.php?section=Weekender&title=from-nets-to-carpets-and-cash&id=110335.

De Mel, S., Mckenzie, D., and Woodruff, C. (2008). 'Returns to Capital in Microenterprises: Evidence from a Field Experiment', *The Quarterly Journal of Economics* 123(4): 1329–72.

De Mel, S., Mckenzie, D., and Woodruff, C. (2010). 'Who Are the Microenterprise Owners? Evidence from Sri Lanka on Tokman v. de Soto'. In J. Lerner and A. Schoar, eds, *International Differences in Entrepreneurship*. Boston, MA: National Bureau of Economic Research.

Deegan, C. (2013). 'The Accountant Will Have a Central Role in Saving the Planet . . . Really? A Reflection on Green Accounting and Green Eyeshades Twenty Years Later', *Critical Perspectives on Accounting* 24: 448–58.

Deegan, C. (2014). 'An Overview of Legitimacy Theory as Applied within the Social and Environmental Accounting Literature'. In J. Bebbington, B. O'Dwyer, and J. Unerman, eds, *Sustainability Accounting and Accountability*. London: Routledge.

De Neve, E., Krekel, C., and Ward, G. (2019), 'Employee Wellbeing, Productivity and Firm Performance', Centre for Economic Performance Discussion Papers, DP1605, LSE.

Doh, J. and Guay, T. (2006). 'Corporate Social Responsibility, Public Policy, and NGO Activism in Europe and the United States: An Institutional-Stakeholder Perspective', *Journal of Management Studies* 43(1): 47–73.

Dolan, Catherine (nd). 'The Ambiguity of Mutuality: Discourse and Power in Corporate Value Regimes', unpublished manuscript.

Dowling, J. and Pfeffer, J. (1975). 'Organization Legitimacy: Social Values and Organizational Behaviour', *Pacific Sociological Review* 28(1): 122–36.

EU (2014). *Directive 2014/95/EU of the European Parliament and of the Council.* Brussels: European Union.

eftec, RSPB, and PwC (2015). 'Developing Corporate Natural Capital Accounts', Final Report for the Natural Capital Committee.

Eccles, R. G. and Krzus, M. P. (2010). *One Report: Integrated Reporting for a Sustainable Strategy.* New Jersey: Wiley & Sons, Inc.

Eccles, R. G. and Krzus, M. P. (2014). *The Integrated Reporting Movement: Meaning, Momentum, Motives, and Materiality.* New Jersey: Wiley & Sons, Inc.

Elkington, John (1998). 'Partnerships from Cannibals with Forks: The Triple Bottom Line of 21st-Century Business', *Environmental Quality Management* 8(1): 37–51.

Erdal, David (2011). *Beyond the Corporation: Humanity Working.* London: Penguin.

Errasti, Anjel, Bretos, Ignacio, and Nunez, Aitziber (2017). 'The Viability of Cooperatives: The Fall of the Mondragon Cooperative Fagor', *Review of Radical Political Economies* 49(2): 188.

EVPA (2019). *Practical Guide to Measuring and Managing Impact.* https://evpa.eu.com/knowledge-centre/publications/measuring-and-managing-impact-a-practical-guide

Fafchamps, M., Mckenzie, D., Quinn, D., and Woodruff, D. (2014). 'Microenterprise Growth and the Flypaper Effect: Evidence from a Randomized Experiment in Ghana', *Journal of Development Economics* 106: 211–26.

Fankhauser, Sam and Thomas K. J., eds, (2016). *The Economics of Climate-Resilient Development.* Cheltenham: Edward Elgar Publishing.

Field, E., Pande, R., Papp, J., and Rigol, N. (2013). 'Does the Classic Microfinance Model Discourage Entrepreneurship among the Poor? Experimental Evidence from India', *American Economic Review* 103(6): 2196–226.

Fischer, G. (2013). 'Contract Structure, Risk-Sharing, and Investment Choice', *Econometrica* 81(3): 883–939.

Flecha, Ramon and Ngai, Pun (2014). 'The Challenge for Mondragon: Searching for the Cooperative Values in Times of Internationalization', *Organization* 21(5).

Ford, Tamasin et al. (2014). 'The Cocoa Crisis: Why the World's Stash Is Melting Away', *The Guardian*, 21 November, https://www.theguardian.com/lifeandstyle/2014/nov/21/cocoa-crisis-world-chocolate-stash-melting-away.

Freiner, Linda (2016). 'Zurich: Changing Lives along Java's Bengawan Solo', Zurich Insurance Group, June, https://www.www.zurich.com/en/knowledge/articles/2016/06/changing-lives-along-javas-bengawan-solo.

Friedrichs, R. W. (1970). *A Sociology of Sociology.* New York: Free Press.

Frooman, J. and Murrell, A. (2005). 'Stakeholder Influence Strategies: The Roles of Structural and Demographic Determinants', *Business and Society* 44(1): 3–31.

GHG (2015). 'The Greenhouse Gas Protocol: A Corporate Accounting and Reporting Standard', revised edition. The Greenhouse Gas Protocol.

Gambhir, R. S. and Gupta, T. (2016). 'Need for Oral Health Policy in India', https://www.ncbi.nlm.nih.gov/pmc/articles/PMC4849117/

Gartenberg, C., Prat, A., and Serafeim, G. (2016). 'Corporate Purpose and Financial Performance', *Organization Science* 30: 1–18.

Geert Hofstede (2001). *Culture's Consequences Comparing Values, Behaviors, Institutions and Organizations Across Nations*. Tilburg University, Netherlands.

Geibler, J.V., Cordaro, F., Kennedy, K., Lettenmeier, M., and Roche, B. (2016). 'Integrating Resource Efficiency in Business Strategies: A Mixed-Method Approach for Environmental Life-Cycle Assessment in the Single-Serve Coffee Value Chain', *Journal of Cleaner Production* 115: 62–74.

Gerhardt, S. (2010). *The Selfish Society: How We All Forgot to Love One Another and Made Money Instead*. London: Simon & Schuster.

Gewirth, Alan (1978). 'The Golden Rule Rationalized', *Midwest Studies in Philosophy* 3: 133–47.

Gladwin, T. N., Kennelly, J. J., and Krause, T. S. (1995). 'Shifting Paradigms for Sustainable Development: Implications for Management Theory and Research', The Academy of Management Review 20(4): 874–907.

Glasbergen, Pieter (2007). 'Setting the Scene: The Partnership Paradigm in the Making'. In P. Glasbergen, F. Bierman, and A. P. J. Mol, eds, *Partnerships, Governance and Sustainable Development*. Cheltenham: Edward Elgar Publishing.

Global Reporting Initiative, 2016. GRI 101: Foundation. https://www.globalreporting.org/media/55yhvety/gri-101-foundation-2016.pdf?page=23

Goodman, J. C., Hebb, T., and Hoepner, A. G. F. (2014). 'Shareholder Dialogue behind the Scenes: Addressing the Bulk of the Iceberg', Proceedings of the 2014 Academy of Management Meeting, Philadelphia.

Googins, Bradley K. and Rochlin, Steven A. (2000). 'Creating the Partnership Society: Understanding the Rhetoric and Reality of Cross-Sectoral Partnerships', *Business and Society Review* 105(1): 127–44.

Granovetter, Mark (1985). 'Economic Action and Social Structure: The Problem of Embeddedness', *American Journal of Sociology* 91(3): 481–510.

Gray, R. (1992). 'Accounting and Environmentalism: An Exploration of the Challenge of Gently Accounting for Accountability, Transparency and Sustainability', *Accounting Organizations and Society* 17: 399–425.

Gray, R. (1994). 'Corporate Reporting for Sustainable Development: Accounting for Sustainability in 2000 AD', *Environmental Values* 3: 17–45.

Green, S. (2009). *Good Value: Reflections on Money, Morality an Uncertain World*. London: Allen Lane.

Greenovate Europe (2012). 'Guide to Resource Efficiency in Manufacturing: Experiences from Improving Resource Efficiency in Manufacturing Companies', https://www.greenovate-europe.eu/sites/default/files/publications/REMake_

Greenovate%21Europe%20-%20Guide%20to%20resource%20efficient%20manufacturing%20%282012%29.pdf.

Griffin, Dale and Tversky, Amos (1992). 'The Weighting of Evidence and the Determinants of Confidence', *Cognitive Psychology* 24: 411–35.

Gudeman, Stephen (2009). 'Necessity or Contingency: Mutuality and Market'. In C. Hann and K. Hart, eds, *Market and Society: The Great Transformation*. Cambridge: Cambridge University Press.

Guay, T., Doh, J., and Sinclair, G. (2004). 'Non-Governmental Organizations, Shareholder Activism, and Socially Responsible Investments: Ethical, Strategic, and Governance Implications', *Journal of Business Ethics* 52(1): 125–39.

Guesné, J.M. and Ménascé, D. (2014). "Sharing Cities: an innovative partnership between the Bel Group and street vendors," *Journal of Field Actions, Field Actions Science Reports*, Special Issue 12.

Gulati, R., Puranam, P., and Tushman, M. (2012). 'Meta-Organization Design: Rethinking Design in Interorganizational and Community Contexts', *Strategic Management Journal* 33(6): 571–86.

Gunter, G. and Matthias, M. (2015). 'Foundation-Owned Firms in Germany: A Field Experiment for Agency Theory', ZBW-Deutsche Zentralbibliotek für Wirtshaftswissenschaften, Leibniz-Informationszentrum Wirtschaft.

Hansmann, H. and Thomsen, S. (2013). 'Virtual Ownership and Managerial Distance: The Governance of Industrial Foundations', Copenhagen Business School Working Paper

Hare, D. (2009). *The Power of Yes*. London: Faber.

Hebb, T., Hoepner, A. G. F., Rodionova, T., and Sanchez, I. (2018). 'Power and Shareholder Saliency'. In Helen Borland, Adam Lindgreen, Joelle Vanhamme, Francois Maon, Veronique Ambrosini, Beatriz Palacios Florencio, eds, *Business Strategies for Sustainability: A Research Anthology*. London: Gower Publishers.

Helliwell, J. F., Huang, H. (2009). How's the Job? Well-Being and Social Capital in the Workplace. Industrial and Labor Relation Review 63(2), 205–27.

Helliwell, J. F. and Wang, S. (2011). Trust and Wellbeing. International Journal of Wellbeing, 1(1).

Helm, D. (2015). *Natural Capital*. New Haven, CT: Yale University Press.

Henderson, Rebecca and Norris, Michael (2015). '1worker1vote: MONDRAGON in the U.S.', *Harvard Business Review*, 28 February.

Hoepner, A. G. F., de Aguiar, T. R. S., and Majithia, R. (2013). 'The Level of Compliance with the International Code of Marketing of Breast-Milk Substitutes: Does It Matter to Stock Markets?' *Journal of Business Ethics* 119(3): 329–48.

Houston, Holly and Wyer, Terry (2012). 'Why Sustainable Cocoa Farming Matters for Rural Development,' Center for Strategic and International Studies, 6 September, https://www.csis.org/analysis/why-sustainable-cocoa-farming-matters-rural-development.

Hower, M. (2015). 'Dell Cuts E-Waste with Recycled Carbon Fiber', GreenBiz, 23 October, https://www.greenbiz.com/article/dell-cuts-e-waste-recycled-carbon-fiber

IPCC (International Panel On Climate Change: Geneva) (2018). 'Global Warming of 1.5°C'. An IPCC Special Report on the impacts of global warming of 1.5°C above pre-industrial levels and related global greenhouse gas emission pathways. Geneva: International Panel on Climate Change. https://www.ipcc.ch/sr15/.

Ivanova, M. (2016). 'Shareholder Activism and the Ethical Harnessing of Institutional Investors—The Unique Case of ShareAction Critical Perspectives on International Business', *Critical Perspectives on International Business* 12(2): 189–214.

Jackson, K. T. (2016). 'Economy of Mutuality: Merging Financial and Social Sustainability', *Journal of Business Ethics* 133(3): 499–517.

Jackson, Matthew O. (2009). *Social and Economic Networks*. Princeton , NJ: Princeton University Press.

Johnson, S. (2015). 'Here Be Modern Day Fossil Fuel Dragons', *Financial Times*, 5 February.

Kahneman, Daniel (2011). *Thinking Fast and Slow*. London: Penguin Books.

Karim, L. (2008). 'Demystifying Micro-Credit: The Grameen Bank, NGOs, and Neoliberalism in Bangladesh', *Cultural Dynamics* 20(1): 5–29.

Kasurinen, T. (2002). 'Exploring Management Accounting Change: The Case of Balanced Scorecard Implementation', *Management Accounting Research* 13: 323–43.

Kitsara, Irene (2014). 'E-Waste and Innovation: Unlocking Hidden Value', *Wipo Magazine*, June, http://www.wipo.int/wipo magazine/en/2014/03/article0001.html.

Kustin, Bridget, et al. (2018). '"Mutuality" through Time: Corporate Possibilities for New Economic Thinking', unpublished manuscript.

Lazonick, Willian and O'Sullivan, Mary (2000). 'Maximizing Shareholder Value', *Economy and Society* 29(1): 13–35.

Liedtke, C., Bienge, K., Wiesen, K., Teubler, J., Greiff, K., Lettenmeier, M., and Rohn, H. (2014). 'Resource Use in the Production and Consumption System: The MIPS Approach', *Resources* 3: 544–74.

Mcdonnell, M. and King, B. (2013). 'Keeping up Appearances: Reputational Threat and Impression Management after Social Movement Boycotts', *Administrative Science Quarterly* 58(3): 387–419.

Mace, G. (2019). 'The Ecology of Natural Capital Accounting', *Oxford Review of Economic Policy* 35(1): 54–67.

Mackey, J. and Sisodia, R. (2013). *Conscious Capitalism: Liberating the Heroic Spirit of Business*. United States: Harvard Business Review Press.

MacLeod, Greg (1997). *From Mondragon to America: Experiments in Community Economic Development*. Sydney, Nova Scotia: Cape Breton University Press.

Mars, Incorporated (2017). 'Who We Are: The Five Principles: Freedom', http://www.mars.com/global/about-us/five-principles/freedom.

Maslow, A. H. (1943). 'A Theory of Human Motivation', *Psychological Review*, 50(4), 370–96.

Masterman, M. (1970). 'The Nature of a Paradigm'. In I. Lakatos and A. Musgrave, eds, *Criticism and the Growth of Knowledge: Proceedings of the International*

Colloquium in the Philosophy of Science, London, 1965. Cambridge: Cambridge University Press.

Mayer, Colin (2013). *Firm Commitment*. Oxford: Oxford University Press.

Mayer, Colin (2015). 'The Meaning of Fair Return and Mutuality in Business', unpublished manuscript, Saïd Business School, University of Oxford, 4 June.

Mayer, Colin (2018). *Prosperity: Better Business Makes the Greater Good*. Oxford: Oxford University Press.

Mazzucato, M. (2018). *The Value of Everything: Making and Taking in the Global Economy*. London: Allen Lane/Penguin Random House.

Michie, Joznathan (2011). 'Promoting Corporate Diversity in the Financial Services Sector', *Policy Studies* 32(4): 309–23.

Michie, Jonathan (2017). 'The Importance of Ownership'. In J. Michie, J. Blasi, and C. Borzaga, eds, *The Oxford Handbook of Mutual, Co-operative, and Co-owned Business*, Oxford: Oxford University Press.

Michie, Jonathan and Oughton, Christine (2013). 'Measuring Diversity in Financial Services Markets: A Diversity Index', Working Paper 097_DP113, The Centre for Financial and Management Studies, The School of Oriental and African Studies, University of London.

Michie, Jonathan and Oughton, Christine (2014). 'Corporate Diversity in Financial Services: An Updated Diversity Index', Building Societies Association, London, https://www.bsa.org.uk/BSA/files/6b/6b587676-ebcb-41df-aa12-eb4f006b8ee7.pdf.

Milne, M. J. and Gray, R. (2013). 'W(h)ither Ecology? The TBL, the GRI, and the Institutionalisation of Corporate Sustainability Reporting', *Journal of Business Ethics* 118: 13–29.

Montgomery, R. (1996). 'Disciplining or Protecting the Poor? Avoiding the Social Costs of Peer Pressure in Micro-Credit Schemes', *Journal of International Development* 8(2): 289–305.

Monzón, Jose Luis and Chaves, Rafael (2017). 'Recent Evolutions of the Social Economy in the European Union', European Economic and Social Committee, European Union, Brussels.

NCC (2016). *Natural Capital Protocol*. London: Natural Capital Coalition.

Naranjo-Gil, D., Maas, V., and Hartman, F. G. H. (2009). 'How CFOs Determine Management Accounting Innovation: An Examination of Direct and Indirect Effects', *European Accounting Review* 18(4): 667–95.

Norton, B. G. (1991). *Toward Unity in Environmentalists*. New York: Oxford University Press.

Ostrom, E. and Ahn, T. K., eds (2003). *Foundations of Social Capital*. Cheltenham: Edward Elgar.

Ownership Commission (2012). 'Better Owned Firms Are the Key to Responsible Capitalism', Mutuo, London, http://www.mutuo.coop/ownershipcommission/.

Pendleton, Andrew (2001). 'Employee Share Ownership and Human Capital Development: Complementarity in Theory and Practice', *Economic and Industrial Democracy* 32(3): 439–57.

Pina-Cabral, João de (2013). 'The Two Faces of Mutuality: Contemporary Themes in Anthropology', *Anthropological Quarterly* 86(1): 257–75.

Platteau, Jean-Philippe (1994a). 'Behind the Market Stage Where Real Societies Exist: Part I—The Role of Public and Private Order Institutions', *Journal of Development Studies* 30(3): 533–77.

Platteau, Jean-Philippe (1994b). 'Behind the Market Stage Where Real Societies Exist: Part II—The Role of Moral Norms', *Journal of Development Studies* 30(4): 753–815.

Polanyi, Karl (1944). *The Great Transformation*. New York: Holt, Rinehart, and Winston.

Porter, Michael and Kramer, Mark (2011). 'Creating Shared Value', *Harvard Business Review* 89(1–2): 62–77.

Pounds, N. (2001). *The History of the English Parish Church*. Oxford: Oxford University Press.

Putnam, R. D. (2000). *Bowling Alone: The Collapse and Revival of American Community*. New York: Simon & Schuster.

RSPB (2018). 'Accounting for Nature: A Natural Capital Account of the RSPB's Estate in England', https://www.rspb.org.uk/globalassets/downloads/documents/positions/economics/accounting-for-nature.pdf.

Rabin, Matthew (2002). 'Inference by Believers in the Law of Small Numbers', *Quarterly Journal of Economics* 117: 775–816.

Rahman, A. (1999). 'Micro-Credit Initiatives for Equitable and Sustainable Development: Who Pays?' *World Development* 27(1): 67–82.

Rangan, S. (2015). *Performance and Progress: Essays on Capitalism, Business, and Society*. Oxford: Oxford University Press.

Rangan, S. (2018). *Capitalism beyond Mutuality? Perspectives Integrating Philosophy and Social Science*. Oxford: Oxford University Press.

Reed, B. (1978). *The Dynamics of Religion: Process and Movement in Christian Churches*. London: Darton, Longman & Todd.

Reid, E. and Toffel, M. (2009). 'Responding to Public and Private Politics: Corporate Disclosure of Climate Change Strategies', *Strategic Management Journal* 30(11): 1157–78.

Ritthoff, M., Rohn, H., and Liedtke, C. (2002). 'Calculating MIPS: Resource Productivity of Products and Services', Wuppertal Spezial 27e. Wuppertal Institute, Wuppertal.

Roche, B. and Jakub, J. (2017). *Completing Capitalism: Heal Business to Heal the World*. Oakland, CA: Berret-Koehler Inc.

Roelents, Bruno et al. (2012). 'The Resilience of the Cooperative Model: How Worker Cooperatives, Social Cooperatives, and Other Worker-Owned Enterprises Respond to the Crisis and its Consequences', CECOP—CICOPA The European Confederation of Cooperatives Industrial and Service Cooperatives, Brussels.

Roll, Kate and Dolan, Catherine (nd). 'Remote Engagement: Corporations, Risk, and Spanning the Institutional Voids at the Base of the Pyramid', unpublished manuscript.

Roland Benabou, Efe A. Ok (2001). 'Social Mobility and the Demand for Redistribution: The Poum Hypothesis', *The Quarterly Journal of Economics*, 116(2): 447–87.

Roodman, D. and Morduch, J. (2014). 'The Impact of Microcredit on the Poor in Bangladesh: Revisiting the Evidence', *Journal of Development Studies* 50(4): 583–604.

Rubin, James (2015). 'E-Waste: The Circular Economy's Achilles Heel,' *edie newsroom*, 26 June, https://www.edie.net/library/E-Waste–The-circular-economy-s-achilles-heel/6611.

Sainsbury, D. (2013). *Progressive Capitalism: How to Achieve Economic Growth, Liberty and Social Justice*. London: Biteback Publishing.

Saldinger, Adva (2014). 'Can (Ghana's) Cocoa Farmers Ever Emerge from Poverty?' *Devex*, 6 August, https://www.devex.com/news/can-ghana-s-cocoa-farmers-ever-emerge-from-poverty-83883.

Sandel, Michael (2012). *What Money Can't Buy*. London: Allen Lane.

Saurat, M. and Ritthoff, M. (2013). 'Calculating MIPS 2.0', *Resources* 2(4): 581–607.

Schein, Edgar (2010). *Organization Culture and Leadership*. San Francisco, CA: Jossey-Bass.

Schmidt-Bleek, F. (1994). *How Much Environment Do Humans Need? The Measure of Ecological Economies (Wieviel Umwelt braucht der Mensch? Das Maß für ökologisches Wirtschaften)* (in German). Berlin: Birkhäuser.

Schoar, A. (2010). 'The Divide between Subsistence and Transformational Entrepreneurship', *Innovation Policy and the Economy* 10(1): 57–81.

Selsky, John W. and Parker, Barbara (2005). 'Cross-Sector Partnerships to Address Social Issues: Challenges to Theory and Practice', *Journal of Management* 31 (6): 849–73.

Sennett, R. *Together: The Rituals, Pleasures and Politics of Cooperation* (London: Allen Lane, 2012)

Slavin, Terry and Ley, Rebecca (2017). 'Female Cocoa Farmers "Key to Divine Chocolate's Success,"' Ethical Corporation, 15 March, http://www.ethicalcorp.com/female-cocoa-farmers-key-divine-chocolates-success.

Soule, E., Tinsley, C., and Rivoli, P. (2017). 'A Social Enterprise Link in a Global Value Chain: Performance and Potential of a New Supplier Model', Georgetown University Women's Leadership Institute, Georgetown University, Washington, DC, http://womensleadershipinstitute.georgetown.domains/on-purpose-kate-spade/.

Stanley, Chris (2013). 'Topic Guide: Engaging Suppliers in Sustainability', Best Foot Forward, May, http://www.wrap.org.uk/sites/files/wrap/Engaging%20suppliers%20in%20sustainability%20Topic%20Guide%20-%20final%20v1.pdf.

Strong, M. (2009). *Be the Solution: How Entrepreneurs and Conscious Capitalist Can Solve All the World's Problems*. New Jersey: John Wiley & Sons.

Suchman, M. C. (1995). 'Managing Legitimacy: Strategic and Institutional Approaches', *Academy of Management Review* 20(3): 571–610.

Surminski, Swenja and Oramas-Dorta, Delioma (2013). 'Flood Insurance Schemes and Climate Adaptation in Developing Countries', *Journal of Disaster Rick Reduction* 7: 154–64, http://eprints.lse.ac.uk/66294/1/Binder1.pdf.

Tandon, S. (2004). 'Challenges to the Oral Health Workforce in India', *Journal of Dental Education* 68: 28–33.

Tanner, K. (2010). 'Is Capitalism a Belief System?' *Anglican Theological Review* 92(4): 617–35.

Thomsen, Steen and Rose, Caspar (2004). 'Foundation Ownership and Financial Performance: Do Companies Need Owners?' *European Journal of Law and Economics* 18(3): 343–64.

UN (2015). 'Transforming our World: The 2030 Agenda for Sustainable Development', http://www.un.org/ga/search/view_doc.asp?symbol=A/RES/70/1&Lang=E.

Vock, Marlene, van Dolen, Willemijn, and Kolk, Ans (2014). 'Micro-Level Interactions in Business-Nonprofit Partnerships', *Business & Society* 53(4): 517–50.

WEF (2018). *The Global Risks Report 2018*, 13th edition. Geneva: The World Economic Forum.

Wanyama, Frederick (2014). 'Cooperatives and the Sustainable Development Goals: a contribution to the post-2015 development debate,' International Labour Organization, Geneva.

Williams, R. (2012). 'From Faust to Frankenstein: Markets Alone Should Not Determine our Conception of What Is Desirable', *Prospect* (23 April): 75.

Williams, Sandra L. (2011). 'Engaging Values in International Business Practice', *Business Horizons* 54: 315–24.

Williamson, O. E. (1991). 'Comparative Economic Organization: The Analysis of Discrete Structural Alternatives', *Administrative Science Quarterly* 36(2): 269–96.

Wilson, E. O. (2016). *Half-Earth: Our Planet's Fight for Life*. New York: Liveright Publishing Corporation.

Winderl, Thomas (2014). 'Disaster Resilience Measurements: Taking Stock of Ongoing Efforts in Developing systems for Measuring Resilience', United Nations Development Programme, February, http://www.preventionweb.net/files/37916_disasterresiliencemeasurementsundpt.pdf.

World Wild Life Fund (2018). Living Planet Report. https://www.worldwildlife.org/pages/living-planet-report-2018.

Xiong, Xue, Nie, Fengying, Bi, Jieying, and Waqar, Muhammad (2017). 'The Research on the Path of Poverty Alleviation of E-Commerce: A Case Study of Jing Dong', *Journal of Simulation* 5(2).

Index

Note: Tables and figures are indicated by an italic "*t*" and "*f*" following the page number.

For the benefit of digital users, indexed terms that span two pages (e.g., 52–53) may, on occasion, appear on only one of those pages.